Epiphanius of Cyprus

Epiphanius of Cyprus

IMAGINING AN ORTHODOX WORLD

Young Richard Kim

UNIVERSITY OF MICHIGAN PRESS

ANN ARBOR

Published in the United States of America by the
University of Michigan Press
Manufactured in the United States of America
♾ Printed on acid-free paper

2018   2017   2016   2015   4   3   2   1

A CIP catalog record for this book is available from the British Library.

Library of Congress Cataloging-in-Publication Data

Kim, Young Richard, 1976–.
Epiphanius of Cyprus : imagining an orthodox world / Young Richard Kim.
   pages   cm
Includes bibliographical references and index.
ISBN 978-0-472-11954-7 (hardcover : acid-free paper)
   1. Epiphanius, Saint, Bishop of Constantia in Cyprus, approximately 310–403.
   2. Orthodox Eastern Church—Bishops—Biography.   I. Title.
BX395.E65K56   2015

                                        270.2092—dc23

For Betty

Acknowledgments

Many individuals and institutions contributed to the completion of this project, and I hope the reader will forgive me for overindulging in my expressions of gratitude. This book began as a dissertation at the University of Michigan, Ann Arbor, supervised by Raymond Van Dam. Epiphanius has been at the center of my research interests for well over a decade, and this monograph is the culmination of hours and hours spent reading his writings and reflecting on his life.

My graduate school education was profoundly influenced by Sara Ahbel-Rappe, H. D. Cameron, John V. A. Fine Jr., the late Traianos Gagos, Diane Hughes, and the late Sabine MacCormack. I am especially grateful to David Potter for serving on my dissertation committee, reading the letters of Jerome with me, and teaching me about living the academic life with excellence and a sense of humor. And I owe my sincerest thanks to Ray for mentoring me and modeling the life of a gentleman scholar and teacher.

I have been the beneficiary of boundless support from my colleagues at Calvin College. I am grateful to the Board of Trustees and Claudia Beversluis, Matt Walhout, and Cheryl Brandsen in the Office of the Provost for Calvin Research Fellowships awarded in 2009 and 2011 and a sabbatical leave in 2012–13. My colleagues in the Department of History have been a joy to work with, and I am ever appreciative of our mutual encouragement, good humor, and friendship. I am also grateful to my fellow professors in the Department of Classics for their camaraderie and support. Gratitude is also due to Megan Berglund, Manager of Grant Proposals, for inspiration and guidance. I was a recipient of a finishing grant from the Calvin Center for Christian Scholarship, and I wish to express my thanks to the governing board and to director Susan Felch.

Much of the research I conducted and the time spent writing this book were made possible by a grant from the Cyprus Fulbright Commission for the 2012–13 academic year. My family and I are indebted to the current and former CFC staff, Daniel Hadjittofi, Anna Argyrou, Kyproula Kyriakidou, Gülsen Öztoprak, Revy Payiata-Chishios, and Sondra Sainsbury. I worked primarily under the auspices of the Cyprus American Archaeological Research Institute, and I am thankful to its director Andrew McCarthy and staff (Vathoulla Moustoukki, Fodoulla Christodoulou, Katerina Mavromichalaou) for facilitating my work. I must also thank Thomas Davis, former director, for his encouragement. I am grateful to Katherine Kearns and the other Fulbright fellows for our memorable social gatherings, and to Professor Chris Schabel at the University of Cyprus for the resources he made available to me. I had several opportunities to share my research while overseas, and I wish to acknowledge Jaime Alvar of the Universidad Carlos III de Madrid, and Georgios Deligiannakis and Stefanos Efthymiadis of the Open University of Cyprus. I would like to thank the Arnott, Botros, Ginting, Hughes/Kong, Loucas/Otterbacher, Malayatoor, Piper, and Royster/Mateen families and Saint Paul's Cathedral for making our experience abroad in Cyprus such a joyful and transformative experience. I am also indebted to Terry Monoyios for masterful lessons in Modern Greek.

I also would like to acknowledge the generosity of the Department of Antiquities of the Republic of Cyprus and its acting director at the time, Dr. Marina Solomidou-Ieronymidou, for permission to photograph several churches and icons. In addition, I thank His Beatitude the Archbishop of Cyprus Chrysostomos II and The Most Reverend Neophytos, Metropolitan of Morphou for granting me the same privileges. I must also express my gratitude to The Most Reverend Vasilios, Metropolitan of Constantia-Ammochostos for his hospitality and generosity. In addition, I am indebted to Ms. Spiroula Chrysi for her assistance at the church of Agios Nikolaos tis Stegis.

A book is never the product of just one author. The contributions of other scholars, in the way of suggestions, corrections, comments, and questions, blend together to produce a more refined work of scholarship, and my monograph is no exception to this. Without the insightful and critical readings of my colleagues and friends, this book would be severely lacking. I must thank Mark DelCogliano, David Eastman, Richard Flower, Nathan Howard, David Hunter, Andrew Jacobs, Scott Manor, Wendy Mayer, Ellen Muehlberger, Taylor Petrey, Claudia Rapp, and Greg Smith. Despite the best efforts of all of these individuals, all of the remaining shortcomings and errors in this book are my own.

ACKNOWLEDGMENTS   ix

I presented many of the ideas in this book at several conferences (the International Conference on Patristics Studies in Oxford, "Shifting Frontiers in Late Antiquity") and annual meetings (Byzantine Studies Association, International Congress on Medieval Studies, North American Patristics Society), and I was the direct beneficiary of numerous comments and observations that have helped me improve my work. Portions of chapter 6 are reprinted with permission from the publishers of "The Transformation of Heresiology in the Panarion of Epiphanius of Cyprus," in Shifting Genres in Late Antiquity, edited by Geoffrey Greatrex and Hugh Elton, with the assistance of Lucas McMahon (Farnham: Ashgate, 2015), 53–65, Copyright ©2015. Parts of chapter 7 were previously published in *Episcopal Elections in Late Antiquity*, Arbeiten zur Kirchengeschichte 119, edited by J. Leemans, P. Van Nuffelen, S. Keough, and C. Nicolaye (Berlin: Walter de Gruyter, 2011), 411–22, and reproduced with permission.

My interest in history and the study of the ancient world began at a relatively young age and burgeoned during my undergraduate years at UCLA. I am particularly grateful to my early teachers and mentors, especially Mary Hope Griffin, Robert Gurval, Charlie McNelis, David Myers, and Claudia Rapp. I would also like to pay tribute to my high school European history teacher, the late Carl Hoist, for getting me started.

I must also thank Ellen Bauerle at the University of Michigan Press for her encouragement and willingness to consider my book at a very early stage. I am also indebted to Susan Cronin, Mary Hashman, and the other staff members at the press for further assistance in the publication process. I am grateful to the two anonymous readers, whose insightful comments and suggestions greatly improved my manuscript. Lisa Eary was an indispensable resource for copyediting, proofreading, and indexing.

I am profoundly thankful for the love and support of friends, whose patience and indulgence of my interests are deeply appreciated. In particular, I would like to thank Jonathan Baek, Nate and Aminah Bradford, Jae Cho, Peter Choi, Samuel Girguis, Tim Gombis, Dae Young Jeong, Joel E. Kim, Reggie Dh. Kim, David Boksung Lee, Paul Lim, Chuck Roeper, Andi and Cynthia Song, David Sung, Doug and Susie Vander Griend, Byunghoon Woo, Mathew Yang, and Sung Yi. There are so many others I have failed to include, and for these omissions I offer my sincerest apologies.

Last, I must thank the most important people in my life, my family. My parents Hai Joon Kim and Youn Hwan Kim have sacrificed so much for me and my siblings, and through their dreams and determination they made possible the blessed lives we now live. My sister, Young-In Kim, and brother-in-law, Charles Park, have also been unceasingly supportive, and I am thankful for my brother, Young-Bin Kim, and niece Emily. I am also grateful to my parents-in-law, Tae Kil and Oak Choon Kim, for their boundless care and provision, and to Steven Kim and Esther Chung-Kim for their familial support. My sons Ewan and Rhys make each day sweeter, funnier, and more joyful; and even though they are too young to understand how much they are also a part of this book, any quality contained herein is in part due to the welcome diversions they provide every day. Finally, I dedicate this book to my wife Betty, who knows me best and loves me with all of my shortcomings, always 사랑.

s.d.g.

Contents

Abbreviations

Ancient Sources

In the footnotes, I have followed generally the abbreviation conventions of G. Lampe, *A Patristic Greek Lexicon* (Oxford: Oxford University Press, 1961) for Greek Patristic authors and titles of primary sources, with the notable exceptions of the *Ancoratus* (*Anc.*) and the *Panarion* (*Pan.*). For classical Greek authors not in Lampe, I have adopted the conventions of H. Liddell and R. Scott, *A Greek-English Lexicon* (Oxford: Oxford University Press, 1996) and for references to Latin authors, P. Glare, *Oxford Latin Dictionary* (Oxford: Oxford University Press, 1968) and A. Blaise and H. Chirat, *Dictionnaire latin-français des auteurs chrétiens* (Turnhout: Éditions Brepols S.A., 1954), whenever possible. For first citations, I include the titles of sources in full, then abbreviate as below in subsequent references.

Ancient Sources

Acta Archelai	*Act. Archel.*
Ambrose of Milan	Ambr.
Epistulae	*Ep.*
Ammianus Marcellinus	Amm.
Res gestae	*Res gestae*
Apophthegmata Patrum	*Apophth. Patr.*
Athanasius	Ath.
apologia ad Constantium	*apol. Const.*
apologia (secunda) contra Arianos	*apol. sec.*
apologia de fuga sua	*fug.*
contra gentes	*gent.*
de decretis Nicaenae synodi	*decr.*
de sententia Dionysii	*Dion.*
epistula ad Afros episcopos	*ep. Afr.*
epistula ad episcopos Aegypti et Libyae	*ep. Aeg. Lib.*
epistula de synodis Arimini et Seleuciae	*syn.*
epistula ad Jovianum	*ep. Jov.*
epistulae ad Serapionem	*ep. Serap.*
historia Arianorum ad monachos	*h. Ar.*
orationes tres adversus Arianos	*Ar.*
tomus ad Antiochenos	*tom.*
vita Antonii	*v. Anton.*
Basil of Caesarea	Bas.
adversus Eunomium libri tres	*Eun.*
epistulae	*ep.*
Clement of Alexandria	Clem.
stromateis	*str.*
Cyril of Jerusalem	Cyr. H.
catecheses illuminandorum	*catech.*
Epiphanius	Epiph.
Ancoratus	*Anc.*
de mensuris et ponderibus	*mens.*
Panarion	*Pan.*
Eusebius of Caesarea	Eus.
chronicon	*chron.*
demonstratio evangelica	*d.e.*
de vita Constantini	*v. C.*
historia ecclesiastica	*h.e.*
praeparatio evangelica	*p.e.*
Gregory of Nazianzus	Gr. Naz.
orationes	*orat.*
Gregory of Nyssa	Gr. Nyss.
epistulae	*ep.*
Hilary of Poitiers	Hilar.
De Synodis	*Syn.*
Hippolytus	Hipp.
refutatio omnium haeresium	*haer.*
Historia acephala	*h. aceph.*

Irenaeus	Iren.
adversus haereses	*haer.*
Jerome	Jer.
Aduersus Ioannem Hierosolymitanum liber	*Adu. Io. Hier.*
Adversus Rufinum libri III	*Ruf.*
De uiris illustribus liber	*Vir. ill.*
Epistulae	*Ep.*
Vita S. Hilarionis eremitae	*Vit. Hil.*
Josephus	Jos.
Antiquitates Judaicae	*AJ*
contra Apionem	*Ap.*
Julius Africanus	Afric.
chronicon	*chron.*
Justin Martyr	Just.
Apologiae	*1, 2 apol.*
dialogus cum Tryphone Judaeo	*dial.*
Nicander	Nic.
Alexipharmaca	*Alex.*
Theriaca	*Ther.*
Origen	Or.
commentarii in Jo.	*Jo.*
de principiis	*princ.*
homiliae in Jos.	*hom. in Jos.*
selecta in Gen.	*sel. in Gen.*
Palladius	Pall.
dialogus de vita Joannis Chrysostomi	*v. Chrys.*
Philostorgius	Philost.
historia ecclesiastica	*h.e.*
Rufinus	Ruf.
Eusebii historia ecclesiastica a Rufino translata et continuata	*Hist.*
Socrates	Socr.
historia ecclesiastica	*h.e.*
Sozomen	Soz.
historia ecclesiastica	*h.e.*
Tatian	Tat.
oratio ad Graecos	*orat.*
Tertullian	Tert.
Aduersus Iudaeos	*Iud.*
Aduersus Marcionem	*Marc.*
De praescriptione haereticorum	*Praescr.*
Theodoret	Thdt.
historia ecclesiastica	*h.e.*
Theophilus of Antioch	Thph. Ant.
ad Autolycum	*Autol.*
vita Epiphanii	*v. Epiph.*

Modern Sources

ACW	Ancient Christian Writers
BASP	*Bulletin of the American Society of Papyrologists*
CCSL	Corpus Christianorum Series Latina
CSCO	Corpus Scriptorum Christianorum Orientalium
CSEL	Corpus Scriptorum Ecclesiasticorum Latinorum
DHGE	*Dictionnaire d'histoire et de géographie ecclésiastiques*
FC	The Fathers of the Church
GCS	Die griechischen christlichen Schriftsteller der ersten drei Jahrhunderte
HTR	*Harvard Theological Review*
JECS	*Journal of Early Christian Studies*
JEH	*Journal of Ecclesiastical History*
JTS	*Journal of Theological Studies*
LCL	Loeb Classical Library
SC	Sources chrétiennes
StPatr	Studia Patristica
VC	*Vigiliae Christianae*
ZAC	*Zeitschrift für antikes Christentum*
ZKG	*Zeitschrift für Kirchengeschichte*
ZNW	*Zeitschrift für die neutestamentliche Wissenschaft und die Kunde des älteren Kirche*

Sigla

In my translations of ancient sources, I occasionally use the following based on the various critical editions listed in the bibliography.

< >	editorial restoration/conjecture inserted into the text
< ?>	editorial restoration or emendation suggested in the critical apparatus
[ ]	words added by the translator for the sake of clarity
( )	citations of scriptural passages and allusions

Introduction

Epiphanius of Cyprus was late antiquity. His life, deeds, and writings, and the development of his thought and beliefs, were deeply involved in the process of negotiating the cultural legacy of the Greco-Roman world and its apparent incompatibilities with an increasingly Christianized world. Some Christian intellectuals found a way to reconcile past and present by selectively embracing aspects of the classical tradition. Epiphanius, however, seemingly maintained an uncompromising stance, and throughout his writings he rhetorically constructed (and demolished) a straw man that embodied an unholy hybrid of classical culture and Christian heresy. This image of Epiphanius the anti-intellectual fundamentalist has stood the test of time, but it is unfortunately a tremendous disservice to the complexity and originality that was this (in-)famous heresiologist. It is high time Epiphanius received his just due for his unique contributions to the history of late antiquity and late ancient Christianity. For too long, he has lurked in the shadows of his more illustrious contemporaries, and modern scholars have largely relegated him to the lunatic fringe. Furthermore, he has been the victim of more enlightened sensibilities that have little tolerance for intolerance and a zealous dislike of religious dogmatism. Certainly there is no denying that Epiphanius maintained strong convictions and acted on them in ways that seem perhaps less than fair or charitable. But these were not the actions of a simple-minded buffoon or Bible-thumping demagogue. His complexity of thought and belief has been underappreciated or ignored altogether, and so this book offers a fresh look at the life and work of this eminently fascinating and provocative man.

The Reception of Epiphanius, Past and Present

Epiphanius of Cyprus was many things to many people, past and present.[1] To his admirers, he was an ascetic exemplar, venerable pastor and bishop, capable administrator, defender of the orthodox faith, biblical scholar, and heresy-hunter. After his death, his reputation and legacy for holiness and orthodoxy gave way to hagiography, a cult site, and a continuous celebration of his feast day on May 12.[2] Jerome, his ally during the Origenist controversy, included the Cypriot bishop in his catalog of illustrious men,[3] and Jerome narrated several anecdotes that epitomized Epiphanius's popularity. For example, when Epiphanius was visiting the city of Jerusalem, Jerome described how "a crowd of all ages and both sexes flocked together to him, offering their little ones, warmly kissing his feet, plucking at the fringes of his clothes."[4] The fifth-century ecclesiastical historian Sozomen simply concluded, "I think that he is entirely the

---

1. Numerous biographical sketches of Epiphanius are available in a wide variety of dictionaries and encyclopedias, although the most useful and informative include B. Altaner, *Patrologie: Leben, Schriften, und Lehre der Kirchenväter* (Freiburg: Herder, 1950), 271–74; W. Schneemelcher, "Epiphanius von Salamis," in *Reallexikon für Antike und Christentum, Band 5* (Stuttgart: Hiersemann, 1962), c. 909–27; P. Nautin, "Épiphane (Saint) de Salamine," in *DHGE* 15 (Paris: Letouzey et Ané, 1963), c. 617–31; C. Riggi, "La figura di Epifanio nel IV secolo," *StPatr* 8, no. 2 (1966): 86–107; J. Dummer, "Die Sprachkenntnisse des Epiphanius," in *Die Araber in der alten Welt* 5, no. 1, ed. F. Altheim and R. Stiehl (Berlin: Walter de Gruyter, 1968), 392–435.
    See also the substantial biographical details synthesized in the following monographs: J. Dechow, *Dogma and Mysticism in Early Christianity: Epiphanius of Cyprus and the Legacy of Origen*, Patristic Monograph Series 13 (Macon, GA: Mercer University Press, 1988), 25–124; A. Pourkier, *L'hérésiologie chez Épiphane de Salamine*, Christianisme Antique 4 (Paris: Beauchesne, 1992), 29–47; O. Kösters, *Die Trinitätslehre des Epiphanius von Salamis: Ein Kommentar zum "Ancoratus,"* Forschungen zur Kirchen- und Dogmengeschichte 86 (Göttingen: Vandenhoeck & Ruprecht, 2003), 17–76. See also the introduction by G. Aragione, "Una 'storia' universale dell'eresia: Il Panarion di Epifanio," in *Epifanio di Salamina: Panarion, Libro primo*, Letteratura Cristiana Antica, Nuova serie 21, ed. G. Pini (Brescia: Morcelliana, 2010).
2. *Itinerarium Antonini Placentini* 1 mentioned Cyprus and the tomb of Epiphanius as the first stop on a pilgrimage originating from Constantinople. For Epiphanius as saint, see C. Rapp, "The *Vita* of Epiphanius of Salamis: An Historical and Literary Study," 2 vols., DPhil. diss., Worcester College, Oxford University, 1991; eadem, "Epiphanius of Salamis: The Church Father as Saint," in *"The Sweet Land of Cyprus": Papers Given at the Twenty-Fifth Jubilee Spring Symposium of Byzantine Studies, Birmingham, March 1991*, ed. A. Bryer and G. Georghallides (Nicosia: Cyprus Research Centre for the Society for the Promotion of Byzantine Studies, 1993), 169–87. Also interesting is Epiphanius's ubiquity in Cypriot church paintings, in which he is sometimes paired with Barnabas, the apostolic father of the church on the island. See references to Epiphanius in A. Stylianou and J. Stylianou, *The Painted Churches of Cyprus: Treasures of Byzantine Art* (London: Trigraph for the A.G. Leventis Foundation, 1985); and D. Mouriki, "The Cult of Cypriot Saints in Medieval Cyprus as Attested by Church Decorations and Icon Painting," in *"Sweet Land,"* 237–77.
3. Jerome (henceforth Jer.), *De uiris illustribus liber* 114. For Epiphanius's relationship with Jerome, see J. Kelly, *Jerome: His Life, Writings, and Controversies* (London: Duckworth, 1975), 195–209.
4. Jer., *Aduersus Ioannem Hierosolymitanum liber* 11. This episode and its circumstances are discussed in greater detail in the final chapter of this volume.

most famous man under heaven, so to speak."[5] While separating fact from fiction is certainly difficult, the hagiographical memory underscores the extent of Epiphanius's popularity and reputation during his lifetime. Among contemporary scholars, Calogero Riggi stands out for his many publications on various aspects of Epiphanius's thought and theology and for the esteem with which he held *il santo di Salamina*.[6] In many of his studies, Riggi acknowledges the negative contemporary perceptions of Epiphanius, but at the same time his own interpretations exhibit an overt reverence and admiration for the bishop.[7] The monograph-length study of the *Ancoratus* by Oliver Kösters offers another favorable portrayal of Epiphanius as a pastor and biblical scholar, whose overarching concern was soteriological and whose rigidly dogmatic persona became manifest when he perceived that the orthodox faithful were under attack.[8]

To his detractors, Epiphanius was a narrow-minded zealot, a divisive meddler, and a subpar scholar with a penchant for harsh rhetoric, hyperbole, and invective. John of Jerusalem, who was unjustly accused by Epiphanius of being an Origenist, apparently thought of him as "a vainglorious old man."[9] The ninth-century Constantinopolitan patriarch and bibliophile Photius did not think very highly of Epiphanius as a writer: "His style is poor, and of such a level as is proper of one who is not guided by Attic elegance," a sentiment that has carried over into modern assessments.[10] Because of Epiphanius's seeming intransigence and dogmatic obstinacy, scholars have generally maintained a rather negative perception of him. Richard Hanson describes him as "another second-rate theologian standing in the tradition of Athanasius" and "a writer

5. Sozomen, *historia ecclesiastica* 6.32.4.
6. For *il santo*, see C. Riggi, "Catechesi escatologica dell' 'Ancoratus' di Epifanio," *Augustinianum* 8, no. 1 (1978): 164. Professor Riggi has written over two dozen articles on Epiphanius and published a critical edition of *Panarion* 66 (on Manichaeism) and a translation (Italian) of the *Ancoratus*. See the substantial listing in the bibliography.
7. See S. Fotiou, "Orthodoxia as Orthopraxia according to Saint Epiphanius of Salamis," *Phronema* 24 (2009): 51–63, for an example of rather uncritical admiration. Also noteworthy is the "ΑΓΙΟΣ ΕΠΙΦΑΝΙΟΣ" institute established by the Holy Bishopric of Constantia-Ammochostos, which hosted a 2008 conference dedicated to Epiphanius and published proceedings in T. Giagkou and C. Nassis, eds., *ΑΓΙΟΣ ΕΠΙΦΑΝΙΟΣ ΚΩΝΣΤΑΝΤΙΑΣ ΠΑΤΗΡ ΚΑΙ ΔΙΔΑΣΚΑΛΟΣ ΤΗΣ ΟΡΘΟΔΟΥ ΚΑΘΟΛΙΚΗΣ ΕΚΚΛΗΣΙΑΣ: ΠΡΑΚΤΙΚΑ ΣΥΝΕΔΡΙΟΥ* (Thessaloniki: Ekdoseis Mygdonia, 2012).
8. Kösters, *Trinitätslehre*, 46.
9. Jer., *Adu. Io. Hier.* 11 (or at least, this sentiment is what Jerome attributed to John). The Origenist controversy will be the focus of final chapter in this book, but for the seminal study, see E. Clark, *The Origenist Controversy: The Cultural Construction of an Early Christian Debate* (Princeton: Princeton University Press, 1992).
10. Photius, *Bibliotheca* Codex 122. Altaner, "In his writing he is often imprecise, superficial, and verbose and, as Photius (Cod. 122) had already noted, generally lacked in cultivated form as well as the Attic spirit." "Epiphanius," 272.

who is narrow-minded at best and very silly at worst."[11] Frank Williams, who translated the entire *Panarion* into English, offers the following judgment: "It is Epiphanius' inflated self-esteem which renders him least attractive. It is clear that he considered his own scholarship superior to most, and his own word on any question of importance decisive; once he had pronounced, nothing need be added. Nor was he given to regarding opponents with respect."[12] In addition to apparent personality defects, Epiphanius also involved himself in a number of ecclesiastical affairs in which he seems to have overestimated and overstepped his authority and appeared the (passive) aggressor.[13] I will discuss these episodes in greater detail in subsequent chapters and will argue that they were ultimately reflections of Epiphanius's personal formation and self-perception. In some sense, he could not help but behave in the ways he did. Finally, Epiphanius's shortcomings and character flaws were further magnified by the fact that he was a contemporary of some of the greats of the patristic tradition: "In fact, Epiphanius seems to be a complete stranger to classical *paideia* and is, in this regard, a unique exception among the grand authors of this age."[14] The sheer brilliance of these illumined men, the Cappadocians, Chrysostom, Jerome, and Augustine to name a few, and the productivity of their pens have far outshone the lowly bishop from Cyprus and his bulky and verbose heresiology.

Despite the generally negative views of Epiphanius that have held sway in contemporary scholarship, scholars still recognize that a debt is owed to him for his transmission of otherwise lost texts and documents: "There cannot be any doubt that Epiphanius' writings remain precious because they preserve much invaluable material for the history of the Church and theology."[15] This incidental preservation in reality is a reflection of Epiphanius's attention to sources. He was explicit in his introduction about how he compiled the source material for his heresiology:

11. R. Hanson, *The Search for the Christian Doctrine of God: The Arian Controversy, 318–381* (Edinburgh: T&T Clark, 1988), 658.
12. For the translation, see F. Williams, *The Panarion of Epiphanius of Salamis*, 2 vols. (with revised volumes), Nag Hammadi and Manichaean Studies 35, 36, 63, 79 (Leiden: Brill, 1987, 1994, 2009, 2012). Quotation is from Williams, *Panarion* (1987), xxv.
13. Epiphanius traveled to Antioch in late 376 or early 377 in an attempt to resolve the Meletian schism (*Panarion* 77.20.5–23.6, henceforth *Pan.*) and to Rome to appear before Pope Damasus in 382 over the same issue (Jer., *Epistulae* 108). Epiphanius went to Jerusalem in 393 to confront Bishop John on Origenism (Jer., *Adu. Io. Hier.*), and he spent his final days in Constantinople attempting to depose John Chrysostom (Socrates, *historia ecclesiastica* 6.10.1–14.12; Soz., *h.e.* 8.14.1–15.7).
14. Nautin, "Épiphane," 625.
15. J. Quasten, *Patrology*, vol. 3 (Westminster, MD: Newman Press, 1960), 385.

Some of what is about to come for the knowledge of the reader <concerning> heresies and schisms we know from love of study; and some we have gained from hearsay; and for some things we happened upon them with our own ears and eyes. And we are confident that we can give an account, from accurate reports, of the origins and teachings of some, but of others [only] a part of what happens among them.[16]

Epiphanius mentioned by name a wide variety of authors and texts that he (allegedly) consulted in writing the *Panarion*; clearly, conducting research or at least claiming to have done so was a priority for him. Fortunately, he incorporated source materials that were written by both orthodox and heterodox and thus preserved several significant texts for which modern scholars are indeed indebted.[17]

Clearly, modern receptions and perceptions of Epiphanius span a wide scale, from admiration to begrudging appreciation to detestation, and perhaps in some way each and all of these reflect different aspects of the man. But at the same time, any single view taken as definitive would only be a caricature, for no one perspective fully explains who he was. My purpose for this summary, however, is not to bemoan or criticize modern scholars for their perceptions of Epiphanius. Rather, my intention is quite the opposite. This book and the scholarship upon which it builds will testify to the vibrant and varied *interest* that Epiphanius's life and work have generated over the centuries, an interest that stretches back into the late Byzantine world, was revived by the Protestant reformer Philipp Melanchthon, was given further depth with the 1622 edition of Petau (later reproduced by Migne) and the five-volume edition of Dindorf (1859–62), and endures today.[18] Furthermore, the incalculably important work of Karl Holl in his publication of the editions of the *Ancoratus* and the *Panarion* in the old Griechischen Christlichen Schriftsteller series and the subsequent revisions by Jürgen Dummer and Christoph Markschies have established the

---

16. *Pan.*, Proem 2, 2.4. All translations of the *Panarion* are my own.
17. For example, the Greek text of a large section from Irenaeus, *adversus haereses* (*Pan.* 31.9.1–32.9), the letter of the Gnostic Ptolemy to Flora (*Pan.* 33.3.1–7.10), a large portion of Methodius, *de resurrectione mortuorum* (*Pan.* 64.12.1–62.15), and letters attributed to Basil of Ancyra and George of Laodicea (*Pan.* 73.2.1–22.8).
18. For Melanchthon's interest in Epiphanius, see K. Holl, *Die handschriftliche Überlieferung des Epiphanius (Ancoratus und Panarion)*, Texte und Untersuchungen zur Geschichte der altchristlichen Literatur 36.2 (Leipzig: J.C. Hinrichs, 1910), 1–13. Also see K. Bretschneider, ed., *Philippi Melanthonis Opera Quae Supersunt Omnia*, Corpus Reformatorum 1 (Halle: C.A. Schwetschke et Filium, 1834), 1110, 1112, for letters Melanchthon wrote to his friend Oporinus (who edited the printed edition) on his discovery and interest in volumes of Epiphanius's writings. Rapp, "*Vita*," 32–43, provides an interesting survey of ancient, medieval, and modern interest in the life and works of Epiphanius.

necessary textual foundation for continued studies of Epiphanius.[19] In addition, there are numerous translations of Epiphanius's works into various modern languages, including the aforementioned translation of the *Panarion* by
Frank Williams and my own translation of the *Ancoratus*. The bibliography lists
all that are generally accessible.[20]

Three important monographs deserve brief mention, and the reader will
certainly notice the presence and influence of these works on this book.[21] Jon
Dechow's *Dogma and Mysticism in Early Christianity: Epiphanius of Cyprus and
the Legacy of Origen* offers a significant, thorough exploration of how Epiphanius (mis)interpreted, (mis)understood, and (mis)constructed a particular theology of Origen to create an "Origenism" and to generate a conflict that was
ultimately a reflection of the larger problem of how the struggle over orthodoxy
and heresy "mediates the transition to Christianity's subsequent doctrinal, spiritual, and cultural development."[22] Aline Pourkier's *L'hérésiologie chez Épiphane
de Salamine* situates Epiphanius in the broader heresiological tradition and
closely examines not only how he drew on the works of his predecessors but
also how he added his own innovations, organized his entries, and executed his

---

19. K. Holl, *Epiphanius (Ancoratus und Panarion)*, in *Die griechischen christlichen Schriftsteller der ersten
drei Jahrhunderte* (Leipzig: J.C. Hinrichs Buchhandlung, 1915, 1922, 1933), in three volumes, with
revised editing for volumes 2 and 3 by J. Dummer (Berlin: Akademie Verlag / Walter de Gruyter,
1980, 1985) and volume 1 by C.-F. Collatz and M. Bergermann and (Berlin: Walter de Gruyter,
2013).

    Holl's edition, however, was not without faults, as contemporary and later critics noted his pen-
chant for conjecture. For discussions on the development and update of the *GCS* editions, see J.
Irmscher, "Die Epiphaniosausgabe der 'Griechischen Christlichen Schriftsteller,'" *Helikon* 22–27
(1982–87): 535–41; J. Dummer, "Zur Epiphanius-Ausgabe der 'Griechischen Christlichen Schriftsteller,'" in *Texte und Textkritik: Eine Aufsatzsammlung*, Texte und Untersuchungen zur Geschichte
der altchristlichen Literatur 133 (1987), 119–25. Holl's conjectures in the so-called *Anakephalaiosis*,
a synopsis of the *Panarion* included and integrated into the critical edition, have also been criticized.
See L. Abramowski, "Die Anakephalaiosis zum Panarion des Epiphanius in der Handschrift Brit.
Mus. Add. 12156," *Le Muséon* 96, nos. 3–4 (1983): 217–30; O. Knorr, "Die Parallelüberlieferung zum,
'Panarion' des Epiphanius von Salamis. Textkritische Anmerkungen zur Neuausgabe," *Wiener Stu-
dien* 112 (1955): 113–27.

20. Y. Kim, *Saint Epiphanius: Ancoratus*, FC 128 (Washington, DC: Catholic University of America
Press, 2014). All translations of the *Ancoratus* in this book come from this volume.

21. Two other recent books are notable, although both examine specific issues related to Epiphanius. C.
Osburn, *The Text of the Apostolos in Epiphanius of Salamis*, The New Testament in the Greek Fathers
6 (Atlanta: Society of Biblical Literature, 2004), examines all of Epiphanius's New Testament citations
of Acts and the Pauline and Catholic epistles and finds his "edition" to be of the Later Egyptian type.
S. Bigham, *Epiphanius of Salamis, Doctor of Iconoclasm? Deconstruction of a Myth*, Patristic Theological Library 3 (Rollinsford, NH: Orthodox Research Institute, 2008), revives a now century-long
debate about the role of Epiphanius's writings in the dispute over Iconoclasm and assertively concludes that the iconoclastic documents later attributed to Epiphanius were forgeries.

22. Dechow, *Dogma*, 12.

plan to serve his rhetorical ends.[23] Finally, Oliver Kösters's *Die Trinitätslehre des Epiphanius von Salamis: Ein Kommentar zum "Ancoratus"* is a comprehensive theological commentary on Epiphanius's first major (and largely neglected) work, the *Ancoratus*. While the *Ancoratus* was not the most organized text, Kösters's thorough analysis has demonstrated the depth of Epiphanius's biblical knowledge and overarching soteriological concern and how his unique thinking ought to be taken into account in broader examinations of the development of Trinitarian theology in the late fourth century. These monographs, in addition to several significant recent articles,[24] mark an important shift in the scholarly view of and approach to Epiphanius as a theologian, bishop, and controversial figure in the world of late antiquity.[25]

A critical biography, however, is missing from the corpus of Epiphanian studies, and this monograph seeks to fill this gap. Its goal is to offer a nuanced but critical understanding and appreciation of Epiphanius in his own right, primarily through an in-depth study of his magnum opus, the *Panarion*, the "Medicine Chest." Rather than mine the *Panarion* as a source of information on the beliefs and practices of *others*, this study examines it as a window into the man himself. I will demonstrate how we can read the text as a reflection of Epiphanius's own formation, convictions, and worldview, even as he dedicated his energy to the rhetorical construction and destruction of the heterodox. The *Panarion* contains detailed autobiographical anecdotes, and I will explore Epiphanius's personal recollections as seminal moments that shaped and influenced how he executed his role as a bishop and heresy-hunter. Furthermore,

---

23. For earlier examinations of Epiphanius's understanding of heresy and heresiology, see P. Fraenkel, "Histoire sainte et hérésie chez Saint Épiphane de Salamine, d'après le tome I du *Panarion*," *Revue de théologie et de philosophie* 12 (1962): 175–91; E. Moutsoulas, "Der Begriff 'Häresie' bei Epiphanius von Salamis," StPatr 7 (1966): 362–71; C. Riggi, "Il termine 'hairesis' nell'accezione di Epifanio di Salamina (*Panarion*, t. I; *De fide*): *Salesianum* 29 (1967): 3–27; G. Vallée, *A Study in Anti-Gnostic Polemics: Irenaeus, Hippolytus, and Epiphanius*, Studies in Christianity and Judaism 1 (Waterloo, ON: Wilfrid Laurier University Press, 1981); F. Young, "Did Epiphanius Know What He Meant by Heresy?," StPatr 17 (1982): 199–205.

24. Notably, R. Lyman, "The Making of a Heretic: The Life of Origen in Epiphanius' *Panarion* 64," StPatr 31 (1997): 445–51; eadem, "Ascetics and Bishops: Epiphanius on Orthodoxy," in *Orthodoxy, Christianity, History*, Collection de L'École Française de Rome 270, ed. S. Elm, E. Rebillard, A. Romano (Rome: École française de Rome, 2000), 149–61; J. Schott, "Heresiology as Universal History in Epiphanius' *Panarion*," ZAC 10 (2007): 546–63; A. Jacobs, "Matters (Un-)Becoming: Conversions in Epiphanius of Salamis," *Church History* 81, no. 1 (2012): 27–47; B. Stefaniw, "Straight Reading: Shame and the Normal in Epiphanius's Polemic against Origen," *JECS* 21, no. 3 (2013): 413–35; A. Jacobs, "Epiphanius of Salamis and the Antiquarian's Bible," *JECS* 21, no. 3 (2013): 437–64.

25. C. Markschies, "Epiphanios von Salamis," in *Der Neue Pauly, Band 3* (Stuttgart: Verlag J.B. Metzler, 1997), 1153, recently noted: "The theological originality of Epiphanius and the source value of his polemic are now judged more favorably."

Epiphanius's construction and inclusion of these personal stories, which I believe were rooted in actual experiences, reveal how he wanted others to understand him and imagine his life. I examine the narratives of these moments within the broader historical developments taking place during Epiphanius's lifetime in order to underscore how his self-construction and presentation paralleled historical changes that were unfolding in the later Roman Empire. The *Panarion* as a work of heresiology has much to show us about the writer himself, and ultimately this biography is about situating and understanding Epiphanius as a unique figure in the world of late antiquity.

Reading Heresiology, Reading the Panarion, Reading Epiphanius

The Christian tradition of heresiology began in the second century and evolved well into the Byzantine world and beyond.[26] Early Christians began to compose its representative texts in the midst of great diversity and flux, as different, sometimes competing and seemingly incompatible forms of Christianity each promoted particular practices and doctrines. At the same time, certain Christian thinkers and their communities advocated the importance of the ecclesiastical hierarchy and submission to the teachings and authority of legitimately appointed church leaders, and the rhetoric of orthodoxy and heresy became an important tool in affirming this ecclesiology.[27] The apologist Justin Martyr was the first to write a Christian heresiology, followed later by Hegesippus, Irenaeus, and Hippolytus.[28] The North African Tertullian (himself a later "here-

---

26. For the evolution of heresiology from antiquity to the Byzantine world and scholarly approaches to it, see A. Cameron, "How to Read Heresiology," *Journal of Medieval and Early Modern Studies* 33, no. 3 (2003): 471–92. See also J. Henderson, *The Construction of Orthodoxy and Heresy: Neo-Confucian, Islamic, Jewish, and Early Christian Patterns* (Albany: State University of New York Press, 1998), for a broader examination of the genre in several religions.

27. For developments in the meaning and understanding of "heresy" from the original Greek usage, see M. Simon, "From Greek Hairesis to Christian Heresy," in *Early Christian Literature and the Classical Intellectual Tradition: In Honorem Robert Grant*, ed. W. Schoedel and R. Wilken (Paris: Beauchesne, 1979), 101–16; H. von Staden, "Hairesis and Heresy: The Case of the *hairesis iatrikai*," in *Jewish and Christian Self-Definition, Vol. 3: Self-Definition in the Greco-Roman World*, ed. E. Sanders (Philadelphia: Fortress Press, 1982), 76–100; A. Le Boulluec, *La notion d'hérésie dans la littérature grecque IIe–IIIe siècles*, 2 vols. (Paris: Études Augustiniennes, 1985), 42–51; R. Norris, "Heresy and Orthodoxy in the Later Second Century," *Union Seminary Quarterly Review* 52 (1998): 43–59.

28. Justin Martyr mentioned a "treatise against all heresies" (*1 apologia* 26), which unfortunately does not survive. Hegesippus's *Hypomnemata* was preserved in fragments by Eusebius. Irenaeus's *adversus haereses* survives in five books, while Hippolytus's work survives in eight books and is known by dif-

tic") also wrote several important treatises against specific heresies, although not in the genre of heresiology per se.[29] And the late antique heresiologists included Epiphanius, Theodoret of Cyrrhus, Filastrius of Brescia, Augustine, and John of Damascus.

The genre of heresiology is notoriously tedious and lends itself to significant interpretative challenges.[30] Historians and theologians of bygone generations typically took heresiologies at face value and thereby affirmed a grand narrative in which the "orthodox" version of the history of the church was granted a privileged position in opposition to the various "heretical" deviations from the "true" and "right" belief. By now, the twentieth-century paradigm shift in scholarly understanding of orthodoxy and heresy is quite familiar to those who study early Christianity.[31] The recognition of early diversity and of manifold Christianities has reoriented contemporary approaches to the development and function of notions of orthodoxy and heresy, and scholars have recognized just how highly rhetorical and polemical heresiologies were in their construction of heresies and heretics.[32] The development of heresiology was also part of

---

ferent names, *Elenchos*, *Refutatio omnium haeresium*, and *Philosophumena*, depending on which books are referred.

   For Justin Martyr as the first heresiologist, see Le Boulluec, *La notion*, 36–91, and see 92–112 on Hegesippus. On Hippolytus as the author of the *Refutatio*, I follow M. Marcovich, *Hippolytus, Refutatio omnium haeresium*, Patristische Texte und Studien 25 (Berlin: Walter de Gruyter, 1986), 8–17, but his authorship is disputed. Pourkier, *L'hérésiologie*, 63–70, argues that the author of the *Elenchos* was "Josipe," following P. Nautin, *Hippolyte et Josipe: Contribution à l'histoire de la littérature chretienne du IIIe siècle* (Paris: Éditions du Cerf, 1947). See also A. Brent, *Hippolytus and the Roman Church in the Third Century: Communities in Tension before the Emergence of a Monarch-Bishop*, Supplements to Vigiliae Christianae 31 (Leiden: Brill, 1995).

29. On Tertullian, see T. Barnes, *Tertullian: A Historical and Literary Study* (Oxford: Oxford University Press, 1971). Another text, Pseudo-Tertullian, *Adversus omnes haereses*, was incorrectly attributed to him, although it does appear to borrow from the lost *Syntagma* of Hippolytus.

30. Cameron says modern scholarship has accused heresiology of "a lack of originality and superficiality" and that most scholars view heresiologies as "a source of information rather than as performative or functional texts." So she offers suggestions as to how they ought to be read and used as historical sources. "How to Read," 473–74.

31. Initiated by W. Bauer, *Rechtgläubigkeit und Ketzerei im ältesten Christentum* (Tübingen: Mohr, 1934). Most Anglophone scholars work with the useful translation by R. Kraft and G. Krodel, *Orthodoxy and Heresy in Earliest Christianity* (Philadelphia: Fortress Press, 1971), which also includes a useful discussion of the reception of the book, written first by Georg Strecker in his 1964 edition and expanded by Kraft. See also D. Harrington, "The Reception of Walter Bauer's 'Orthodoxy and Heresy in Earliest Christianity' during the Last Decade," *HTR* 73, nos. 1–2 (1980): 289–98; T. Robinson, *The Bauer Thesis Examined: The Geography of Heresy in the Early Christian Church* (Lewiston: Edwin Mellen Press, 1988); M. Desjardins, "Bauer and Beyond: On Recent Scholarly Discussions of Αἵρεσις in the Early Christian Era," *Second Century* 8, no. 2 (1991): 65–82. More recently, L. Ayres, "The Question of Orthodoxy," *JECS* 14, no. 4 (2006): 395–98, considers further how post-Bauer thesis scholarship has developed.

32. Le Boulluec, *La notion*, is seminal in this regard. For a broader examination and synthesis of how Christianity deployed rhetorical discourse in its self-identification and construction (and that of the

a much broader Christian appropriation and reinterpretation of classical culture and its literary genres.[33] Christians became engaged in a project of asserting total command over human knowledge, especially that of the classical tradition, and rendering the sum total of this collective erudition into a monolithic testament to the Christianization of civilization. Furthermore, the dynamic push and pull between Christianity and Judaism also affected the development of heresiological discourse, and the intersection and parting of the two "religions" has been a fruitful locus of recent scholarly inquiry.[34]

The constructed nature of heresiologies makes it quite difficult (but perhaps not impossible) to discern and reconstruct the *real* beliefs and practices of those deemed and condemned as heretics. Furthermore, fortuitous discoveries of texts once condemned as heretical, like those found in the Nag Hammadi corpus, have upended the traditional and triumphalist narrative of Irenaeus,

---

other), see A. Cameron, *Christianity and the Rhetoric of Empire: The Development of Christian Discourse*, Sather Classical Lectures 55 (Berkeley: University of California Press, 1991).

Rebecca Lyman has done much to explore the implications of the constructed nature of "orthodoxy" and "heresy": see "Making"; eadem, "The Politics of Passing: Justin Martyr's Conversion as a Problem of 'Hellenization,'" in *Conversion in Late Antiquity and the Early Middle Ages: Seeing and Believing*, ed. K. Mills and A. Grafton (Rochester, NY: University of Rochester Press, 2003), 36–60; eadem, "A Topography of Heresy: Mapping the Rhetorical Creation of Arianism," in *Arianism after Arius: Essays on the Development of the Fourth Century Trinitarian Conflicts*, ed. M. Barnes and D. Williams (Edinburgh: T&T Clark, 1993), 45–62; eadem, "Origen as Ascetic Theologian: Orthodoxy and Authority in the Fourth-Century Church," in *Origeniana Septima: Origenes in den Auseinandersetzungen des 4. Jahrhunderts*, Bibliotheca Ephemeridum Theologicarum Lovaniensium 137, ed. W. Bienert and U. Kühneweg (Leuven: Leuven University Press, 1999), 187–94; eadem, "Ascetics."

33. See H. Inglebert, *Interpretatio Christiana: Les mutations des saviors (cosmographie, géographie, ethnographie, histoire) dans l'Antiquité chrétienne (30–630 après J.-C.)*, Collection des Études Augustiniennes, Série Antiquité 166 (Paris: Institut d'Études Augustiniennes, 2001).

34. See D. Boyarin, *Dying for God: Martyrdom and the Making of Christianity and Judaism*, Figurae: Reading Medieval Culture (Stanford: Stanford University Press, 1999); idem, *Border Lines: The Partition of Judaeo-Christianity* (Philadelphia: University of Pennsylvania Press, 2004), with some modification in idem, "Rethinking Jewish Christianity: An Argument for Dismantling a Dubious Category (to which is Appended a Correction of My *Border Lines*)," *Jewish Quarterly Review* 99, no. 1 (2009): 7–36. See also S. Cohen, "A Virgin Defiled: Some Rabbinic and Christian Views on the Origins of Heresy," *Union Seminary Quarterly Review* 36, no. 1 (1980): 1–11, who offers an earlier, suggestive attempt at connecting parallel developments in Rabbinic Jewish and patristic Christian conceptions of heresy (although not in the more direct way argued by Boyarin).

For further studies on how Christians constructed the Jews as heretics, see A. Cameron, "Jews and Heretics: A Category Error?," in *The Ways That Never Parted: Jews and Christians in Late Antiquity and the Early Middle Ages*, Texts and Studies in Ancient Judaism 95, ed. A. Becker and A. Reed (Tübingen: Mohr Siebeck, 2003), 345–60. Many essays in this volume are also useful in further exploring the relational dynamic of Judaism and Christianity in the early centuries of the Common Era. Also important is A. Jacobs, *Remains of the Jews: The Holy Land and Christian Empire in Late Antiquity*, Divinations: Rereading Late Ancient Religion (Stanford: Stanford University Press, 2004), 44–51; idem, *Christ Circumcised: A Study in Early Christian History and Difference*, Divinations: Rereading Late Ancient Religion (Philadelphia: University of Pennsylvania Press, 2012), especially 100–114, for Epiphanius's construction and location of "Jews" in his heresiological discourse.

Hippolytus, and Epiphanius.[35] Thus recent study of heresiologies has become less about the subjects they purported to refute and more about the authors who wrote them and the experiences and circumstances that shaped their conceptions of and beliefs about the world around them. This shift in scholarly understanding and approaches to heresiology is also part of a much larger conversation about the development of Christianity. In much recent scholarship, a turn to critical theory and alternative methodologies to reading early and late ancient Christian texts has changed the way many scholars study and write about the early church, including the conception, development, and deployment of the rhetoric of orthodoxy and heresy.[36] My own study of Epiphanius is indebted to developments in the last few decades that have reoriented scholarship away from traditionally pietistic narratives of the history of Christianity toward new readings with particular emphasis on the late ancient Christian use and meaning of words, the realities and ideologies of empire, and the construction of "self" and "other" identities.[37] This book builds on the body of scholarship that has transformed how we read heresiologies and their authors and contributes to the ongoing discussion of how we study these and other patristic texts.[38]

35. Consider the challenges to and reinterpretations of the traditional understanding and narrative of the heresies identified as "Gnostic" or "Gnosticism." See F. Wisse, "The Nag Hammadi Library and the Heresiologists," *VC* 25, no. 3 (1971): 205–23; idem, "Gnosticism and Early Monasticism in Egypt," in *Gnosis: Festschrift für Hans Jonas*, ed. B. Aland (Göttingen: Vandenhoeck & Ruprecht, 1978), 431–40; E. Pagels, *The Gnostic Gospels* (New York: Random House, 1979); Vallée, *Study*.

  And more recently, see M. Williams, *Rethinking "Gnosticism": An Argument for Dismantling a Dubious Category* (Princeton: Princeton University Press, 1996); K. King, *What is Gnosticism?* (Cambridge, MA: Harvard University Press, 2003), especially 20–54, 149–217, and contrast with C. Markschies, *Gnosis: An Introduction*, trans. J. Bowden (London: T&T Clark, 2003); B. Pearson, *Gnosticism and Christianity in Roman and Coptic Egypt*, Studies in Antiquity and Christianity (London: T&T Clark, 2004), especially 201–23. D. Brakke, *The Gnostics: Myth, Ritual, and Diversity in Early Christianity* (Cambridge, MA: Harvard University Press, 2010), offers a via media.

36. See E. Clark, *History, Theory, Text: Historians and the Linguistic Turn* (Cambridge, MA: Harvard University Press, 2004), for developments in historiography and literary theory that have reconfigured how different academic disciplines understand history, the meaning and function of language, and the nature of "texts," "contexts," and "narratives." Clark also suggests how different theoretical frameworks might inform the ways scholars study late ancient Christianity.

  For reflections on the challenges and changes in the approach to church history by North American scholars, as well as the influence of theoretical approaches to the study of early Christianity, see D. Brakke, "The Early Church in North America: Late Antiquity, Theory, and the History of Christianity," *Church History* 71, no. 3 (2002): 473–91.

37. See the articles in E. Iricinschi and H. Zellentin, eds., *Heresy and Identity in Late Antiquity*, Texts and Studies in Ancient Judaism 119 (Tübingen: Mohr Siebeck, 2008).

38. See for example the collection of essays in D. Martin and P. Cox Miller, eds., *The Cultural Turn in Late Ancient Studies: Gender, Asceticism, and Historiography* (Durham, NC: Duke University Press, 2005). The introduction by Martin offers a useful survey of how recent scholarship has approached the study of late ancient Christianity. Also see Clark, *History*, 156–85.

If a text like the *Panarion*, which long ago may have been considered a reliable source of information on heretics and their beliefs and practices, is actually fraught with rhetorical and polemical exaggerations, misrepresentations, and constructions of the heretical "other," the question then remains how (and perhaps if) we ought to read and utilize it. It is a question well worth pursuing, and I return to the point that the *Panarion* has much to say about the late antique man who conceived and wrote it. I have found essential Averil Cameron's assertion that rather than reading heresiologies merely as sources of information, which can only yield unsympathetic reactions to such texts, we must think of them as "performative or functional texts."[39] I have argued elsewhere that we might "read" the *Panarion* as a sort of collective biography in which the sum of the biographical details that Epiphanius provided on various heresiarchs built a composite image of the "unholy man."[40] I also extrapolated from the *Panarion* a novel conception of the geography of the Roman Empire that envisioned the borders defined not by Roman-ness but by belief. Therefore, in Epiphanius's imagination, the orthodox became the new citizens, while the heretics became the new barbarians.[41]

In this book, which builds on ideas I explored in my doctoral dissertation,[42] I read the *Panarion* as an "autobiography," that is, I "read" Epiphanius himself. A fundamental premise in this study is that specific, real experiences in Epiphanius's life, which he packaged and inserted into the *Panarion*, were formative in shaping his outlook on the world, informing his policies as a bishop, and influencing his behavior as a heresy-hunter. At the same time, his recollections were the products of his imagination, and he constructed his life to provide readers with an idealized public image situated in strategic loci in his heresiology. Thus I believe it is possible to "read" Epiphanius in these episodes both as a historical person and a rhetorical persona, but I also recognize that this double reading presents some methodological difficulty and necessitates a careful negotiation between the author (Epiphanius) and his text (*Panarion*), and the text and its reader.

For a critical study of Epiphanius's life and work, I have utilized an uncon-

39. Cameron, "How to Read," 473–74.
40. Y. Kim, "Reading the *Panarion* as Collective Biography: The Heresiarch as Unholy Man," *VC* 64, no. 4 (2010): 382–413.
41. Y. Kim, "Epiphanius of Cyprus and the Geography of Heresy," in *Violence in Late Antiquity: Perceptions and Practices*, ed. H. Drake (Burlington: Ashgate, 2006), 235–51.
42. Y. Kim, "The Imagined Worlds of Epiphanius of Cyprus," PhD diss., University of Michigan, Ann Arbor, 2006.

ventional chapter framework that needs some explanation. In each of three "biographical" chapters, I analyze both the historical circumstances in which a particular period of Epiphanius's life unfolded and the specific, first-person episode as he presented it in order to extrapolate and construct a composite picture of the historical and literary Epiphanius. I have paired each of these biographical chapters with a thematic chapter, each exploring through wide readings of the *Panarion* broader aspects of Epiphanius's thinking, convictions, and imagining of the world. The core chapters thus form a series of couplets organized into three parts: beginnings, transitions, and ascents. Epiphanius narrated and inserted into his heresiology his recollections of pivotal life experiences that both molded him and informed how he imagined himself—monk-bishop, arbiter of orthodoxy, heresy-hunter—and how he imagined the world around him, one that reflected a primordial struggle between right and wrong belief and practice. This worldview was deeply influenced by the life and legacy of Athanasius and was always threatened by the poisonous threat of heresies and heretics. The final chapter examines Epiphanius's life after the *Panarion*, when he essentially "lived out" the "Epiphanius" we will have seen take shape in the *Panarion*. This book is not a traditional biography but a complex examination of the intersection of words and deeds, convictions and tensions, perceptions and practices that undergird the pages of the *Panarion*, and my study seeks to understand Epiphanius on his own terms, in his own *imagined* orthodox world.

PART ONE

Beginnings

CHAPTER 1

"But the Merciful God Rescued Me from Their Depravity"

Epiphanius in Egypt

Monastic Beginnings

At the end of Book 6 of his *Ecclesiastical History*, Sozomen surveyed the most outstanding monks of the fourth century by region. In the section dedicated to Palestine, he included Epiphanius among the greats.[1] Sandwiched between the mention of Epiphanius's monastic settlement in Palestine and his rise as metropolitan of Cyprus is a brief description of his early training: "Instructed from youth by the finest monks and, on account of this, having spent a great deal of time in Egypt, he became most notable for his monastic philosophy among both the Egyptians and the Palestinians."[2] According to Sozomen, Epiphanius spent a significant part of his youth in Egypt. If this was true, we can assume that the monastic instruction he received there was an essential component of his educational background.[3] However, we must also maintain a degree of cau-

---

1. Soz., *h.e.* 6.32.1–5.
2. Soz., *h.e.* 6.32.3.
3. For an earlier assessment of Epiphanius's educational background, see C. Riggi, "La scuola teologica di Epifanio e la filologia origeniana," in *Crescita dell'uomo nella catechesi dei padri (Età Postnicea): Convegno di studio e aggiornamento Facoltà di Lettere cristiane e classiche (Pontificium Institutum Altioris Latinitatis), Roma 20–21 marzo 1987*, ed. S. Felici (Roma: LAS, 1988), 87–104. Riggi is right to emphasize the importance of the (Pachomian) monastic milieu in Epiphanius's educational formation; although, as we will see below, Riggi's overemphasis on the existence and influence of a defined and recognizable Origenism in early fourth-century Egypt is problematic. Riggi, in his typically hagiographical way, argues that Epiphanius came to represent a via media between the extremes of Anthropomorphite and Origenist theologies.

tion not to accept this account too readily, since Sozomen was writing in the fifth century and may have been drawing on a hagiographic tradition that celebrated Epiphanius as an ascetic and orthodox champion.

Much is uncertain about the dates of Epiphanius's birth, youth, and time in Egypt. Generally, scholars place his birth circa 315, which is extrapolated from more firmly established dates in his life (although even these are disputed), namely his rise to the metropolitan bishopric on Cyprus (either 366 or 367) and the date of his death (either 402 or 403). Palladius in his *Dialogue on the Life of John Chrysostom* wrote: "The blessed Epiphanius, bishop of Constantia in Cyprus, governed the church there for thirty-six years," and Jerome writing in 393 added the following detail: "He is still alive up to this day and presently in extreme old age."[4] Depending on what Jerome meant by "extreme old age," we can suggest that Epiphanius was in his middle to late seventies at this point (393) and thus accept a range for his birth between 310 and 320, for an average of circa 315. Again, when Epiphanius made his way to Egypt remains uncertain and is further complicated by the biographical sketch found at the beginning of the *Ancoratus*.[5] Nevertheless, if we take circa 315 as the date of his birth and assume that his elementary education in letters and grammar was completed in his homeland, his sojourn to Egypt for further study could have started when he was around fifteen, circa 330.[6] This date is important because it places a young

---

4. Palladius, *dialogus de vita Joannis Chrysostomi* 16.206–7. Jer., *Vir. ill.* 114 (*superest usque hodie et in extrema iam senectute*).

   For reasons to be explained in the conclusion, I argue for the date of his death in 403, and thus the beginning of his episcopate to 367. For the date of Jerome's *On Illustrious Men*, see P. Nautin, "La date du De viris inlustribus de Jérôme, de la mort de Cyrille de Jérusalem et de celle de Grégoire de Nazianze," *Revue d'histoire ecclésiastique* 56 (1961): 33–35. Also, both Nautin and Pourkier affirm the 366 (election) and 402 (death) dates.

5. The relevant section reads: "Our holy and great father Epiphanios was from Eleutheropolis in Palestine, where he became a father of monks. He first <practiced?> asceticism, withdrawing into Egypt, and persevering <there> until his return in his twentieth year of life, when he returned back to the country around Eleutheropolis and built a monastery there" (this translation and all subsequent quotations of the *Ancoratus* from Kim, *Saint Epiphanius*, 51). This would leave Epiphanius in Egypt until about 335, although there is no indication of when he first left his homeland. However, Holl, *Überlieferung*, 65, indicates that this short summary of his life was a later addition, and hence Kösters, *Trinitätslehre*, 77–80, argues that we ought to regard its chronology with caution.

6. Pourkier, *L'hérésiologie*, 29, has suggested that Epiphanius might have received some education with a rhetorician in Alexandria, although there does not appear to be any clear evidence to substantiate this. However, it is possible that he did live in Alexandria for at least part of his educational experience, whatever form it was. Epiphanius's encounter with certain Gnostic women, an episode that is at the heart of this chapter, seems to affirm that he was at least in an urban setting with bishops. Cf. Nautin, "Épiphane," 618.

   Both the order of education and the age suggested here are entirely conjectural, but based on the

Epiphanius in Egypt in the aftermath of the Council of Nicaea and in the midst of the escalating Arian controversy and the rise and travails of Athanasius. Epiphanius also learned to practice his asceticism in an Egypt, where the institutions of monasticism were still developing and in flux.

Ultimately, it is difficult to answer exactly why the Palestine-born Epiphanius made his way to Egypt and what he intended to learn and become. However, from his own life and pen we can observe that Epiphanius exhibited extreme hostility toward secular education and Greek culture, that is, all that was encompassed in the tradition of classical *paideia*.[7] No one epitomized this danger more than Origen, whom Epiphanius described as a onetime orthodox Christian who was ruined by his "secular" learning.[8] In the conclusion of his refutation of Origen, Epiphanius argued, "Thus you, Origen, your mind blinded by your Greek education (Ἑλληνικῆς παιδείας), have vomited poison for your followers and have become noxious food for them, by which you yourself have been harmed while harming more people."[9] In addition, Epiphanius's consistent repudiation of classical learning went hand in hand with his rejection of an "academic" Christianity, characteristic of Alexandria, in which theology, philosophy, and the Christian life were explored and mediated by prominent, independent Christian teachers who, together with their circles of devoted followers, posed particular threats to the ecclesiastical hierarchy.[10]

---

study of H. Marrou, *Histoire de l'éducation dans l'antiquité, deuxième édition* (Paris: Éditions du Seuil, 1950), 359–60. Dechow, *Dogma*, 32, places Epiphanius's arrival in Egypt c. 330 and Pourkier, *L'hérésiologie*, 29–34, c. 326–c. 331 (depending on his birth year). Kösters, *Trinitätslehre*, 20–29, pushes his arrival into Egypt earlier, c. 325 around the age of ten, partly because Epiphanius's theological formation needed time to incubate and develop.

7. J. Dummer, "Epiphanius von Constantia und Homer," *Philologus* 119, no. 1 (1975): 84–91, notes that Epiphanius's classical knowledge was often derived from intermediary sources. On the social and political function of *paideia* in late antiquity, see P. Brown, *Power and Persuasion in Late Antiquity: Towards a Christian Empire* (Madison: University of Wisconsin Press, 1992), 3–70. On the complicated relationship and responses Christians had to *paideia*, see Inglebert, *Interpretatio*, 257–78, 443–49. For a useful examination of Roman education in late antiquity, with ample references, see E. Watts, *City and School in Late Antique Athens and Alexandria*, Transformation of the Classical Heritage 41 (Berkeley: University of California Press, 2006), 1–23.

8. *Pan.* 64.3.1: "For Origen was at that time of the orthodox and catholic faith."

9. *Pan.* 64.72.9. See Kim, "Reading," 406–12. This was all the more ironic because Origen himself was cautious about how much philosophy a Christian could use before becoming corrupted; cf. Origen, *epistula ad Gregorium Thaumaturgum* (*philocalia* 13). Epiphanius, of course, did not consider at all the subtle arguments Origen made regarding the relationships between true Christianity, heresy, Greek philosophy, and pagan religion. See Le Boulluec, *La notion*, 439–545, for a thorough examination.

10. D. Brakke, *Athanasius and Asceticism* (Baltimore: Johns Hopkins University Press, 1995), 57–79, sees the rejection of academic Christianity as a central feature of Athanasius's revised program of asceti-

Epiphanius frequently made self-deprecating remarks about his own education, perhaps with a pinch of false or contrived humility, as for example when he invoked "my customary calling on God's help for my lack of education" in his entry against Origen.[11] This was by the fourth century a well-established rhetorical trope with which a speaker could ingratiate himself to an audience with feigned humility and render himself that much more persuasive.[12] Perhaps here is a hint that Epiphanius viewed his initial secular educational pursuits with a sense of disdain (due to failure?), and he emphasized throughout his writings the supremacy of Christian knowledge over, above, and to the exclusion of that of the world.[13] In the second preface to the *Panarion*, as he began his massive exposition on orthodoxy and heresy, Epiphanius made clear the only true source of knowledge:

> Neither through my own ability nor from my own reasoning do I proceed, but as God, master of all and merciful one, revealed to his prophets, and through them he deemed me worthy of the knowledge of the whole subject, according to what is allowed to human nature. And while I begin to examine these things forthwith, in the first place I come not to a small struggle, but I am even exceedingly afraid, having undertaken not a chance matter. And I call upon holy God himself, and his only-begotten Son, Jesus Christ, and the Holy Spirit, in order that he might shine upon our impoverished mind for an illumination of knowledge concerning these things.[14]

Sozomen's observation that Epiphanius was trained at a young age in a monastic context and later became renowned for his own particular "monastic philosophy" seems the most fitting basis for understanding Epiphanius's educational background and personal formation, even if he had initially moved to

---

cism, especially for women. See also R. Williams, *Arius: Heresy and Tradition* (London: Darton, Longman, and Todd, 1987), 82–91; Watts, *City*, 143–203. For Epiphanius, Origen was the quintessential academic Christian corrupted by Greek philosophy and culture.

On Alexandria in general, see C. Haas, *Alexandria in Late Antiquity: Topography and Social Conflict* (Baltimore: Johns Hopkins University Press, 1997).

11. *Pan.* 64.72.2. Epiphanius imagined a dichotomy of the undereducated but orthodox Christian, taught by God (Epiphanius), and the overeducated heretic corrupted by his worldly knowledge (Origen).

12. For example, D. Martin, *The Corinthian Body* (New Haven: Yale University Press, 1995), 47–68, argues that the Apostle Paul effectively utilized self-deprecation to augment his argument.

13. See Inglebert, *Interpretatio*, 443–49, on the conflicting attitudes of Christians with respect to the relationship between secular knowledge and Christian faith. Inglebert argues that Epiphanius ultimately failed in his attempt to define Christian culture strictly on religious grounds.

14. *Pan.* Proem 2, 1.2

Egypt to pursue a more traditional education. In other words, Epiphanius and his admirers would have us believe that his education was ascetically Christian. We must, however, again remain cautious in accepting too readily Epiphanius's obvious self-construction as well as the "Epiphanius" remembered by later writers. He was by no means an uneducated or even undereducated person. Although medieval and modern scholars have disparaged his writing style, Epiphanius's own work displayed a breadth of secular and sacred knowledge, a keen ability to employ rhetoric to attack his enemies, and a depth of theological and biblical engagement, all of which were characteristic of someone with a solid educational foundation.

Nevertheless, Epiphanius was renowned and remembered as a monastic exemplar in other ancient sources.[15] In addition to Sozomen's observations, Jerome in his hagiography of the famed ascetic Hilarion wrote: "Epiphanius, bishop of Salamis in Cyprus, . . . since he abided with Hilarion exceedingly, has written his praise in a brief letter that is read by the masses."[16] Not only was Epiphanius personally familiar with Hilarion and presumably his way of life, but he also carried on the legacy of his "teacher" in a lost letter that was apparently read by many. Furthermore, Jerome described how Hilarion was instructed by none other than Antony, which suggests that Epiphanius had at least an indirect connection with the famed Egyptian ascetic.[17] Kösters conjectures that Hilarion might have mentored Epiphanius in the context of an anchoritic community and that certain aspects of Hilarion's monasticism would have been influential in his disciple's life.[18] While it is ultimately impossible to determine to what extent, if any, Epiphanius learned from either ascetic exemplar, clearly the monastic milieu of his early life became an important part of his transmitted biography. This is further evident in the anonymous fifth-century collection of sayings by celebrated desert fathers, the so-called *Apophthegmata Patrum*, which included various sayings attributed to Epiphanius.[19] In one anecdote, we find an inversion of Jerome's picture of Epipha-

---

15. On the paucity of information from Epiphanius himself on his monastic views and teachings, see I. Bugár, "Epiphanius of Salamis as Monastic Author? The So-Called *Testamentum Epiphanii* in the Context of Fourth-Century Spiritual Trends," StPatr 42 (2006): 73–81.

16. Jer., *Vita S. Hilarionis eremitae* 1.

17. Jer., *Vit. Hil.* 3; Dechow, *Dogma*, 32–33.

18. Kösters, *Trinitätslehre*, 24. The *Vita Epiphanii* 13, also emphasized the vital influence of Hilarion on Epiphanius.

19. On what we can potentially learn of early Egyptian monasticism from the *Apophthegmata*, see D. Burton-Christie, *The Word in the Desert: Scripture and the Quest for Holiness in Early Christian Monasticism* (Oxford: Oxford University Press, 1993); G. Gould, *The Desert Fathers on Monastic Community* (Oxford: Oxford University Press, 1993); W. Harmless, *Desert Christians: An Introduction to the Literature of Early Monasticism* (Oxford: Oxford University Press, 2004), 167–273. But see criti-

nius as disciple of Hilarion when the latter recognized the former's exemplary asceticism: "Forgive me, your [Epiphanius's] way of life is better than mine."[20]

The various sources that shed some light on the life of Epiphanius were of course composed well after the events they purported to describe. With the exception of Jerome, none of the other authors knew Epiphanius personally. Thus it was clear that by the end of the fourth century, an imagining of Epiphanius was already in development. As we will see throughout this book, Epiphanius himself engaged in constructing his persona in the *Panarion* as he "remembered" particular episodes from his lifetime and incorporated them into his heresiology to serve a variety of rhetorical purposes. We should not read Epiphanius's own recollections at face-value, just as we would not read other parts of the *Panarion* for straightforward descriptions of the beliefs and practices of the heresies and heretics he refuted. However, neither should we dismiss the autobiographical stories outright as mere fabrications. I maintain that despite the obvious self-construction, the stories were nevertheless grounded in real experiences. So we must tread carefully between being overly dismissive of Epiphanius's recollections and too accepting of what were clearly narratives stemming from his memory and imagination. Epiphanius wanted his readers to envision him in a particular way, and he deliberately constructed a past for himself, built on a foundation of real-life experiences, to legitimize and lend greater authority to the work he was undertaking in the *Panarion*. But before discussing Epiphanius's imagined youth, we will examine developments in early fourth-century Egypt that would have comprised the ecclesiastical and monastic milieu in which he gained his education and had his first "encounter" with heresy.

Monastic Trends

We are well informed of the rich and complex developments in ascetic practice and spirituality that gave rise to different but related traditions of monasticism in the deserts of Egypt (and neighboring regions) in the third and

---

cisms in S. Rubenson, "Origen in the Egyptian Monastic Tradition of the Fourth Century," in *Origeniana Septima*, 319–37.

20. *Apophth. Pat.* E 4 (translation from B. Ward, *The Sayings of the Desert Fathers: The Alphabetical Collection* [Kalamazoo: Cistercian Publications, 1975], 49). Another notable detail about the Epiphanius that appeared in this collection was that he was clearly identified as a bishop who continued to live the monastic life.

fourth centuries.[21] We are also aware of the important dynamic between ascetic practice and spiritual authority that presented a number of challenges to Christians, especially those within the ecclesiastical hierarchy, who, along with imperial and local administrators, were threatened by the social, political, and spiritual functions of holy men who operated beyond the confines of the church.[22] Thus these Christians attempted to control the impact and legacy of these exemplars, especially after their deaths, by carefully constructing their biographies and supervising their cult sites. These were important and perhaps necessary rhetorical strategies for enfolding these holy men within the institutional church, or at least for maintaining a vigilant eye upon them.[23]

---

21. For a starting point, see D. Chitty, *The Desert a City: An Introduction to the Study of Egyptian and Palestinian Monasticism under the Christian Empire* (Oxford: Blackwell, 1966). See also P. Rousseau, *Ascetics, Authority, and the Church in the Age of Jerome and Cassian* (Oxford: Oxford University Press, 1978), with second edition (Notre Dame, IN: University of Notre Dame Press, 2010), 9–76; idem, *Pachomius: The Making of a Community in Fourth-Century Egypt*, Transformation of the Classical Heritage 6 (Berkeley: University of California Press, 1985); C. Griggs, *Early Egyptian Christianity, from Its Origins to 451 C.E.*, Coptic Studies 2 (Leiden: Brill, 1990); Burton-Christie, *Word*; Gould, *Fathers* (which challenges some of the arguments of Rousseau, *Ascetics*); J. Goehring, "The Encroaching Desert: Literary Production and Ascetic Space in Early Christian Egypt," *JECS* 1, no. 3 (1993): 281–96; S. Elm, *"Virgins of God": The Making of Asceticism in Late Antiquity* (Oxford: Oxford University Press, 1994), especially 226–372 for Egypt; the collection of essays in J. Goehring, *Ascetics, Society, and the Desert: Studies in Early Egyptian Monasticism*, Studies in Antiquity and Christianity (Harrisburg, PA: Trinity Press International, 1999); and Harmless, *Desert*.
    For studies on more practical concerns in Egyptian Christianity and monasticism, see J. Goehring, "The World Engaged: The Social and Economic World of Early Egyptian Monasticism," in *Gnosticism and the Early Christian World. In Honor of James M. Robinson*, ed. J. Goehring, C. Hedrick, J. Sanders, with H. Betz (Sonoma, CA: Polebridge Press, 1990), 134–44 (also in Goehring, *Ascetics*, 39–52); R. Bagnall, *Egypt in Late Antiquity* (Princeton: Princeton University Press, 1993), 293–303; A. Martin, *Athanase d'Alexandrie et l'église d'Égypte au IVe siècle (328–373)*, Collection de L'École française de Rome 216 (Paris: École française de Rome, 1996), 707–63; E. Wipszycka, *Moines et communautés monastiques en Égypte (IVe–VIIIe siècles)*, Journal of Juristic Papyrology, Supplement XI (Warsaw: Faculty of Law and Administration of Warsaw University, Institute of Archaeology of Warsaw University, Raphael Taubenschlag Foundation, 2009).
22. This dynamic was famously studied by Peter Brown for Syria in "The Rise and Function of the Holy Man in Late Antiquity," *Journal of Roman Studies* 61 (1971): 80–101. But also see the following important examinations of the dynamics and potential tensions between asceticism and spiritual authority, especially from the perspective of the ecclesiastical hierarchy: Rousseau, *Ascetics*; H. Chadwick, "Bishops and Monks," StPatr 24 (1993): 45–61; Brakke, *Athanasius*, 80–141; Haas, *Alexandria*, 258–67; D. Caner, *Wandering, Begging Monks: Spiritual Authority and the Promotion of Monasticism in Late Antiquity*, Transformation of the Classical Heritage 33 (Berkeley: University of California Press, 2002); C. Rapp, *Holy Bishops in Late Antiquity: The Nature of Christian Leadership in an Age of Transition*, Transformation of the Classical Heritage 37 (Berkeley: University of California Press, 2005), 56–152. For the challenge to imperial authority, see Brown, *Power and Persuasion*.
23. For example in Athanasius's *vita Antonii*. Bagnall states succinctly: "The church hierarchy valued monasticism, but wanted to control it, and official views of the monks tend to be colored by the need to make them fit into approved forms." *Egypt*, 295. See also M. Gaddis, *There Is No Crime for Those Who Have Christ: Religious Violence in the Christian Roman Empire*, Transformation of the Classical Heritage 39 (Berkeley: University of California Press, 2005), 230–50.
    The *vita Antonii* is an intensely scrutinized and disputed text. For a summary of the textual and

There is no better example than Athanasius's construction of the life of Antony:

Though the sort of man he [Antony] was, he honored the rule of the Church with extreme care, and he wanted every cleric to be held in higher regard than himself. He felt no shame at bowing the head to the bishops and priests; if even a deacon came to him for assistance, he discussed the things that are beneficial, and gave place to him in prayer, not being embarrassed to put himself in a position to learn.[24]

Athanasius's imagined Antony, the ascetic par excellence, clearly subsumed himself under the authority of the ecclesiastical hierarchy. Furthermore, bishops like Athanasius took the literary control of an ascetic a step further. Because church leaders recognized the powerful influence those who wielded a spiritual authority acquired through their commitment to asceticism, they sought to control and utilize living monks by ordaining them into the ecclesiastical hierarchy as a practical means of direct oversight.[25]

---

historical problems (with references to earlier scholarship), see S. Rubenson, *The Letters of St. Antony: Origenist Theology, Monastic Tradition and the Making of a Saint*, Bibliotheca Historico-Ecclesiastica Lundensis 24 (Lund: Lund University Press, 1990), 126–32; Harmless, *Desert*, 111–13; Wipszycka, *Moines*, 227–80; but also earlier H. Dörries, "Die Vita Antonii als Geschichtsquelle," *Nachrichten von der Akademie der Wissenschaften in Göttingen, Philologisch-Historische Klasse* 14 (1949): 359–410. On questions of Athanasian authorship, see M. Tetz, "Athanasius und die Vita Antonii: Literarische und theologische Relationen," *ZNW* 73 (1982): 1–30; T. Barnes, "Angel of Light or Mystic Initiate? The Problem of the *Life of Antony*," *JTS* 37, no. 2 (1986): 353–68; A. Louth, "St Athanasius and the Greek *Life of Antony*," *JTS* 39, no. 2 (1988): 504–9; D. Brakke, "The Authenticity of the Ascetic Athanasiana," *Orientalia* 64 (1994): 17–56; idem, "The Greek and Syriac Versions of the *Life of Antony*," *Le Muséon* 107 (1994): 29–53; Martin, *Athanase*, 481–90.

On the construction and control of the life of Antony to serve other purposes, see R. Gregg and D. Groh, *Early Arianism: A View of Salvation* (Philadelphia: Fortress Press, 1981), 131–59; M. Williams, "The *Life of Antony* and the Domestication of Charismatic Wisdom," *JAAR Thematic Studies* 48, nos. 3–4 (1982): 23–45; Rubenson, *Letters*, 132–44; J. Goehring, "The Origins of Monasticism," in *Eusebius, Christianity, and Judaism*, ed. H. Attridge and G. Hata (Detroit: Wayne State University Press, 1992), 238–40 (also in Goehring, *Ascetics*, 13–35); Brakke, *Athanasius*, 135–38, 201–65; Watts, *City*, 177–81; R. Van Dam, *The Roman Revolution of Constantine* (Cambridge: Cambridge University Press, 2007), 319–29.

24. Ath., *vita Antonii* 67 (trans. from R. Gregg, *Athanasius: The Life of Antony and The Letter to Marcellinus*, Classics of Western Spirituality [Mahwah, NJ: Paulist Press, 1980]). Gregg and Groh see this as an aspect of Athanasius's attempt to address the "anticlerical bias among monastics." *Arianism*, 139.

25. They did this even if the candidate refused and fled from ordination; cf. Ath., *epistula ad Dracontium*. On the tensions that emerged between commitment to the monastic enterprise and the ecclesiastical hierarchy, and the subsequent developments that brought them into alignment, see Rousseau, *Ascetics*; Elm, "*Virgins*," 354–72 (specifically on Athanasius and the careful negotiation of his relationships with different ascetics); Brakke, *Athanasius*, 99–110; Martin, *Athanase*, 680–98; A. Sterk, *Renouncing the World yet Leading the Church: The Monk-Bishop in Late Antiquity* (Cambridge, MA: Harvard University Press, 2004), 119–40; Rapp, *Bishops*, 137–52. The process of subsuming monasticism un-

Monarchial Christians who emphasized the authority of the bishop in a tightly administered ecclesiastical hierarchy employed other rhetorical strategies to mold ascetic practice into a form that resonated with their views of proper church leadership. One very important locus for observing the intersection of asceticism and the church as institution was in the discourse of orthodoxy and heresy. For example, Athanasius's construction of the life of Antony includes a distinct sense that Antony served as a proxy for expressing Athanasius's own theological convictions: "Only do not defile yourselves with the Arians, for that teaching is not from the apostles, but from the demons, and from their father, the devil; indeed, it is infertile, irrational, and incorrect in understanding, like the senselessness of mules."[26] Thus in the *Life of Antony*, the ascetic discipline pursued by Antony that resulted in closeness to God and augmented personal holiness was also connected to his submission and obedience to the ecclesiastical hierarchy and his affirmation of orthodox belief over and against heresy.[27] Such a careful, ideologically driven construction of the life of the monk Antony suggests a perceived threat among Christians committed to "orthodox" leadership and doctrine. Indeed, as monasticism continued to take root and spread in Christian culture through the fourth century, several trends within it unfolded into varying theological and practical trajectories, some of which were thought dangerous and eventually deemed heretical. These developments necessitated a response, and thus "orthodox" writers recast the ascetic enterprise as necessarily connected to both obedience to ecclesiastical authority and commitment to correct belief.[28]

Within this context of early monastic diversity and competition, perhaps no other figure embodied the perceived dangers of asceticism gone awry than Origen and his theology. By the late fourth century, Epiphanius was well aware that the ascetic enterprise itself, that pathway to discipline, holiness, and divine intimacy, could also become corrupted under the wrong influences, especially Greek culture.[29] Rebecca Lyman has demonstrated how Epiphanius framed Origen's descent into heresy as an internal failure, a breakdown of ascetic discipline paired

---

der church control was long and contentious, and only at the Council of Chalcedon in 451 was this principle inscribed into canon law; cf. Gaddis, *No Crime*, 316–17.

26. Ath., *v. Anton.* 82 (trans. Gregg).

27. Brakke: "The social function of Athanasius's presentation of Antony as exemplar, both in its form and behavioural content, is to reinforce episcopal Christianity and its unchanging doctrine." *Athanasius*, 262. See also Martin, *Athanase*, 490.

28. See J. Goehring, "Monastic Diversity and Ideological Boundaries in Fourth-Century Egypt," *JECS* 5, no. 1 (1997): 61–84.

29. Hence an emphasis by some ascetics on the repudiation of secular learning and "starting over" with Scripture as the only needed "textbook." See Burton-Christie, *Word*, 43–61. We must bear in mind, however, that perceptions of the dangers of Origen were not characteristic of Egyptian monasticism in the *early* fourth century. On this, see Rubenson, *Letters*; idem, "Origen."

with a "dangerous" brilliance that compelled him to "speak" error.[30] Epiphanius exerted a great deal of intellectual energy attacking Origen's theological speculations and conclusions, which he believed were rooted in the Alexandrian's overallegorizing exegesis of Scripture.[31] For Epiphanius, the rejection of Origen was not just about an intellectual theology. At the heart of his concern was the impact Origen's theology had on the Christian life, especially that of the ascetic.

This anxiety is reflected in a significant portion of the *Ancoratus*, a theological exposition in the form of a letter written in 373/4 to Christians in Pamphylia, in which Epiphanius specifically attacked Origen's allegorizing of the Fall of Adam and Eve and their ejection from Eden and his denial of an actual, bodily resurrection. In his reflections on the latter issue, Epiphanius denigrated those who were influenced by Origen, even criticizing them as more foolish than pagans:

> And concerning those who appear to be Christians (being persuaded by Origen and confessing that the resurrection of the dead, both of our flesh and the body of the Lord, that holy one which has been received from Mary, and saying that this flesh is not raised, but another in place of this is given from God), how rather would we not say of them that they have a more impious notion and a heresy more foolish than the opinion among the Hellenes and the rest?[32]

Epiphanius then explicitly emphasized the absolute necessity of the resurrection of the human, physical body:

> For first, if another [flesh] in place of this is raised according to their argument, the judgment of God is not just, according to their myth, judging another flesh in place of the one that sinned or bearing another body to the glory of the royal

---

30. Lyman, "Making," 448–50.
31. I say overallegorizing here because nearly every theologian of the fourth century, including Epiphanius, engaged in some form of allegorical reading of Scripture. Indeed, the neat categories of "literal" and "allegorical" exegesis and the assumed geographical locales that preferred one or the other are false impositions made by modern scholars, as studied by F. Young, *Biblical Exegesis and the Formation of Christian Culture* (Cambridge: Cambridge University Press, 1997). See Stefaniw, "Straight Reading," 427–31, for Epiphanius's rejection of Origen's textuality.
    For Epiphanius's construction of the charges against Origen's theology, see Dechow, *Dogma*, 243–390; idem, "From Methodius to Epiphanius in Anti-Origenist Polemic," *Adamantius* 19 (2013): 10–29.
32. *Anc.* 87.2.

inheritance of heaven in place of the body that has toiled with fasts and sleeplessness and mortifications in the name of God.[33]

If in the resurrection an alternate body replaces the original body, then the ascetic disciplines that were applied to it in this life would be for naught.[34] Here we see an important underlying connection in Epiphanius's thinking: a vital link existed between orthodoxy and orthopraxy. In his understanding of the faith, a believer fundamentally could not practice the latter without the former. In other words, a person could not act rightly unless that person believed rightly. Thus Epiphanius's concern for ascetic discipline and its continued practice was intimately connected to what he understood to be orthodox belief, and a true Christian had to remain both personally vigilant and under the vigilance of the orthodox church to ensure that holy practice was rooted in right belief.

The issues just described formed much of the story of the latter half of Epiphanius's life, and we will return to his battle against Origenism in the last chapter. While Origen and his reception, influence, and legacy in Egyptian monasticism were especially significant for Epiphanius in the 370s, when he composed both the *Ancoratus* and *Panarion*, perhaps we should be careful not to assert too strongly the extent of his anti-Origenist convictions before the written proof, especially in the early years of his life. Indeed, we must resist the temptation to divide early Egyptian monasticism into an artificial dichotomy between pro- and anti-Origenist communities, if we can say that such even

---

33. *Anc.* 87.3. See Clark, *Controversy*, 86–104. For the evolving perspectives and attitudes toward the body in late ancient Christianity, see P. Brown, *The Body and Society: Men, Women, and Sexual Renunciation in Early Christianity*, Lectures on the History of Religions 13 (New York: Columbia University Press, 1988).

34. The objection to Origen's privileging of the soul over the body in connection to its implications for the ascetic life was expressed earlier by Methodius of Olympus. See L. Patterson, *Methodius of Olympus: Divine Sovereignty, Human Freedom, and Life in Christ* (Washington, DC: Catholic University of America Press, 1997), especially 141–99. See also J. Dechow, "Origen and Corporeality: The Case of Methodius's *On the Resurrection*," in *Origeniana Quinta: Papers of the 5th International Congress, Boston College, 14–18 August 1989*, Bibliotheca Ephemeridum Theologicarum Lovaniensium 105, ed. R. Daly (Leuven: Leuven University Press, 1992), 509–18; J. Behr, *The Nicene Faith*, Formation of Christian Theology 2 (Crestwood, NY: St Vladimir's Seminary Press, 2004), 38–48. Epiphanius reproduced a lengthy passage from Methodius, *de resurrectione mortuorum* in *Pan.* 64.12.1–62.15.

Epiphanius's concern over the bodily resurrection was also central to his Christology, especially in his orthodox understanding of Christ's assumption of full humanity; cf. *Anc.* 64–66, 75–79. E. Clark, "New Perspectives on the Origenist Controversy: Human Embodiment and Ascetic Strategies," *Church History* 59, no. 2 (1990): 156–57, also makes the important observation that Epiphanius's critiques against Origenism expanded in the 390s in the aftermath of disputes over Jovinian's views on marriage and reproduction.

existed in the early fourth century.[35] However, this is not to say that Origen and his thinking were not influential in early Egyptian monasticism. As many scholars have shown, Origen's thought and theology were important elements.[36] The main point here is that the operative monasticisms during Epiphanius's period of training exhibited theological and practical diversity, development, and degrees of interaction, much of which has been "hidden" by the polemics and rhetoric of later sources, including those by Epiphanius himself.[37]

Hieracas and the Hieracites

Hieracas and his ascetic movement were part of the Egyptian milieu in which Epiphanius would have learned and practiced his monasticism, and the Hieracites and their views must have influenced Epiphanius's perceptions of and convictions about the relationship between ascetic practice and orthodox belief and the ecclesiastical hierarchy as well as his understanding of the nature of the church, his ecclesiology. According to Epiphanius, Hieracas was a highly educated ascetic who promulgated a vision of Christian life and community that included repudiation of marriage.[38] Hieracas taught that male and female ascetics dedicated to virginity should live in community and worship together to the exclusion of all others.[39] While older scholarly interpretations understood

35. See Dechow, *Dogma*, 96–124, who tries to find the anti-Origenist influences that would have solidified Epiphanius's convictions, namely in Peter of Alexandria, Methodius, and Eustathius of Antioch. This is echoed also in Riggi, "La scuola." However, see Kösters, *Trinitätslehre*, 22–23, for the difficulty in evaluating Epiphanius's early anti-Origenism.
36. See Dechow, *Dogma*, 139–240, for an examination of Origenism among the monks in Lower and Upper Egypt, although his discussion examines the entire fourth century, not just Epiphanius's early years in Egypt. An important case of the (universal?) influence of Origen in the early fourth century can be found in the figure of Antony himself, the "founder" of Egyptian monasticism. See Rubenson, *Letters*, 59–88, 105–25; idem, "Origen," 320–24; in contrast with R. Williams, *Arius*, 89. Rubenson's argument is also supported by the thought and legacy of Didymus the Blind. See R. Layton, *Didymus the Blind and His Circle in Late-Antique Alexandria: Virtue and Narrative in Biblical Scholarship* (Urbana: University of Illinois Press, 2004), especially 85–158.
   For useful summaries of Origen's theology and its impact in the Trinitarian debates of the early fourth century, see L. Ayres, *Nicaea and Its Legacy: An Approach to Fourth-Century Trinitarian Theology* (Oxford: Oxford University Press, 2004), 20–30; Behr, *Nicene*, 37–59.
37. For the monastic diversity and fluidity of communities of the fourth century (especially in contrast to older received narratives), see Goehring, "Diversity," 61–84, especially 72–82, in relation to the Origenist controversy. See also Wisse, "Gnosticism"; Bagnall, *Egypt*, 303–9.
38. For an introduction to Hieracas and a critical examination of Epiphanius's account, see J. Goehring, "Hieracas of Leontopolis: The Making of a Desert Ascetic," in *Ascetics*, 110–33. See also Elm, "*Virgins*," 339–42.
39. See Brakke, *Athanasius*, 44–57, on the conflicting visions of Christianity promoted by Athanasius and Hieracas, especially on the question of human nature and free will and the relationship between ascetic communities and the church.

Hieracas's movement as one of withdrawal, James Goehring argues that the form of ascetic practice Hieracas established early in the development of the monastic movement must be situated in the context of the city and not in the deserts of Egypt, and that the clash of ideologies within the urban setting resulted in tension with the hierarchical church: "it was in fact the formation and practices of his innovative separatist ascetic association that sharpened the conflict between him and the episcopacy."[40] For Athanasius, who harshly condemned Hieracas, one of the central problems was his form of asceticism that functioned separately from the oversight and authority of the church.[41]

Fundamental to Epiphanius's condemnation of Hieracas, however, was heterodox theology. Hieracas denied a bodily resurrection: "For this man also maintains that the flesh is not raised up at all, but only the soul."[42] But immediately following this blunt assertion, Epiphanius remarked: "But the man was astonishing in his asceticism and capable of persuading souls. For example, many Egyptian ascetics were led away with him. For I know that concerning the resurrection of the dead, he denied the resurrection of the flesh, having received his pretexts from Origen or vomiting them from his own thinking."[43] Thus Hieracas, despite his notable asceticism, was condemned for his mistaken belief. He may have demonstrated orthopraxy, but he did not possess orthodoxy and was justifiably condemned.[44] "His way of life (πολιτεία) is in vain. For to be satisfied with lifeless things, together with false belief . . . this is not a school of life and hope and salvation."[45] Furthermore, the insinuation that Hieracas had derived his ideas from Origen is significant, and Epiphanius made yet another direct link between Hieracas and Origen in their respective denials of Paradise as an actual place.[46] The effect of this connection was the establishment of a succession of heresiarchs, a long-standing notion in the tradition of

---

40. Goehring, "Hieracas," 131. Also Brakke, *Athanasius*, 48. Chitty is entirely dismissive of the influence of Hieracas on monasticism. *Desert*, 4.

41. Ath., *First Letter to Virgins* 22–30.

42. *Pan.* 67.1.5. Cf. *Anc.* 82.3.

43. *Pan.* 67.1.6. The connection of Hieracas to Origen is important because it speaks to the influence of Origen's theology in the context of early Egyptian monasticism.

44. Epiphanius also emphasized the link between orthopraxy and orthodoxy in his refutation of the Archontics, whom he encountered in Palestine. See the discussion in chapter 3.

45. *Pan.* 67.7.8.

46. On Origen's denial of an earthly Paradise, see *Anc.* 54–55. Perhaps a connection can be made between Hieracas's view on marriage and the later dispute during the Origenist controversy that Origen's theology of bodiless souls before the Fall would have rendered marriage and reproduction as curses, not blessings. See Clark, "Perspectives," 156–59.

Christian heresiology.[47] However, Epiphanius also recognized that Hieracas's assertion that the Holy Spirit had been Melchizedek was drawn not from Origen but a faulty exegesis of Hebrews 7:3, which in turn tainted the heresiarch with the problem of heretical innovation.[48] Hieracas apparently defended his belief by citing a noncanonical text, the so-called "Ascension of Isaiah," which for Epiphanius only further substantiated his condemnation.[49] Not only did heresiarchs breed other heresiarchs, but the successors either took the heretical notions of their "teachers" and made them worse or invented entirely novel, even more corrupt ideas. These ideas were common themes within the panoply of heresiological rhetoric. In his condemnation of Hieracas's heterodox beliefs, Epiphanius expanded Athanasius's heresiological polemic by adding the dimension of mistaken belief to an unorthodox way of life.

His entire entry on the Hieracites exhibits Epiphanius's typical haphazard discussion of heretical beliefs and practices. He intermingled his denunciation of Hieracas's beliefs on the resurrection with reflections on the heresiarch's teaching on marriage and the condemnation of children who die prematurely. Hieracas apparently excluded children who died "before knowledge" from the hope of heaven because they had not "contended" in the life of faith.[50] Epiphanius cited a number of biblical passages to refute this notion and to assert the innocence of babies, thus positing a more moderate understanding of their spiritual status.[51] Epiphanius agreed with Hieracas that virginity was the "pride of the holy catholic and apostolic Church."[52] But unlike Hieracas, Epiphanius also recognized marriage as an honorable institution.[53] Hieracas ostensibly believed that marriage was established in the Old Testament but was no longer acceptable after the coming of Christ. Therefore, those who chose to marry in

---

47. See Le Boulluec, *La notion*, 40, 80–91, 162–73; Pourkier, *L'hérésiologie*, 53–63; Kim, "Reading," 393–400, on succession. This strategy was also deployed in other religious traditions; see Henderson, *Construction*, 120–57.

48. *Pan.* 55.5.1–5 (the entry against the Melchizedekians), 67.2.8–3.2.

49. *Pan.* 67.3.4–5.

50. *Pan.* 67.2.7.

51. Cf. *Pan.* 67.4.4–5.5.

52. *Pan.* 67.6.3.

53. *Pan.* 67.6.3–8. For example in *Anc.* 98.8 in his defense of bodily resurrection, Epiphanius wrote: "Elijah was [living] in virginity, in order that he might declare to the world the preeminence of virginity, as well as immortality, and the incorruption [associated] with the body. But in order that the resurrection and the permanence of the body might not be believed to be only in the case of virginity, Enoch was not a virgin, but was temperate and begot children. And these two men are living, preserving the body and soul for the sake of hope."

See Elm, *"Virgins,"* 337–38; Brakke, *Athanasius*, 44–57. Consider also the balanced (but complicated) perspective offered much earlier by Clement of Alexandria, *stromateis* 3.5–6 (40.1–56.3). See D. Buell, *Making Christians: Clement of Alexandria and the Rhetoric of Legitimacy* (Princeton: Princeton University Press, 1999), especially 32–49.

the post-Incarnational dispensation could not inherit the promise of heaven.[54] Thus it seems that again Epiphanius opted for a more moderate and accommodating position, in many ways parallel to that of Athanasius.[55]

It was quite possible that during his stay in Egypt, Epiphanius knew and perhaps even interacted with the Hieracites, and the *Vita* of Epiphanius even claimed that he confronted and refuted Hieracas directly.[56] While Epiphanius may have admired the ascetic discipline of the heresiarch, he ultimately found him unacceptable in his orthodox world because Hieracas tainted his commendable monastic practice with erroneous beliefs. But not only was Hieracas condemned for mixing asceticism with heresy, he was equally culpable for taking his ascetic convictions too far. Thus Epiphanius's brief discussion and refutation of the Hieracites underscored his ecclesiology. Like Athanasius, Epiphanius believed that the church consisted of a diversity of believers, some further along the journey of holiness than others, but all partakers of God's salvation.[57] Christianity was large and wide enough to accommodate both those who pursued the highest virtue of virginity and those who chose marriage, and Epiphanius's own experiences and encounters with the Hieracites as a young man in Egypt may have informed and influenced his own convictions about asceticism, the ideal of virginity, marriage, and the nature of God's church on earth.

The Melitian Schism

Melitius was another figure who played an important role in the development of Egyptian Christianity in the early fourth century.[58] Epiphanius discussed

---

54. *Pan.* 67.1.7–9.
55. Cf. Ath., *epistula festivalis* 10.4; *epistula ad Amunem*. Epiphanius also apparently maintained a relatively moderate position on the issue of remarriage; cf. *Pan.* 59.3.1–11.6, especially 4.8–12. However, scholars have disagreed on Epiphanius's intended meaning as well as the reading of the text itself. See A. Condamin, "St. Épiphane a-ti-il admis la légitimité du divorce pour adultère?," *Bulletin de Littérature Ecclésiastique* 1 (1900): 16–21; H. Crouzel, "Les Pères de l'Église ont-ils permis le remariage après séparation?," *Bulletin de Littérature Ecclésiastique* 70 (1969): 3–43; C. Riggi, "Nouvelle lecture du Panarion 59,4 (Épiphane et le divorce)," StPatr 12 (1975): 129–34; P. Nautin, "Divorce et Remariage chez Saint Épiphane," *VC* 37, no. 2 (1983): 157–73; H. Crouzel, "Encore sur Divorce et Remariage selon Épiphane," *VC* 38 (1984): 271–80.
56. *v. Epiph.* 49.
57. Brakke, *Athanasius*, 50.
58. On the Melitius and the Melitian Schism, see L. Barnard, "Athanasius and the Meletian Schism in Egypt," *Journal of Egyptian Archaeology* 59 (1973): 181–89; A. Martin, "Athanase et les Mélitiens (325–335)," in *Politique et théologie chez Athanase d'Alexandrie*, Théologie Historique 27, edited by C. Kannengiesser (Beauchesne: Paris, 1974), 31–61; L. Barnard, "Some Notes on the Meletian Schism in Egypt," StPatr 12 (1975): 399–405; R. Williams, "Arius and the Meletian Schism," *JTS* 37, no. 1 (1986): 35–52; idem, *Arius*, 32–41; Bagnall, *Egypt*, 306–9; Elm, "*Virgins*," 342–47; Martin, *Athanase*, 219–319; H. Hauben, "The Melitian 'Church of the Martyrs' Christian Dissenters in Ancient

Melitius and the schism he created in *Panarion* 68, and in many ways the entry reads like a history of Christianity in Egypt in this period. A closer examination of the entry reveals two different narratives stitched together. In the first part, Epiphanius, likely drawing on Melitian sources, discussed Melitius and the cause for the schism.[59] In the second part, Epiphanius to a large extent assumed the Athanasian narrative of the Melitian "conspiracy" with a faction of Arians led by Eusebius of Nicomedia.[60] We will focus here on the first part of the entry and on the figure of Melitius himself, what he represented for Epiphanius, and the potential ideas and convictions the schism may have engendered in the young Epiphanius.

Melitius was a bit of a dilemma for Epiphanius. On the one hand, Epiphanius recognized Melitius as entirely orthodox in his beliefs: "He belonged to the catholic Church and was of the orthodox faith. For his faith did not change at any time from the holy catholic Church."[61] Unlike Hieracas, who succumbed to heretical beliefs, Melitius remained orthodox. In fact, Epiphanius made it quite clear that Melitius did not innovate a new heresy; rather, "He caused a schism, though he certainly did not cause a change to the faith."[62] The first half of *Panarion* 68 paints a vivid picture of the church under duress in a time of persecution and includes a prison scene in which Melitius and Peter, the bishop of Alexandria, along with some loyal supporters, found themselves awaiting execution.[63] Epiphanius described the bishop Melitius as a kind of second-in-command and personal assistant to Peter.[64] A dispute arose between them over the *lapsi*, those who had committed some act of idolatry during persecution,

---

Egypt," in *Ancient History in a Modern University, Vol. 2. Early Christianity, Late Antiquity and Beyond*, edited by T. Hillard, R. Kearsley, C. Nixon, A. Nobbs (Grand Rapids, MI: Eerdmans, 1998), 329–49; and the collection of previously published articles and updated bibliography in H. Hauben, *Studies on the Melitian Schism in Egypt (AD 306–335)*, edited by P. Van Nuffelen (Burlington, VT: Ashgate, 2012).

59. For a discussion of Epiphanius's engagement with and use of Melitian sources in the construction of this particular entry, see Martin, *Athanase*, 222–24, 279–86, but more importantly, H. Hauben, "Épiphane de Salamine sur le schisme mélitien," *Salesianum* 67, no. 4 (2005): 737–70.

60. In chapter 4, I will discuss in greater detail the alleged alliance between the Melitians and the party led by Eusebius of Nicomedia, primarily as a reflection of Epiphanius's adoption of Athanasius's version of the events that unfolded in the early fourth century over Arian theology.

61. *Pan.* 68.1.1.

62. *Pan.* 68.1.4.

63. The scene was laid out in *Pan.* 68.1.5–3.9. Hauben, "Épiphane," 744–52, demonstrates the completely mangled chronology and erroneous information in Epiphanius's narrative. Also Williams, "Schism," 36–37. On what we can reconstruct of the life of Peter, see T. Vivian, *St. Peter of Alexandria: Bishop and Martyr*, Studies in Antiquity and Christianity (Philadelphia: Fortress Press, 1988).

64. *Pan.* 68.1.5–6. See Martin, *Athanase*, 262–67, 286–90.

and their request for "mercy through repentance."[65] The imprisoned Melitius, along with other confessors, argued for the rigid position of denying forgiveness, although they did offer the concession of allowing penance for restoration to the church (though not to positions of leadership) *after* the end of persecution and the restoration of peace.[66] However, according to what Epiphanius had either heard or read, Peter articulated the opposing perspective: "Let us receive those who repent, and let us arrange a penance for them to hold fast to the church. And let us not prevent them from clerical offices."[67] In both points of view, Epiphanius found something admirable, describing Peter's argument as one for "for mercy and clemency" and Melitius's for "truth and zeal."[68] The prison scene finished with Peter setting up a curtain to divide the room, with some joining him, but with many bishops, presbyters, and other prisoners siding with Melitius.[69] According to Epiphanius's narrative, Peter was then martyred, while Melitius and others were exiled to mines in Palestine.[70] Furthermore, Melitius, even while incarcerated, ordained clergy and established churches, thus overreaching his ecclesiastical authority and creating a schism in the church.[71]

While Epiphanius's account of events is not without problems, it served a rhetorical purpose as the heresiologist drew on different sources and arranged the details to construct a particular picture of the Egyptian church in the early fourth century. Although Melitius remained entirely orthodox in his beliefs, he acted in ways that violated the proper order of the ecclesiastical hierarchy. But even this "crime" received no direct condemnation from Epiphanius.[72] The issue of the *lapsi* was mentioned just once more, later in the narrative, and Epiphanius clearly felt torn as he composed this particular section of the entry.[73] He

---

65. *Pan.* 68.2.1. On the problem of the *lapsi* amid persecution, see Martin, *Athanase*, 269–76, but especially 290–96, for comparisons with earlier problems in North Africa in the time of Cyprian. Vivian offers a through examination of the account of Epiphanius and concludes that it is not to be trusted. *Peter*, 27–36

66. *Pan.* 68.2.4.

67. *Pan.* 68.3.1. On what Peter actually may have believed about penance for the lapsed, including clergy (and contradicting Epiphanius's account), see Vivian, *Peter*, 139–62.

68. *Pan.* 68.3.2.

69. This story is dramatic, but fictitious. See Vivian, *Peter*, 27, n. 90.

70. On the martyrdom of Peter, see Vivian, *Peter*, 40–50, 64–86.

71. *Pan.* 68.3.5–8. On the sources and circumstances for the conflict between Peter and Melitius, which presented a rather different picture than Epiphanius painted, see Martin, *Athanase*, 224–38. Vivian argues in fact that the dispute between them was over ecclesiastical authority. *Peter*, 20–23.

72. Contrast this with Ath., *apologia (secunda) contra Arianos*, 59.1.

73. *Pan.* 68.6.4, in his later discussion of the Melitians conspiring with the Arians. Epiphanius also discussed "lapsed" Christians extensively in *Pan.* 59, and exhibited a moderate, if not forgiving, position

could find very little worthy of condemnation in Melitius, especially in doctrinal matters, and Epiphanius even credited the schismatic bishop with identifying and condemning Arius and his heretical teaching in Alexandria.[74] Furthermore, ordaining clergy outside of one's authority or jurisdiction was a practice Epiphanius himself would engage in years later, and thus it is not surprising that he gave little direct criticism of Melitius.[75]

Hans Hauben argues that the Melitians resisted and rejected the efforts of the bishops of Alexandria to assert a monarchial form of leadership over the church in Egypt.[76] They opposed the systematic program advanced by Athanasius to subjugate all the disparate and at times competing elements of Christianity in Egypt under the control of the metropolitan bishop.[77] As we will see in chapter 4, Epiphanius not only admired Athanasius as a hero of the faith and defender of orthodoxy, he also assumed much of Athanasius's narrative of the fourth century, one that constructed a theological and ideological battle between the orthodox and the Arian conspiracy. This was the other reason Epiphanius condemned the Melitians: they had conspired with the Arian heretics. So while their founder may not have done anything serious enough to deserve condemnation as a heresiarch, his successors did. Thus Epiphanius the young monk learned and practiced his asceticism among diverse and developing practices in the cities and deserts of Egypt, and he must have encountered and perhaps even interacted with Melitian Christians. But he would have witnessed in them a schismatic community that challenged the burgeoning authority of the see of Alexandria and thus unacceptably of Athanasius himself.

---

on those who repented of committing major sins after they had been baptized. See C. Riggi, "Différence sémantique et théologique entre ΜΕΤΑΜΕΛΕΙΑ et ΜΕΤΑΝΟΙΑ en Épiphane, Haer. LIX," StPatr 18, no. 1 (1985): 201–6.

74. *Pan.* 68.4.1, 69.3.5. This detail may have been derived from supporters of Melitius; cf. Williams, "Schism," 46–47. On the complicated and at times conflicting traditions about the relationship between Arius and Melitius, see Martin, *Athanase*, 241–53, who argues that the explicit link between the schismatic and the heresiarch was a later tradition characteristic of an "Alexandrian tradition" that retroactively connected the two men for rhetorical and apologetic purposes. Epiphanius, however, portrayed Melitius in opposition to Arius, and thus must have been drawing on markedly different sources.

75. For Epiphanius's strategic use of improper ordinations, see chapter 7. According to *Pan.* 68.3.6–9, Melitius performed many of these ordinations en route to the mines of Phaeno in Palestine, an account that Martin, *Athanase*, 276–79, argues was constructed by Epiphanius based on what he had read in Eusebius's *De martyribus Palestinae.*

76. Hauben, "Melitian," 336. See also Martin, *Athanase*, 224–61, 286–90, 761–63.

77. This process may very well have begun under Alexander; cf. Williams, "Schism," 50–52. See also Martin, *Athanase*, 117–29, 141–201, for a thorough discussion of the central ecclesiastical authority of Alexandria over all of the surrounding provinces of Egypt. This authority was affirmed as a unique phenomenon in the sixth canon of Nicaea. See also Haas, *Alexandria*, 245–58, on the authority of the patriarch of Alexandria.

The Episode (Panarion 26.17.1–18.6)

The preceding discussion has offered a survey of important trends in early fourth-century Egyptian Christianity that comprised the diverse and fluid environment in which Epiphanius learned and practiced asceticism. In his educational formation, his convictions and attitudes were surely influenced by the people and practices he encountered, including the female denizens of a particular Christian sect. We turn now to the autobiographical episode that he included in the *Panarion*, beginning with a translation of the passage:

17.1 But what other thing shall I say? Or how will I shake off this soiled labor, since I wish and I do not wish to speak, though I am compelled, lest I appear to conceal something of the truth, and I am fearful, lest I, in revealing the awful things of these people, defile or smite or incite those who are led astray by pleasure and desires toward being overly concerned about this matter. (2) Nevertheless, would that I, and the entire <congregation?>[78] of the holy catholic Church, and all who read this book remain unharmed by such a wicked suggestion and mischief of the devil! (3) For if I undertake to talk about the other things that are said and done by them (how many are such things, and still so many are greater and <worse>[79]), I shall reduce them. But if I also wish to match a fitting remedy, like a medicine of healing, to each thing they say, for a great burden I labor in putting together this work.

(4) For even I, O beloved, happened upon this heresy myself, and I was taught the very things in person from the mouths of those who actually attempt this [heresy]. Thus some self-deceived women not only offered this sort of talk to me and revealed such things to me, but they, like that destructive and wicked Egyptian wife of the chief cook, were also attempting with babbling audacity to drag me down, yearning for me in my youth. (5) But the one who stood by holy Joseph then, also stood with me. And then when I, unworthy and insufficient, called upon that one who rescues, was shown mercy and escaped their destructive hands, I was able, singing a hymn to the all holy God, to say, "Let us sing to the Lord, for he is gloriously magnified. He cast the horse and rider into the sea" (Exod 15:1). (6) For not by a similar power of the righteousness of that man [Joseph], but by my groaning toward God was I shown mercy and saved. For reproached by the destructive women themselves, I was laughing at them, as

---

78. The word in the text is ἐλπίς, although Holl suggests an emendation of σύστασις.
79. Another conjecture from Holl (χείρω).

such women were insinuating to one another (indeed, jesting), that "we were not able to 'save' the young man, but we handed him over into the hands of the archon to be destroyed." (7) Inasmuch as whoever of them is prettier, she puts herself forward as bait, so that through her they allege that they "save" those who are being deceived instead of destroying them. And then there is blame for the one who is ugly by those who are prettier. She says, "I am a chosen vessel, able to save those who are being deceived, but you could not prevail!" (8) So those women who were teaching this enticing myth were most attractive in the outward form of their appearance, but they had in their minds of depravity all the ugliness of the devil. But the merciful God rescued me from their depravity, so that after I read their books and came to know their true mind and was not carried away, I escaped and was not enticed. (9) Then I also made haste to point them out to the bishops in that place, and to find out the names of those hidden in the church. And they were expelled from the city, about eighty, and the city was purged of their tare-like and thorny growth.

18.1 But someone, who has remembered my promise above,[80] perhaps also might commend me, as I declared before that I encountered some of them. And I have come to know some through their writings and others through reports and testimonies of trustworthy men who were able to point out the truth to me. Thus here also, frankly, I have not passed by the opportunity, but I have indicated what one of the heresies we encountered is like. (2) And I am able to speak plainly concerning this [heresy], on account of what I did not do (God forbid!), but having learned accurately from those who prevailed upon me to this (but did not succeed). But they lost their hope of my destruction, and they did not attain the goal of their plot against my wretched soul, which was attempted by them and the devil inside them. Thus singing together with the most holy David, I am able to say that "their blows were weapons of babes" (Ps 63:8) and what follows, and that "their toil will turn round to their own head, and their injustice will come down upon the crown of their head" (Ps 7:17). (4) So as I, having encountered and fled and recognized them, discerning and condemning them, having been saved, passed them by, thus also I exhort you, recognizing, having recognized and condemning <their noxious doctrine?>, to pass them by, so that you will not fall upon the poison of the depravity of these serpents. (5) But if ever you might even encounter any from this snake-like school, at once picking up the wood prepared for us by the Lord, on which our Lord Christ fixed, <and> at once hurling it against the head of the snake, may you say that "Christ

80. Cf. *Pan.* 25.3.3, 25.7.1–2.

has been crucified on our behalf, leaving for us a model" (1 Pet 2:21) of salvation. (6) For he would not have been crucified, if he was not possessing flesh. And having flesh and being crucified, he crucified our sin. I am held by faith of the truth, and I am not carried away by the bastard error of the snake and by the deceitful whispering of his teaching.

The Arbiter of Knowledge

Epiphanius placed this narrative toward the end of the entry on the Gnostics, after that of the Nicolaitans, who were identified by the ancient heresiologists as a heresy of the Apostolic era (cf. Rev 2:6).[81] He linked the "Gnostics" or "Borborites"[82] ("filthy ones") to this heretical pedigree, and he dedicated the first part of his refutation to deriding their mythological schema of the cosmos and the various texts that explained it.[83] Epiphanius's attack, however, also exhibits a significant shift away from attacking just heretical beliefs and teachings and focusing instead on denigrating the behavior of these heretics: "Narrating such things, those who join together with the heresy of Nicolaus for the sake of knowledge have fallen from the truth, not only turning aside the minds of those persuaded by them but also enslaving their bodies and souls to fornication and promiscuity."[84] Again we see the common heresiological theme of heretical suc-

---

81. Cf. Iren., *haer.* 1.26.3; Hipp., *haer.* 7.36.2–3. Epiphanius made this link deliberately; see J. Dummer, "Die Angaben über die gnostische Literatur," in *Koptologische Studien in der DDR* (Halle: Wissenschaftliche Zeitschrift der Martin-Luther-Universität, 1965), 194–95. For a commentary on this entry, see P. Wälchi, "Epiphanius von Salamis: *Panarion haereticorum* 25," *Theologische Zeitschrift* 53, no. 3 (1997): 226–39.

82. S. Gero considers the "Borborites" a Gnostic sect encountered by Epiphanius in Egypt, which, however, may have originated and certainly persisted in Syria and Mesopotamia beyond the fourth century, although much of his evidence is based on later sources, many of them hagiographical or polemically driven. "With Walter Bauer on the Tigris: Encratite Orthodoxy and Libertine Heresy in Syro-Mesopotamian Christianity," in *Nag Hammadi, Gnosticism, and Early Christianity*, ed. C. Hedrick and R. Hodgson (Peabody, MA: Hendrickson, 1986), 287–307.

83. For an introduction to Epiphanius's entries on the Gnostics, a consideration of their place in the broader corpus of "gnostic" literature, and select translations, see B. Layton, *The Gnostic Scriptures* (New York: Doubleday, 1987), 199–214. For a useful commentary, see M. Tardieu, "Épiphane contre les gnostiques," *Tel Quel* 88 (1981): 64–91.
    In the entry, Epiphanius also used several other names to describe the sect(s): "Koddians," "Stratiotics," "Phibionites," "Zacchaeans," "Barbelites." For the derivations of these names, see Dummer, "Die Angaben," 209–11; Tardieu, "Épiphane," 83–84. In *Pan.* 25.2.1, Epiphanius also named the "Phibionites," the disciples of "Epiphanes," "Stratiotics," "Levites," and "Borborites." This naming was a method to reinforce the notion of heresiological succession.

84. *Pan.* 26.3.3; cf. 25.2.5. In his transition from *Pan.* 25 to 26, Epiphanius also made the succession explicit: "As bodies are corrupted by other bodies through 'grafting,' a savage itch, or leprosy, thus in part the so-called <Gnostics> are connected to these, having taken their pretexts from Nicolaus himself and those who came before him, I mean Simon and the others" (25.7.2).

cessors innovating and further corrupting the beliefs and practices of their predecessors. The infamous entry continues with a detailed exposition of the alleged lurid practices of a heresy given over completely to "libertine" behavior,
and it concludes with the account of his personal encounter with the sect.[85]

Epiphanius presented himself as someone in a terribly awkward, even dangerous position as he hesitated about whether to describe the various behaviors
of these heretics. But at the same time, he felt obliged to disclose them to his
readers: "I would not dare to speak out on the whole of this thing, unless I was
compelled by something, on account of the excess of the grieving spirit in me
concerning the things done vainly by them."[86] He then included explicit descriptions of the alleged things these heretics did as acts of devotion and liturgy
to God and the corresponding theological and exegetical justifications for
them.[87] For our purposes, questions on the reliability and authenticity of
Epiphanius's account are of less importance than his rhetorical presentation of
himself and the heretics.[88] This episode is about Epiphanius "imagining" himself and constructing for his readers a persona that augmented his authority as
an expert on heresies and an arbiter of orthodoxy. Again after discussing several examples, Epiphanius reflected on the tension he felt: "And in truth these
things ought not be spoken or deemed worthwhile to be written in a treatise,
but buried as if some reeking corpse exuding a pestilent stench, in order that

---

85. I use scare quotes here because this notion is derived from the rhetorical construction of such behavior by heresiologists who were polemically opposed to them. J. Goehring uses the term for lack of a
better alternative. "Libertine or Liberated: Women in the So-Called Libertine Gnostic Communities," in *Images of the Feminine in Gnosticism*, Studies in Antiquity and Christianity, ed. K. King
(Philadelphia: Fortress Press, 1988), 329–44. See J. Buckley, "Libertines or Not: Fruit, Bread, Semen
and Other Body Fluids in Gnosticism," *JECS* 2, no. 1 (1994): 15–31, for an argument on why this
category does not work, though she is not necessarily dismissive of the possibility that such rituals
occurred. Williams, however, is completely critical of the "two option" (ascetic vs. libertine) Gnostic
ethic as a false construct by modern scholars that is rooted in the misinterpretations and distortions
of the ancient heresiologists. *Rethinking*, 163–88. Contrast with W. Speyer, "Zu den Vorwürfen den
Heiden gegen die Christen," *Jahrbuch für Antike und Christentum* 6 (1963): 129–35; S. Benko, "The
Libertine Gnostic Sect of the Phibionites According to Epiphanius," *VC* 21 (1967): 103–19; Gero,
"Bauer"; and Goehring, "Libertine," 338–44, who all take these descriptions as largely reliable. Williams criticizes such views. *Rethinking*, 182–83.
86. *Pan.* 26.3.4.
87. See Benko, "Libertine," for translations and descriptions.
88. Williams discusses and dismisses Epiphanius's alleged firsthand experiences. He is right to argue that
based on his presentation in the entry, it is apparent that Epiphanius never personally witnessed any
of the lurid rituals he alleged took place. *Rethinking*, 179–84. Nevertheless, I would argue that some
experience or encounter, however minor, did leave a lasting impression on the young Epiphanius and
played a part in the shaping of his heresiological outlook, and Williams seems to leave some room for
the possibility (182).

people might not be ruined through hearing."[89] The problem was that he conceded that the heresy still existed and thus was obliged to write about it.[90]

The ostensible purpose of his statements of hesitation was to warn his readers about the potential dangers that lay in even reading or hearing about the practices of heretics. But at the same time, the practical effect was twofold. First, the reader cannot help but be drawn into the world Epiphanius described and be impressed by the seeming breadth of his knowledge. He listed several of the sources from which the Gnostic practices allegedly derived, including "Noria," a "Gospel of Perfection," a "Gospel of Eve," "Questions of Mary," "Greater Questions of Mary," "Lesser Questions of Mary," "Apocalypses of Adam," "Birth of Mary," and a "Gospel of Philip," and he repeatedly gave the impression that he had studied these texts, although it is not entirely certain that he did.[91] He also claimed that he acquired some of his information "through reports and testimonies of trustworthy men," but he provided no other information about who these people were.[92] Thus Epiphanius became the gatekeeper of this knowledge. Second, the reader and listener are then compelled to follow Epiphanius, and him alone, in this journey through the liturgical life of this Gnostic heresy. He gave the distinct impression that he wanted his readers to know that he had come to the very brink, the breaking point between a life of holiness and licentiousness, but that he, through the help of God, had been able to overcome and resist temptation: "And I am able to speak plainly concerning this [heresy], on account of what I did not do (God forbid!), but having learned accurately from those who prevailed upon me to this (but did not succeed)."[93] Thus only someone who had such experience and fortitude in the face of destruction could instruct others on how to resist the allures of heresy. But it was not just the basic information and the means for refutation that Epiphanius provided for his readers in the *Panarion*. He included an account of his own firsthand experience, however inflated, which amplified his expertise, and he strategically situated the autobiographical episode at the end of the entry, which had the added effect of verifying all of the information he had provided before.

---

89. *Pan.* 26.14.4.
90. *Pan.* 26.14.5.
91. *Pan.* 26.1.3, 26.2.5, 26.2.6, 26.8.1–2, 26.12.1, 26.13.2. Williams makes the point that the "Gospel of Philip" quoted in the entry is different from the text of the same name from Nag Hammadi. *Rethinking*, 180. In fact, Epiphanius never quoted from any sources that testified directly to the alleged practices he described. See Dummer, "Angaben," 191–219, for a discussion of these sources and their shared points of contact and the source-critical problems associated with them.
92. *Pan.* 26.18.1.
93. *Pan.* 26.18.2.

The Church Infested

Specific features of this autobiographical story shed light on Epiphanius's attitudes and convictions and the circumstances in which they developed. For one, he seemed to recognize that heresy could be a phenomenon *internal* to the church.[94] Earlier writers in the heresiological tradition emphasized the sharp contrast between orthodox and heretic, true and false, good and evil, and the mentality they seemed to promote was one of vigilance. True believers were to act as guards armed with knowledge drawn from heresiological treatises to enable them to discern error that "moreover is adorned cunningly in seductive dress, that it may deceive the more ignorant by its outward appearance, and (as ridiculous as it is to say), it presents itself as more true than the Truth."[95] Irenaeus suggested to his readers that he wrote his heresiology so that "you, knowing these things, may make them clear to all who are with you and may warn them to guard themselves from the depth of madness and this blasphemy against God."[96]

Epiphanius certainly echoed these sentiments and goals for his own writing, but he also emphasized that heresy and heretics had to be purged from within the walls of the orthodox church. They were at times "hidden in the church."[97] Like weeds and wild animals that run rampant in the wilderness, heretics could infiltrate the city and the church. Therefore orthodox Christians had a double responsibility. They had to be guardians protecting the entryway, and they had to act as gardeners and hunters, with the result that "they [heretics] were expelled from the city, about eighty [in number], and the city was purged of their tare-like and thorny growth."[98]

Dangerous Women

The striking emphasis on the attractiveness of these women accentuates the very real temptation that the young Epiphanius must have felt, and the fact that he knew how the more attractive members ridiculed the more homely betrayed a more than casual familiarity. Epiphanius's encounters with these heretical women represented a pivotal moment in his life, a tipping point between the

94. See Lyman, "Making," for how Origen exemplified for Epiphanius the problem of heresy as an internal danger.
95. Iren., *haer.* 1.Preface.2.
96. Iren., *haer.* 1.Preface.2.
97. *Pan.* 26.17.9.
98. *Pan.* 26.17.9.

preservation of his chastity and orthodoxy and succumbing to the desires of the flesh and heresy, and this experience would impact and shape his thinking about how and where women belonged in the church.

The prominence of women in a variety of "Gnostic" groups, whether historical or largely rhetorical, was a source of concern for the heresiologists and reflected a broader attitude among patristic writers who constructed a particular "*topos* of 'feminine weakness' to produce a variety of ideological effects."[99] For example, the potential threat to patriarchal authority embodied in the female leadership of the Montanist movement is a well-known locus of the negative heresiological construction of women.[100] In the fourth century, the advent of the ascetic movement entailed a veritable revolution in Christian perspectives on what it meant to be male or female, the nature and function of the body, and what would happen to the body in the final consummation of all things.[101] Epiphanius matured during this time of shifting frontiers in thinking and practice. Furthermore in the specific context of Egypt, he witnessed the efforts of Athanasius to effect a programmatic change in perception of the ideal Christian woman as a "bride of Christ" or virgin dedicated to a life of chastity and devotion to Jesus only in the context of the hierarchical church.[102] Epiphanius certainly would have been familiar with these devout women who repre-

---

99. Cf. Tert., *De praescriptione haereticorum* 41. On the "orthodox" concern over women and the feminine in Gnosticism, see Pagels, *Gospels*, 48–69; V. Burrus, "The Heretical Woman as Symbol in Alexander, Athanasius, Epiphanius, and Jerome," *HTR* 84, no. 3 (1991): 229–48. On "feminine weakness" and the patristic construction of an "ideology of woman," especially through "stereotyping, naturalizing, and universalizing" rhetorical strategies, see E. Clark, "Ideology, History, and the Construction of 'Woman' in Late Ancient Christianity," *JECS* 2, no. 2 (1994): 155–84, quotation from 166. See also E. Clark, "Devil's Gateway and Bride of Christ: Women in the Early Christian World," in *Ascetic Piety and Women's Faith: Essays on Late Ancient Christianity*, Studies in Women and Religion 20 (Lewiston: Edwin Mellen Press, 1986), 23–60. As we will see, Epiphanius's personal anecdote might also be understood as part of this ideological construction, but also more explicitly connected to the rhetoric of heresy.

　　Interestingly, Goehring suggests that the women described by Epiphanius were real and understood themselves to be involved, "as part of the salvation process, an attempt to win a convert and gather more 'light' for God." He also emphasizes the heresiologists' presentation of women as "simpletons," perhaps a rhetorical means to criticize the apparent high regard and role the Phibionites had for women. "Libertine," 341.

100. See C. Trevett, *Montanism: Gender, Authority and the New Prophecy* (Cambridge: Cambridge University Press, 1996), especially 151–97.

101. See throughout Brown, *Body*, for a thorough examination of the evolution in the Christian thinking on and treatment of the body.

102. Brakke, *Athanasius*, 17–79. For the development of female ascetic ideals and practices, see Brown, *Body*, 259–84; Elm, "*Virgins*"; Martin, *Athanase*, 197–200; T. Shaw, "Askesis and the Appearance of Holiness," *JECS* 6, no. 3 (1998): 485–500; Wipszycka, *Moines*, 567–611. For a broader examination of conceptions of the ideal woman, see K. Cooper, *The Virgin and the Bride: Idealized Womanhood in Late Antiquity* (Cambridge, MA: Harvard University Press, 1996).

sented an antithesis to the women he described in his personal encounter with the Gnostic sect. The picture he painted in his autobiographical account was that the women were the active recruiters for the sect. Thus they operated in the public sphere, free to interact with whom they chose. Furthermore, the women themselves taught their ideas and doctrines, a trend that Athanasius emphatically sought to curb.[103]

For Epiphanius, the sharp contrast between the submissive and sequestered virgins and the proactive and public Gnostic women must have made an impression. In the decades following his education and experiences in Egypt, Epiphanius certainly had time to formulate his own understanding of the ideal woman, and he offered in one of his writings what he thought was an ideal image of the way a Christian woman should behave. In the *Ancoratus*, he twice lauded Sarah for her proper behavior:

> [The phrase] "so Sarah laughed, being inside the house" (Gen 18:12) intends to show her modesty as a model for those who wish to be pious in truth, in order that when they receive strangers they may serve from their own labors on the one hand, on the other hand because of modesty they may not show their face to men. For that blessed woman fully prepared [herself] and having prepared was not appearing to the face of the angels, putting forth a model of modesty to subsequent generations.[104]

And:

> Therefore not being ignorant was he asking, but in order that he [God] might inspire her "daughters," the ones who "proclaim godly fear" (1 Tim 2:10), to learn the struggle of that woman [Sarah], whenever they may endeavor to minister to saints out of their own labors. For that woman, taking the initiative in so great a service, herself making unleavened loaves and preparing so great a service together with her own maidservants, was not seeing the faces of those being served, [thus] leaving behind a model of suitable prudence for our times.[105]

Unlike the Gnostic women who freely went about the city and within the church attempting to lure young men into their heresy, the ideal woman Sarah exhibited

103. However, Athanasius's efforts were directed more specifically against freethinking and free-speaking women in philosophically inspired intellectual circles; see Brakke, *Athanasius*, 57–79.
104. *Anc.* 39.5–6.
105. *Anc.* 109.5–6.

a sense of modesty, choosing not to appear before the men (angels) who were Abraham's guests and preparing to minister to them through unseen hospitality.

Tell the Bishop

Finally, that Epiphanius made it a priority to inform the local bishops about his discovery of heretics within the church is telling because it intimates that he recognized the authority of the ecclesiastical hierarchy and that he understood it to be the means by which heretics should be expelled from the church. Epiphanius would take this understanding and use it to its full effect during his tenure as metropolitan of Cyprus. This moment also represents his first act of heresy-hunting, and as we shall see in the ensuing chapters, this activity would become one of the defining and culminating features of his career.[106]

Epiphanius spent the formative years of his young life in Egypt, where he witnessed the church undergoing sweeping changes. The later hagiographical tradition emphasized his monastic training; and while this was most certainly central to his personal development, he also embraced and practiced a form of asceticism with distinct characteristics. For Epiphanius, the life of the church and the life of the monk were one and the same. His monasticism was one that submitted to the ecclesiastical hierarchy, whose representative leaders, men like Athanasius, labored tirelessly to rein in or to expel the practitioners of extreme or potentially heretical forms. A personal encounter with certain women belonging to a "libertine" Gnostic sect must have been a shock to the young man's system. Tempted by the allure of very attractive and active women, Epiphanius could have succumbed to their wiles, but he resisted. These women then became the antithesis in his thinking of the ideal Christian woman, one who was submissive and hidden from the public eye. He must have been alarmed to find some of these heretics within his local congregation, and he learned that heresy was a phenomenon internal to the church that had to be eradicated. Epiphanius also recognized the bishop to be not only the locus of authority in the church but also the instrument through which orthodox Christians could identify and expel heresy. These developments, initiated early in his life and education, would play a tremendously important role in the formation of Epiphanius, heresy-hunter and author of the *Panarion*.

---

106. It is not entirely clear who these bishops were or where they administered. Epiphanius was certainly familiar with the churches in and around Alexandria; cf. *Pan.* 69.2.2–4.

CHAPTER 2

Reimagining the Ancient Past

Epiphanius the Historian

Epiphanius "remembered" a pivotal moment of his youth and presented himself as a model of resistance to temptation, submission to ecclesiastical authori-
ties, and vigilance against the constant threat of heresy to the church. Later
writers followed suit and imagined a version of the young Epiphanius as an
ascetic exemplar mentored by the legendary Hilarion. In this chapter, the reimagining of beginnings remains the essential theme. But rather than looking
again at how Epiphanius reimagined the early part of his own life, we will explore his archaeology of humanity, how he conceived and constructed a history
of human beliefs, culture, and depravity. Although he was by no means the first
Christian writer, let alone ancient writer, to rewrite history to serve a particular
rhetorical end, Epiphanius nevertheless offered a unique revision of history.[1]
But it will also be clear that Epiphanius was inspired by established traditions
and drew on the thematic content of the pseudepigraphic Jewish book *Jubilees*,
writings from the Christian chronographic tradition, and the works of Eusebius of Caesarea.[2]

---

1. As Inglebert argues, Christian beliefs about Jesus as the Messiah, the Incarnation, and future expec-
    tations of his return necessitated a reinterpretation of history. *Interpretatio*, 302–15. Still thoughtful
    is A. Momigliano, "Pagan and Christian Historiography in the Fourth Century A.D.," in *The Conflict
    between Paganism and Christianity in the Fourth Century*, ed. A. Momigliano (Oxford: Oxford Uni-
    versity Press, 1963), 79–99. See A. Droge, *Homer or Moses? Early Christian Interpretations of the
    History of Culture*, Hermeneutische Untersuchungen zur Theologie 26 (Tübingen: J.C.B. Mohr [Paul
    Siebeck] Verlag, 1989) for a study of how early Christian apologists reinterpreted history.
2. The connection between the *Panarion* and the chronographic tradition has been observed and stud-
    ied by W. Adler, "The Origins of the Proto-Heresies: Fragments from a Chronicle in the First Book
    of Epiphanius' *Panarion*," *JTS* 41, no. 2 (1990): 472–501.

Epiphanius dedicated the first twenty entries of the *Panarion* to heresies that appeared *before* the Incarnation, including four Greek philosophical schools and twelve sects stemming from Judaism. However, the first four "mother" heresies, entitled "Barbarism," "Scythianism," "Hellenism," and "Judaism," together comprised a reinterpretation of history and culture. Epiphanius envisioned a form of proto-orthodox Christianity existing from the beginning of humanity and a gradual but steady diversification and deterioration of human depravity following the Fall.[3] The names of these four entries were ostensibly inspired by Colossians 3:11: "In that renewal there is no longer Greek and Jew, circumcised and uncircumcised, barbarian, Scythian, slave and free; but Christ is all and in all!" (NRSV), although Epiphanius's truncated quotation was, "for in Christ there is no barbarian, no Scythian, no Hellene, no Jew."[4] The apparent emphasis of this verse was Christian unity and the deconstruction of ethnicity, gender, culture, and social distinctions in the new dispensation of the church. Epiphanius, however, reinterpreted its meaning as identifying a primordial state of humanity having a pure, correct belief followed by periods of division and descent, with each subsequent era exhibiting worse forms of depravity and culminating in two separate but equally flawed heretical traditions, Hellenism and Judaism.[5] Thus Epiphanius found inspiration for a divisive scheme in a biblical verse ostensibly proclaiming the unity and equality of all believers.[6]

Throughout his revisionist history of moral degeneracy, Epiphanius retroactively identified and traced a form of proto-orthodox Christianity in which even Adam, the first man, knew and believed in the Triune God. Therefore, history and culture progressed forward along two parallel tracks, one a continued preservation and transmission of orthodox belief and the other a steady decline into worse and worse manifestations of sin and depravity. Epiphanius reconstructed ante- and postdiluvian history to match his own convictions about the history of religion, characterized by this dichotomy of orthodoxy and heresy, and incorporated all of this into the beginning of the *Panarion* as four separate heresiological entries. This reconstruction might appear rather odd, and modern scholarship has decried his inconsis-

3.   Inglebert argues that it was precisely the choice to extend the existence of heresy before Christ that allowed Christian thinkers to reassess humanity according to Christian criteria. *Interpretatio*, 418.
4.   *Pan.* 1.1.9. He also may have drawn from Gal 3:28.
5.   Boyarin, "Rethinking," 19. See D. Buell, *Why This New Race: Ethnic Reasoning in Early Christianity* (New York: Columbia University Press, 2005).
6.   Young, "Epiphanius," 202.

tent and at times confusing definition of heresy.[7] But ultimately Epiphanius's identification of these epochs of history reflected his comprehensive understanding of orthodoxy and heresy, whose existence he could trace back to the beginning of the human experience.[8]

Jubilees and Reimagining Genesis

Jubilees is a second-century BCE pseudepigraphic text that provides an account of revelations received by Moses during his forty-day retreat on Mount Sinai.[9] It fills in different gaps in Genesis, supplementing details and explanations of the biblical account to augment the credibility of the Genesis narrative.[10] The author of *Jubilees* emphasized the absolute necessity of using a 364-day solar year and attempted to establish and maintain a precise chronological scheme, arranging the book into forty-nine-year jubilee periods. A major theme that undergirds the narrative is the transcendence of the Mosaic Law, and the author wanted his readers to understand that Jewish laws and festivals were practiced long *before* Moses received them. The origin of evil also received careful attention, and the author blamed heavenly beings known as "Watchers," who intermarried with women and whose children fought one another, and demons led by a Satan-like figure called Mastema for bringing it.[11] The postdiluvian ac-

---

7. Again, see Young, "Epiphanius," although her criticisms are counterbalanced well by Schott, "Heresi-ology."
8. See the helpful discussions in Fraenkel, "Histoire," 188–91; Moutsoulas, "Begriff," 365–71; Riggi, "Il termine." Moutsoulas examines how Epiphanius's concept of heresy was not only applicable to false belief, but also to a false way of life. This idea fits well with the scheme discussed below in which Epiphanius set the negative developments of the first four eras of human history in contrast to a pure, natural human state. Moutsoulas, however, understands Epiphanius's application of the term "heresy" to the first four heresies to be neutral, whereas Riggi correctly views his use as entirely negative.
9. See J. VanderKam, *The Book of Jubilees* (Sheffield: Sheffield Academic Press, 2001). The most intact version of *Jubilees* has survived in an Ethiopic translation, and quotations are drawn from R. Charles, *The Book of Jubilees or The Little Genesis*, Translations of Early Documents Series I, Palestinian Jewish Texts (Pre-Rabbinic) (New York: Macmillan, 1917), revised by C. Rabin in *The Apocryphal Old Testament*, ed. H. Sparks (Oxford: Oxford University Press, 1984), 10–139. See also another translation and introduction by O. Wintermute, "Jubilees: A New Translation and Introduction," in *The Old Testament Pseudepigrapha, Vol. 2*, The Anchor Bible Reference Library, ed. J. Charlesworth (New York: Doubleday, 1985), 35–142. On its complicated transmission and use by Christian writers, see W. Adler, "The *Chronographiae* of Julius Africanus and Its Jewish Antecedents," *ZAC* 14, no. 3 (2011): 496–524, especially 510–14.
10. See J. van Ruiten, *Primaeval History Interpreted: The Rewriting of Genesis 1–11 in the Book of Jubilees*, Supplements to the Journal for the Study of Judaism 66 (Leiden: Brill, 2000).
11. Cf. Gen 6:1–4. Many Christian authors also took up the myth of these angelic creatures for a variety of rhetorical purposes, in some cases drawing on the Enochic tradition. See J. VanderKam and W. Adler, eds., *The Jewish Apocalyptic Heritage in Early Christianity*, Compendia Rerum Iudaicarum ad Novum Testamentum 4 (Minneapolis: Fortress Press, 1996), 60–88. See Adler, "*Chronographiae*,"

count focused on the division of mankind and the rise of Abraham and the Jewish patriarchs, with Jacob as a central figure. The author portrayed Abraham, the patriarch par excellence, in the most positive light. Because he emphasized the long-standing traditions of obedience to the Mosaic Law and the festival calendar, the deepest motivation of the author of *Jubilees* may have been to warn his readers about the dangers of mixing Jewish culture with Greek. In other words, *Jubilees* is a reimagined and reconstructed history of ancient humanity with the express purpose of legitimizing and reinforcing the convictions and values of the author and his contemporary readers. It belongs to a larger tradition of alternate versions of human history written to achieve particular rhetorical ends, usually to demonstrate the longevity of the author's civilization and thus the superiority of that culture over another, in this case Jewish in opposition to Greek.[12]

Epiphanius certainly knew of this book, and he referenced it in his entry against the Sethians, both as "Jubilees" and "The Little Genesis."[13] He apparently drew on information from *Jubilees* to explain how the sons of Adam had wives and children and why at that time it was lawful for brothers to marry sisters.[14] Epiphanius most likely used an intermediate work that included stories from *Jubilees*, although undoubtedly he was aware of some of the thematic content of the original.[15] While they wrote centuries apart, Epiphanius and the author of *Jubilees* both retroactively projected a particular tradition of "orthodoxy," and they both reimagined the book of Genesis to suit their rhetorical goals. The author of *Jubilees* imagined the existence and observance of a proto–Mosaic Law in the antediluvian world and in the life and journey of Abraham. The other patriarchs were consistently portrayed as faithful observers of a divine law that was only later articulated by God to Moses, and yet they knew how and when to celebrate the festivals of the Jewish calendar. With a parallel rhetorical strategy, Epiphanius retroactively introduced a form of pre-Incarnation, proto-orthodox Christianity that the patriarchs believed and faithfully practiced. Adam, Abraham, and Moses all recognized and followed a form of the true Christian faith: "And in unity the Trinity was always pro-

---

508–12, for how Christian writers from the fourth century forward historicized the Watchers accounts of *Enoch* and *Jubilees*.

12. A robust tradition of Jewish historiography during the Hellenistic period sought to establish either Abraham or more often Moses as the father and founder of culture; see Droge, *Homer*, 12–35.

13. *Pan.* 39.6.1

14. Cf. *Jubilees* 4.9–17; *Pan.* 39.6.2–7.1.

15. This is suggested by Adler, "Origins," 476.

claimed and believed in by the most outstanding of them, that is, by the prophets and those who were sanctified."[16] Thus the important concept Epiphanius drew from his reading of *Jubilees* (or an epitome of it) was the reimagining and retelling of the Genesis narrative to reflect his own particular convictions and understanding of the world.

Ancient Chronography

Another literary tradition that influenced Epiphanius's reimagining of human history was chronography, which developed from a long-standing interest of Near Eastern cultures in preserving a record of the primordial and prehistoric past. The *Babylonica* of Berossus (ca. 290 BCE) and the *Aegyptiaca* of Manetho (third century BCE) are two examples of texts in this tradition.[17] Both authors were natives of their respective cultures, flourishing sometime after the conquests of Alexander of Macedon. They wrote in Greek for Greek audiences, and the main purpose of the research, compilation, and narration of their respective histories was to provide their readers with a glimpse into the history of their venerable, ancient civilizations that Alexander had conquered. Both emphasized the longevity and accomplishments of their peoples and cultures. The Babylonians and the Egyptians had long-standing traditions of king-lists, chronicles, and archival information that traced their lineages back to the primordial world, and other cultures like the Assyrians and Phoenicians claimed to have similar records. The detailed descriptions of ancient dynasties and rulers were a subtle jab at the relatively young chronology of the Greeks, and Berossus and Manetho subtly demonstrated the superiority of their own cultures using the argument that longevity was a marker of sophistication.[18] Jewish au-

---

16. *Pan.* 4.5.5.
17. For an introduction to both authors as well as a collection and translation of fragments and comparative tables, see G. Verbrugghe and J. Wickersham, *Berossus and Manetho, Introduced and Translated: Native Traditions in Ancient Mesopotamia and Egypt* (Ann Arbor: University of Michigan Press, 1996). See also S. Burstein, *The Babyloniaca of Berossus*, Sources and Monographs, Sources from the Ancient Near East 1.5 (Malibu: Undena Publications, 1978); and W. Adler, *Time Immemorial: Archaic History and Its Sources in Christian Chronography from Julius Africanus to George Syncellus* (Washington, DC: Dumbarton Oaks Research Library and Collection, 1989), 24–27, especially for references to modern scholarship on both authors.

    Droge discusses the importance of the work of Hecataeus of Abdera, whose propagandist account of Egyptian history (specifically in opposition to Greek) spawned other "nationalist" histories. *Homer*, 5–8.
18. Schott, "Heresiology," 557.

thors in the Hellenistic period also composed accounts of their history that
established the antiquity of their people over the Greeks, and perhaps no author
exemplified this tradition more than Josephus.[19]

Greek writers composed their own chronographies, although they faced
what was perhaps the embarrassing reality that their history and culture did not
compare in antiquity with the Babylonians, Egyptians, or even Jews.[20] Still, Hellenistic writers like Eratosthenes (276–194 BCE) and Apollodorus (born ca. 180
BCE) established a tradition of Greek scientific chronography.[21] But for both
writers, "history" began in 1184 BCE with the fall of Troy, and anything prior to
this was relegated to the realm of myth.[22] The Hellenistic chronographic tradition tended to focus on the Greek world (specific regions and cities) and did
not fully consider the cultures and traditions of outside civilizations, perhaps
because the Greeks recognized that their culture was simply not as old as others. Nevertheless, Castor of Rhodes (ca. 60 BCE) later attempted to compose a
world chronicle that placed the Greeks on par with the cultures of the Near
East, although he ignored sources like Manetho and Berossus.[23]

Christian apologists were very interested in the works of authors like Berossus and Manetho because they wanted to demonstrate the longevity of their
faith, especially against the charges of pagan intellectuals that Christianity was
something new and therefore unreliable and not worthy of respect.[24] Even
though Christians disagreed with the antediluvian details of the *Babylonica* and
Aegyptiaca, they took up these works (or redactions or epitomes of them) and
recast their chronologies to construct a long history and ancient pedigree for
Christianity by linking it directly with the history of the Israelites.[25] Going even

19. See Droge, *Homer*, 35–47; Inglebert, *Interpretatio*, 370–74, 481–93; Adler, *"Chronographiae,"* 514–
   19.
20. This was in fact Josephus's criticism of the Greeks; cf. Josephus, *contra Apionem* 1.6–18. See Inglebert, *Interpretatio*, 372–74.
21. See A. Mosshammer, *The "Chronicle" of Eusebius and Greek Chronographic Tradition* (Lewisburg, PA:
   Bucknell University Press, 1979), 84–112, for an historical survey of the Greek chronographic tradition.
22. Wacholder, "Chronology," 463–64. This is in part why Greek writers resisted the use of Near Eastern
   works like that of Berossus; cf. Inglebert, *Interpretatio*, 299–300, 464–67.
23. Wacholder, "Chronology," 464–65. A parallel tradition of writing universal history also integrated
   non-Greek information and sources; cf. Inglebert, *Interpretatio*, 468–73, 522–24.
24. For example, Tatian, *oratio ad Graecos* 36; Theophilus of Antioch, *ad Autolycum* 3.21, 29. On the
   criticism with regard to age, Droge observes that "the assertion of modern origin was equivalent to
   the charge of historical insignificance." *Homer*, 44.
25. For the Jewish and Christian use of the chronographies of Berossus and Manetho, see Adler, *Immemorial*, 20–42. Josephus also drew on the works of Manetho and Berossus; cf. Jos., *Ap.* 1.73–105,
   1.128–60.
      For a succinct summary of the challenges chronographers faced and solutions they developed in

further, some Christian thinkers sought to bolster the credibility of their faith by tying it to the archaic past, all the way back to the Genesis narrative.[26] One of the main problems they faced, however, in drawing on these Near Eastern works lay in the specific dating of events and persons who lived before the Flood, as the pagan authors' accounts were of course significantly different from the biblical reckoning of antediluvian history.[27] Thus Christians (and Jews) had to figure out ways to explain away or refute the details in these works that conflicted with their own understanding of human history drawn from Genesis.[28] Nevertheless, the survival of these pagan texts owes a great deal to Christian writers who preserved portions of the originals in their reconciliations of the conflicting details. By taking advantage of chronographic sources generally neglected by the Greeks, Christians were able to highlight the relatively short history of Greek civilization and thus imply its cultural and religious inferiority.

Julius Africanus

Significant disagreements, however, developed even among Christian writers on the chronology of the Genesis account. The six-day creation was a debated issue, with some understanding the days as allegorical ages and others as literal days. Some Christians, like Julius Africanus (ca. 160–ca. 240 CE) in his *Chronography*, were interested in establishing fixed chronological markers because of their millenarian interests.[29] Africanus, the first of the Christian chronogra-

---

reconciling the primordial chronologies of the Babylonians and Egyptians, see W. Adler, "Berossus, Manetho, and '1 Enoch' in the World Chronicle of Panodorus," *HTR* 76, no. 4 (1983): 422–42; idem, *Immemorial*, 50–55.

26. See Adler, *Immemorial*, 18–20, and idem, "Eusebius' *Chronicle* and Its Legacy," in Attridge and Hata, *Eusebius*, 468–74.

27. See Adler, *Immemorial*, 68–71.

28. For developments in Jewish chronography prior to the appropriation by Christians, see B. Wacholder, "Biblical Chronology in the Hellenistic World Chronicles," *HTR* 61 (1968): 451–81; Adler, "Chronographiae."

29. See Mosshammer, *Chronicle*, 146–57, for Africanus and the chiliast tradition. For a broader introduction to Africanus and his writings, see M. Wallraff, ed., *Iulius Africanus: Chronographiae, The Extant Fragments*, GCS NF15, with U. Roberto, K. Pinggéra, trans. W. Adler (Berlin: Walter de Gruyter, 2007), xiii–lxvii. This volume compiles all fragments and secondary references attributable to Africanus in ancient and medieval sources. An especially important source was Georgius Syncellus, the eighth/ninth-century Byzantine chronographer. I will cite fragments from Africanus according to the scheme of this volume.

See also W. Adler, "Sextus Julius Africanus and the Roman Near East in the Third Century," *JTS* 55, no. 2 (2004): 520–50, particularly for his examination of Africanus's other, more controversial work, the *Kestoi*.

phers, believed in a 6,000-year course of the earth beginning with Creation and culminating in the advent of the Kingdom of Heaven. Therefore, chronography was a means to calculate when the consummation of history would occur.[30] Africanus's efforts were undergirded by the idea that he could organize all of human history into "one great chronological system," and he tried to incorporate disparate branches of history, including those of the Near Eastern and Hellenistic traditions and *Jubilees*.[31] Unfortunately, much of Africanus's work is now lost, and the textual tradition presents several problems.[32]

Epiphanius never specifically mentioned or cited Africanus; thus we must be careful in assuming a direct engagement with the *Chronography*. Nevertheless, the chronographic data that Epiphanius integrated into his historical scheme reflected parallels with that of Africanus, although again it is likely that Epiphanius acquired this information through an intermediate source.[33] The main thematic influence that Africanus had upon Epiphanius was the willingness to conceive and calculate human history from the first humans to the Flood and afterward to synchronize important biblical events and figures with those of other cultures. The extension of human history to the very beginning was certainly important to Africanus and his millenarian conception of the cycle of time. But as we shall see, it was equally important for Epiphanius's understanding of the earliest existence of orthodox Christianity and the development of heresy.

Epiphanius apparently drew on a variety of Christian chronographic works, picking and choosing information and calculations that served his needs, which at times led to confusion and errors. But ultimately, he was less concerned with accuracy and consistency than with rewriting human history to fit his convictions about orthodoxy and heresy. He attempted to project this parallel history of orthodoxy and heresy all the way back to the beginning of history. Hence, he reimagined the ancient past to underscore his belief that a form of orthodox Christianity began with Adam and continued through the genera-

---

30. Inglebert, *Interpretatio*, 383–84. Eus., *historia ecclesiastica* 6.31.1–3, spoke admiringly about Africanus.
31. Wallraff, *Africanus*, xxiii. Adler argues that Africanus's *Chronicle* attests to "a very early stage in the Christian transmission of the *Book of Jubilees*." "Origins," 482. This is also in contrast to the *Chronicle* of Hippolytus, whose focus was not a universal synthesis but a continuation of the biblical narrative. Because of Hippolytus's limited integration of information from the Greek tradition, I argue that his work was less influential on Epiphanius's reimagined history in the *Panarion*. See Inglebert, *Interpretatio*, 497.
32. Wallraff, *Africanus*, xxix–lv.
33. Adler, "Origins," 484.

tions down to his own time and that heresy was always the product of the steady worsening of human sinfulness. For Epiphanius, Christianity was older than Judaism, and orthodoxy was older than heresy.

Eusebius of Caesarea

No writer had a greater impact and influence on conceptions of history and culture among Christians in late antiquity than Eusebius of Caesarea.[34] Epiphanius's writings betray that he read and consulted the works of Eusebius, and he must have struggled to maintain a balance between admiration for Eusebius's erudition and contributions and disdain for his well-known commitment to a subordinating theology of the Son.[35] Nevertheless, Eusebius's works were undeniably important and influential on Christians across the theological spectrum, and in the *Panarion*, we can observe thematic content from the *Chronicle*, *Onomasticon*, *Ecclesiastical History*, *Preparation for the Gospel*, and the *Demonstration of the Gospel*.[36]

Eusebius was the first Christian author who attempted to compile and compare the disparate chronographic traditions and offer a synchronized product.[37] Thus one could make the case, as Eusebius himself did, that his work was an innovation, and the *Chronicle*, with its year-by-year synchronization of all Greek and Near Eastern kingdoms, was indeed innovative.[38] The first part of his *Chronicle*, commonly called the *Chronography*, is a collection of source material and discussions of different chronological systems used by various ancient

---

34. Momigliano, "Historiography," 87–94; R. Grant, *Eusebius as Church Historian* (Oxford: Oxford University Press, 1980); T. Barnes, *Constantine and Eusebius* (Cambridge, MA: Harvard University Press, 1981), 126–47; A. Johnson, *Ethnicity and Argument in Eusebius' "Praeparatio Evangelica"* (Oxford: Oxford University Press, 2006).
35. Cf. *Pan.* 29.4.3.
36. See C.-F. Collatz and A. Rattmann, *Epiphanius IV: Register zu den Bänden I–III (Ancoratus, Panarion haer. 1–80 un De fide) nach den Materialen von Karl Holl*, GCS Neue Folge 13 (Berlin: Walter de Gruyter, 2006), 273–77, for a list of references of where Epiphanius may have consulted and used these writings.
37. C. Kannengiesser suggests the pivotal influence of Origen on Eusebius, particularly for the methodology of compiling the canons together. "Eusebius of Caesarea, Origenist," in Attridge and Hata, *Eusebius*, 435–66. On the "pure scholarship" of the *Chronicle*, see Barnes, *Constantine*, 106–25. For a thorough study of the extant versions of the text and manuscript tradition, see Mosshammer, *Chronicle*, 29–83.
38. On Eusebius's claim, see Eus., *praeparatio evangelica* 10.9.2 and the preface to his *Chronicle*. See B. Croke, "The Originality of Eusebius' *Chronicle*," *American Journal of Philology* 103 (1982): 195–200; Inglebert, *Interpretatio*, 504–5.

peoples. In the second part, the *Chronological Canons*, Eusebius took various regnal lists and offered a method of synchronization with Olympiad years.[39] The first part thus constituted the "rescarch" phase of his overall project, and the work allowed him to synchronize biblical dates with notable dates from Greek history. Ultimately, this work demonstrated the longevity and antiquity of Hebrew history, which was one of Eusebius's main goals, particularly as a response to the criticism leveled against Christianity by the pagan philosopher Porphyry.[40] In a subtle attack on Greek culture, Eusebius attempted to demonstrate the relative lateness of the Trojan War, that watershed Greek event, in comparison to Moses.[41] Like the apologists before him, Eusebius desired to show that the pivotal events in Greek history all occurred after Moses and that any Greek accomplishment was either learned or plagiarized from other people, thereby subordinating the Greek past and its culture to biblical and barbarian history.[42]

Eusebius maintained a greater sense of caution than Africanus about the extent to which humans could know and calculate the chronology of antedilu-

39. See J. Karst, *Eusebius Werke V, Die Chronik*, GCS 20 (Leipzig: J.C. Heinrichs'sche Buchhandlung, 1911); cf. Mosshammer, *Chronicle*, 65–66. For citations to the *Chronography*, I will refer to the pages and line numbers of the translation by Karst.

The *Chronological Canons* survives almost entirely extant in the Latin translation of Jerome, who incorporated material from it into his own *Chronicle*. For a discussion of Eusebius's influences and place in the broader tradition of chronicle writing, see B. Croke, "The Origins of the Christian World Chronicle," in *History and Historians in Late Antiquity*, ed. B. Croke and A. Emmett (Oxford: Pergamon Press, 1983), 116–31.

On the dating of the *Canons* (between 306 and 313), see R. Burgess, "The Dates and Editions of Eusebius' *Chronici Canones* and *Historia Ecclesiastica*," *JTS* 48, no. 2 (1997): 471–504. On the structure of the *Chronicle*, problems in transmission, and important themes, see Barnes, *Constantine*, 111–20.

40. Burgess, "Dates," 479. For a broad study of Eusebius's antipagan polemic in the *praeparatio evangelica* and *demonstratio evangelica*, see Kofsky, *Eusebius of Caesarea against Paganism*, Jewish and Christian Perspectives Series 3 (Leiden: Brill, 2000), and on his response to Porphyry in his *Against Porphyry*, see M. Frede, "Eusebius' Apologetic Writings," in *Apologetics in the Roman Empire: Pagans, Jews, and Christians*, ed. M. Edwards, M. Goodman, S. Price (Oxford: Oxford University Press, 1999), 235–40. For examinations of Porphyry's anti-Christian polemic, see B. Croke, "Porphyry's Anti-Christian Chronology," *JTS* 34.1 (1983), 168–85; R. Wilken, *The Christians as the Romans Saw Them* (New Haven: Yale University Press, 1984), 126–63; Kofsky, *Eusebius*, 17–36.

41. Eus., *p.e.* 10.4.5–11, 10.9.1–28.

42. Cf. Tat., *orat.* 31, 36–40; Thphl. Ant., *Autol.* 3.21, 23, 39. See Johnson, *Ethnicity*, 126–52. Contrast also with Clem., *str.* 1.15–17 (66.1–89.4), 5.4–5 (19.1–31.5), 5.14 (89.1–141.3), who was more optimistic about the contributions of the Greeks and in particular how their philosophers possessed the truth in part. Although in much of *str.* 1.21, Clement demonstrated that major events in Greek history were posterior to Moses. See Le Boulluec, *La notion*, 263–360. Clement's perspectives, by and large, would have been completely antithetical to Epiphanius. On Eusebius as an apologetic writer, see E. Gallagher, "Eusebius the Apologist: The Evidence of the *Preparation* and the *Proof*," StPatr 26 (1993): 251–60; Frede, "Apologetic"; Johnson, *Ethnicity*, 198–233.

vian history, and he allegorically interpreted the Genesis account before the Fall.[43] That Eusebius, under the influence of Origen, would assert this is not surprising.[44] He understood the time in Eden as chronologically indeterminate and nonphysical and that only after the Fall was the human soul encased in flesh. Eusebius was also antichiliast, and he remained suspicious of those who claimed to know how to determine the dates for the beginning and end of the world.[45] Because Eusebius doubted a chronicler's ability to reckon the chronology of the primordial past, he avoided beginning his historical works from Adam. Rather, the life of Abraham was a more suitable chronological reference point, and thus his *Chronological Canons* began with Abraham in the year 2016 BCE.[46] In his *Preparation for the Gospel*, Eusebius painted a picture of human history that prioritized Moses over Plato and the primacy of Jewish law over Greek philosophy, but he also posited a theory that distinguished the "Hebrews" from the Jews and identified Christians as the direct descendants of the former, who believed and practiced the right religion.[47] Thus Eusebius reimagined and manipulated the history of human developments to legitimize the longevity and supremacy of Christianity over both Judaism and paganism.

Another important Eusebian contribution to the context in which Epiphanius developed his own ideas was the schema of the *Ecclesiastical History*. Eusebius essentially invented a literary genre through the synthesis of biblical and classical approaches to history.[48] His thematic ordering of church history, from Christ to his own times, combined the chronologies of the Roman emperors, bishops and other prominent Christians, and heretics. He envisioned an unfolding of the divine economy in which Christian truth was passed down from Jesus to his disciples and through the generations of the church, which resulted

43. See Adler, *Immemorial*, 46–50; Inglebert, *Interpretatio*, 382. For example, "For in the beginning, after the first life in blessedness, the first man, who thought the divine command inferior, fell straightaway into this mortal and perishable life and exchanged the former divinely-inspired delight for this accursed earth." Eus., *h.e.* 1.2.18.

44. See for example Origen, *homiliae in Gen.* 1.13. Of course Epiphanius vehemently attacked Origen's allegorical understanding of Eden and the nature of humanity pre-Fall; cf. *Anc.* 54–63. See the analysis of Epiphanius's critique of Origen's teaching on Eden and the Fall in Dechow, *Dogma*, 334–42.

45. Cf. Eus., *chronicon* (Karst) 36.16–37.9.

46. Inglebert, *Interpretatio*, 505.

47. A. Johnson provides broad discussions of Eusebius's "ethnic argumentation" and "narrative of descent" as apologetic tools in opposition to the criticisms of pagans and Jews. "Identity, Descent, and Polemic: Ethnic Argumentation in Eusebius' *Praeparatio Evangelica*," *JECS* 12, no. 1 (2004): 23–56; idem, *Ethnicity*. See Droge, *Homer*, 168–93, for a discussion of Eusebius's use of the history of culture in the *p.e.*, as well as Inglebert, *Interpretatio*, 514–15. See also Gallagher, "Apologist." Frede shows how Eusebius argued that Platonism was in fact a derivative of Scripture. "Apologetic," 240–50.

48. Inglebert, *Interpretatio*, 321–23, 504–7, 533–36. See also Grant, *Eusebius*.

in confrontation with and persecution by the Roman Empire. At the same time, Eusebius imagined a succession of those who deviated from the truth and corrupted the pure, original message.[49]

The influence of Eusebius in Epiphanius's work is undeniable, which perhaps should come as no surprise. While both men flourished during the same century, the elder Eusebius died (ca. 339) well before Epiphanius emerged on the ecclesiastical stage. Each was deeply invested and interested in defending his understanding of the Christian faith, and their work exhibited a comprehensive, encyclopedic approach to their subjects. Although we might situate each man on opposing ends of the theological spectrum, they shared many of the same literary and rhetorical goals and participated in a common mission that witnessed the triumph of the Christian faith and church. Eusebius accomplished much of the hard work of reimagining human history, filling in and aligning the details with already established traditions, and Epiphanius, whether he liked it or not, was one of the beneficiaries of Eusebius's vision and literary accomplishments.

Epiphanius's Imagined History *(Panarion 1–8)*

The first four entries of the *Panarion* comprise an amalgam of different literary traditions that deal with human history and reckoning time. In the tradition of *Jubilees*, Epiphanius would have seen how a reimagining of Genesis could be used to emphasize specific developments and themes that aligned with his own convictions. In Julius Africanus, he would have understood that calculating archaic time in precise terms, even of the antediluvian world, was possible. Epiphanius was not a chronographer. Nevertheless, he attempted to integrate numerical calculations to establish a chronological scheme through which he then traced the progression of history, culture, and depravity. His date calculations were clearly borrowed and adapted from other sources, and numerical accuracy was certainly not his forte.[50] The years, however, were not as important to Epiphanius as the effect they would have on his readers, and the data he provided served to demonstrate how "orthodox" Christianity had existed from the very beginning and how far human sinfulness had degenerated since the

---

49. Grant, *Eusebius*, 84–96.
50. Adler identifies the numerous inaccuracies in Epiphanius's calculations, based in part on his adding corrections for two different timeline traditions for the period from Adam to the Flood. "Origins."

Fall. From Eusebius, Epiphanius learned that history had to be understood as Christian history and that the faith, or at least the character of it, had existed from the beginning. Furthermore, he would have recognized the schema in which Hellenism and Judaism both might be conceived as heresies.[51] According to Eusebius, Judaism was a corruption of a pure "Hebrew" faith, and Hellenism merely copied and mutilated what was true from a much older and venerated people and culture.[52] Epiphanius worked all of these themes drawn from this diversity of literary traditions into his reimagining of history.

Barbarism: Humanity before the Flood

According to Epiphanius, "Barbarism" was the first human era, which began appropriately with Adam, who was "created from the earth and received the breath of God."[53] The choice of "barbarism" as the moniker to describe this earliest period also may have been strategic, because it would seem to imply that all subsequent developments and achievements in human civilization emerged from barbarians, not Greeks.[54] This theoretical starting point is significant because it undermines any credit owed to Greek culture for its contributions to humanity, and in fact, Epiphanius attempted to show that Greek culture, broadly categorized as Hellenism, was the result of human corruption and decline, not progress and evolution.[55]

Just as Adam was an earthly creation, Eve was created from the "same body" and the "same breath," which again highlighted the physical, bodily creation of man and woman.[56] Epiphanius's emphasis on the embodied creation of the first humans was important for contemporary debates relating to the body, particularly in response to notions attributed to Origen that the pre-Fall Adam and Eve did not have physical bodies and only received them after they had sinned.[57] Adam, in his original created state, was "simple and

51. Including the sects of Judaism as part of the Christian heresiological tradition was established long before by Justin Martyr; cf. Le Boulluec, *La notion*, 70–78. Likewise, Hippolytus did much to establish the Greek philosophical tradition as part of heresiology.

52. Johnson, *Ethnicity*, 94–125.

53. *Pan.* 1.1. Cf. *Anc.* 61.6.

54. See Droge, *Homer*, 49–193, for how Christian apologists repeatedly tried to demonstrate the antiquity of Judaism, and by association Christianity, against Greek claims to have been the inventors of philosophy and other skills beneficial to humanity.

55. Compare the argument laid out by Eusebius in his *p.e.* See Droge, *Homer*, 185–87.

56. *Pan.* 1.2.

57. Cf. *Anc.* 62; *Pan.* 64.4.5–8, 64.63.5–65.28. This is the so-called "Garments of Skins" problem. Critics of Origen claimed that he taught that the garments of skin given to Adam and Eve were their physical

innocent, not having acquired any other name, nor having acquired an additional name from an opinion, doctrine, or distinct way of life."[58] Adam and Eve lived in a pure state of existence that had not been divided or variegated by any opinions or thoughts.[59] Epiphanius, however, was careful to frame this state of innocence in terms of "opinion, doctrine, or distinct way of life," that is, according to belief and practice.

Epiphanius then discussed Adam and Eve's male and female offspring and included the first numerical calculation and reference point, that Adam lived 930 years.[60] The period of the first five descendants of Adam, beginning with Seth, then Enosh, Kenan, Mahalael, and Jared (cf. Gen 5:5–20),[61] is notable, as Epiphanius explains:

> As the tradition that has come to us has it, thenceforth the practice of base arts (κακομηχανία) began (ἤρξατο) to exist (γίνεσθαι) in the world: and from the beginning (ἀπ' ἀρχῆς), through the disobedience of Adam, then through the fratricide of Cain, and now in the time of Jared and beyond, [came] witchcraft and magic, licentiousness, adultery, and injustice.[62]

---

bodies, which would imply that they had existed in a soul-like state before the Fall (cf. Or., *selecta in Gen.* 3.21; *homiliae in Lev.* 6.2). This view influenced Eusebius as well (cf. Eus., *p.e.* 7.18.3–10), and he notably resisted any attempt to impose a chronological framework upon the time of Eden.

    For Epiphanius's rejection of this teaching, see Dechow, *Dogma*, 315–33. On the centrality of debates on the body and soul in the Origenist controversy, see Clark, "Perspectives"; eadem, *Controversy*, especially 86–104, on Epiphanius. Furthermore in Epiphanius's view as he outlined it in his entry on Origen, the allegorical interpretation of the Fall implied another heretical idea, the loss of God's image: "He says that Adam lost the image of God. Thence he also says that the Bible signifies that the garments of skin are bodies, as it says 'he made garments of skin for them and clothed them'" (*Pan.* 64.4.9).

    In *Anc.* 54, Epiphanius correspondingly insisted on the earthly, physical reality of the Garden of Eden, which again Origen understood allegorically (*sel. in Gen.* 2.8–9) as the location of the pre-Fall souls of Adam and Eve. Epiphanius repeated his criticism in Jer., *Ep.* 51.5.

58. *Pan.* 1.1.
59. Adler: "Primitive mankind could not even contemplate heresy, because there was neither the instinct nor the aptitude to do so." "Origins," 472.
60. *Jubilees* 4.1–8, named two of the daughters (Awan and Azura) born to Adam and Eve in addition to Cain and Abel, and it specified that they had nine more children. *Jubilees* 4.30; Jos., *Antiquitates Judaicae* 1.83 gave 930 years for Adam's life.
61. Cf. *Jubilees* 4.9–15.
62. *Pan.* 1.3. As Droge points out in his discussion of Theophilus of Antioch's *Ad Autolycum*, the use of terms such as ἀρχή and γίγνομαι and their related forms were important markers in ancient discussions of cultural history because they distinguished "cardinal foundings or inaugurations." *Homer*, 111. However, unlike Theophilus and other Christian apologists who articulated a progression of human culture, Epiphanius presented one of degeneration.

Presumably, the "tradition" to which Epiphanius referred is *Jubilees*.[63] This statement marks the beginning of Epiphanius's reimagined history of culture characterized by degeneration and corruption over time. He indicated here that the inception of this decline was the "disobedience" of Adam, which in turn was punctuated by Cain's fratricide. Although Epiphanius posited that for the first time "base arts" were practiced in the world, they were still free of any association with different beliefs or ideas: "There was no other opinion (γνώμη), no changed belief, but one language and one race that had been sown on the earth at that time."[64] There was not yet any heterodoxy. Another important facet of Epiphanius' account of human depravity is the lack of reference or blame assigned to demonic powers, which was a common idea among various Christian writers to explain the proliferation of wickedness.[65] Epiphanius's rendering of the events reflects a "highly denatured and rationalized form," which is an important aspect of his broader understanding of the development of heresy.[66] Human beings alone initiated wrong beliefs and wrong practices. Thus, the onus of responsibility fell on them.

The narrative moves quickly to the Flood, brought on by the "just judgment of God."[67] Epiphanius provided no explanation for why God destroyed all living things through the cataclysm, although the earlier list of human failings must have played a part in the divine judgment. But as we shall see, Epiphanius did offer further commentary in his entry "Scythianism."[68] Noah and his progeny survived the Flood, along with all manner of living things, some in twos and others in sevens, and this event marked the passing of ten generations from the time of Adam, comprising a total of 2,262 years.[69]

---

63. Adler, "Origins," 476.

64. *Pan.* 1.4.

65. Eus., *d.e.* 4.9 (158c–160d). See Droge, *Homer*, 54–59. For Justin Martyr, demonic powers were also at the root of heresy; cf. Le Boulluec, *La notion*, 64–67.

66. Adler, "Origins," 477. This emphasis on human responsibility contrasts with the *Jubilees* account, which focused on the machinations of the demonic figure Mastema and the corruption introduced by the Watchers.

67. *Pan.* 1.6.

68. *Jubilees* 5.2, 7.21, attributed the proliferation of human sin to the corruption of the Watchers, who initially came to earth to teach men how to live rightly, but then married the daughters of men and produced giant sons. Both *Jubilees* and Epiphanius identified the time of Jared as a key moment in human corruption. Cf. *Jubilees* 4.15, 4.22 5.1–11; *1 Enoch* 6–11. See van Ruiten, *Primaeval History*, 188–92, and VanderKam, *Jubilees*, 34–35. This is echoed in Jos., *AJ* 1.73.

    Africanus, in contrast with *Jubilees*, implied that the Flood occurred because of human wickedness. He interpreted the "sons of God" not as angelic beings, but as the descendants of Seth who later intermingled with the descendants of Cain; cf. Julius Africanus, *chronicon* F23. See Adler, *Immemorial*, 114–15.

69. *Pan.* 1.7–8. Cf. Jos., *AJ* 1.82. The year 2,262 for the Flood is characteristically from Africanus's sys-

Epiphanius concluded the era of "Barbarism" with important comments on the condition of humanity following the postdiluvian recovery:

> There was not yet heterodoxy, no differentiated people, no name of a heresy, not even idolatry, since each man was living by his own opinion (γνώμη), for there was not one law. For each person became a law unto himself and was living by his own opinion, just as in the usage of the Apostle, not only of [the term] barbarism, but also of others. For he says, "In Christ Jesus there is no barbarian, no Scythian, no Greek, no Jew" [Col 3:11]); the eponym of the time then, in the ten generations, was called "Barbarism."[70]

Epiphanius underscored the absence of heterodoxy and heresy and perhaps also betrayed his inconsistent or very flexible use of the term "heresy." Although the heresiological entry itself is entitled "Barbarism," it seems that no heresy existed in the era of barbarism. Rather, people lived in an era of relative morality, as each determined his or her way of life according to individual "opinion." There was no organized or uniform law, hence the appellation "Barbarism." The idea that primitive people lived in a kind of wild, perhaps even animal-like state was certainly not uncommon in antiquity, and this theory usually presaged discussions of human progress and civilization.[71] But again we will see Epiphanius's inversion of this model.

Scythianism: The Flood and Aftermath

In this relatively short entry, Epiphanius offered some of his most important thoughts on the history of human culture and depravity and the development of orthodoxy and heresy.[72] The narrative continues with the resting of Noah's ark and his postdiluvian settlement and planting of his famous vineyard (Gen

---

tem; cf. Afric., *chron.* F16b, in Wallraff, *Africanus*, 29, and see 35, n. 2, for why Africanus dated the Flood in 2,262 (to account for a discrepancy in the age of Methuselah). However, in his letter to John of Jerusalem, Epiphanius gave 2,242 years (cf. Jer., *Ep.* 51.6), which is consistent with the numbering in the LXX. Cf. Thphl. Ant., *Autol.* 3.24; Eus., *chron.* (Karst) 38.4.

70. *Pan.* 1.9.

71. For example, Berossus, *Babyloniaca* 1.4, described earliest man in a state of nature living "without laws just as wild animals" (translation Burstein, *Babyloniaca*, 7). Berossus believed that men became civilized after divine revelation from the gods at Babylon, and writers in other traditions made similar arguments about their respective gods and peoples.

72. Adler discusses Epiphanius's flexible use of "Scythianism." "Origins," 488–90.

9:20).[73] Epiphanius omitted the cultural mandate to "be fruitful and multiply" (Gen 8:17, 9:1) and the rainbow covenant; rather, he mentioned that Noah's descendants down to a fifth generation comprised 659 years, excluding Shem.[74] He then proceeded with a list of the descendants of Shem:[75] Arpachshad, Kenan, Shelah, Eber,[76] and Peleg.[77]

Humanity's Natural State

At this point in the entry, Epiphanius transitioned to an important cultural and theological excursus. He reiterated that even after the earth was destroyed by the Flood, there was "no heresy, no other opinion, but they were only called men, of 'one tongue and one language' (Gen 11:1). There was only impiety and piety, the law according to nature and error according to nature, of each person's own will, not from a teaching nor from books. There was not Judaism, not Hellenism, not some heresy."[78] Epiphanius indicated that humans still lived in a primitive, natural state, again in accordance with each individual's will. But his mention of the absence of Judaism and Hellenism foreshadowed the two paths of the future decline of humanity. He then made makes the following profoundly important observation:

> In a way, the faith now presently dwelling in the holy catholic Church of God was existing from the beginning and was revealed again later. For the one who wishes to see truthfully, from his own investigation, <it is possible to see that> the catholic and holy Church is the beginning of all things. For Adam, the first-formed, had been formed not circumcised, but uncircumcised in the flesh. He

73. *Pan.* 2.1.
74. *Pan.* 2.2.
75. Cf. *Anc.* 59.4, 114.7. The narrative of Shem played an important role in the *Ancoratus* as a refutation of the charge that God was unjust in allowing the Israelites to conquer Canaan. According to *Anc.* 114, Ham's son Canaan illicitly seized the land of Palestine and its environs from Shem's descendants, and thus the later invasion by the Israelites was God's just, but patient response to the earlier crime. Cf. *Jubilees* 10.28–34.
    By listing Kenan as the son of Arpachshad, Epiphanius followed the text of the LXX and departed from Africanus and Eusebius, who both only accounted for the first antediluvian Kenan. Cf. Wallraff, *Africanus*, 29, n. 1 and 37–41; Adler, "*Chronographiae*," 500–501.
76. The name of the Hebrews, the practitioners of the right religion before Judaism, came from Eber. Cf. Thphl. Ant., *Autol.* 3.24; Hipp., *haer.* 10.30.5; Eus., *p.e.* 7.6.1–4, 7.8.20, 11.6.39–40. Johnson, *Ethnicity*, 114–15.
77. Peleg was an important figure in the chronography of Africanus, who dated Peleg's death in the 3,000th year after creation, marking the halfway point in the 6,000-year cycle of human history. See Adler, "*Chronographiae*," 500–501, 519–23.
78. *Pan.* 2.3.

was not an idolater, and he knew God as Father and Son and Holy Spirit, for he was a prophet.[79]

Epiphanius indicated that a form of the faith believed in his own day existed from the beginning of humanity, only to be revealed again at a later time, presumably with the Incarnation, and that the "Church," even if not in an explicit way, had existed from the beginning as well.[80] Furthermore Adam, the first man and prophet, knew a Triune God, and "therefore not having circumcision, he was not a Jew."[81] Epiphanius interpreted circumcision as a clear marker of difference that demarcated the Jew. Through his emphasis on Adam's noncircumcision but proto-orthodox belief, he made the separation between Judaism and Christianity a moot point because they were never joined, and the latter most certainly did not emerge from the former. Indeed in Epiphanius's vision of history, Judaism emerged from Christianity! He projected back into human history the existence of the "Church" and an orthodox theology, and he offered some (weak) exegetical proof "that Adam knew that the Father said to the Son, 'let us make man'" (Gen 1:26).[82] Epiphanius then remarked, "So what was this, neither having circumcision nor worshipping idols, but that he, showing just a little, exhibited the character of Christianity."[83] These claims have the twofold effect of giving Christianity a greater antiquity and establishing a specific proto-orthodox faith at the beginning of human history.[84] Furthermore, Epiphanius listed additional biblical patriarchs who exhibited this "character of Christianity": Abel, Seth, Enosh, Enoch, Methuselah, Noah, and Eber, down to Abraham.[85] This list represents an appropriation of the patriarchs of pre-Mosaic Judaism into the fold of orthodox Christianity.[86]

---

79. *Pan.* 2.4.
80. See Buell, *New Race*, 70–84, on the "rhetoric of restoration." Schott argues that Epiphanius held a view of orthodoxy that was "fundamentally a-historical and a-cultural." It was impervious to the effects of human depravity and cultural decline and continued to exist "among the patriarchs typologically." "Heresiology," 560–61. See also Riggi, "Il termine," 10–13.
81. *Pan.* 2.5. On the manifold and complex interpretations that early and late ancient Christians made with regard to circumcision (especially on the body of Christ), see Jacobs, *Circumcised*.
82. Cf. Eus., *p.e.* 7.15.1–18; *h.e.* 1.2.6, but with a clear subordinating theology.
83. *Pan.* 2.5.
84. Cf. Eus., *h.e.* 1.4.1–15. Eusebius certainly conceived of a Christian prehistory over and against Judaism and Hellenism, although he emphasized that the moral conduct (and monotheism) of patriarchs like Abraham reflected the hallmarks of Christianity. See Kofsky, *Eusebius*, 100–136.
85. *Pan.* 2.6. Eus., *p.e.* 7.8.1–39; *d.e.* 1.2, listed and described "righteous men" and "friends of God," including Enosh, Enoch, Noah, Melchizedek, Abraham, Isaac, Jacob, Job, Joseph, and Moses.
86. Again, Eus., *d.e.*, 1.2, developed a concept of a "third religion" between Judaism and Hellenism that was practiced by righteous men before the advent of Christianity.

In the postdiluvian world, "Piety and impiety, faith and unbelief were operative then. Faith maintained the image of Christianity, and unbelief maintained the character of impiety and transgression, contrary to the law according to nature, up to the time mentioned before."[87] Epiphanius thus imagined a dichotomous world in which only the two extremes of faith and unbelief existed, with the former reflecting the image of the proto-orthodox Christianity passed down from Adam and the latter exhibiting the "character of impiety and transgression," which was *contrary* to the natural law that would have maintained a right belief.

Biblical History Resumed

The entry returns to the historical retelling of Genesis with the fifth generation after the Flood, when the descendants of Noah's sons repopulated the world, with seventy-two leaders and chieftains.[88] Together they departed from Mount Lubar, where the ark had rested, and settled in the plain of Shinar (Gen 11:2), which according to Epiphanius was originally Assyrian land, but later held by the Persians.[89] Therein they were called "Scythians," hence the name of the era, and they conspired to construct the tower and city of Babylon. The narrative continues with the familiar Tower of Babel story (cf. Gen 11:3–9), after which God "scattered their tongues about and divided from one into seventy-two, according to the number of men found, whence these men were also called 'Meropes' because of the divided speech.[90] And a blast of wind laid low the tower."[91] The entry concludes with additional details about the distribution of lands among the people scattered from Babel.[92]

Although the justification for the appellation "Scythianism" is ambiguous, Epiphanius presented this "heresy" as a distinct period of history. The uncir-

---

87. *Pan.* 2.7. Cf. Eus., *p.e.* 7.6.1–4, on the Hebrews living "according to nature" and receiving truth from God.

88. The number was derived from Genesis 10 in the LXX. In *Anc.* 59, Epiphanius listed the names of the descendants of Shem, and in *Anc.* 112–14, he recorded the lands claimed by each of Noah's sons and the different peoples who emerged from each lineage.

89. *Pan.* 2.9–10.

90. Adler discusses the double meaning of this term, literally "dividing the tongue," but referring to the division of peoples and the division of the earth. "Origins," 489.

91. *Pan.* 2.11. On the destructive wind, cf. *Jubilees* 10.26.

92. In *Anc.* 112–13, Epiphanius offered an extensive list of the peoples who descended from Noah's sons and the territories they inherited. Inglebert discusses briefly how *Jubilees* reflected a Jewish reaction to Hellenistic influence, in this case in geography. *Interpretatio*, 118–19. The author of *Jubilees* incorporated certain features of the Greek conception of geography, namely the division of the earth into three continents, and assigned a part to each of Noah's sons. Christian writers including Epiphanius later appropriated this idea in their own works.

REIMAGINING THE ANCIENT PAST   63

cumcised, non-Jewish Adam believed in a Triune God and exhibited the character of Christian faith, so orthodox Christianity existed from the beginning of humanity. In this era, people lived according to either impiety or piety, faith or unbelief, and neither Hellenism nor Judaism had yet come into existence.

Hellenism: Cultural Decay

"Hellenism" in Late Antiquity

In this strategically titled entry, Epiphanius continued his reimagined history of culture and depravity. By the fourth century, "Hellenism" and paganism were synonymous. Thus Epiphanius's designation of this era must have invoked a variety of implications about Greek culture and pagan religion, namely that they were part of the larger development of heresy.[93] Throughout his career, Epiphanius exhibited an intense hostility toward classical culture, *paideia*, which he argued was responsible for corrupting true faith into heresy. In late antiquity, *paideia* was an important cultural and social currency shared among elites across the Roman Empire and was one of the markers of distinction between those who had power (or access to it) and those who did not.[94] But despite his vocal opposition, Epiphanius's own connection to *paideia* was perhaps more complicated than he made it out to be.[95] His writings reveal that he knew how to use secular knowledge and words for all their rhetorical potential, thus betraying at least some traditional learning, but he assumed a public stance that denigrated classical culture. However, many of his contemporaries across the Mediterranean world who struggled over the relationship between their own (secular) educational backgrounds and their Christian faith came to more nuanced conclusions. For example Basil of Caesarea, despite misgivings about his own academic pursuits, used the language and ideals of *paideia* to pursue patronage and to execute it.[96]

---

93. On the meaning of Hellenism by this time, see G. Bowersock, *Hellenism in Late Antiquity* (Ann Arbor: University of Michigan Press, 1990), 1–13.
94. See throughout Brown, *Power and Persuasion*.
95. See R. Lyman, "Hellenism and Heresy," *JECS* 11, no. 2 (2003): 209–22, for a discussion of the complicated negotiation in which Christians were engaged regarding the relationship between the faith and the surrounding Hellenistic culture.
96. For a broad study of Basil, see P. Rousseau, *Basil of Caesarea*, Transformation of the Classical Heritage 20 (Berkeley: University of California Press, 1994). See also R. Van Dam, *Kingdom of Snow: Roman Rule and Greek Culture in Cappadocia* (Philadelphia: University of Pennsylvania Press, 2002), 159–202, on how Basil and Gregory of Nazianzus (and Julian) each dealt with the relationship between culture and faith.

But the late fourth century was also a time of significant shifts and transitions, especially in ecclesiastical leadership.[97] The bishop and the monk, once separated as two different expressions of the Christian faith and representatives of two different modes of authority, one within and one beyond the walls of the church, were becoming fused into a new model of leadership.[98] Basil embodied this changing ideal, and he drew on his family background, education, asceticism, and social connections to carry out his duties as bishop. One could argue, however, that he still functioned within the established political and social landscape of elites in late antiquity. Epiphanius, on the other hand, offered a variation on the emerging forms of Christian leadership. His power was rooted not in wordly learning or social connections, but in the rhetoric of orthodoxy and heresy, as he made himself the arbiter of right and wrong. His patronal prestige was augmented by his biblical and theological expertise. Other Christians looked to him for help, and he was happy to tell others the correct way to live and to believe. He would have his readers imagine that he had no need for the currency of *paideia* and the access to other elites it could provide, because his authority was founded on his encyclopedic biblical knowledge and mastery of the contours of heresy and orthodoxy. Thus in *Panarion* he could condemn as heresy (albeit rhetorically) Hellenism and its implicit connection to *paideia*.

"Hellenism" in the *Panarion*

Epiphanius continued his reimagining of Genesis with the idea that during construction of the Tower of Babel and the city of Babylon, the "beginning of the taking of counsel and tyranny" occurred.[99] This observation was about human political organization. People in previous eras had lived according to their own natural inclinations, but they now lived under the rule of individuals. "Nimrod (Νεβρώδ), the son of Cush the Ethiopian, ruled as king," and he was a founder of cities "in the land of Assyria."[100] The Greeks apparently equated this same Nimrod with Zoroaster, who moved further east and eventually settled in Bactria.[101] "Thenceforth, unlawful things were disseminated upon the earth, for this man became an inventor of bad teaching, astrology, and magic, as some say about this of Zoroaster."[102] Epiphanius, however, rejected the Nimrod-

---

97. See throughout, Rapp, *Bishops*.
98. See Sterk, *Renouncing*, 13–92.
99. *Pan.* 3.1.
100. *Pan.* 3.2.
101. On the equation of Nimrod and Zoroaster, see Pseudo-Clement, *homiliae Clementinae* 9.4–5. See also Inglebert, *Interpretatio*, 526.
102. *Pan.* 3.3.

Zoroaster connection, arguing that this Nimrod was "the giant" (cf. Gen 10:8) and far apart in time from the Persian prophet.[103]

> Pelcg begets Reu; Reu [begets] Serug, which means "provoked," from whom idolatry and Hellenism began among men (as the knowledge which has come to me has it). But not yet in statutes or reliefs made of stones, or wood, or wrought silver or gold or any other material, but only through paintings and images, the thinking of man discovered evil for itself. And through its free reason and mind, it discovered what was unlawful, instead of goodness.[104]

Epiphanius insinuated that "Hellenism" was intimately linked with the invention of idolatry and, as we will continue to see, unveiled a sort of hierarchy in its development, with this era only exhibiting painted images.[105] He also explained how the human mind is "free" to exercise its own will and thereby choose between what is evil and what is good, which again had the effect of situating the fault for error squarely among humans and not demonic powers.[106]

Serug's son was Nahor, who was the father of Terah (Gen 11:22–25), and during their time "came to be the molding of images from the knowledge of the working of clay and pottery, from the skill (τέχνης) of this man, Terah."[107] We see here the next phase in the development of idolatry from pictures to clay objects, and we also witness the invention of a "skill" applied to an Old Testament figure. Attributing all of the most important skill discoveries to non-Greek innovators was an important rhetorical tool in the arguments of Near Eastern, Jewish, and later Christian writers who sought to minimize or eliminate the unique contributions of the Greeks to human society.[108] All of these developments reached the twentieth generation of mankind and 3,332 years.[109]

---

103. Eus., *p.e.* 10.9, placed Zoroaster in the time of Ninus the Assyrian.
104. *Pan.* 3.4. *Jubilees* 11.4–6, had the beginning of idolatry in the time of Serug.
105. Epiphanius outlined a similar progression of idolatry in *Anc.* 102.7.
106. A point made by Adler, "Origins," 477. See also Iren., *haer.* 4.37.1–7, on the centrality of human freedom in his antiheretical arguments. Athanasius in *contra gentes* also developed the idea that evil originated with the soul's pursuit of corruptible things, and one of the first results of the wayward soul is idolatry.
107. *Pan.* 3.5. *Jubilees* 11.16, had Terah as an idolater, but his son Abram turning away from this. Adler states: "What we can say in any case is that Epiphanius' story of Serug and the rise of Hellenism is a reworking of historical and chronological traditions from Eusebius' *Canons* and Julius Africanus, combined with apocryphal expansion based loosely on Jewish sources, most notably the *Book of Jubilees*." "Origins," 481–82.
108. Cf. Clem., *str.* 1.16 (74.1–80.6); Eus., *p.e.* 10.6.1–9. See Droge, *Homer*, 86–91, 110–18.
109. *Pan.* 3.5. According to Africanus's chronology (Afric., *chron.* F16), the birth of Terah would have been at 3,132 years. Adler suggests that Epiphanius attempted to correct, albeit poorly, Africanus's

Terah, who was the father of Abram, Nahor, and Haran (Gen 11:26), "from the time when he set up a rival to God, making one through his working of clay, was rightly repaid the like for the things he had done, and he was provoked to jealousy by his own son."[110] This era still exhibited the hallmarks of "Scythianism" in lacking any "heresy," but idolatry ran rampant and worsened with euhemeristic practices.[111] Idolatry began first when people "made gods of ill-fated tyrants or sorcerers who deluded the world" and later did the same with "Kronos, Zeus, Rhea, and Hera and their ilk. Then they worshiped Akinakes, and the Sauromatians of the Scythians [worshiped] Odryses and the forefather of the Thracians."[112] The entry ends with the following observations:

> This entire period of time comprised thenceforth the beginning of the receiving of error in the aforementioned season, confusing the ways of men. Thereupon authors and historians, having borrowed the mythological error of the Egyptians <carried it over to the other nations?>,[113] whence the things of sorcery and magic were discovered. These things were carried over into Greece from the time of Cecrops. And it was at this time that Ninus and Semiramis the Assyrians were contemporaries with Abraham and the sixteenth dynasty of the Egyptians. Only the people of Sicyon were then being ruled by kings, of whose kingdom the beginning happened with Europs.[114]

Epiphanius reiterated the long-standing perspective popular among the Christian apologists that all things religious and cultural antedated the Greeks.[115] In this case, the originators of the practices of sorcery and magic were the Egyptians, and Epiphanius notably blamed "authors and historians" for disseminating these errors. He echoed the established tradition that Cecrops brought Hellenism to Greece from Egypt, and he synchronized Cecrops, the first king of Attica, with the Assyrian rulers Ninus and Semiramis and with Abraham.[116]

---

omission of the second postdiluvian Kenan. "Origins," 478–79. This error led to subsequent calculation errors.

110. *Pan.* 3.7. Cf. *Jubilees* 12.14, which had Haran dying in a fire, while Ps.-Clem., *recog.* 1.31, alluded to an incestuous crime.

111. *Pan.* 3.9–10. Euhemerism was an important aspect of the Christian understanding of the history of culture; see Droge, *Homer,* 125–38.

112. *Pan.* 3.10.

113. This is Holl's conjecture.

114. *Pan.* 3.11–12. Cf. Clem., *str.* 1.21 (102.5), who identified Aigialaos as first king before Europs.

115. Schott argues that the very idea that an "inventor" of a particular cultural or religious practice transplanted his discovery to Greece was an implicit argument for the ethnic inferiority of the Greeks. "Heresiology," 558.

116. Eus., *p.e.* 10.9.10, identified Cecrops as a contemporary of Moses, not Abraham, and he synchronized

REIMAGINING THE ANCIENT PAST   67

Epiphanius drew on a number of different traditions in his attempt to establish a chronographic schema without fully working out all of the details, which led to inconsistent and sometimes contradictory synchronizations. Indeed to establish his rhetorical claim that Greek culture originated in earlier corruptions of humanity, Epiphanius had to rework the chronology to fit his thematic plan and historical narrative. But he made his overall point here well enough, that the Greeks had learned wicked things from an older culture and that the rise of "Hellenism" was characterized by the development of idolatry.

Judaism: Religious Decay

True and False Monotheism

Just as the appellation "Hellenism" would have invoked particular associations, "Judaism" was equally fraught with negative meaning. By Epiphanius's lifetime, the so-called "parting of the ways" between Jews and Christians, with their respective polemic of heresy against each other and any who would occupy the theological and cultural space in between, had long since begun.[117] Furthermore by the late fourth century, the homeland of the Jews, centered at Jerusalem, was experiencing a rapid and radical expropriation and transformation by Christians and their developing notion of a holy land. The Jews were physically and rhetorically losing ground. Nevertheless, a polemical debate concerning the relationship between Jews and Christians continued to occupy the minds of Christian thinkers, and this issue was exacerbated by pagan intellectual criticisms of Christianity as an offshoot of Judaism.[118] Eusebius did much in his own writings to combat these attacks, and he developed a theory that posited a differentiation between the Hebrew religion, which bore the character of Christianity, and Judaism, which began with the Mosaic Law.[119] Epiphanius adopted

Abraham with Ninus and Semiramus. Eusebius was roundly criticized by later chronologists for the Cecrops-Moses synchronization; see Adler, "Origins," 480–81.

117. See Boyarin, *Border Lines*. For what Epiphanius knew about the Judaism of his own day, see J. Lieu, "Epiphanius on the Scribes and the Pharisees (*Pan.* 15.1–16.4)," *JTS* 39, no. 2 (1988): 509–24.

118. The novelty of Christianity was one of the classic criticisms of Celsus. On Celsus and Origen, see H. Chadwick, *Origen: Contra Celsum, Translated with an Introduction and Notes* (Cambridge: Cambridge University Press, 1953), especially the introduction, ix–xxxii; Wilken, *Christians*, 94–125; R. Hoffman, *Celsus on the True Doctrine: A Discourse Against the Christians* (Oxford: Oxford University Press, 1987); M. Frede, "Celsus' Attack on the Christians," in *Philosophia Togata II: Plato and Aristotle at Rome*, ed. J. Barnes and M. Griffin (Oxford: Oxford University Press, 1997), 218–40; idem, "Origen's Treatise *Against Celsus*," in Edwards, Goodman, Price, *Apologetics*, 131–55. See also Droge, *Homer*, 72–81, for a discussion of Celsus's criticisms vis-à-vis Justin Martyr's defense of Christianity as the true ancient "philosophy," and Le Boulluec, *La notion*, 52–60.

119. See for example, Eus., *d.e.* 1.2.

and adapted this scheme, attributing to Adam and the patriarchs a belief in the Triune God and a faith that exhibited the character of true Christianity. The entry "Judaism" continues Epiphanius's reimagining of the Genesis narrative and the underlying belief that orthodox Christianity had been known and passed down from the beginning of humanity and that human sinfulness continued its steady degeneration into Hellenism and Judaism.

The entry commences with Abraham, "faithful in uncircumcision, in the very character of the holy catholic Church, and most perfect in piety, a prophet in knowledge, one who acquired in life a Gospel way of living."[120] The argument that Abraham was righteous before he was circumcised had roots in the writings of Paul (cf. Rom 4), and this became an important theme among Christians who tried to appropriate Abraham as their true forefather and to distinguish Judaism and the Law from the righteous form of faith that preceded them.[121] God mandated circumcision for Abraham when he was ninety-nine, and this marker was the characteristic feature of Judaism.[122] This command was given in the twenty-first generation, in the year 3,431 after the foundation of the world, and marked the beginning of the era of "Judaism."[123] Epiphanius curiously remarked that after Abraham there was "not yet an eponym of a heresy, except the name of his religion. Therefore, they were called 'Abramians' from Abraham."[124] Perhaps this appellation was yet another means of distinguishing the Jews and Judaism from the righteous faith of Abraham and an echo of the Eusebian idea that before Judaism, the Hebrews had a pure, correct belief.[125] The entry continues with descriptions of Abraham's sons, Ishmael and Isaac, and their descendants, and Epiphanius also applied the name "Isaacians" to the "race of the religious."[126] He then placed Job in the succession of patriarchs as a

---

120. *Pan.* 4.1.1. Cf. Iren., *haer.* 4.25.1.

121. Cf. Just., *dialogus cum Tryphone Judaeo* 23; Iren., *haer.* 4.5.5, 4.21.1; Eus., *h.e.* 1.4, *p.e.* 7.8.22–25, *d.e.* 1.6 (14a-b). See Buell, *New Race*, 94–115.

122. Jacobs examines Epiphanius's critique of the Ebionite view of circumcision. *Circumcised*, 108–14. Epiphanius argued in *Panarion* 30 that the true purpose of the circumcision of Abraham and his progeny was "to keep them from forgetting the God of their fathers when enslaved by the idolatrous" (108), but that Christ's circumcision marked the true fulfillment of Jewish prophecy. Jacobs demonstrates how Epiphanius simultaneously rejected and appropriated circumcision, especially as located on the body of the Messiah, to denigrate the hybridity that was the Ebionite Jewish-Christian religion, but at the same time to create a hybrid of his own, "orthodoxy." See also Boyarin, "Rethinking," 22–27.

123. *Pan.* 4.1.3–4. According to Epiphanius's calculations, Abraham's birth would have been in year 3,332 after creation, while Africanus had 3,202 and Eus., *chron.* (Karst) 42.32, had 3,184.

124. *Pan.* 4.1.5.

125. Cf. Eus., *p.e.* 7.6.1–4, *d.e.* 1.6 (12c–16d). According to Eus., *p.e.* 7.8.37–39, *d.e.* 1.6 (17a–18d), the Hebrews became corrupted during their sojourn in Egypt at which time they became known as Jews, and the Law was intended to correct them. See Johnson, *Ethnicity*, 94–125.

126. *Pan.* 4.1.5–8.

direct descendant of Isaac through Esau, with the name Jobab (cf. Gen 36:33–34), which became Job shortly before his trials.[127] The narrative includes quick summaries of the life of Jacob and Joseph, the descent of the Israelites into Egypt (where they lived for five generations), and the Exodus.[128]

Heathen Beliefs and Practices

At this point, Epiphanius steered away from retelling Genesis to focus instead on developments among the Gentile cultures. Incorporating various elements from Christian chronographic writings, he discussed the development of Greek religion and philosophy. To the modern reader, these descriptions in the "Judaism" entry might appear peculiar and perhaps better suited to "Hellenism." But we must bear in mind that in these first four entries, Epiphanius was imagining developmental "eras" in human history and not individual "heresies" per se. It is also noteworthy that up to this point in his schema, "heresy" as an organized phenomenon did not yet exist. Humans practiced idolatry, magic, sorcery, and other dark arts, but heresy as a proper category would only come later under the Greek philosophers. The narrative continues: "It was in that time that Inachus was becoming known in Greece, whose daughter was Io, also called Atthis, from whom also now Attica is called. And from her was [born] Bosporus, from whose name the city on the Black Sea is called. Egyptians call her Isis, whom they also worship as a god. There is also a river with the same name as this man, thus called Inachus."[129] The synchronization of Moses with Inachus was a tradition established by earlier apologists and chronographers, but Eusebius decided instead to make Inachus a contemporary of Isaac and Jacob, thus pushing the chronology of Moses later, contemporaneous with Cecrops.[130] Epiphanius assumed the older tradition in an attempt to "correct" what he must have thought was an error in Eusebius's reckoning, but what resulted was a mangled chronology with Cecrops predating Inachus.[131]

The comments that follow are important because they related to further developments in Epiphanius's history of culture and human depravity:

---

127. *Pan.* 4.1.10. Cf. Afric., *chron.* F31. Contrast, however, with Eus., *p.e.* 7.8.30, who considered Job not of the Jewish people, although at 9.25.1–4, the quotation from Alexander Polyhistor (quoting Aristeas) attested to the Jobab connection. But compare with Eus. *d.e.* 1.6 (14d). Gallagher suggests: "His [Eusebius's] inclusion of Job among the 'ancient friends of God' is designed to indicate that the true religion was not limited to a particular physical lineage among the Hebrews but was available to all who demonstrated piety and virtue." "Apologist," 225.

128. *Pan.* 4.1.11–2.4.

129. *Pan.* 4.2.5. Cf. Clem., *str.* 1.21 (106.1); Afric., *chron.* F34; Eus., *p.e.* 2.1.28, 10.9.20, on Io and Isis.

130. Cf. Tat., *orat.* 38; Clem., *str.* 1.21 (101.1–5); Afric., *chron.* F34, F50; Eus., *p.e.* 10.10.15–20. On earlier synchronizations of Moses and Inachus, see Wacholder, "Chronology," 470–72.

131. Whereas in Tat., *orat.* 39; Clem., *str.* 1.21 (102.1–2); Eus., *p.e.* 10.9.18–19, Inachus predated Cecrops.

Thence the mysteries and rites among the Greeks had their beginning, having been invented for bad earlier among the Egyptians and Phrygians and Phoenicians and Babylonians and carried over to Greece from the land of the Egyptians by Cadmus[132] and Inachus himself, who earlier was called Apis and established Memphis.[133] But they [mysteries and rites] also received their beginning from Orpheus and some others (7) and later were organized into heresies in the time of Epicurus and Zeno the Stoic and Pythagoras and Plato, from whose time they began to grow strong, up to the time of the Macedonians and Xerxes, king of the Persians (after the first destruction of Jerusalem and captivity of Nebuchadnezzar and Darius) and the period under Alexander the Macedonian. (8) For Plato was becoming known at that time, and those before him, Pythagoras, and afterwards Epicurus. Whence indeed, as I said earlier, it gave rise to the occasion, and writings among the Greeks came, (9) and after this time, the celebrated heresies of the philosophers. They agree with one another in error, and they weave together the same kind of knowledge of idolatry and impiety and atheism, but in the same error they break off from one another.[134]

Epiphanius reiterated the common apologetic claim that Greek religion and its different expressions originated not with the Greeks but with other peoples. But he then made an important transition in which he explicitly alluded to the later organization of heresies, which happened in direct connection to the representatives of four "schools" of philosophy. Although they promulgated different beliefs, each school developed as a heresy, weaving together "the same kind of knowledge," idolatry and atheism. The idea that the forms of heresy derived from Greek philosophy would be characterized by the worship of false gods and denial of the one God fits well with Epiphanius's scheme established earlier, that Adam and the patriarchs were "orthodox" men who believed in a Triune God and had a faith that reflected a proto-orthodox Christianity. The charge that philosophies conflicted with one another but ultimately promulgated the same error was a familiar trope in the Christian apologetic tradition and was a reversal of the pagan charge that Christianity's own divisiveness was proof of its folly. Amid his discussion and critique of Greek philosophy, Epiphanius also

---

132. Cf. Clem., *str.* 1.21 (106.1); Eus., *p.e.* 1.6.4, 10.4.4, 10.5.1. In Eusebius's narrative, Cadmus transmitted Phoenician religion and letters to the Greeks, while Orpheus did the same with Egyptian religion and customs; cf. Johnson, "Identity," 39–41.

133. See Adler, "Origins," 481, on the problematic merging of Inachus and Apis.

134. *Pan.* 4.2.6–9.

made important links to the cultural development of "writings," in other words, the literature of the Greeks. Thus in Epiphanius' scheme, the Greek literary tradition, the heart of *paideia*, developed in conjunction with the rise of heresy under the Greek philosophers.

Greek Philosophy

In a strategic rhetorical move, Epiphanius interrupted his entry on Judaism and inserted brief entries on four different schools of Greek philosophy, the "Stoics," "Platonists," "Pythagoreans," and "Epicureans."[135] Epiphanius's heresiological predecessors already established a tradition of linking heresy with Greek philosophy, so the inclusion of four in the *Panarion* was by no means an innovation.[136] Furthermore, in the treatise called the *Exposition of the Faith* appended to the *Panarion*, Epiphanius included a condemnatory laundry list of philosophers with occasional snippets about their beliefs. He clearly obtained these names from a source that provided such basic information, so he was not completely unfamiliar with aspects of Greek philosophy. But at the same time, he was clearly not well versed in the intricacies of the different traditions. The inclusion of these four sects in the *Panarion* must have been a deliberate choice, and not surprisingly each represented a valuable point of attack against philosophical trends prevalent in the fourth century.[137] The selection of Plato and Pythagoras echoed the works of Porphyry, the vocal critic of Christianity who had written biographies of Pythagoras and Plotinus, the founder of Neoplatonism. The entries on the Stoics and Epicureans represented the Hellenistic philosophies that continued to enjoy popularity in the late Roman world.[138]

135. *Pan.* 5, 6, 7, 8, respectively. On the expansion of the catalog of heresies by including pagan philosophy and religion, see Inglebert, *Interpretatio*, 424–26. Pourkier argues that Epiphanius's presentation of these philosophies reflects his shallow familiarity with classical culture. *L'hérésiologie*, 96–99.
136. Notably Hippolytus, *refutation omnium haeresium*, but also see Iren., *haer.* 2.14.1–9. For Epiphanius's use of the nonextant *Syntagma* of Hippolytus, see R. Lipsius, *Zur Quellenkritik des Epiphanios* (Vienna: Wilhelm Braumüller, 1865). Scholars disagree about the authorship of the *refutatio*, as indicated in the introduction, n. 28, although I accept Hippolytus as the author.
    Another example of heresiological condemnation of Greek philosophy and linkage with heresy can be found in Tert., *Praescr.* 7, in which he accused Valentinus of borrowing from Plato and Marcion from Zeno the Stoic.
137. They also reflected the "four chairs" of philosophy established in Athens; cf. Pourkier, *L'hérésiologie*, 98.
138. See G. Clark, "Philosophic Lives and the Philosophic Life: Porphyry and Iamblichus," in *Greek Biography and Panegyric in Late Antiquity*, Transformation of the Classical Heritage 31, ed. T. Hägg and P. Rousseau (Berkeley: University of California Press, 2000), 29–51. On the biography of Plotinus, see M. Edwards, "Birth, Death, and Divinity in Porphyry's *Life of Plotinus*," in Hägg and Rousseau, *Greek Biography*, 52–71.

Epiphanius's refutation of the Stoics is the longest of the four, although he exhibited only a cursory familiarity with the basic ideas of Stoicism.[139] He began with the Stoic notion of deity, that "God is a mind, or of the entire invisible vault, I mean of heaven, earth, and the rest, like a soul in a body," which was apparently his understanding of basic Stoic cosmology.[140] Epiphanius also attacked Stoic belief in the "transferences of souls and transmigrations of bodies" and assertion that "the soul is part of God, and immortal."[141] Epiphanius correctly identified Zeno as the founder of this school and offered varying traditions about his origins. After attacking the Stoic teaching on matter as coexistent with God and the existence of fate and fortune, Epiphanius gave a brief disclaimer before proceeding: "Therefore, however much our abbreviated discussion shall prevail as a remedy for the most pitiable condition of this man, rather than going in detail through the great bulk of the matter, I will drive through the main points. But merely scratching the surface so that I not digress, I will answer this man."[142] Perhaps he was veiling his general ignorance of Stoicism by appealing to brevity for his readers' sake. Epiphanius then introduced a sort of mock dialogue with Zeno in which he refuted the aforementioned teachings about the nature of God and matter, transmigration of souls and bodies, and fate.[143] The matter of fate incensed Epiphanius greatly, and he expressed frustration at the implication that fate controls the behavior of humans, thereby relieving them of personal moral responsibility: "Rather than he who was compelled to do the deed, the stars that imposed the necessity ought to pay the price."[144] Exasperated by such an idea, Epiphanius interrupted his discussion with an emotional outburst:

But I shall speak on these things in some other way. Let the diatribes cease! Let the sophists and rhetoricians and grammarians, physicians and other profes-

---

139. Cf. Hipp., *haer.* 1.21.1–5, on the Stoics. For an introduction to the basic teachings of Stoicism, see the classic A. Long, *Hellenistic Philosophy: Stoics, Epicureans, Stoics*, 2nd ed., (Berkeley: University of California Press, 1986), 107–209.

140. *Pan.* 5.1.1.

141. *Pan.* 5.1.3.

142. *Pan.* 5.1.6.

143. *Pan.* 5.2.1–3.1.

144. *Pan.* 5.3.1. Eusebius, in Book 6 of the *p.e.*, also wrote extensively against pagan conceptions of fate. See Inglebert, *Interpretatio*, 221–33, for a discussion of the relationship between astrology and fate, and how Christians, building on Jewish and Greek philosophical arguments, ultimately rejected the practice of astrology. The concepts of human freedom and moral responsibility were central to this. On the Roman view and practice of astrology, see T. Barton, *Power and Knowledge: Astrology, Physiognomics, and Medicine under the Roman Empire*, The Body, in Theory (Ann Arbor: University of Michigan Press, 1994), 27–94, including 62–69, on Christians.

sions, and a countless multitude of handicrafts and skills stop! No one should teach any longer, if for men the procuring of knowledge depends naturally on fate and not on learning from letters. For if fate made a person educated and most learned, let him not learn from a teacher, but let the thread-spinning Fates conceive knowledge into him naturally, according to the sound of your boasting, through the error of your arguments.[145]

Rather than engaging in a philosophical critique of these Stoic teachings, Epiphanius turned to invective and a caricature of the Stoic teaching on fate.

The next three entries display even less engagement with philosophical ideas. Clearly, Epiphanius was no fan of Plato, and he attributed to him the same beliefs in the "transference and transmigration of souls, and polytheism, and other idolatries and superstitions."[146] Epiphanius, however, also seemed to recognize (reluctantly) that Plato "knows God" and understood God to be the originator of all things. This mirrored the views of older apologists who viewed Plato as the philosopher closest to the truth about God among all the pagans of the past.[147] Still, Epiphanius qualified this apparent praise by mentioning that Plato also believed in a second and third cause; and with a quotation from the *Timaeus*, Epiphanius offered proof that Plato had changed his mind about the origin of matter, positing at one time that it was "contemporaneous with God," which echoed the criticism of the Stoics.[148]

The entry on the Pythagoreans is even shorter, and Epiphanius lumped together Pythagoras and the Peripatetics (presumably Aristotle and his successors) into one heresy.[149] Again, Epiphanius conceded that they "characterize God as one," but they nevertheless erred in their belief in the "immortality and transmigration of souls and the destruction of bodies."[150] The entry ends with a

---

145. *Pan.* 5.3.2. Compare the tenor of this with Tat., *orat.* 25–26.

146. *Pan.* 6.1.1. Cf. Hipp., *haer.* 1.19.6–13, on the gods and the transmigration of souls.

147. Cf. Just., *1 apol.* 59–60; Iren., *haer.* 3.25.5; Eus., *p.e.* 11.1.1–13.13.66. For example, Droge examines Justin Martyr's generally optimistic view of Plato (and the Stoics), as well as that of Eusebius, although even he accused Plato of plagiarism. Both, however, insisted on the superiority of Christianity and the Hebrew wisdom on which it was based. *Homer*, 49–81, 168–93. See also Le Boulluec, *La notion*, 52–60; Kofsky, *Eusebius*, 282–86; Johnson, *Ethnicity*, 137–42.

148. *Pan.* 6.1.3. Cf. Hipp., *haer.* 1.19.1–5. Epiphanius quoted from Plato, *Timaeus* 38B.

149. See Pourkier, *L'hérésiologie* 96, on the possible source for the connection of the Pythagoreans and Peripatetics. Epiphanius's connection between Pythagoras and Aristotle is less sensible, since by the fourth century there was a strong link between Plato and Pythagoras, with some asserting that their philosophies were essentially the same or that Plato himself was a Pythagorean, whereas Epiphanius's predecessor Hippolytus made strong connections between the two philosophies (both of which were derived from the Egyptians), and he attributed the heresy of Valentinus to both; cf. Hipp., *haer.* 6.21.1–3, 6.29.1–2, 6.37.1–6.

150. *Pan.* 7.1.1. Cf. Hipp., *haer.* 1.2.11, 6.25.4, on the immortal soul; 6.26.1–3, on transmigration.

brief biographical note that Pythagoras died in Media and his assertion, "God is a body, that is, heaven, and that the sun and moon and other stars and planets in heaven are his eyes and other parts, just as in a man."[151] However, Epiphanius offered neither refutations nor any concluding thoughts or transitions.

The final entry against the Epicureans begins with the charge that Epicurus taught that there is no Providence, that all things are composed of atoms, and that all things came to exist by chance.[152] Epiphanius then described the Epicurean "egg" cosmography and the origin of matter and brought the entry to a swift conclusion. For all intents and purposes, these entries on the four schools of Greek philosophy have little to do with providing any systematic account of the respective teachings of each school or with appropriate refutations. Rather, the conspicuous presence of these named schools, identified as separate heresies and interjected in his reimagined history of humanity, while shallow, serves an intended rhetorical effect. Epiphanius insinuated that Greek philosophy was heresy and the product of human depravity, not enlightenment or achievement.

Judaism Resumed: The History of Israel

The continuation of the entry on Judaism marks the end of the reimagining of Genesis and a transition toward the biblical history of the Israelites. Epiphanius, however, restarted the entry by reiterating a point that he had made earlier, that idolatry was the first error perpetrated by humans, with the added detail that "poets, prose-writers, historians, astronomers, and those who introduced other kinds of error, having accustomed their minds to manifold wicked causes and ways of life, darkened and confounded the notions of humanity."[153] The blame for the proliferation of the error of idolatry fell on those who wrote literature and on those who observed the stars, with both skills representing aspects of *paideia*.[154] In Epiphanius's reckoning, at this point in history "all things were divided into Hellenism and Judaism," although Judaism actually was not called such until after "<five> successors."[155] Epiphanius proceeded to outline the succession of the tribe of Judah (whence the eponym "Jews"), beginning with Nahshon (cf. Num 1:7), to the accession of David as king. He then

---

151. *Pan.* 7.1.2.
152. *Pan.* 8.1.1. Cf. Hipp., *haer.* 1.22.1–5, on the Epicureans. See Long, *Philosophy*, 14–74.
153. *Pan.* 4.2.1.
154. Eus., *p.e.* 2.5.4, discussed the category of ancient men who, although the reason to seek after God was instilled within them, upon looking to the heavens began to worship the luminaries in the sky, which was the origin of one form of idolatry.
155. *Pan.* 4.2.2.

recapitulated the division of humanity that he had described up to this point, and he again invoked Colossians 3:11, but this time adding "but a new creation" to the previously truncated verse.[156] In his brief explanation of this verse that he projected backward to refer to primordial humanity and not to the post-Incarnational dispensation, Epiphanius stated, "Since it was new from the beginning, when creation was created, it did not have an any more distinctive name."[157] This comment underscores the broad theme he has been developing: that at creation, no other name existed to describe human beliefs (and thus no heresy); that a pure human state existed with a belief characteristic of true Christianity; and that only in subsequent developments in human history, that is, in the devolution of human depravity, did new appellations become necessary to characterize the different ways in which humans veered from the original right belief.

The narrative resumes with a summary of biblical history from Abraham's circumcision in his ninety-ninth year through the stories of Isaac and Jacob to the Exodus. Epiphanius's focus in this abbreviated account was on the purpose and meaning of circumcision. God commanded Abraham to bear this mark "in order that his seed, when they became foreigners in another land, might not turn away from the name of God," and his descendants continued this practice up to the time of the Exodus.[158] However, in the second year of their departure from Egypt, Moses gave to the Israelites the Law, whose purpose Epiphanius understood to be that of "a teacher, giving commands physically, but having a spiritual expectation."[159] The question of the Law presented a number of problems for Christians, especially in light of pagan attacks that criticized them for abandoning the ancestral customs of their Jewish forebears. Some Christian apologists argued that the dispensation of the Law was a positive for humanity, and that later cultures like the Greeks had learned about it from Moses and were thus able to bring order to their societies and practice justice.[160] Epiphanius's summary of the Law entails the following practices: "to circumcise; to observe the Sabbath; to tithe of all their produce and as many as are born among

---

156. The quotation here reads, "For in Christ there is no barbarian, no Scythian, no Hellene, no Jew, but a new creation."

157. *Pan.* 4.3.3.

158. *Pan.* 4.4.1, 4.4.2–7. Cf. Eus., *p.e.* 7.8.24.

159. *Pan.* 5.5.4.

160. Cf. Just., *1 apol.* 44. Jewish apologists made this argument first, as for example Josephus, *Ap.* 2.154–56. See Droge, *Homer*, 12–48, 59–65. Eus., *d.e.* 1.3, however, argued that the Law of Moses was intended only for the nation of the Jews; cf. Iren., *haer.* 4.15.1–16.5. Contrast with Ath., *de incarnatione* 12.5.

them, from man or animal; to give of the first-fruits, on the fifteenth and thirti-eth [day]; and to know God alone and to serve him."[161] Epiphanius did not have anything negative to say about the Law, and in fact he reiterated the very impor-tant theme he developed earlier about the maintenance of an "orthodox" wor-ship, even at this time: "So the Name was heralded in unity, and in unity the Trinity was always proclaimed and believed in by the most outstanding of them, that is, by the prophets and those who were sanctified."[162] Thus we have a clear connecting point from the declaration that Epiphanius had made earlier about the orthodox belief of Adam and the patriarchs that now includes Moses. Even the dispensation of the Law did not yet result in the corruption that was Judaism, and a continuity of orthodox worship existed from Creation to the Exodus.[163]

The Failure of the Jews

The Jews in the desert also received "prophetic utterances about the coming Christ," even if the Hebrew Scriptures at times referred to him as "'prophet,' al-though he was God, and 'angel,' although he was Son of God."[164] Epiphanius then listed what he understood to be the canonical books of the Hebrew Scriptures, to which he added the Wisdom of Sirach and the Wisdom of Solomon as apocry-phal books of disputed canonicity. He explained that all of these books taught the Jews the Law as a preparation for the coming of Christ and that the Jews would have been counted among the righteous had they accepted "his divinity and his incarnate *parousia*, since the types were in the Law, but the truth was in the Gospel."[165] The failure of the Jews—and hence the heresy of Judaism—was their denial of the prophesied Christ. Furthermore, the physical circumcision that was mandated by the Law was "subordinate in time until the 'great' circumcision, that is, baptism, which circumcised us from our sin and sealed us in the name of God."[166] Thus physical circumcision was a type for the future sacrament of bap-

161. *Pan.* 4.5.4.
162. *Pan.* 4.5.5. Schott states: "For Epiphanius, the Law itself also represents a collection of orthodox traces or signs." "Heresiology," 562.
163. This contrasts with Eusebius's narrative in the *p.e.* 7.8.37–39, in which he argued that the Hebrews were corrupted during their stay in Egypt and hence became "Jews" when they received the correc-tive Law from Moses. See Johnson, *Ethnicity*, 137–42.
164. *Pan.* 4.5.6.
165. *Pan.* 4.6.6.
166. *Pan.* 4.6.7. Jacobs examines the link Christians made between circumcision and baptism throughout. *Circumcised.* See also J. Verheyden, "Epiphanius on the Ebionites," in *The Image of the Judaeo-Christians in Ancient Jewish and Christian Literature*, Wissenschaftliche Untersuchungen zum Neuen Testament 158, ed. P. Tomson and D. Lambers-Petry (Tübingen: J.C.B. Mohr [Paul Siebeck], 2003), 182–208, especially 200–205.

tism, and the Jews failed to recognize this. Similarly, they erred in their understanding of the Sabbath, which again Epiphanius interpreted as a sign that "was
restraining us for the great Sabbath, that is, for the rest of Christ, in order that in
Christ we might take a Sabbath from sin."[167] Because of their failures, the Jews
were "thrown out of the vineyard (cf. Matt 21:41) and the Gentiles entered in."[168]
The Jews were guilty of breaking all of the laws, and their only recourse, the only
way for them to be saved, was through the Gospel.[169]

Epiphanius reiterated the idea that before the Jews were Jews, they were
called "Abramians"[170] according to the name of "Abraham, the patriarch of piety" and "Israelites" from the name of Jacob.[171] But in the time of David, after
the division of the Jews into twelve tribes, they were called "Jews." The narrative
continues with further summary of biblical history, including the division into
two kingdoms and the succession of kings after Rehoboam drawn from Matthew 1:7–11. This history occasions another excursus, this time on the accuracy
of the Matthean lineage, which some doubters had apparently tried to fix.[172]
However, before offering his explanations, Epiphanius made makes an interesting comment about his work:

> Let no one doubt about this, but rather let him [the reader] marvel at the preci-
> sion, in a helpful way being set down here for the sake of useful learning for those
> earnest persons who desire to understand the finer points of the Scriptures. They
> will have been compelled straightaway after the assistance to be appreciative, hav-
> ing gained the exact content that was removed in the Gospel by certain ignorant
> people on account of an ambiguity, as though an emendation.[173]

In what appears to be not a little bit of self-aggrandizement, Epiphanius suggested that his reader should marvel not only at the minor correction he was
making here about the genealogy of Matthew, but also at the breadth and accuracy of all that he presented up to this point. This was a declaration of Epiphanius's expertise. Ultimately, the biblical proficiency Epiphanius spoke of here
was the implicit foundation for his authority.

---

167. Cf. *Anc.* 116.5–6; *Pan.* 4.6.8; cf. 30.32.1–12. On the identification of Christ as the "great Sabbath," see
   P. Devos, "ΜΕΓΑ ΣΑΒΒΑΤΟΝ chez saint Épiphane," *AnBoll* 108, nos. 3–4 (1990): 293–306.
168. *Pan.* 4.7.1.
169. *Pan.* 4.7.1–3.
170. Holl supplied the term as an emendation to the text.
171. *Pan.* 4.7.5.
172. *Pan.* 4.8.1–4. Cf. *Anc.* 59.4, for the succession of kings.
173. *Pan.* 4.8.1.

The Rise of the Samaritans

After this excursus, Epiphanius resumed the narrative of biblical history beginning with the Babylonian captivity and the request of the exiles to have Nebuchadnezzar send Assyrian colonists to Israel.[174] The settlers, with idols in tow,
established themselves in Samaria, but were ravaged by wild beasts and reported their sufferings back to Babylon (cf. 2 Kings 17:24–26). The exiles informed the king that God had mandated that the people who lived in this land
had to abide by the Law and that no idolatry would be tolerated (cf. 2 Kings
17:26), and so the king sent Ezra from Babylon to instruct the settlers on how to
live according to the Law (cf. 2 Kings 17:27–28).[175] Epiphanius said that these
events transpired during the thirtieth year of captivity, and that after another
forty years, the Babylonian captivity came to an end.[176] The work of Ezra in
Samaria was significant because it established another category and succession
of four heresies that would follow Judaism, that of the Samaritans. This, however, also presented an incongruity in Epiphanius's overall scheme, because
thus far he had built a structure of four heresies and four corresponding epochs
of human history, but elsewhere, Epiphanius identified "Samaritans" as the fifth
"mother" heresy.[177] This discrepancy has not gone unnoticed in modern scholarship, hence the criticism of Epiphanius's inconsistency and ambiguous definition of heresy.[178] In the *Panarion*, however, here at the end of the entry on Judaism, Epiphanius expounded on his theory of heresy, namely, that heresy always
breeds heresy. Alluding back to the proliferation of languages and peoples after
the collapse of the Tower of Babel, Epiphanius argued that the religion of Israel,
when it was brought to the Assyrian colonists, "became divided."[179] He concluded the entry with the following: "And then error began, and discord was
sown, away from the one fear of God, into many falsified opinions, just as each
person formed an opinion for himself and thought to be trained in the letter [of
the Law] and to expound, according to his own will."[180] The Samaritan heresy
and its offshoots (Essenes, Gorothenes, Sebuaeans, and Dositheans) were heresies that "began from sacred Scripture" and were thus different from the first

---

174. *Pan.* 4.8.5–6.
175. *Pan.* 4.8.9–10.
176. *Pan.* 4.8.11. Cf. Cf. Thphl. Ant., *Autol.* 3.25.
177. *Anc.* 12.7–8.
178. See Fraenkel, "Histoire," 181–84; Young, "Epiphanius," 201–2; Pourkier, *L'hérésiologie*, 87–90.
179. *Pan.* 4.9.3.
180. *Pan.* 4.9.4

four entries.[181] Despite his earlier identification of the Samaritans as a mother heresy, here their heresy is subsumed under Judaism.

Conclusion

We have examined Epiphanius's broad, sweeping reimagining of primordial and biblical history. By the time he sat down to pen the first pages of the *Panarion*, a long tradition of Jewish and Christian literature that sought to reinterpret and integrate the history revealed in Scripture with the histories of other old and venerable cultures had developed. In the Jewish tradition, *Jubilees* had recast the Genesis narrative to prove the pre-Mosaic existence and practice of the Law, and later Christian writers drew on this work to elaborate their own ideas about the history of the earliest humans. Christian apologists writing in the second and third centuries did much to portray the Christian faith as the true expression of the religion revealed in the Hebrew Scriptures in response to pagan intellectual criticisms about the novelty that was Christianity.[182] Julius Africanus, the first Christian chronographer, synchronized human history beginning with Adam to express his particular millenarian view and expectations for the future. Eusebius also rewrote aspects of human history in several works to underscore the eventuality of the triumph of the Christian faith and its people, the "third nation" or "third race," over the Greeks and Jews.[183] These historical and chronographic works were not merely attempts at reconciling or synchronizing peoples, places, and events with already established traditions from the Near East and Greece. They had an underlying rhetorical purpose, namely to demonstrate the longevity and thus superiority of Jewish culture compared to all others, and Christian writers appropriated the history told in the Hebrew Scriptures and made it their own while simultaneously disconnect-

181. *Pan.* 9.1.1.
182. See A. Cameron, "Apologetics in the Roman Empire: A Genre of Intolerance?," in *"Humana Sapit": Études d'antiquité tardive offerts à Lellia Cracco Ruggini*, Bibliothèque de l'Antiquité Tardive 3, ed. J.-M. Carrié and R. Testa (Turnhout: Brepols, 2002), 219–27, for a discussion of "apologetic" not as a distinct literary genre but a "tone or method" of argument that served both defensive and offensive functions. Her discussion is built primarily vis-à-vis a critical examination of Edwards, Goodman, Price, eds., *Apologetics*.
183. Eusebius posited a model of Christianity as the middle of the two extremes of the polytheism of Hellenism and the slavish dependence on ritual of the Jews; cf. Eus., *d.e.* 1.6 (22b–d). See Gallagher, "Apologist"; Johnson, "Identity."

ing contemporary Jews from their Judaic heritage.[184] Furthermore, all of these works exhibited a sense of totalizing command of knowledge. The breadth of detail, the accuracy of calculations, and the mastery of esoteric data proved the expertise of each author and hence the absolute correctness of the ideas he was promoting. While Epiphanius may have drawn on abbreviated or epitomized versions of these works, he was no stranger to their themes.

Using Scripture as his starting point, he constructed a narrative of the human experience from its beginnings in an original, pure state of existence in which the prime man, Adam, knew and believed in a Triune God. After the Fall, human depravity began a long, slow, but steady descent into mistaken beliefs and mistaken practices. This was a simple world in which piety and impiety and natural law and human freedom soon gave way to two broad heretical trajectories. The first was Hellenism, which was an already loaded term in the fourth century, and in the *Panarion* it represented the third era of human history in which idolatry developed and spread, eventually making its way into Greece and becoming an integral part of its culture. This idolatry manifested itself in a variety of ways, in paintings, physical objects, worship of the heavenly bodies, and finally in philosophy. Although the different schools of philosophical thought promoted various ideas about the cosmos and the human experience, they were all nevertheless guilty of idolatry because they failed to recognize the one God. The second trajectory of human depravity was Judaism, and here Epiphanius focused on the patriarchs, who maintained the right belief in a Triune God even after having received the Law and whose descendants fell into heresy when they failed to recognize the prophecies and types of Christ revealed in the Hebrew Scriptures and fulfilled in the Incarnation. While Epiphanius may have concluded his reimagined history in these four entries, the *Panarion* itself was a continuous unfolding of human history cast in terms of the steady preservation of orthodox Christianity and the proliferation of a succession of heresies that existed both before and after the incarnate *parousia* of Christ. Thus the *Panarion*, a quintessential heresiology, was also a work of history.

---

184. This was part of the process of Christian identify formation through its separation from Judaism. See the discussion in J. Lieu, "The Forging of Christian Identity," *Mediterranean Archaeology* 11 (1998): 71–82; eadem, *Christian Identity in the Jewish and Graeco-Roman World* (Oxford: Oxford University Press, 2004).

PART TWO

Transitions

CHAPTER 3

Monastic Discipline and Orthodox Faith in Late Roman Palestine

Abba Epiphanius

In his youth, Epiphanius spent several years in Egypt, where he acquired an education and devoted himself to the church and to the ascetic life. He also had significant interactions with women belonging to a certain "Gnostic" group, whom he resisted and reported to the local bishops. Epiphanius's training and experiences in Egypt were formative and laid the foundation for his convictions about his own lifestyle, doctrine, and relationship to the church. In his ascetic practice, he emphasized the centrality of the real, complete, human body. The discipline with which he would master it had to reflect the truth of a larger reality that Eden, Adam and Eve, the Incarnation, and the final resurrection all had to be embodied. This conviction set the stage for the dispute over Origen's theology that consumed the final years of Epiphanius's life.

Epiphanius's ecclesiology was also profoundly shaped by his time in Egypt. There he eschewed some of the more extreme positions of Hieracas and Melitius with respect to the church and its members, but he also recognized the susceptibility and vulnerability of the church to heresy. Epiphanius witnessed many of the early years of the "Arian" controversy, and he claimed firsthand experience with the long-standing threat of Gnosticism. He came to recognize that the church needed protection and strong leadership. Fortunately, Epiphanius found a Christian hero and model to emulate. During his stay in Egypt, the rising star of Athanasius, the protégé of Alexander, undoubtedly made an impression on Epiphanius.[1] Even in those early embattled years of the famed Al-

---

1. "Not long after Theonas's death, Athanasius arrived. And a synod of bishops from everywhere was

exandrian's administration, Epiphanius must have admired the confluence of orthodoxy and orthopraxy embodied in Athanasius. This esteem would only grow in the years to come as the ecclesiastical controversies and struggles of the fourth century and Athanasius's central role in them as the defender of ortho-doxy unfolded. Epiphanius found in Athanasius a model for a strong, perhaps even ruthless episcopal leader, and his own future would reflect this type of leadership.

But before Epiphanius assumed the title of bishop and the reins of control in Cyprus and before he became an arbiter of orthodoxy and full-fledged heresy-hunter, he took another important transitional step in his personal for-mation, the "second phase" of his biography. Sometime after 335, he returned to his homeland and established a monastery, perhaps on his own family's land.[2] Sozomen wrote specifically that Epiphanius "fixed his abode near the village of Bēsandoukē (ἀμφὶ Βησανδούκην),[3] where he was born, of the district of Eleu-theropolis" and apparently was quite successful. "They [Epiphanius and He-sychas] and their companions advanced to the apex of virtue and added greater honor to their monasteries there."[4] According to Jerome, at some point Epipha-nius was ordained a "presbyter of the monastery" and "was listened to by Eu-tychius," the bishop of Eleutheropolis.[5] However, the exact locations of Epipha-nius's birth village and monastery remain uncertain.[6] The type of monastic

---

convened, and thus the appointment of this man took place. And the throne was restored to a worthy man and for whom it was prepared according to the will of God and according to the testimony and command of the blessed Alexander." *Pan.* 68.7.4.

2. His age when he returned home is uncertain, although the biographic preface of the *Ancoratus* stated that he was age twenty. Thus with the conjectured date of his birth ca. 315, his return to Palestine would have been ca. 335. Schneemelcher, "Epiphanius," c. 911; Dummer, "Sprachkenntnisse," 412, n. 4; Dechow, *Dogma*, 36–37, work with age twenty for his return, although Nautin, "Épiphane," c. 617, attributes this age to a copyist's speculation and thus remains cautious. Pourkier, *L'hérésiologie*, 35, assumes age thirty (ca. 339/40), while Kösters, *Trinitätslehre*, 29, offers a similar range between twenty-five and thirty (ca. 335, depending on his birth year).

    The connection to family land derives from the hagiographic tradition; cf. *v. Epiph.* 5–6. This is, however, purely speculative, although Nautin, "Épiphane," c. 618; Pourkier, *L'hérésiologie*, 35, n. 22 accept the possibility. Dechow, *Dogma*, 32; Kösters, *Trinitätslehre*, 30, are more circumspect.

3. Nautin, "Épiphane," c. 617, lists the orthographical variations of the name of the village in manu-scripts of Jerome (*becos adhuc, vetus adduci, bos addici*) and Peter the Deacon (*Bycoyca*). In the Hil-berg edition, Jer., *Ep.* 82.8, reads *Becos Abacuc* to refer to the name of Epiphanius's monastery.

4. Soz., *h.e.* 6.32.1–3.

5. Jer., *Adu. Io. Hier.* 4. See Pourkier, *L'hérésiologie*, 19, n. 1, for a brief description of Eleutheropolis; also Rapp, "Vita," 109–12. The possible role of Eutychius in Epiphanius's departure from Palestine to be-come bishop of Cyprus will be discussed in chapter 5.

6. Eleutheropolis / Beth Govrin is approximately 40 km southwest (as the crow flies) of Jerusalem; cf. R. Talbert, ed., *Barrington Atlas of the Greek and Roman World* (Princeton: Princeton University Press, 2000), 70.

organization and lifestyle this community adopted is also not evident, although we could make the case that Epiphanius's training in Egypt would have influenced how he led his community.[7] The hallmarks of Epiphanius's convictions were submission to the ecclesiastical hierarchy, relative moderation but firm physical discipline in ascetic practice, and vigilance over doctrinal orthodoxy. Beyond these broad assumptions, we are left with little specific information about his leadership of this community, although we do know that he maintained a close relationship with his monastery long after he left.[8]

Epiphanius inserted two autobiographical anecdotes in the *Panarion* that belong to his monastic phase. Again, we must be mindful that Epiphanius reimagined and constructed these life stories and included them to serve particular rhetorical ends and to convey a particular self-image upon his readers. Nevertheless, we will examine closely these two episodes—his meeting with Joseph of Tiberias and Eusebius of Vercelli and his confrontation of the Archontic Peter—and argue that they were real experiences that reflected the ongoing development of Epiphanius's convictions. As we have done, we will "read" these episodes both as historical moments in his life and as examples of rhetorical self-fashioning.

At the Home of Joseph of Tiberias (Panarion 30.5.1–8)

In the entry against the Ebionites, Epiphanius included a lengthy excursus on the conversion story of Joseph of Tiberias, a onetime high official at the court of the Jewish Patriarch. After becoming a Christian, Joseph was promoted by Constantine to the rank of count and given permission and funds to build churches in Palestine.[9] Other scholars have examined the problematic content of this story and its implications for understanding the relationship between Judaism and Christianity in late antiquity.[10] Our interests, however, lie in a par-

---

7. See Kösters, *Trinitätslehre*, 30, n. 80, regarding an earlier suggestion that the community was Pachomian.
8. See chapter 7.
9. *Pan.* 30.4.4–12.9. For Epiphanius on the Ebionites, see G. Koch, "A Critical Investigation of Epiphanius' Knowledge of the Ebionites: A Translation and Critical Discussion of *Panarion* 30," Ph.D. diss., University of Pennsylvania, Philadelphia, 1976; Verheyden, "Epiphanius on the Ebionites"; Jacobs, *Remains*, 44–51; idem, *Circumcised*, 100–18.
10. Koch includes an excursus on the Joseph narrative, which he considers in relation to what we can ascertain about Jewish-Christianity in fourth-century Palestine and the Ebionites. "Investigation," 374–83. S. Goranson makes a more careful and thorough study and is critical of Koch's limited ap-

ticular story within the larger story, specifically the context and occasion in which Epiphanius met Joseph and heard his conversion story from him:

5.1 Joseph discussed <this> with me, for I heard all these things from his own mouth and not from another person, in his old age, when he was about seventy or even more. For I lodged with him in Scythopolis. (2) He had moved from Tiberias and acquired notable property there in Scythopolis. In his home, Eusebius of blessed memory, from Italy, the bishop of the city of Vercelli, was entertained as a guest, as he had been exiled by Constantius on account of his orthodox faith. And I and other brothers were there to visit this man, and we were lodged with him. (3) Having met with Joseph at his house and asking things about him and finding out that he had been prominent among the Jews, I inquired about both the reason and how he had come to Christianity, and I heard all these things plainly [from him] and not from someone else's report. (4) For which reason, because of the translations into Hebrew that are in the treasuries, I also thought that the things that the man went through were worthy of mention for the edification of the faithful. Not as of secondary importance have I provided the entire reason of the aforementioned Joseph. (5) For the man was deemed worthy to become not only a faithful Christian but also one who very much denounced the Arians. For in that city, I mean Scythopolis, this man alone was orthodox, and everyone else Arian. And if he was not a count and the rank of count was not preventing persecution of him by the Arians, the man would not have consented to live in the city, especially with Patrophilos[11] the Arian bishop being exceedingly strong in wealth and austerity and in his acquaintance and *parrēsia* with the emperor Constantius.

(7) But in the city there was another younger person of Hebrew lineage who

---

proach to the Joseph story. "The Joseph of Tiberias Episode in Epiphanius: Studies in Jewish and Christian Relations," PhD diss., Duke University, Durham, NC, 1990. See also the updated reflections and references in idem, "Joseph of Tiberias Revisited: Orthodoxies and Heresies in Fourth-Century Galilee," in *Galilee through the Centuries: A Confluence of Cultures*, Duke Judaic Studies 1, ed. E. Meyers (Winona Lake, IN: Eisenbrauns, 1999), 335–43. See also F. Manns, "Joseph de Tibériade, un judéo-chrétien du quatrième siècle," in *Christian Archaeology in the Holy Land: New Discoveries*, Studium Biblicum Franciscanum Collecto Maior 36, ed. G. Bottini, L. di Segni, E. Alliata (Jerusalem: Franciscan Printing Press, 1990), 553–60; T. Thornton, "The Stories of Joseph of Tiberias," *VC* 44 (1990): 54–63.

More recently Jacobs situates Joseph's conversion story in a broader consideration of Epiphanius's negotiation of the boundary that separated Judaism and Christianity, such that the latter was made to absorb the former, and thus Epiphanius "closed" the frontier zone that separated them and asserted his discursive control over it. "Matters," 42–44.

11. Cf. Socr., *h.e.* 2.43.10.

believed orthodoxly, who did not dare <to associate with me?> in public, but he was visiting with me in secret. (8) And Joseph told me something plausible and laughable, and I think forthwith that he was speaking the truth. For he was saying that when his wife had died, fearing lest somehow the Arians might seize him and ordain him as a cleric (for often flattering him to persuade him to their heresy, they were promising him greater promotions, if necessary to ordain him bishop), he said that because of this he took a second wife in order that he might escape from their ordinations.[12]

At this point the excursus ends, and Epiphanius returns to the narrative of Joseph, his conversion, and his church-building efforts. Epiphanius's visit to the home of Joseph took place sometime between 355 and 361, some two decades after he had returned to his native Palestine. Unfortunately, we are uncertain about Epiphanius's activities in the prior years, although again we can assume he was putting into practice what he had learned in Egypt and helping others to do so as well.

If it is a truism that a person is defined by the company he or she keeps, then Epiphanius certainly gave his readers a distinct impression about the kinds of people with whom he associated. Eusebius of Vercelli was in Palestine after he had been exiled by Constantius after the Council of Milan in 355 because he refused to condemn Athanasius during its proceedings.[13] Thus by virtue of being a defender of Athanasius, Eusebius would have made Epiphanius's short list

---

12. *Pan.* 30.5.1–8. For a broad survey of the city of Scythopolis, see J. Binns, *Ascetics and Ambassadors of Christ: The Monasteries of Palestine, 314–631* (Oxford: Oxford University Press, 1994), 121–47. For an examination of the religious and social diversity, tensions, and ritualized violence in the city, see H. Sivan, *Palestine in Late Antiquity* (Oxford: Oxford University Press, 2008), 157–75.

13. Ath., *apologia ad Constantium* 27; *apologia de fuga sua*; Jer., *Vir. ill.* 96; Socr., *h.e.* 2.36.1–5; Soz., *h.e.* 4.9.1–10. On Eusebius's life and surviving writings, see V. De Clercq, "Eusèbe de Verceil," in *DHGE* 15 (Paris: Letouzey et Ané, 1963), c. 1477–83. Most importantly, see D. Williams, *Ambrose of Milan and the End of the Nicene-Arian Conflicts* (Oxford: Oxford University Press, 1995), 49–68, 238–42, and the collection of essays in E. dal Covolo, R. Uglione, G. Vian, eds., *Eusebio di Vercelli e il suo tempo*, Biblioteca di scienze religiose 133 (Rome: LAS, 1997), and in particular M. Simonetti, "Eusebio nella controversia ariana," 155–79. On his exile, see T. Barnes, *Athanasius and Constantius: Theology and Politics in the Constantinian Empire* (Cambridge, MA: Harvard University Press, 1993), 117–18; Williams, *Ambrose*, 58–62; Ayres, *Nicaea*, 133–37; D. Washburn, "Tormenting the Tormenters: A Reinterpretation of Eusebius of Vercelli's Letter from Scythopolis," *Church History* 78, no. 4 (2009): 731–55, especially n. 6, on the modern debate about the reasons for his exile. Eusebius was later recalled with the accession of Julian.

In the *Panarion*, Epiphanius maintained a generally ambivalent, if not positive attitude toward the Roman emperors of the fourth century (with the exception of Julian), even though they were by and large heretics according to Epiphanius's own standards of orthodoxy. This position was strategically and rhetorically driven. See Y. Kim, "Bad Bishops Corrupt Good Emperors: Ecclesiastical Authority and the Rhetoric of Heresy in the *Panarion* of Epiphanius of Salamis," StPatr 47 (2010): 161–66.

of worthy allies. After Eusebius arrived in Palestine, he opposed the bishop of Scythopolis, Patrophilus, a notorious supporter of Arius and opponent of Athanasius.[14] Eusebius later participated in a church council held in 362 in Alexandria over which Athanasius presided, and Eusebius became a key advocate in the Latin West of the developing "pro-Nicene" position.[15] For Epiphanius, Eusebius's western connection was important because for much of Epiphanius's career, he remained in the theological minority in the Greek East, and he found greater agreement with the positions of the majority of western bishops among whom Athanasius also found tremendous support. It should come as no surprise, as we will see in chapter 6, that Epiphanius traveled to Rome in 382 to meet Damasus in order to argue for Paulinus's legitimacy as rightful bishop of Antioch.

Epiphanius underscored Eusebius's credentials as an orthodox Christian, which at the same time gave Joseph the host an understood association with orthodox Christianity.[16] In Joseph's story, we find Epiphanius building a particular picture of this Jewish convert that highlighted the fact that not only did a prominent Jew become a Christian, he also became a particular kind of Christian, one who denounced the Arians as heretics.[17] Epiphanius also set Joseph in opposition to the Arian bishop Patrophilus. In other words, Joseph had converted to orthodox Christianity, and his association with Epiphanius and Eusebius solidified their minority cadre of righteous believers in a Palestine surrounded by conspiring heretics.[18] Epiphanius also derided the lengths to which the Arians would go to solidify their power by insinuating that they conspired to forcibly ordain Joseph, ostensibly because of his position and influence, and that they treated the sacred office as a tool for bribery. Furthermore, Epiphanius made an important rhetorical point about himself in his retelling of this story:

---

14. On Patrophilus's support for Arius, see Ath., *epistula de synodis Ariminum et Seleuciae* 1.3; Soz., *h.e.* 1.15.10–12; Theodoret, *historia ecclesiastica* 1.6.13–14. On the opposition to Athanasius, see Ath., *apologia contra Arianos* 87.1–3; Socr., *h.e.* 1.35.1–3. On Patrophilus, see Washburn, "Tormenting," 734–36, and throughout for his conflict with Eusebius. See also Simonetti, "Eusebio," 159–62.

15. Cf. Ath., *Tomus ad Antiochenos* 10.3; Soz., *h.e.* 5.12.1–5. For his involvement in the proceedings at Alexandria, see Simonetti, "Eusebio," 162–65, and for his activities in the West, Williams, *Ambrose*, 66–68; Simonetti, "Eusebio," 166–70.

16. For Eusebius as stalwart of pro-Nicene Christianity during the Arian controversy, see Hanson, *Search*, 507–8; Simonetti, "Eusebio," 155–70; Ayres, *Nicaea*, 178.

17. I use "Arians" only in the sense that Epiphanius wanted his readers to understand that a cohesive, identifiable group of heretics known as such existed. This was, of course, an ancient construct built largely through the efforts of Athanasius. See Ayres, *Nicaea*, 105–30; D. Gwynn, *The Eusebians: The Polemic of Athanasius of Alexandria and the Construction of the "Arian Controversy"* (Oxford: Oxford University Press, 2007).

18. On the circumstances of Eusebius's stay with Joseph, see Washburn, "Tormenting," 747–48. On Eusebius's exile and alleged maltreatment by Patrophilus, see Simonetti, "Eusebio," 159–62.

he was completely anti-Arian in this period of monastic administration. Indeed, knowing the theological and ecclesiastical environment of mid-fourth-century Palestine is important for understanding Epiphanius's stay there, and the environment perhaps had an important bearing on his eventual departure to Cyprus. Aline Pourkier suggests that Palestine in 350s was characterized by the presence of diverse heresies and that ongoing debates over the Council of Nicaea and the meaning and acceptance of the term *homoousios* were particularly lively and nourished by ecclesiastical rivalries. She does well in identifying the different and often conflicting theological strands in both the Greek East and Palestine, and she briefly discusses the competing visions of Marcellus of Ancyra, the Homoiousians, the Homoians, and the Anomoians.[19] Pourkier thus maintains that Epiphanius was a Nicene Christian "surrounded by Arians and Semi-Arians."[20]

We must, however, be cautious here in attributing to Epiphanius too overt or strong a position in the 330s and 340s, especially an expressed commitment to Nicaea and any technical meaning of *homoousios*.[21] In the mid-fourth century, Christians were still very much developing their understanding and articulation of the relationship between the Father and the Son (and later the Holy Spirit). Of course this is not to say that Epiphanius did not believe in the correlative divinity of the Son and the Father and in a Trinitarian doctrine of the Godhead. When he wrote the *Ancoratus* and the *Panarion* in the 370s, he was explicit about the use of *homoousios* to define the relationship of the persons within the Godhead.[22] Furthermore, by this time Epiphanius also asserted Nicaea as a clear standard for orthodoxy.[23] But we will see that Epiphanius evolved in his theological understanding of and language used for the Trinity. We have no direct evidence that allows us to conclude that prior to the 350s, he explicitly confessed *homoousios* as the measure of orthodoxy. But we can gener-

---

19. Pourkier *L'hérésiologie*, 35–38.
20. Pourkier *L'hérésiologie*, 37.
21. Kösters, *Trinitätslehre*, 31–33.
22. For example, *Anc.* 6.4: "to say *homoousios* is the bond of the faith." See the next chapter for further discussion.
23. Cf. *Pan.* 69.11.1, 70.9.6, 73.23.8, 73.34.3. In *Anc.* 118.14, he made clear the baseline standard represented at Nicaea: "And this is the faith handed down from the holy Apostles and <affirmed / written down?> in a church [at] the holy city by all the holy bishops together then, more than 310 in number." There had been earlier scholarly debate about the meaning of the "holy city," with Holl arguing that it referred to the universal church. GCS 25, 147. However, subsequent work by B. Weischer affirms the identification of Nicaea because the creed quoted in the *Anc.* was originally the Nicene Creed before it was later modified by a scribe to the Niceno-Constantinopolitan creed. "Die ursprüngliche nikänische Form des ersten Glaubenssymbols im Ankyrōtos des Epiphanius von Salamis: Ein Beitrag zur Diskussion um die Entstehung des konstantinopolitanischen Glaubenssymbols im Lichte neuester äthiopistischer Forschungen," *Theologie und Philosophie* 53, no. 3 (1978): 407–14.

ally assume that he followed the trajectory of Athanasius, who initially made little recourse to Nicaea and *homoousios* as standards of orthodoxy.[24] Only in the 350s with the composition of his *On the Decrees of the Council of Nicaea* and in subsequent writings did Athanasius make the famous council, its creed, and its vocabulary hallmarks of orthodox Christianity.[25] Thus when Epiphanius met with Joseph and Eusebius of Vercelli sometime in the mid-350s or early 360s, the "orthodox" Nicene position, at least as conceived by Athanasius, had only recently been articulated in more explicit terms.

Of course in the mid-370s when Epiphanius recalled and wrote the account of his meeting with Joseph, the theological and ecclesiastical battle lines were clearer, and the debates and alliances among the interested parties had plenty of time to shift and harden. We will examine these shifting theological frontiers in the next chapter and will now simply reiterate Epiphanius's rhetorical touches to his story. He wanted his readers to know about his association with Eusebius of Vercelli, a western stalwart of orthodoxy, and with Joseph of Tiberias, a high-ranking convert from Judaism who was also decidedly anti-Arian. In turn, Epiphanius accentuated his own orthodoxy during his administration of his monastery and by implication throughout his life. Thus Epiphanius's reimagination of his meeting with Joseph of Tiberias, although only a brief excursus in the larger narrative of Joseph's conversion, has provided us a rare glimpse into Epiphanius's time as abbot of a monastery. Still, we must remember that he wrote this account some decades after the purported events and that his narrative was constructed to reflect how he wanted his readers to imagine him as a man who always associated with orthodox, anti-Arian Christians.

Heresy-Hunting the Archontics (Panarion 40.1.1–9)

The other significant autobiographical episode from Epiphanius's Palestinian monastic phase was his confrontation with the heresy of the Archontics, which

---

24. Cf. Ath., *orationes tres adversus Arianos* 1.7. In these orations, written beginning in the 340s, Athanasius mentioned *homoousios* just once.

25. Cf. Ath., *de decretis Nicaenae synodi*. Recent scholarship has demonstrated that Athanasius appealed to Nicaea and *homoousios* beginning in the 350s, quite removed from the events of 325 and in response to changing political and theological circumstances. See Ayres, *Nicaea*, 85–104, 140–44; idem, "Athanasius' Initial Defense of the Term Ὁμοούσιος: Rereading the *De decretis*," *JECS* 12, no. 3 (2004): 337–59; X. Morales, *La théologie trinitaire d'Athanase d'Alexandrie*, Collection des Études Augustiniennes, Série Antiquité 180 (Paris: Institut d'Études Augustiniennes, 2006), 285–93.

was apparently a fourth-century Gnostic sect with close affinities to later Se-thian Gnosticism.[26] The narrative is found in *Panarion* 40, and I have translated the relevant section:

1.1 A heresy of Archontics follows these, but it is not borne in many places, or only in the province of Palestine. Forthwith they brought over their poison even into Greater Armenia, but also this weed already has been scattered (2) in Lesser Armenia by a certain man from Armenia who lived in the land of Pales-tine in the time of Constantius, about the time of his death. His name was Eu-taktos (but rather "disorderly"), and having learned this wicked doctrine, he then returned to his homeland and taught this way. (3) He received it, as I said, in Palestine (as from a snake's poison) from Peter a certain old man (unworthily named Peter!) who lived in the district of Eleutheropolis <and> Jerusalem, three milestones beyond Hebron. They call the village *Kapharbaricha.*[27]

(4) First, this old man possessed an astonishing garment, full of hypocrisy. For in truth on the outside he had been clothed in a sheep's fleece, but it was not known that on the inside he was a rapacious wolf. For since he was remaining in a certain cave, he was appearing to be an anchorite, who indeed gathered many people for renunciation, and indeed he was called "father" because of his old age and appearance. He distributed his possessions to the poor, and each day he was giving alms. (5) In his youth he was counted among many heresies, but in the time of Aetius the bishop he was accused and then proven to be among the heresy of the Gnostics. He was deposed from the presbyterate (for he was ordained once as presbyter), and was exiled from that place by Aetius after his conviction. And going forth he dwelt in Arabia in Kokabe, wherein the roots of the Ebionites and the Nazoraeans began, as I indicated also in many heresies concerning this place. (6) Later, as if having come to his senses in old age, he came back, secretly bearing in himself this venom and being unrecognized by all; until when finally from what words he whispered in the ears of certain peo-ple, this wretch, having been convicted by us, was anathematized and refuted by my most puny self. (7) And then he settled in his cave, loathed by all and for-saken by the brethren and by most who care for their lives.

26. This group is known only through Epiphanius. See H.-C. Puech, "Archontiker," in *Reallexikon für Antike und Christentum* 1 (Stuttgart: Hiersemann Verlags, 1950), c. 633–43; L. Painchaud, "L'écrit sans titre du codex II de Nag Hammadi (II.5) et la *Symphonia* d'Épiphane (*Pan.* 40)," StPatr 18, no. 1 (1985): 263–71; R. Van Den Broek, "Archontics," in *Dictionary of Gnosis and Western Esotericism*, ed. W. Hanegraaff (Leiden: Brill, 2006), 89–91.
27. In Talbert, *Barrington*, 69, the village is Caphar Baricha.

(8) The aforementioned Eutaktos lodged with this old man, if at any rate he was "orderly," having come through from Egypt and having received the wicked doctrine from the old man. As though great merchandise, receiving this poison, he carried it away into his homeland. For he was starting out from Lesser Armenia, as I said, close to Satale. (9) When he returned anyway to his homeland, he was polluting many people of Lesser Armenia, having become acquainted to their misfortune with certain wealthy men, high-ranking women, and certain other honored persons, through which illustrious men he destroyed many people there. But the Lord more quickly wiped him out from life, except that he had scattered his weed.[28]

Because Epiphanius specifically mentioned the death of Constantius in his narrative, we can date this episode to sometime in the late 350s or early 360s, as the emperor died on 3 November 361. These events occurred chronologically close to Epiphanius's meeting with Eusebius and Joseph, but it remains uncertain which took place first. Nevertheless, the narrative is important for our study because through it Epiphanius underscored important details about his personal formation, self-construction, and heresiological methods.[29]

Eutaktos

The vilification of the disciple Eutaktos features three ideas that are relevant to Epiphanius's approach to heresiology. First, he indicated the geographical reach of this particular heresy. Epiphanius wanted to inform his orthodox Christian readers what heretics believed and did and also where they were located. Throughout the *Panarion*, Epiphanius consistently included geographical information in his refutations, and collectively they paint a picture of the ubiquity of heresy and thus the necessity for the active vigilance of the orthodox faithful.[30] Second, through the figure of Eutaktos, Epiphanius again emphasized the *diadochē* of heresy: heretics always bred other heretics, and heresy spread from one region to another by this mechanism. Eutaktos learned this heresy in Palestine, but he also took it back to his homeland and spread it there. This "move-

---

28. *Pan.* 40.1.1–9.
29. Jacobs examines this episode as an example of Epiphanius's (failed) attempt to "enforce internal ecclesiastical boundaries." "Matters," 36–37. Epiphanius exemplified the late ancient project of asserting ecclesiastical authority along an unstable frontier zone (with varied results) as part of a larger development in identity formation and management of status and difference.
30. In Kim, "Geography," I suggest Epiphanius's orthodox world was surrounded by a "heresy-belt."

ment" of heresy across space represented an antithesis to the spread of the Gospel and reflected Epiphanius's historical vision discussed in the previous chapter: that from the beginning, right belief was passed down through the generations, but humanity also steadily descended into depravity and heresy, which spread from one generation and one place to the next. Third, Epiphanius used the name "Eutaktos," meaning something like "well-ordered," as an occasion to resort to name-calling and sarcasm, and Epiphanius mentioned twice this play on words. In fact throughout the *Panarion*, Epiphanius seemed to enjoy any opportunity to comment on the ironic names of certain heresiarchs and their followers.[31]

Peter the Hermit

The description of the heresiarch Peter the Hermit bears the hallmarks of Epiphanius's sometimes sarcastic wit as he scoffed at the misnomer "Peter." Furthermore, the image of a wolf in sheep's clothing, invoking the warning of Christ in Matthew 7:15, reflects more of the same rhetorical flair, and the details about Peter's youth and his penchant for associating with heretics serve to foreshadow his future demise.[32] That he was ordained a presbyter highlights the danger of heresy as an *internal* problem.[33] Peter's exile afforded him the opportunity to dwell among yet more heretics, the Ebionites and Nazoraeans, in the east in Arabia. Andrew Jacobs's examination of the porousness of the imagined boundary between orthodox and heretic, Jewish and Christian highlights well the problem of a figure like Peter in Epiphanius's thinking.[34] For Epiphanius, it was just as easy to become an orthodox Christian and a leader in the church as it was to unbecome one. As "easy" as it was for Aetius to identify Peter as a heretic and to exile him, so also could Peter return (stealthily) among the orthodox and once again promulgate his heresy. No physical wall separated the orthodox from the heretic, those who belonged from those who did not. Thus for one such as Epiphanius, who could only imagine a binary world, there were

---

31. For example, the "madness" of Mani (*Pan.* 66.1.5).
32. Cf. Iren., *haer.* 1.preface.2, 3.16.8, for heretic wolves appearing like sheep; also Ath., *epistula ad episcopos Aegypti et Libyae* 3. On the deceptive wolf theme, see T. Shaw, "Wolves in Sheep's Clothing: The Appearance of True and False Piety," StPatr 29 (1997): 127–32. On the dangerous subtlety of heresy, see Henderson, *Construction*, 163–69.
33. See Lyman, "Making," for an examination of Origen as the prime example of this internal danger. See also Kim, "Reading," 401–6.
34. See Jacobs, "Matters."

limits to what he could do in his battle against heresy. He had little recourse but to wage his battles with words, at least when he was writing in the mid-370s.

The Palestinian landscape of the mid-fourth century was very much characterized by monastic variety, with some ascetics preferring isolation and others communal organization.[35] Arguably the most famous of the earliest monks in Palestine was Hilarion. As Jerome described in his *Life of Hilarion*, this ascetic was known for his austere lifestyle and dedication to isolation as well as his tremendous power and charisma.[36] Epiphanius, although the head of a monastic community, never made any explicit criticisms of eremitic practice. Rather, the problem with Peter was his pretense of asceticism, and Epiphanius bemoaned the fact that Peter was able to gather people to him for the sake of "renunciation."[37] Peter possessed a false charisma and a baseless authority. But as a "father" only in appearance, he was able to deceive others and thereby propagate his heresy.[38] Therefore, Peter's "cave" represented not only the locale where this "wolf in sheep's clothing" maintained the sham of worldly renunciation, but after Epiphanius's confrontation with him, it also became the place of Peter's isolation.[39] Again, the underlying problem of confronting heresy at this time was that Epiphanius did not have any physical means to prevent Peter from spreading his heretical ideas. He could only identify and isolate the poison or pathogen, as if placing the heresiarch in a sort of reverse rhetorical quarantine, so that the healthy, that is, the orthodox, would avoid and shun the deadly heretic. Alas, Eutaktos could not resist the heresiarch's wiles, and thus the Archontic heresy reproduced itself and spread. The best Epiphanius could do was to attempt to marginalize Peter. Only in the future under different ecclesiastical and political circumstances could the orthodox use more than words to confront and eradicate heresy.

One key difference between this narrative and that of Epiphanius's encounter with the Gnostic women in Egypt was the protagonist. In his youth, Epipha-

---

35. See Chitty, *Desert*, 82–100; Binns, *Ascetics*, primarily for the fifth and sixth centuries; B. Bitton-Ashkelony and A. Kofsky, "Monasticism in the Holy Land," in *Christians and Christianity in the Holy Land: From the Origins to the Latin Kingdoms*, Cultural Encounters in Late Antiquity and the Middle Ages 5, ed. O. Limor and G. Stroumsa (Turnhout: Brepols, 2006), 257–91, especially 257–71 for Palestinian monasticism before the fifth century.
36. Cf. Jer., *Vit. Hil.* Although see Bitton-Ashkelony and Kofsky, "Monasticism," 259–61, on the problems of deriving our historical knowledge of Palestinian monasticism from what was clearly a hagiographic work modeled on the *Life of Antony*.
37. *Pan.* 40.1.4.
38. On the important connection between ascetic practice and authority, see Rapp, *Bishops*, 100–152.
39. Jacobs suggests that Peter was part of Epiphanius's monastic community and only dwelt in the cave after his expulsion. "Matters," 36.

nius seemed almost to succumb to the temptation of heresy. But in this episode, he exhibited a noticeable confidence. No longer do we see a potentially break-able young man. Instead we witness a proactive, orthodox Christian. Rather than reporting the heresy to the local bishops, we see Epiphanius himself con-fronting the heresiarch. Again with some rhetorical flair and a hint of self-deprecation, he informed his readers that "his puny self" opposed Peter. Clearly at this point in his career, Epiphanius believed that he possessed the authority to refute, convict, and anathematize Peter, and he must have felt justified in part because of his ordination by Bishop Eutychius. Thus Epiphanius defended or-thodoxy with an authority rooted in both his ascetic practice and his confirma-tion within the ecclesiastical hierarchy. This event represented a significant transition in Epiphanius's evolution as a heresy-hunter.

Palestine Reimagined[40]

Epiphanius administered his homeland monastery for some thirty years before he became the lead bishop of Cyprus. While he presumably remained in the vicinity of Eleutheropolis for much of this time, he must have felt the presence and pull of two neighboring *poleis*, Caesarea and Jerusalem.[41] The former, the metropolitan, was linked to the legacies of Origen and Eusebius and thus em-bodied both the great potential of Christian faith and the tremendous danger of heresy.[42] But Caesarea would begin to see its primacy challenged and impor-tance slowly decline through the course of the fourth century. Perhaps this was just as well for Epiphanius, who took his battle against Origen and Origenism elsewhere.[43] However, Jerusalem was essentially undergoing a revolution, and undoubtedly the Palestine Epiphanius left as a youth was rapidly transitioning into something else after his return. And as the transformation of both the per-ceptions and physical landscape of his homeland were already under way when

---

40. Sivan, *Palestine,* is an insightful recent study of Palestine from the late Roman to Islamic periods.

41. See O. Irshai, "From Oblivion to Fame: The History of the Palestinian Church (135–303 CE)," in Li-mor and Stroumsa, *Christians and Christianity,* 91–139, for a useful survey of the church in Palestine in the period following the Bar-Kokhba revolt up to the Tetrarchic persecution.

42. See L. Levine, *Caesarea under Roman Rule,* Studies in Judaism in Late Antiquity 7 (Leiden: Brill, 1975), 113–34. On Origen's transformative role, see Irshai, "Oblivion," 131–36.

43. On the decline, see Levine, *Caesarea,* 135–39; Z. Rubin, "The See of Caesarea in Conflict with Jeru-salem from Nicaea (325) to Chalcedon (451)," in *Caesarea Maritima: A Retrospective after Two Mil-lennia,* Documenta et Monumenta Orientis Antiqui 21, ed. A. Raban and K. Holum (Leiden: Brill, 1996), 559–74.

Epiphanius established his monastery, these changes became concretely mani-fest in new buildings, modes of piety, and political tensions.[44] Epiphanius's homeland and its biblical capital, Jerusalem, were being reimagined as the Holy Land. While the effects of this extreme makeover did not necessarily affect Epiphanius directly during his leadership of his monastery, the changes occur-ring in Jerusalem set the stage for his later conflicts with Bishop John over the-ology and ecclesiastical polity and are thus worthy of some exploration here. Our excursus also may provide some clues as to why Epiphanius, a Palestinian native, became not the bishop of Caesarea or Jerusalem but of ancient Salamis (Constantia in his day) in Cyprus.

Before the Holy Land

When Epiphanius was born, the once great home of the Temple, the very dwell-ing place of the glory of God, had been transformed into a pagan city, Aelia Capitolina.[45] This was ultimately the result of decades of tension between the Jews and the Romans, which culminated in the Bar Kokhba revolt (132–35 CE): "In Jerusalem he [Hadrian] founded a city in place of the one razed, which he named Aelia Capitolina. And when he built instead a temple to Jupiter at the location of the temple of the god, a war neither small nor of a short duration was incited."[46] After they were defeated, the Jews were expelled from Jerusalem. Hardly more than ruins remained where the Temple once stood, and any cir-cumcised man was forbidden to enter the city precinct.[47] But despite losing the central focus of cult life and access to Jerusalem, the Jews appeared to have continued to flourish in the cities and villages of Palestine.[48] Still, for almost

---

44. See E. Hunt, *Holy Land Pilgrimage in the Later Roman Empire AD 312–460* (Oxford: Oxford Univer-sity Press, 1982); R. Wilken, *The Land Called Holy: Palestine in Christian History and Thought* (New Haven: Yale University Press, 1992); J. Taylor, *Christians and the Holy Places: The Myth of Jewish-Christian Origins* (Oxford: Oxford University Press, 1993); J. Prawer, "Christian Attitudes toward Jerusalem in the Early Middle Ages," in *The History of Jerusalem: The Early Muslim Period 638–1099,* ed. J. Prawer and H. Ben-Shammai (Jerusalem: Yad Izhak Ben-Zvi, 1996), 311–48; Sivan, *Palestine,* 187–229. On the role of Cyril of Jerusalem in the elevation of the city, see J. Drijvers, *Cyril of Jerusa-lem: Bishop and City,* Supplements to Vigiliae Christianae 72 (Leiden: Brill, 2004).
45. On the transformation, see Irshai, "Oblivion," 96–102.
46. Dio Cassius, 69.12.1. However, one must be cautious with Dio's account, since he never visited Jeru-salem. It is unclear whether the razing of the city was a result of the revolt or the cause of it. For the period following the revolt, see Drijvers, *Cyril,* 1–11.
47. Cf. Dio Cassius, 69.12.21; Tert., *Aduersus Iudaeos* 13.3. On the effects of Hadrian's policies on the Jews, see Drijvers, *Cyril,* 8–11.
48. See D. Groh, "Jews and Christians in Late Roman Palestine: Towards a New Chronology," *Biblical Archaeologist* 51, no. 2 (1988): 80–96, for challenges to older views of a decline in Jewish life in Pal-

two centuries Jerusalem was forgotten by the broader Roman Empire to the extent that in the early fourth century, Eusebius reported an account of a magistrate conducting a trial in Caesarea who was totally confounded at the mention of Jerusalem.[49] For the Romans, the city was Aelia Capitolina, and Caesarea was the provincial capital.[50]

What had been a tragic series of events for Jews was to many Christians a sure sign of divine retribution for the murder of Christ. The Jews were proven to be no longer the favored people of God, and the physical remains of the destroyed Jerusalem and a pagan temple replacing the Temple symbolized the failure of Judaism to accept Christ as Messiah. In the previous chapter, we saw the lengths to which Christians writers in the fourth century, including Epiphanius, engaged in a literary, rhetorical deconstruction and reinterpretation of Jewish identity, separating them from the Jews from their ancestral patriarchy and rendering them a corruption of the true "Hebrew" religion revealed by God. In many ways this view was affirmed by the physical destruction of the Jewish homeland. Although Jerusalem was a city central to the story of Christianity and its stones were trod upon by Christ himself, many Christians in the early centuries were content to leave the city to its pagan destiny or to reinterpret its significance altogether.

Christian chiliasts anticipated a future kingdom on earth centered in Jerusalem and therefore did not repudiate the city as a sign of Jewish failure.[51] However, other theologians like Origen rejected millenarian acceptance of a holy land located on earth, opting instead to downplay the importance of Judaea in Christian eschatology.[52] In his highly allegorical interpretations of the Bible, he

---

estine after the destruction of the Temple. See also D. Sperber, *The City in Roman Palestine* (Oxford: Oxford University Press, 1998), who examines Rabbinic sources and argues that in the third and fourth centuries, land gradually transferred from Jewish to non-Jewish possession. This in turn led to the slow but steady change in perception from a land forsaken by God because of the Jewish murder of Christ to a Christian Holy Land.

49. Eus., *de martyribus Palestinae*, in the *recensio prolixior* 11ff. Eusebius provided an account of the exchange between the Roman magistrate Firmilian and a Christian during an interrogation. The judge asked the location of "Jerusalem" and ultimately concluded that the Christians had established a new city somewhere in the East.

50. For an examination of Caesarea in antiquity, see Levine, *Caesarea* and the essays in T. Donaldson, ed., *Religious Rivalries and the Struggle for Success in Caesarea Maritima*, Studies in Christianity and Judaism 8 (Waterloo, ON: Wilfrid Laurier University Press, 2000). On Aelia, see Drijvers, *Cyril*, 1–5.

51. Cf. Just., *dial.* 80–81; Tert., *Aduersus Marcionem* 3.24. See R. Wilken, "Early Christian Chiliasm, Jewish Messianism, and the Idea of the Holy Land," *HTR* 79, nos. 1–3 (1986): 298–307; idem, *Land*, 76–78. Iren., *haer.* 4.4.1–3, however, showed that although he was a chiliast, his hopes for the future were not staked in the temporal revival of the city of Jerusalem.

52. Or., *Contra Celsum* 7.28–29. See Wilken, *Land*, 78.

emphasized the importance of a heavenly city promised for Christians upon Christ's return.[53] Elsewhere Origen described the existence of the earthly Jerusalem as a "shadow and copy" of the heavenly truth.[54] Along with the earthly city, "There was a temple, an altar, and a visible worship; there were priests and high priests," and these symbols were all types of what were to come in the future. However, with the descent of "Truth" from heaven in the form of Christ, the "shadows and copies have fallen." The Incarnation resulted in the destruction of the earthly Jerusalem, and worship was no longer to be offered in the earthly Temple but in "spirit and in truth." Origen comforted the Jew who would come seeking the earthly city of Jerusalem by telling him to search for a heavenly city, the "heavenly Jerusalem that is the mother of all."[55]

Eusebius echoed the sentiments of his spiritual hero.[56] In the *Demonstration of the Gospel*, he developed an extensive theological argument against the Jewish claim that the promises of God were reserved only for them. For Eusebius, the destruction of Jerusalem and the Temple was proof that God had not only abandoned the Jews but also that his new covenant was intended for all nations.[57] Furthermore, Eusebius would have had practical problems with the rapid elevation of Jerusalem's status as a holy city because Caesarea was the metropolitan of Palestine, and the bishop residing there held primacy over the region. So the growing ecclesiastical importance of Jerusalem threatened the power of the bishop of Caesarea, that is, of Eusebius himself.[58] However, he was in a particularly difficult situation. On the one hand, he wanted to uphold the authority of Caesarea, but on the other hand, he had to support the emperor

---

53. Or., *de principiis* 4.3.8.
54. Or., *homiliae in Jos.* 17.1, for all quotations in this paragraph B. Bruce, *Origen: Homilies on Joshua*, FC 105 (Washington, DC: Catholic University of America Press, 2002).
55. Cf. Gal 4:26.
56. P. Walker studies Eusebius's attitudes concerning Jerusalem both before and after 325, and examines the strategies Eusebius used in his writings to minimize the special status of Jerusalem. Walker argues that Eusebius was opposed to any reverence for the city and that his theological convictions necessitated an emphasis on a spiritual interpretation of Jerusalem. *Holy City, Holy Places? Christian Attitudes to Jerusalem and the Holy Land in the Fourth Century* (Oxford: Oxford University Press, 1999), 347–401.
57. Cf. Eus., *d.e.* 2.1–3, 6.18 (284a–294c). Thus Julian's later attempt to rebuild the Temple was an attempt to prove the falsity of Christianity; see G. Bowersock, *Julian the Apostate* (Cambridge, MA: Harvard University Press, 1978), 79–93; Drijvers, *Cyril*, 127–52.
58. See Z. Rubin, "The Church of the Holy Sepulchre and the Conflict between the Sees of Caesarea and Jerusalem," in *The Jerusalem Cathedra: Studies in the History, Archaeology, Geography and Ethnography of the Land of Israel* 2 (1982): 79–105; Walker, *City*, 52–57; Sivan, *Palestine*, 194–200. Rubin, however, also shows that the dispute between the cities flared up to a greater extent in the careers of Acacius (Eusebius's successor) and Cyril of Jerusalem. "Caesarea," 560–62. See also Drijvers, *Cyril*, 35–39.

Constantine's newfound favor of Jerusalem, which was solidified in the seventh canon of the Council of Nicaea.[59] Therefore, like Origen, Eusebius emphasized the spiritual importance of Jerusalem, encouraging Christians not to focus so much on the cross or the places where Christ had walked. Eusebius wanted Christians to think about the emptiness of the tomb and not about where it was physically located. Furthermore, Eusebius cited the destruction of the city and the Temple and the dispersion of the Jews as fulfillment of prophecies in the Hebrew Scriptures and proof of the truth of the Gospels.[60]

Even as the importance of the holy places in and around Jerusalem was growing in the late fourth century, certain Christians like Gregory of Nyssa continued to resist and minimize the importance of Palestine in the Christian consciousness.[61] He wrote against the need for believers to journey to the Holy Land "in which the proofs of the visitation of the Lord are visible."[62] Nevertheless, the places associated with Jesus simply could not be ignored, and it was only a matter of time before the Christian perception of the land changed. Even as early as the second century, Christians may have gone on pilgrimage to Jerusalem, although doing so was at that time not a high priority in Christian modes of piety.[63] Eusebius also wrote about a Christian who visited Jerusalem in the early third century for "prayer" and "investigation of sites," and he ultimately had a shift in perspective in conjunction with Constantine's elevation of the city's importance.[64] Furthermore, Eusebius's *Onomasticon* reflects an underlying interest in the geography of Palestine, and his hero Origen toured Pal-

59. Wilken examines Eusebius's commentary on Isaiah, which emphasized that Isaiah's messianic message reflected the reign of a Christian emperor (Constantine) rather than a restoration of Jerusalem to the Jews. *Land*, 78–81.

60. Eus., *d.e.* 1.1 (5–6), 1.6 (18d–25a).

61. On Gregory's attitude (and that of Augustine), see B. Bitton-Ashkelony, "The Attitudes of Church Fathers toward Pilgrimage to Jerusalem in the Fourth and Fifth Centuries," in *Jerusalem: Its Sanctity and Centrality to Judaism, Christianity, and Islam*, ed. L. Levine (New York: Continuum, 1999), 188–203; B. Bitton-Ashkelony, *Encountering the Sacred: The Debate on Christian Pilgrimage in Late Antiquity*, Transformation of the Classical Heritage 38 (Berkeley: University of California Press, 2005), 48–57.

62. Gregory of Nyssa, *epistulae* 2.2–4.

63. For example, Eus., *h.e.* 4.26.14, records that Melito of Sardis visited Palestine to visualize and confirm his Old Testament studies. On the question of early pilgrims, see J. Wilkinson, "Christian Pilgrims in Jerusalem during the Byzantine Period," *Palestine Exploration Quarterly* 108, no. 2 (1976): 75–101; E. Hunt, "Were There Christian Pilgrims before Constantine?," in *Pilgrimage Explored*, ed. J. Stopford (Woodbridge, Suffolk: York University Press, 1999), 25–40.

64. Eus., *h.e.* 6.11.2, described a certain Alexander, a bishop in Cappadocia, who visited Jerusalem. See R. Markus, "How on Earth Could Places Become Holy? Origins of the Christian Idea of Holy Places," *JECS* 2, no. 3 (1994): 257–71, who emphasizes the importance of local holy sites and a desire for a connection to the past that transformed attitudes about sacred time and space.

estine to visit particular holy sites.[65] Thus in the fourth century, the nascent
impulse toward pilgrimage catalyzed the radical transformation of Jerusalem
and its environs. As the influence of Christianity solidified, particular sites became holy because they were the physical manifestations of belief.[66] In other
words, it was one thing for a Christian to believe that Christ had risen from the
dead, but it was a completely different confirmation of faith for a believer to
visit the actual empty tomb. In his catechetical teachings for those preparing for
baptism, Cyril of Jerusalem constantly appealed to the empty tomb and the
places where Christ had ministered as proof of Christian truth, but he also
emphasized the empty tomb for very different reasons. He said, "Others merely
hear, but we see and touch," referring to the very physical connection those in
Jerusalem had to the person of Christ as manifest in the topography of the
city.[67] Christians cultivated a growing obsession with the physical remnants of
Christianity and the power that such places or objects had in affirming and
validating the truth. Jerusalem, therefore, was central because this was the place
where Christ himself had walked, died, and risen. In opposition to Eusebius's
emphasis on the empty tomb, Cyril naturally argued for glorifying the physicality of other holy sites in Jerusalem.[68]

A Holy Land Imagined

With the patronage of Constantine in the early fourth century, Jerusalem experienced a radical transformation, both in its physical appearance and in Christian perception.[69] The land formerly abandoned by the Romans became a holy

65. Walker, *City*, 12. See Hunt, "Pilgrims," for how all of these writings by Eusebius were before the
Constantinian creation of the Holy Land and were thus indicative of earlier Christian (including
Eusebius) interest in sacred, biblical sites and pilgrimage.
66. See G. Frank, *The Memory of the Eyes: Pilgrims to Living Saints in Christian Late Antiquity*, Transformation of the Classical Heritage 30 (Berkeley: University of California Press, 2000), 1–34, for the
importance of the physical senses and their association with the desire to engage in pilgrimage,
particularly to visit holy people. The sacralization of place was of course not limited just to Palestine.
See P. Maraval, *Lieux saints et pèlerinages d'Orient: Histoire et géographie des origines à la conquête
arabe* (Paris: Éditions du Cerf, 1985); idem, "The Earliest Phase of Christian Pilgrimage in the Near
East (before the 7th Century)," *Dumbarton Oaks Papers* 56 (2003): 63–74.
67. Cyril of Jerusalem, *catecheses illuminandorum* 13.22.
68. See Walker, *City*, for the respective roles of Eusebius and Cyril of Jerusalem in the revival of Palestine
as a Christian Holy Land. See also Drijvers, *Cyril*, 153–76; Bitton-Ashkelony, *Encountering*, 57–62;
Sivan, *Palestine*, 200–204.
69. Succinct summaries can be found in Drijvers, *Cyril*, 11–22; L. Perrone, "'Rejoice Sion, Mother of All
Churches': Christianity in the Holy Land during the Byzantine Era," in Limor and Stroumsa, *Christians and Christianity*, 147–54. See also Taylor, *Christians*, 295–332; E. Hunt, "Constantine and Jerusalem," *JEH* 48, no. 3 (1997): 405–24.

place once again under Constantine, and later traditions added the involvement of Constantine's mother, Helena, in the discovery of the True Cross of Christ.[70] Helena's attachment and devotion to the region in particular guaranteed the continued revival of Jerusalem.[71] Under the guidance of Bishop Macarius, new building projects including churches on the sites of Christ's birth, crucifixion, and ascension cemented the newfound importance of Jerusalem and Palestine as a testament to the life and legacy of Christ, and these edifices in turn led to Christians' increasing interest in visiting these sites to experience them firsthand. Thus the fourth-century development of Christian pilgrimage represented a profound change in the conceptual understanding of Palestine as a Holy Land.[72] The brief travel itinerary to Palestine of the Bordeaux Pilgrim in 333 is an early example of this gradual shift in perception,[73] and the journal of the pilgrim Egeria in 381–84 embodied the ongoing development of Christian pilgrimage and embrace of the notion of the Holy Land.[74] At the center of both of these travel accounts is the use of the Bible as a guide to the topography and landscape of Jerusalem and its environs.

Egeria's tour of the Holy Land was essentially lifted from the pages of the Bible, which served as a sort of guidebook for her itinerary.[75] For example, her

---

70. The earliest full account of Helena's discovery of the cross is found in Ambrose, *De obitu Theodosii oratio* 45–47. See Hunt, *Pilgrimage*, 28–49, on the legend of Helena and the Holy Land, but more importantly J. Drijvers, *Helena Augusta: The Mother of Constantine the Great and the Legend of Her Finding of the True Cross*, Brill's Studies in Intellectual History 27 (Leiden: Brill, 1992). See also Hunt, "Constantine," 416–19, on the rhetorical purpose of Helena's travels throughout the East.

71. Cf. Eus., *de vita Constantini* 3.42. Soz., *h.e.* 2.2.1–3.13, gave a detailed account of Helena's involvement in the transformation of Jerusalem. Cf. Socr., *h.e.* 1.17.1–13 and Rufinus, *Eusebii historia ecclesiastica a Rufino translata et continuata* 10.7–8. H. Drake examines Eusebius's silence on the discovery of the cross as a deliberate part of his construction of the image of Constantine. "Eusebius on the True Cross," *JEH* 36, no. 1 (1985): 1–22. An opposing view is offered by Hunt, *Pilgrimage*, 28–49. Wilken throughout discusses the transformation of Jerusalem from a pagan city to a Christian center, as well as the theological changes in understanding the city as Jewish versus Christian. *Land*. Walker describes the drastic changes in Jerusalem. *City*, 15–22.

72. See Wilken, *Land*, 108–22; Frank, *Memory*, 79–133.

73. For different interpretations of the itinerary of the Bordeaux Pilgrim, see Wilkinson, "Pilgrims," 84–88. L. Douglass suggests the traveler may have been a woman. "A New Look at the *Itinerarium Burdigalense*," *JECS* 4, no. 3 (1996): 313–33, but is challenged by S. Weingarten, "Was the Pilgrim from Bordeaux a Woman? A Reply to Laurie Douglass," *JECS* 7, no. 2 (1999): 291–97. See also J. Elsner, "The *Itinerarium Burdigalense*: Politics and Salvation in the Geography of Constantine's Empire," *Journal of Roman Studies* 90 (2000): 181–95.

74. See J. Wilkinson, *Egeria's Travels* (London: S.P.C.K., 1971); H. Sivan, "Who Was Egeria? Pilgrimage and Piety in the Age of Gratian," *HTR* 81, no. 1 (1988): 59–72; eadem, "Holy Land Pilgrimage and Western Audiences: Some Reflections on Egeria and Her Circle," *Classical Quarterly* 38, no. 2 (1988): 528–35.

75. D. Groh suggests that Egeria had used Eusebius's work as a guide, although Eusebius had not yet changed his own views on the Holy Land at the time of its writing. "The *Onomasticon* of Eusebius and the Rise of Christian Palestine," *StPatr* 18 (1983): 23–31. Compare with Hunt, *Pilgrimage*, 83–

vivid descriptions of her trip to Mt. Sinai parallel the events of the Exodus, as when she saw the site of the burning bush, the place where Moses was given the Law by God, and the spot where the glory of God descended to earth in a cloud of smoke.[76] Egeria's travels reflect a reimagining of the geography of the Roman world, and Jerusalem, through its burgeoning status as a Christian city, became an increasingly important center of ecclesiastical interest and ultimately of power and influence. As the apologists and chronographers had done through their literary efforts in prior centuries, Christians in the fourth century were appropriating the physicality of the Hebrew Scriptures. Egeria's description of Egypt and her retracing the steps of the Israelites underscore the new reality that the Exodus and Moses in particular had wandered out of the legacy of the Jews and had become a part of Christian consciousness and history.[77] The same could be said of Abraham.[78]

The topography of Jerusalem in the later Roman world reflected the change in the Christian perception of Palestine. Whereas in the theology of Origen, the destroyed Temple and city proved the demise of Judaism, the transformation of Jerusalem into a Christian city validated the truth of Christianity. Churches and basilicas emerged at a rapid pace, as did the Christianization of the city. Egeria described in great detail the development of a particular liturgy, especially during Holy Week, that included songs, a set movement from building to building and site to site, and a regulated series of ascetic and liturgical practices.[79] On one level, the acceptance of a Christian Holy Land, despite Origen's previous objections to calling it such, symbolized the triumph of Christianity over Judaism. The Holy Land, both in its physical appearance and in its spiritual symbolism, thus became a focal point in the Christian conception and imagination of the world. The church transformed the eastern half of the Roman Empire into an imagined Holy Land, inspired by the initial developments at Jerusalem. Not only did pilgrimage become an important mode of piety for

---

106; idem, "The Itinerary of Egeria: Reliving the Bible in Fourth-Century Palestine," in *The Holy Land, Holy Lands, and Christian History: Papers Read at the 1998 Summer Meeting and the 1999 Winter Meeting of the Ecclesiastical History Society*, Studies in Church History 36, ed. R. Swanson (Suffolk: Boydell Press, 2000), 34–54, highlighting the "takeover" of the Holy Land by monks and its appropriation from a Jewish sacred landscape to a Christian one.

76. Egeria, *Itinerarium* 2.1–5.4.

77. Hunt, *Pilgrimage*, 83–106. For the appropriation and transformation of the Sinai desert as part of the Christian sacred landscape, see Sivan, *Palestine*, 65–77, and see also 249–55, for an examination of how such processes were reflected in Eusebius's *Onomasticon*.

78. Eus., *v. C.* 3.51–53; Soz., *h.e.* 2.4.1–8. Constantine had built a shrine at Mamre dedicated to Abraham. See Taylor, *Christians*, 86–95.

79. Drijvers, *Cyril*, 72–84, 187–90, drawing on Egeria and the *Armenian Lectionary*.

Christians in late antiquity, but actual settlement in the land also became increasingly popular.[80] Jerome settled in the vicinity of Bethlehem and remained there for the rest of his life. He wrote ebulliently about Jerusalem, "our Athens":

> It would take a long time now to survey the time from the ascension of the Lord up to the present day, who of the bishops, who of the martyrs, who of the men eloquent in ecclesiastical doctrine have come to Jerusalem, reckoning themselves to have less of religion, less of science, and not to have received in hand the highest of virtue, as it is said, unless they have adored Christ in those places in which the gospel first shook off the yoke.[81]

The centrality and growing importance of Jerusalem ultimately came to represent the culmination of the Christian appropriation of sacred time and space, over and against that of Judaism and paganism, and believers living in the light of this reality conceptualized and imagined their world in a new way. The Bible and the life of Jesus became the defining features of this world, and Christians who visited and lived in Palestine imagined themselves to be the direct recipients of this heritage.

This was the world in which Epiphanius began his monastic ministry upon returning to his homeland. In many ways, the transitions occurring in Jerusalem and Judaea must have resonated with Epiphanius's reimagining of the Roman world as one that was defined by the Christian faith. Indeed, if Christianity was simply about Christ and the physical reality of his life, death, and resurrection, then Palestine would have been the closest that Epiphanius could have been to Jesus materially and spiritually. But unfortunately there was the problem of theology, of defining and expressing the dogmas of the faith, and Epiphanius was very much a part of this dynamic and contentious process in the fourth century. Ultimately because of his firm convictions and inability to tolerate divergent viewpoints, even a spiritually rich, almost otherworldly region like Palestine, the place where he was born and built his monastery, if it did not match his beliefs, could not be a place where he would live out his imagined reality.

---

80. Settlements were established on the Mount of Olives by Rufinus and Melania, as well as in Bethlehem by Jerome and Paula. See Hunt, *Pilgrimage*, 155–79; Bitton-Ashkelony and Kofsky, "Monasticism," 262–64.
81. Jer., *Ep.* 46.9. On Jerome's attitudes, see Bitton-Ashkelony, *Encountering*, 65–105.

CHAPTER 4

In the Footsteps of Athanasius

Epiphanius the Successor

A Desperate Plea for Help

When Athanasius of Alexandria died on 2 May 373, the storied career of one of late antiquity's most important and polarizing figures came to an end.[1] Like Epiphanius, Athanasius was both loved and despised, regarded by some as a true hero and defender of the orthodox faith and by others as a thug and bully. For one Christian community, however, the death of the famed Alexandrian could not have come at a worse time. Certain believers in Syedra, a city on the southern coast of Anatolia in the region of Pamphylia, were struggling against those whom some polemicists (including Epiphanius) later vilified as the "Pneumatomachoi," the "fighters against the Spirit."[2]

In the first half of the fourth century, the status of the Holy Spirit was over-

---

1. For Athanasius's career and writings, see Barnes, *Athanasius*; Brakke, *Athanasius*; Martin, *Athanase*. For specific examinations of his theology, see K. Anatolios, *Athanasius: The Coherence of His Thought* (New York: Routledge, 1998); Morales, *La théologie*.
2. On the so-called Pneumatomachoi and the debate over the Holy Spirit in the fourth century, see P. Meinhold, "Pneumatomachoi," in *Paulys-Real Encyclopädie, neue Bearbeitung* 21.1 (Stuttgart: J.B. Metzler, 1951), 1066–101; W.-D. Hauschild, *Die Pneumatomachen: Eine Untersuchung zur Dogmengeschichte des vierten Jahrhunderts* (Hamburg: Dissertation zur Evang.–Theologischen Fakultät der Universität Hamburg, 1967); A. Laminski, *Der Heilige Geist als Geist Christi und Geist der Gläubigen: Der Beitrag des Athanasios von Alexandrien zur Formulierung des trinitarischen Dogmas im vierten Jahrhundert*, Erfurter theologische Studien 23 (Leipzig: St. Benno-Verlag GMBH, 1969); Hanson, *Search*, 738–90; M. Haykin, *The Spirit of God: The Exegesis of 1 and 2 Corinthians in the Pneumatomachian Controversy of the Fourth Century*, Supplements to Vigiliae Christianae 27 (Leiden: Brill, 1994). See also the introduction in Kim, *Saint Epiphanius*, 20–33.

shadowed by the raging debate over the relationship between the Father and the Son. Nevertheless, the issue of the Spirit's divinity became contested in this combative theological climate, and some who affirmed the correlative divinity of the Son began to consider how they might do the same for the Spirit.[3] The turn toward the Spirit was in large part reactionary, as theologians of other persuasions came up with varied conclusions. One of the earliest "identifiable" groups that expressly denied the divinity of the Holy Spirit was the so-called Tropikoi, who had caused some distress for Bishop Serapion of Thmuis in Egypt.[4] They apparently maintained an acceptable theology of the Son but subordinated the Spirit to the level of a creature, superior to angels by only a small degree.[5] Serapion needed help, so he sought the theological knowledge of his friend and colleague Athanasius, who in turn replied with a series of letters (c. 359–61) that explicated a theology upholding the divinity of the Spirit.[6] While the Tropikoi were likely unique to the environs of Egypt, a decade later the debate over the status of the Spirit smoldered in Anatolia, where the so-called Pneumatomachoi, represented and led by Eustathius of Sebaste, divided the churches in the early 370s.[7]

The Christians in Syedra were among those divided over this issue, and quite possibly their bishop was either one of the Pneumatomachoi or at least

---

3. See L. Ayres, "Innovation and *Ressourcement* in Pro-Nicene Pneumatology," *Augustinian Studies* 39, no. 2 (2008): 187–206; M. DelCogliano, "Basil of Caesarea, Didymus the Blind, and the Anti Pneumatomachian Exegesis of Amos 4:13 and John 1:3," *JTS* 61, no. 2 (2010): 644–58.

    For earlier Christian understandings of the Holy Spirit, see A. McGowan, "Tertullian and the 'Heretical' Origins of the 'Orthodox' Trinity," *JECS* 14, no. 4 (2006): 437–57 (in particular with respect to the New Prophecy); M. Barnes, "The Beginning and End of Early Christian Pneumatology," *Augustinian Studies* 39, no. 2 (2008): 169–86.

4. I use scare quotes here because scholars are not entirely certain who they were. Their name derives from the accusation that they used certain *tropoi* to (mis-)interpret passages of Scripture that affirmed the divinity of the Spirit. See C. Shapland, *The Letters of Saint Athanasius Concerning the Holy Spirit* (London: Epworth Press, 1951), 32–34; Laminski, *Geist*, 30–35 for different theories. Haykin does not identify the theological pedigree of the Tropikoi but does call them "the first group to whom the name 'Pneumatomachoi' may be properly given." *Spirit*, 18–24 (20). On Serapion, see K. Fitschen, *Serapion von Thmuis: Echte und unechte Schriften sowie die Zeugnisse des Athanasius und anderer*, Patristische Texte und Studien 37 (Berlin: Walter de Gruyter, 1992).

5. Ath., *epistulae ad Serapionem* 1.10.4–12.5.

6. See M. DelCogliano, A. Radde-Gallwitz, L. Ayres, *Works on the Spirit: Athanasius's "Letters to Serapion on the Holy Spirit" and Didymus's "On the Holy Spirit,"* Popular Patristics Series 43 (Crestwood, NY: St. Vladimir's Seminary Press, 2011). On the historical context of their composition, see Martin, *Athanase*, 533–36.

7. On Eustathius, see J. Gribomont, "Eustathe de Sébaste," in *Dictionnaire de spiritualité: Ascétique et mystique, doctrine et histoire* 4.2 (Paris: Beauchesne, 1961), 1708–12; idem, "Eustathe de Sébaste," in *DHGE* 16 (Paris: Letouzey et Ané, 1967), 26–33. Later sources also identified the Pneumatomachoi as "Macedonians," in connection with the Homoiousian Macedonius, who was also onetime bishop of Constantinople and a colleague of Eustathius. See Kim, *Saint Epiphanius*, 26, n. 86.

sympathetic to them.[8] Thus those who affirmed the divinity of the Holy Spirit were compelled to look elsewhere for assistance, and they turned to Epiphanius and sent him two letters, likely from two separate but related groups, sometime after the death of Athanasius.[9] In the first letter, the Syedrans lamented those who blasphemed against the Holy Spirit, but rejoiced that "though many are disturbed, we ourselves stand by the grace of Christ in sound faith and have absolutely not been shaken from the correct and sound teachings. And many of those who seem to have been deceived have been made wholly sound by the grace of our Lord, through the writings of the Bishop Athanasios, worthy of blessed memory, and of your most pious fellow minister Proclianos."[10] Although they had some useful texts in their possession, they needed more help:

> But because remnants of wicked teaching still remain among some, and because it is necessary through you, the experienced farmer, to engraft them to a good olive tree or to cut them off completely (cf. Rom 7:11–22), writing to your piety we ask for this favor, that your reverence consider it worthy to compose texts for our church and to expound the correct and sound faith through a more expansive explanation, in order to strengthen and to make secure the simpler who are in doubt about the faith through your sacred writings, and to put to shame the enemy of the church, the Devil, through your holy prayers."[11]

This was neither the first nor last time other Christians sought Epiphanius's help, as the *Panarion* itself was composed in response to a letter from Acacius and Paul, two Syrian presbyters.[12] In the first letter from the Syedra Christians,

8. See Kösters, *Trinitätslehre*, 91–93.
9. See Kösters, *Trinitätslehre*, 89–107, on the two letters and the circles they represented.
10. *Anc.* Letter 1.3.
11. *Anc.* Letter 1.4.
12. We also have a letter (reproduced in *Pan.* 78.2.1–24.6) in response to Christians in Arabia on the proper theology of Mary; cf. C. Riggi, "La 'lettera agli Arabi' di Epifanio, pioniere della teologia mariana (Haer. 78–79)," in *La Mariologia nella catechesi dei Padri (Età postnicena): Convegno di studio e aggiornamento Facoltà di Lettere cristiane e classiche (Pontificium Institutum Altioris Latinitatis) Roma 10–11 marzo 1989, XXV della Facoltà*, Biblioteca di Scienze Religiose 95, ed. S. Felici (Rome: Editrice LAS, 1991), 89–107. We possess fragments of letters that Epiphanius wrote to believers in Egypt about the proper calculation for Easter and to others on the Apollinarian heresy; cf. K. Holl, "Ein Bruchstück aus einem bisher unbekannten Brief des Epiphanius," in *Festgabe für Adolf Jülicher zum 70. Geburtstag 26. Januar 1927* (Tübingen: J.C.B. Mohr 1927), 159–89, reprinted in Holl, *Gesammelte Aufsätze zur Kirchengeschichte, T. 2* (Tübingen: J.C.B. Mohr [Paul Siebeck], 1928), 204–24; J. Lebon, "Sur quelques fragments de letters attribuées à S. Épiphane de Salamine," in *Miscellanea Giovanni Mercati, Vol. I. Bibbia-Letteratura Cristiana antica*, Studi e Testi 121 (Vatican City: Biblioteca Apostolica Vaticana, 1946), 145–74.

we can make two very important observations about their circumstances. First, they had consulted Athanasius's writings on the proper understanding of the Holy Spirit, most likely the Letters to Serapion.[13] Second, because of the recent passing of the famed bishop of Alexandria, they were compelled to look elsewhere for help and thus wrote to Epiphanius. In other words, other orthodox Christians perceived that Epiphanius represented theological continuity with Athanasius, that the former was a worthy "successor" of the latter as a defender of true Christianity in the ongoing disputes of the era. Thus their appeal to Epiphanius highlights that he was thought to be a theological expert and trustworthy teacher.

Modern scholars have written much on the contentious theological and political disputes of the fourth century, an era that has proven to be ripe for periodic reassessment and reinterpretation.[14] As much as the disputants in the late ancient church argued the minutiae of theology, even down to a single iota, scholars today continue to revisit and reevaluate this period and all of its prickly developments.[15] The story of this most quarrelsome and fascinating era has been told and retold, and without doubt future scholars will continue to repeat the process. But we must also remember that the interpretation and presentation of differing narratives of the theological and ecclesiastical disputes were taking place in real time as the purported events and developments were either unfolding or had recently come to pass. Theology was of course a central field

13. See Kösters, *Trinitätslehre*, 90–91, following Hauschild, *Pneumatomachen*, 33, n. 2. What the writings from Proclianos entailed is unclear.

14. The bibliography is, of course, massive, and I reference here only a representative list of significant scholarly works: M. Simonetti, *La crisi ariana nel IV secolo*, Studia Ephemeridis "Augustinianum" 11 (Rome: Institutum Patristicum "Augustinianum," 1975); T. Kopecek, *A History of Neo-Arianism*, 2 vols. (Cambridge, MA: Philadelphia Patristic Foundation, 1979); Gregg and Groh, *Arianism*; Williams, *Arius*; H. Brennecke, *Studien zur Geschichte der Homöer: Der Osten bis zum Ende der homöischen Reichskirche*, Beiträge zur historischen Theologie 73 (Tübingen: J.C.B. Mohr [Paul Siebeck], 1988); Hanson, *Search*; C. Kannengiesser, *Arius and Athanasius: Two Alexandrian Theologians* (Hampshire: Variorum, 1991), a collection of previously published articles; Barnes and Williams, eds., *Arianism after Arius*; V. Drecoll, *Die Entwicklung der Trinitätslehre des Basilius von Cäsarea: Sein Weg vom Homöusianer zum Neonizäner*, Forschungen zur Kirchen- und Dogmengeschichte 66 (Göttingen: Vandenhoeck & Ruprecht, 1996); J. Lienhard, *Contra Marcellum: Marcellus of Ancyra and Fourth-Century Theology* (Washington, DC: Catholic University of America Press, 1999); R. Vaggione, *Eunomius of Cyzicus and the Nicene Revolution* (Oxford: Oxford University Press, 2000); Ayres, *Nicaea*; Behr, *Nicene*; S. Parvis, *Marcellus of Ancyra and the Lost Years of the Arian Controversy, 325-345* (Oxford: Oxford University Press, 2006); Gwynn, *Eusebians*; K. Anatolios, *Retrieving Nicaea: The Development and Meaning of Trinitarian Doctrine* (Grand Rapids, MI: Baker Academic, 2011).

15. For example, see the introduction by S. Coakley, "Disputed Questions in Patristic Trinitarianism," *HTR* 100, no. 2 (2007): 125–38, and the other articles in the recent special issue of *HTR* dedicated to examinations and critiques of Ayres, *Nicaea and Its Legacy* and responses by the author.

of battle in these conflicts; so too was biblical exegesis.[16] However, my goal in this chapter is not to scrutinize the theological and exegetical arguments, but to consider how Epiphanius imagined and narrated the early years of the struggle for "orthodoxy." He assumed the historical narrative as it was laid out by Athanasius, and his version of ecclesiastical history decried the conspiratorial machinations of a gang of "Arian" heretics, who along with Melitian schismatics shook the very foundations of true Christianity and forced orthodox bishops and clerics into exile.[17] Furthermore, Athanasius modeled the important practice of documentation in the building of his case against his opponents by including numerous letters and documents from both his friends and his enemies to serve as written testimonies to his case.[18]

Scholars now recognize that the classic saga of the battle for the "truth" waged by the orthodox hero Athanasius against the "evil" conspirators led by Eusebius of Nicomedia was in part a product of the imagination and selective presentation of the oft-exiled Alexandrian.[19] But if there was anyone in late antiquity who bought into the Athanasian narrative of this struggle, it was Epiphanius, who through retelling the story implicitly aligned himself as an ally and successor to the "father of orthodoxy," Athanasius.[20] The perceived connection between the Christianities of Athanasius and Epiphanius is the central theme of this chapter. Not only did other people view the two as being in a kind of orthodox succession, but Epiphanius himself imagined this. My aim in this chapter is not to demonstrate that they agreed on everything (because they did not), nor is my method to scour the depths of their theologies to find every intersection. Rather, we will examine vital points of correspondence in the thoughts and deeds of Athanasius and Epiphanius that will underscore their political and theological continuity. The line of succession from Athanasius to Epiphanius also marked an important fourth-century transition from the man largely responsible for waging the rhetorical and real conflict against the "Arians" to the man who would escalate the war against heresy to new heights.

---

16. Ayres introduces this important point and examines it throughout. *Nicaea*, 11–40.
17. Generally the ecclesiastical historians of the late fourth and fifth centuries, Rufinus, Theodoret, Socrates, and Sozomen, took up the Athanasian narrative as well, although Philostorgius offered some useful opposing perspectives.
18. This was a practice, of course, demonstrated effectively by Eusebius of Caesarea.
19. See throughout Gwynn, *Eusebians*.
20. *Pan.* 69.2.3. Perhaps we could argue the same of Gregory of Nazianzus, *orationes* 21.

The Arian-Melitian Conspiracy (Panarion 68)

Two Traditions, Two Perspectives

In chapter 1, we examined Epiphanius's understanding of the early years of the Melitian schism that he framed not in doctrinal terms but as a difficult case of ecclesiological rigidity and ultimately the rejection of the established structure of church leadership. We can discern a heresiological tension in the first part (about a third) of his account in *Panarion* 68, and he repeatedly emphasized that Melitius was *doctrinally* orthodox: "For I often was saying that he was holding nothing [no belief] that has been altered."[21] Thus in the opening section of the entry against the Melitians, Epiphanius likely drew on a source or sources that were friendly to the Melitian perspective. However, after the death of Melitius, whom Epiphanius identified as a "confessor," the rest of the entry takes a markedly different turn. From this point forward, Epiphanius's story of the Melitians is the Athanasian version and part of an "Alexandrian" tradition, and any mixed feelings Epiphanius might have had toward Melitius turned into acerbic hostility against the Melitians as a discernible "party" that conspired with the Arians.[22]

According to Epiphanius's shifting narrative, Bishop Alexander of Alexandria renewed his efforts to end the schism in the Egyptian church and applied forceful pressure upon the Melitians to return them to the fold. In their frustration, the schismatics attempted to make direct recourse to the imperial court to petition for their right to assemble freely.[23] Among the emissaries were Paphnutius, an anchorite whose mother was a confessor, John, one of their respected bishops, and Callinicus, another bishop. Unfortunately, they did not even receive a hearing with the emperor.[24] Epiphanius then reports the following developments:

> Meanwhile, it happened that with Paphnutius, John, and <the> rest, they lingered in parts of Constantinople and Nicomedia. Then they became friends

---

21. *Pan.* 68.3.9.
22. *Pan.* 68.5.1. Cf. Ath., *apol. sec.* 59.4–6; *ep. Aeg. Lib.* 22; *historia Arianorum ad monachos* 78.1–79.5; Soz., *h.e.* 2.22.1–23.8. On the "Alexandrian" tradition, see Martin, *Athanase*, 224–61, and 341–89, on the period from the accession of Athanasius to the Council of Tyre.
23. *Pan.* 68.5.1–2.
24. *Pan.* 68.5.3–5. On John (Archaph), cf. Ath., *apol. sec.* 17.3; Soz., *h.e.* 2.22.2–3. On Paphnutius, see Martin, *Athanase*, 45–48.

with Eusebius, bishop of Nicomedia, and related to him their story (for they knew that he wielded *parrēsia* before the emperor Constantius), and they asked that they be introduced to the emperor through him. (2) But after consenting to present them to the emperor and to carry out the matter of their request, this request was asked of them: that they receive into communion with them Arius, who had "repented" in a pretend way and with dissembling. (3) And they consented to this. And then Eusebius presented them to the emperor and explained their circumstances. And thereafter it was granted to the Melitians to assemble among themselves and not to be disturbed by anyone. (4) Would that the Melitians themselves, who received the perfectly correct form of the truth, had communed after repentance with they who had lapsed rather than with Arius and those with him! (5) For this has come to pass for them, according to the proverb, that fleeing the smoke they have fallen upon the fire. For Arius would not have been able to have a place to stand and *parrēsia*, if not on account of a pretext of this sort, which has become for them up to the present a wicked alliance. For the once pure and absolutely correct in their faith Melitians have comingled with the disciples of Arius. (6) And now the majority has been defiled by the wicked belief of Arius, turning away from the faith in our times. But even if on the one hand some remain, holding the true faith, on the other hand they hold it, but by no means are they recovered from the filthy muck because of their communion with Arius and the Arians.[25]

Again Epiphanius seemed to lament just how close the Melitians were to remaining orthodox, but their desire for legitimacy and the freedom of assembly to pursue their own rigid separatism compelled them to turn to Eusebius of Nicomedia and his *parrēsia* before the emperor.[26] Epiphanius would have his readers believe that the potentially righteous Melitians struck a deal with the devil and turned to heresy, even if some of them clung to the vestiges of whatever orthodox beliefs they had left.

The connection between Eusebius and his "free speech" was very important

25. *Pan.* 68.6.1–6. On the "restoration" of Arius, see, for example, Ath., *h. Ar.* 1.1–2.4. On the willingness of the Melitians to become Arians, see Ath., *h. Ar.* 78.1–5, in which Athanasius (in contrast to Epiphanius) was entirely pessimistic about the beliefs of the Melitians. On the context for the criticisms of the Melitians, see Martin, *Athanase*, 496–502.
26. Cf. Soz., *h.e.* 2.22.1. Ath., *apol. sec.* 59.4, emphasized the initiative of Eusebius in this alliance. Furthermore, Ath., *ep. Aeg. Lib.* 22, accused the Melitians of conspiring with the Arians to satisfy their ambition and greed. See Martin, *Athanase*, 344–48, on the Melitian appeal to the emperor.

in Epiphanius's anti-Arian polemic.[27] Consistently throughout the *Panarion*, Epiphanius emphasized the corrupting power and influence of heretic bishops upon the Roman emperors, even though Constantius and Valens were denigrated in later sources for their support of non-Nicene theology.[28] For strategic or rhetorical reasons, Epiphanius was careful always to portray the emperors in flattering terms. Thus Constantius was "pious and good in many ways."[29] While such characterizations surely must have been at odds with the actual theological preferences of the emperors, the rhetorical effect underscores the conspiratorial success of the heretic bishops: "Their gang of serpents prevailed a second time through Eudoxius, who slithered in and corrupted again the sense of hearing of the most reverent and God-loving Valens, the God-fearing emperor."[30] While Athanasius maintained a markedly negative attitude toward the emperors, especially Constantius, he also consistently stressed the dangerous power wielded by the conspiracy of heretic bishops (and eunuchs): "But when I compare his [Constantius's] letters, I find that this man does not possess a mind according to nature, but that it alone is moved according to the suggestions [of others], and he does not in any way possess a mind of his own."[31]

Enter Athanasius

Epiphanius continued with a brief but smug account of the death of Arius, followed by the death of Bishop Alexander of Alexandria.[32] At this point in Epiphanius's narrative, Athanasius enters the scene, sent as a deacon from Alexander to the imperial court and handpicked by the metropolitan to succeed him. With the unexpected death of Alexander and Athanasius's absence, the Melitians seized the opportunity to install their own choice of bishop, Theonas, in the Egyptian capital. Theonas, however, lived only three months following his consecration, which allowed Athanasius enough time to return, and then "a

---

27. On the function of *parrēsia* in dealing with emperors, see Brown, *Power and Persuasion*, 35–70.
28. See Kim, "Bad Bishops." On Constantius, see throughout, Barnes, *Athanasius*, and for Valens, see N. Lenski, *Failure of Empire: Valens and the Roman State in the Fourth Century A.D.*, Transformation of the Classical Heritage 34 (Berkeley: University of California Press, 2002).
29. *Pan.* 69.12.5.
30. *Pan.* 69.13.1.
31. Ath., *h. Ar.* 69.2. Depending on his personal circumstances, Athanasius exhibited deference to Constantius, as in *apol. Const.*, and open hostility and vitriol as for example in *h. Ar.* 30.1–34.4 and throughout the rest of the work, in which Constantius is described as a forerunner of the Antichrist; see Martin, *Athanase*, 502–18. On bad eunuchs, cf. Ath., *h. Ar.* 38.1–5.
32. On the significance of the manner of Arius's death, see Ath., *epistula ad Serapionem de morte Arii; ep. Aeg. Lib.* 19; Ruf., *Hist.* 10.14.

synod of orthodox bishops from everywhere was hammered together, and thus his appointment took place, and the throne was returned to him, a worthy man, and for whom it was prepared, according to the will of God and according to the testimony and command of <the> blessed Alexander."[33] In no uncertain terms, Epiphanius stressed that Athanasius was the rightful successor to Alexander despite any Melitian claims otherwise. Unfortunately, Athanasius's accession marked only the beginning of his real troubles. The Melitians and Eusebius of Nicomedia intensified their attack against the venerable bishop with well-known accusations: that he committed financial improprieties, that one of his agents broke a sacred vessel, that he murdered a presbyter from Mareotis named Arsenius, and that he acted in general like a thug and gangster, which compelled Constantine to convene the Council of Tyre.[34]

Among the synod attendees was Potamon, a "zealot for the truth and orthodoxy," who as a confessor had been partially blinded during the persecution.[35] He was apparently dismayed that Eusebius of Caesarea was among the adjudicators at the council: "Do you sit, Eusebius, while the guiltless Athanasius is before you? Who could bear such things as they are? Tell me; were you not in the prison with me during the persecution? And I lost my eye for the sake of the truth, but you do not appear to have any part of your body maimed, nor did you bear witness, but you stand alive with nothing mutilated."[36] Thus Epiphanius's narrative sets in opposition the unscathed Eusebius, sitting in judgment upon an innocent Athanasius, and the weighty voice of a confessor whose testimony and protestations are augmented by the very visible reminder of his sufferings. The conspirators, it seems, bore none of the marks of true Christianity. Euse-

33. *Pan.* 68.7.1–4, 69.11.4–7. Cf. Ath., *apol. sec.* 6.4–7; Philostorgius, *historia ecclesiastica* 2.11; Soz., *h.e.* 2.17.1–11. See Martin, *Athanase*, 323–26, on Epiphanius's two accounts, one "Melitian," the other "Arian." On the disputed election of Athanasius, see Barnes, *Constantine*, 230–31; D. Arnold, *The Early Episcopal Career of Athanasius of Alexandria*, Christianity and Judaism in Antiquity 6 (Notre Dame, IN: University of Notre Dame Press, 1999), 36–62; Martin, *Athanase*, 321–39.

34. *Pan.* 68.7.5–8.1. Cf. Eus., *v.C.* 4.42; Ath., *apol. sec.* 60.1–3; Socr., *h.e.* 1.28.1–31.4; Soz., *h.e.* 2.22.1–23.8, 2.25.1–20. See Arnold, *Career*, 103–42 and Barnes, *Athanasius*, 20–25, for the events leading up to Tyre and Athanasius's first exile. For the proceedings, see Arnold, *Career*, 143–63. Cf. Ath., *apol. sec.* 3.1–20.1, which is a letter composed by the participants of a council in Alexandria in 338 and sent to Julius of Rome to explain the false charges leveled against Athanasius at the Council of Tyre. Also see Ath., *apol. sec.* 71.1–81.2, for a series of documents relating to the charges and investigation connected to the Council of Tyre. On the panoply of early charges made against Athanasius, see Martin, *Athanase*, 348–57, and 364–66, for those made specifically at Tyre, and Barnes, *Athanasius*, 25–33, for Athanasius's retroactive self-defense against the charges made by the Arian/Melitian conspiracy.

35. *Pan.* 68.8.3. Martin, *Athanase*, 46.

36. *Pan.* 68.8.4. Ath., *apol. sec.* 8.3, intimated that Eusebius had been accused of sacrificing to idols during his imprisonment.

bius and the other judges sent Ursacius and Valens to Egypt to investigate the charges made against Athanasius, and upon their return, their falsified report served as the justification for his removal from office.[37] Meanwhile Athanasius, fearing the outcome of the proceedings, fled Tyre to seek an audience with Constantine.[38] But despite his pleas of innocence before the emperor, Athanasius was deposed *in absentia* (at least according to Athanasius) by the council in Tyre and ultimately banished by the emperor (first exile), during which time he made his way to the West (Trier).[39] Epiphanius, however, was confused about the different exiles of Athanasius. His suggestion that this first exile was spent in Italy for "more than twelve or fourteen years" would have been impossible. The Council of Tyre took place in 335; and after the death of Constantine in 337, exiled bishops, including Athanasius, were allowed to return to their sees.[40]

Epiphanius's narrative of the ensuing years and subsequent exiles of Athanasius is a jumbled mess of confused details and conflated events, although the main thrust of the report remains the travails of Athanasius at the hands of the heretic conspirators. The story continues with the well-known account of the discovery of Arsenius, alive and with all of his body parts intact, which once again proved that the Arian conspirers resorted to duplicitous tactics to maintain their power and sway at court.[41] With the death of Constantine, Athanasius, who according to Epiphanius's account had by this time solidified his popularity in the West, was allowed to return from exile and reentered Alexandria.[42] However, Epiphanius mistakenly stated that Athanasius resumed his episcopal throne from Gregory of Cappadocia, the "Arian" bishop who was in fact appointed just before Athanasius's second exile.[43] The narrative continues

37. *Pan.* 68.9.1–4; Ath., *apol. sec.* 13.1–14.4, 72.1–76.5. Epiphanius, however, also reported that Ursacius and Valens later repented of their false testimony and wrote to both Athanasius and Julius of Rome to seek restitution; cf. Ath., *apol. sec.* 2.1–4, 58.1–6; *apol. Const.* 1; *h. Ar.* 26.1–5. Nevertheless, the same two bishops later "relapsed" and again turned against Athanasius; cf. *h. Ar.* 29.1–2. On the investigation, see Arnold, *Career*, 157–60; Martin, *Athanase*, 367–76, and 461–65, on the retraction of Ursacius and Valens.
38. Cf. Soz., *h.e.* 2.25.13–14.
39. *Pan.* 68.9.4–6. Cf. Socr., *h.e.* 1.32.1–3; Soz., *h.e.* 2.25.15–20. On whether Athanasius was present for his condemnation by the council, see Martin, *Athanase*, 376–77, and 379–87, on the proceedings at Constantinople. See also Arnold, *Career*, 163–73. Athanasius's opponents (Ath., *apol. sec.* 87.1–3; cf. Socr., *h.e.* 1.35.1–3) insinuated that he intended to halt the grain supply from Alexandria to Constantinople, which was enough for Constantine to send him into exile.
40. *Pan.* 68.9.6.
41. *Pan.* 68.10.1–2. Cf. Ath., *apol. sec.* 8.4–5, 38.1–3, 65.1–70.2.
42. *Pan.* 68.10.3. This would have been in the early summer 338. For these events, see Barnes, *Athanasius*, 34–46; Martin, *Athanase*, 393–400. Thus Epiphanius's earlier assertion of a twelve- to fourteen-year stay in the West would not make sense here.
43. *Pan.* 68.10.4. Cf. Ath., *epistula encyclica*; *apol. sec.* 29.1–30.4; *h. Ar.* 10.1–2; Socr., *h.e.* 2.10.1, 2.11.1–7;

with a compressed account of more condemnations, first at the instigation of Stephen, a onetime bishop of Antioch, in the presence of Emperor Constantius, then another initiated by Stephen's successor, the eunuch Leontius and his supporters.[44] Epiphanius omitted or was confused about many details of the developments of the 340s and 350s (including Athanasius's second exile and return) and instead fast-forwarded his account to the accession of Julian, who "turned to Hellenism after the death of Constantius."[45] Epiphanius did, however, include a brief account of the fate of George of Cappadocia, who came to Alexandria on 24 February 357 to assume the see of Alexandria after Athanasius had been deposed by Constantius at the Council of Milan in 355 and forced to hide in the Egyptian desert.[46] George did not last long in the city because of the popular support of Athanasius (and according to the exiled bishop, outrages committed) and was forced to flee on 2 October 358.[47] But George eventually returned to Alexandria on 26 November 361. Epiphanius then reported that upon George's return, the Alexandrians "killed him, having set him on fire, making him into ashes, and scattering them into the wind."[48]

Thdt., *h.e.* 2.4.1–6. The replacement "Arian" bishop during the first exile was Pistus; cf. Ath., *apol. sec.* 24.1–4. Gregory assumed the see of Alexandria by force on 23 March 339, and he died on 26 June 345. On the alleged atrocities of Gregory, see Ath., *h. Ar.* 12.1–13.3; Thdt., *h.e.* 2.14.1–14. See Haas, *Alexandria*, 270–71. On Athanasius's return from his second exile on 21 October 346, cf. Ath., *h. Ar.* 25.1–4; Socr., *h.e.* 2.23.1–58; Soz., *h.e.*. 3.20.1–21.2. Also see Barnes, *Athanasius*, 87–93; Martin, *Athanase*, 440–47.

44. *Pan.* 68.11.1. Cf. Ath., *ep. Aeg. Lib.* 7; *fug.* 1, 26; *h. Ar.* 4.2, 20.1–5, 28.1; Thdt., *h.e.* 2.9.1–10.2, 2.19.1–15. See Martin, *Athanase*, 438–39.

45. *Pan.* 68.11.1. For example, Epiphanius failed to mention the important councils at Antioch (341), Sardica (343) (which exonerated Athanasius; cf. Ath., *h. Ar.* 15.1–17.3), Sirmium (351), Milan (355), and Rimini/Seleucia (359). For Athanasius's activities during this period, see Martin, *Athanase*, 410–536.

46. Ath., *apol. Const.* 30; *ep. Aeg. Lib.* 7; *fug.* 6–7; *h. Ar.* 75.1–3. Cf. Soz., *h.e.* 4.9.1–10; Ruf., *Hist.* 10.21; Philost., *h.e.* 3.3; Thdt., *h.e.* 2.15.1–10. George was actually chosen to replace Athanasius at the end of 349 at a council in Antioch; cf. Soz., *h.e.* 4.8.3–4. See Barnes, *Athanasius*, 118–19, and Simonetti, "Eusebio," 155–59, for Milan and its aftermath. For a thorough examination of Athanasius's activities while in hiding, especially his literary propaganda, see Martin, *Athanase*, 474–540. For the reputation and career of George, see Martin, *Athanase*, 518–27, 536–40.

47. Cf. *Historia acephala* 1.10–2.6. Haas, *Alexandria*, 280–95, building on idem, "The Alexandrian Riots of 356 and George of Cappadocia," *Greek, Roman, and Byzantine Studies* 32, no. 3 (1991): 281–301.

48. *Pan.* 68.11.2, but also 78.1.1–2. Cf. *H. aceph.* 2.8–10; Ammianus Marcellinus, *Res gestae* 22.11.1–11; Socr., *h.e.* 3.2.1–10; Soz., *h.e.* 4.30.1–2, 5.7.1–9; Philost., *h.e.* 7.2. George died on 24 December. Epiphanius also added more information about George in *Pan.* 76.1.1–7, detailing the abuse he suffered from the pagans of Alexandria and the crimes of avarice he had committed. On the disparate source traditions on George's death, see Brennecke, *Studien*, 116–19. See also Martin, *Athanase*, 536–40; Haas, *Alexandria*, 280–95, especially for how George provoked the pagans of Alexandria. On the "failed martyrdom" of George and its broader implications on the relationship between violence and intolerance, see H. Drake, "The Curious Case of George and the Camel," in *Studies of Religion and Politics in the Early Christian Centuries*, Early Christian Studies 13, ed. D. Luckensmeyer and P. Allen (Strathfield, NSW: St Pauls Publications, 2010), 173–93.

Julian allowed bishops exiled by Constantius to return, which Athanasius did on 21 February 362.[49] Epiphanius made no report of Julian's subsequent banishment of Athanasius, but instead mentioned in passing the death of Julian in Persia.[50] Epiphanius then transitioned abruptly to the succession of the "blessed Jovian, who with much honor and trustworthy letters wrote to Bishop Athanasius, summoned and embraced him, and sent him to his proper throne. The holy church received back its bishop and was encouraged for a time."[51] Again, Epiphanius grossly oversimplified the complex jockeying for the favor of Jovian among all the bishops of the East as soon as word of Julian's death was known.[52] Athanasius was able to secure recognition from Jovian as bishop of Alexandria, but the emperor's reign was short, and "with the death of Jovian, the blessed Athanasius again suffered the same persecutions, rumors, and troubles."[53] The "Arian" conspirators had chosen Lucius as George's successor, and Lucius, along with others in Antioch, had apparently denounced Athanasius before Jovian to no avail.[54] Epiphanius was aware of Lucius and his attempts to claim the see of Alexandria, especially before Valens, who "on account of a disturbance of the people was not willing to expel him [Athanasius]."[55] Only after the death of Athanasius, however, did Valens send Lucius, who "exhibited much wickedness to the church, the city, the people, the bishops, the clerics—those who were under Athanasius and had

---

49. Cf. *h. aceph.* 3.2–4; Thdt., *h.e.*, 3.4.1–2. Barnes dates this edict to 360, before the death of Constantius. *Athanasius*, 154–55.

50. Cf. *h. aceph.* 3.5; Socr., *h.e.* 3.13.13–14; Soz., *h.e.* 5.15.1–3. See Barnes, *Athanasius*, 158–59; Martin, *Athanase*, 565–73.

51. *Pan.* 68.11.3; cf. Ruf., *Hist.* 11.1. Cf. Ath., *epistula ad Jovianum*. This was also the (problematic) impression given later by Soz., *h.e.*, 6.5.2. That Jovian wrote to Athanasius (and others) asking for an exposition of the faith is disputed in modern scholarship. See Brennecke, *Studien*, 171, n. 83; Martin, *Athanase*, 575–76; T. Karmann, *Meletius von Antiochien: Studien zur Geschichte des trinitätstheologischen Streits in den Jahren 360–364 n.Chr.*, Regensburger Studien zur Theologie 68 (Frankfurt am Main: Peter Lang, 2009), 336–37. On Jovian's imperial policies as a Christian, see Brennecke, *Studien*, 158–81; Barnes, *Athanasius*, 159–61; Karmann, *Meletius*, 331–40.

52. Cf. Socr., *h.e.* 3.24.1–25.21. When Athanasius learned of Julian's death, he returned to Alexandria, then left Egypt to seek an audience with Jovian; cf. *h. aceph.* 4.4. See Brennecke, *Studien*, 169–73; Barnes, *Athanasius*, 159–61; Martin, *Athanase*, 573–89; A. von Stockhausen, "Athanasius in Antiochien," *ZAC* 10 (2006): 86–102; Karmann, *Meletius* 335–37.

53. *Pan.* 68.11.3.

54. Cf. *h. aceph.* 4.7; Socr., *h.e.* 3.4.2, 4.1.14. Also appended to the end of Athanasius's letter to Jovian was the petition of Lucius and his supporters against Athanasius. On Lucius, see Barnes, *Athanasius*, 160; Martin, *Athanase*, 588–90, 593–94; von Stockhausen, "Antiochien," 97–101.

55. *Pan.* 68.11.4. Cf. *h. aceph.* 5.1–7; Soz., *h.e.* 6.12.3–16. Epiphanius conflated and oversimplified the sequence of events. Valens issued an edict on 5 May 365 expelling all bishops recalled under Julian, including Athanasius, which led to public unrest in Alexandria. Athanasius secretly left the city on 5 October, but on 1 February 366, news came from Valens allowing Athanasius to retain his see. See Brennecke, *Studien*, 209–12; Barnes, *Athanasius*, 162–63; Martin, *Athanase*, 592–95.

received him in each church, and to Peter, the appointed successor after Athanasius in Alexandria."[56]

Throughout the closing sections of the entry against them, the Melitians do not appear at all as players in the power politics that resulted in the five exiles of Athanasius. This was the story that Athanasius had constructed and Epiphanius repeated. The Melitians were rhetorically subsumed under the broader "Arian" conspiracy that dominated much of the fourth-century proceedings. Epiphanius then offered the following assessment of the contemporary situation:

> And things have transpired thus up to this point. Among the exiled were bishops and presbyters and deacons, but some have been subjected to beheading in Alexandria, and others have been made to fight with wild beasts. Virgins have been killed, and many others slain. Up to this point, the church of God suffers still in these things, because of the aforementioned affair of the Melitians and the Arians, who through such means secured their standing and <the pretext> for strengthening the same system of heretical opinions, I mean, of the Arians. And I will fully describe everything in detail in the refutation against the Arians.[57]

Thus Epiphanius concluded his "refutation" of the Melitians, which had very little to do with heresy. Indeed the entry is essentially a condensed history of the middle decades of the fourth century inspired by the Athanasian version.[58] By no means did Epiphanius recount with complete accuracy and consistency the drama that was Athanasius's life. But he did manage to highlight some of the major themes of the story that Athanasius himself had constructed in his writings: the Arian-Melitian conspiracy, the bad behavior of emperors, the false charges and illegitimate councils, and the wicked machinations of a cadre of heretic bishops. While Epiphanius's narrative functions as a setup for the subsequent refutation of the Arians, it also confirms the degree to which Epiphanius positioned himself in political and ecclesiastical continuity with Athanasius, who also imagined a world strictly demarcated between orthodoxy and heresy.

---

56. *Pan.* 68.11.5. Cf. *h. aceph.* 5.11–14; Socr., *h.e.* 4.20.1–22.6; Soz., *h.e.* 6.19.1–20.12; Thdt., *h.e.* 4.20.1–22.37. See Brennecke, *Studien*, 236–38; Martin, *Athanase*, 789–96.
57. *Pan.* 68.11.6–8. On the abuse of virgins, see for example Ath., *apol. sec.* 15.1–2; *apol. Const.* 33; *h. Ar.* 72.5–6.
58. For example, Ath., *ep. Aeg. Lib.* 22.

A Theological Excursus

Although modern scholarship has tended to minimize Epiphanius's theological sophistication and contributions to the development of Trinitarian dogma, Oliver Kösters's commentary on the *Ancoratus* has done otherwise. My own introduction to and translation of the same work offers further consideration of Epiphanius's doctrinal importance and the unique ideas he posited in the debates of his time. Thus further analysis of Epiphanius's Trinitarian theology, especially in the *Panarion*, and comparisons with other contemporary theologians are potentially fruitful ground for future work that will only deepen our already rich discussions of fourth-century Christianity.

Scholars of fourth-century Trinitarian theology are well aware of the complexities of the philosophical concepts and the specific vocabulary employed by ancient thinkers to articulate their particular understanding of the Godhead. Terms like *hypostasis* and *ousia* (with all of its variant prefixes), and the different formulas that combined them, have begotten countless studies and will no doubt continue to occupy the imaginations of scholars and theologians.[59] As much as these terms are difficult to translate into modern parlance, as in "person" and "substance," the late ancient conceptions and understandings of them were equally fraught with differences in nuance and meaning and change over time. Furthermore, how these ideas cohered with the testimony of Scripture created yet another set of challenges for late ancient theologians. The word *hypostasis* appears in the New Testament, but its meaning and use invariably depend on the context of its user, while *ousia* is equally problematic (and potentially enigmatic).[60] This chapter will not rehash the myriad viewpoints and shifting concepts related to these terms and their uses. Rather, a few cursory observations will provide the necessary framework to observe how Epiphanius initially maintained a one-*hypostasis* theology but ultimately shifted his confession toward a three-*hypostaseis* formula, which in an older tradition of scholarly works was identified as the "Neo-Nicene" confession championed largely by the Cappadocian Fathers.[61] Athanasius, while not fully embracing the latter

59. The bibliography, of course, is immense, but a useful and recent starting point for unraveling the vocabulary and concepts of the early and mid-fourth century is Morales, *La théologie*.

60. See Hanson, *Search*, 181–90; Morales, *La théologie*, 21–79, 235–405. On the development of ancient concepts of *ousia*, see C. Stead, *Divine Substance* (Oxford: Oxford University Press, 1977). Furthermore, both terms were used interchangeably (and problematically) well into the fourth century.

61. Cf. Basil, *epistulae* 125.1; Gregory of Nazianzus, *orationes* 21.35. See J. Zachhuber, "Basil and the Three-Hypostases Tradition: Reconsidering the Origins of Cappadocian Theology," *ZAC* 5, no. 1

formula before his death, also exhibited a willingness to accommodate a three-*hypostaseis* theology, which for many decades was the hallmark of the very theology he opposed and condemned as Arian.

Nicaea and Its Aftermath

The Council of Nicaea was just the first step in the long journey toward defining and articulating the Trinity.[62] The Creed and anathemas that emerged from its proceedings utilized the words *hypostasis* and *ousia* and introduced a loaded, nonbiblical, and highly debated term, *homoousios*. Three separate expressions used this vocabulary. The first proclaimed that the only-begotten Son was "from the *ousia* of the Father."[63] The second said that the Son is *homoousios* with the Father.[64] The third condemned those who "assert [that the Son is] of a different *hypostasis* or *ousia*" from the Father. These expressions forced theologians across the spectrum to contemplate and negotiate how such concepts and vocabulary lined up with the testimony of Scripture and with their own convictions about the nature of the relationship between Father and Son.[65] For Arius, the Son was begotten by the "will and counsel" of the Father and was "made out of nothing." Thus the phrase "from the *ousia* of the Father" presented several theological problems, including the implication of two first principles, a materialist understanding of the generation of the Son, and the attribution of change to the Father.[66] The introduction at Nicaea of *homoousios*, a term already famil-

---

(2001): 65–85, for an excellent recent reassessment of the roots of Basil's famed theological expression. On Basil, see throughout Drecoll, *Entwicklung*; Ayres, *Nicaea*, 187–221; Behr, *Nicene*, 263–324. Also see J. Lienhard, "*Ousia* and *Hypostasis*: The Cappadocian Settlement and the Theology of 'One Hypostasis,'" in *The Trinity: An Interdisciplinary Symposium on the Trinity*, ed. S. Davis, D. Kendall, G. O'Collins (Oxford: Oxford University Press, 1999), 99–121.

62. For the developments leading up to the Council, see Hanson, *Search*, 129–51; Ayres, *Nicaea*, 15–20; Behr, *Nicene*, 62–69. See also J. Behr, *The Way to Nicaea*, The Formation of Christian Theology 1 (Crestwood, NY: St Vladimir's Seminary Press, 2001).

63. See Stead, *Substance*, 223–33.

64. See Stead, *Substance*, 242–66, for a summary explanation of this phrase. In particular, he argues against the idea that the adoption of *homoousios* was an attempt to reflect the prevailing Trinitarian theology of the West.

65. For example, Eus., *epistula ad Caesarienses* (text in H.-G. Opitz, *Athanasius Werke III.1, Urkunden zur Geschichte des arianischen Streites 318-328* [Berlin and Leipzig: Walter de Gruyter, 1934], 42–47; citations from this volume are indicated henceforth by *Urk.*). Cf. Ath., *decr.* 2.3–5; Philost., *h.e.* 2.1; Thdt., *h.e.* 1.13.1–4. Behr summarizes well how the Nicene Creed compelled Eusebius of Caesarea to interpret his theology further. *Nicene*, 150–61.

66. The text of Arius's letter to Eusebius of Nicomedia in *Pan.* 69.6.1–6 (also *Urk.* 1). See Stead, *Substance*, 225, and Ayres, *Nicaea*, 97, on this particular phrase. Cf. Eus., *d.e.* 4.3.11–13; Eusebius of Nicomedia, *epistula ad Paulinum Tyrium* (*Urk.* 8). Ath., *Ar.* 3.60–66, however, attacked the idea that the Son, as the Word, was begotten by an act of the Father's will.

iar from debates in the previous century, was of course deliberately provocative, apparently as a foil against the Eusebian position.[67] Scholars disagree whether Origen used the term in reference to the relationship between Father and Son, but by the fourth century it had associations with various Gnostic authors and with Sabellian theology that made it suspect.[68] In the second half of the third century, the term *homoousios* became connected to and tainted by the theology of Paul of Samosata, who apparently suggested that those who did not agree with him that Christ was a man who became God necessarily had to believe that Christ was *homoousios* with the Father.[69] Thus for many eastern theologians of the early fourth century, the term was inappropriate because of its non-scriptural usage, materialist repercussions, and heretical taint, although Arius (at least according to Athanasius) further rejected it for upholding the equality of Father and Son.[70]

Overall, there was little enthusiasm for this term and for the binding authority of the Council and Creed of Nicaea, and scholars have since recognized that Athanasius himself did not actively defend or use *homoousios* until more than two decades after 325.[71] But when he did, Athanasius strategically used the term to affirm the status of the Son as the Father's Wisdom and Word.[72] He understood it to mean roughly "some sort of equal ontological status and sharing of nature" and used it as a corollary and cipher for "from the *ousia* of the Father," which in turn underscored the Son's intrinsic connection to the Father and absolute difference from creation.[73] Athanasius gave the term a retroactive,

---

67. Ath., *decr.* 19–20; *syn.* 45.7–8; Ambrose, *De fide* 3.15.125. P. Beatrice argues that the origins of this term were pagan (Hermetic), that Constantine had a key role in its introduction at the council, and thus that it was not introduced as an anti-Arian concept. "The Word '*Homoousios*' from Hellenism to Christianity," *Church History* 71, no. 2 (2002): 243–72. Compare with M. Edwards, who argues that Alexander sanctioned and even championed the use of *homoousios* before Nicaea. "Alexander of Alexandria and the *Homoousion*," *VC* 66, no. 5 (2012): 482–502.

68. For Origen, see Simonetti, *La crisi*, 91; Hanson, *Search*, 68–69; Ayres, *Nicaea*, 24; Behr, *Way*, 187–88, and contrast with Stead, *Substance*, 209–14; M. Edwards, "Did Origen Apply the Word *Homoousios* to the Son?," *JTS* 49, no. 2 (1998): 658–70; Beatrice, "Word," 250–51. On the Gnostic and Sabellian use, see Hanson, *Search*, 190–93; Beatrice, "Word," 248–52.

69. See Behr, *Way*, 207–35, for a useful discussion of what we can reconstruct of Paul's theology and its implications in later debates.

70. Ath., *syn.* 15.3, but contrast with 42.1–2. Stead, *Substance*, 244–45. Arius also connected the term with apparent errors in Valentinian, Manichaean, and Sabellian theologies; cf. Ath., *syn.* 16.3. See also Morales, *La théologie*, 335–38.

71. See Ayres, *Nicaea*, 85–130.

72. See Ayres, "Defense," which traces well the development of Athanasius's thinking about and use of *ousia* language.

73. As for example in Ath., *decr.* 19.2–22.5; *syn.* 33.1–36.6, *epistula ad Afros episcopos* 4–5, 8. See Ayres, *Nicaea*, 140–44; Morales, *La théologie*, 285–355.

historical legitimacy by having writers of the third century, namely Theognos-
tos, Dionysius of Alexandria, and Dionysius of Rome, affirm and explain the
orthodoxy of *homoousios*.[74] He also sanitized the association of *homoousios*
with Paul of Samosata, by writing that the bishops who opposed Paul in the
third century had insisted that the "Son is not *homoousios* with the Father" only
out of a sense of caution and in order to avoid any materialist misunderstand-
ing of the term.[75] Furthermore, Athanasius rejected the argument that *homoousios* implied the existence of a preexisting *ousia*, which would thus render Father and Son brothers.[76] Finally against the charge that Scripture did not use
these terms, which Athanasius conceded, he argued that they nevertheless con-
veyed the sense of the Scriptures.[77] Thus by defining what *homoousios* was and
was not on his own terms, Athanasius made it a rhetorical and polemical rally-
ing point and standard of orthodoxy for himself and his supporters, and he
emphasized that *homoousios* was intimately and historically connected with the
Council and Creed of Nicaea. He thus imagined and created a theological and
ecclesiastical scenario in which the binding orthodox decisions of Nicaea were
set in opposition to the views of any who would subordinate the Son to the level
of a creature.[78] Epiphanius was very much in sync with the Athanasian perspective: "To say *homoousios* is the bond of the faith."[79]

 The third phrase in question from the Nicene Creed, that the Son was not
"of a different *hypostasis* or *ousia* from the Father," was an anathema seemingly
aimed at the theology of the Son begotten "out of nothing." In fact it was only in
this anathema that the term *hypostasis* appeared. Although it seemed to equate
the two terms and was for the most part rather ambiguous, John Behr suggests
that it was intended "both to preserve the Son's derivation from the Father (and
not of another *hypostasis*), and also to maintain that he is not a different kind of
being (or of another *ousia*)."[80] Again as Behr points out, Athanasius in his later
defense and discussion of the decisions at Nicaea removed *hypostasis* from the

74. Ath., *decr.* 25.1–26.7; *ep. Afr.* 6. In the case of Dionysius of Alexandria in *de sententia Dionysii*, Athanasius had to "rehabilitate" the bishop and explain certain controversial statements made in the context of his opposition to Sabellianism. See Morales, *La théologie*, 25–29, especially in connection to
the term *hypostasis* in the dispute between the Dionysii.
75. Ath., *syn.* 41.1–46.3 Cf. Bas., *ep.* 52; Hilary of Poitiers, *De Synodis* 86. See the discussion in Morales,
La théologie, 320–34.
76. Ath., *syn.* 51.3–7.
77. Ath., *decr.* 21.1–4.
78. Cf. Ath., *ep. Aeg. Lib.* 5–6.
79. *Anc.* 6.4.
80. Behr, *Nicene*, 158. See also Hanson, *Search*, 167–68.

phrase.[81] The anathema and its meaning were vague, and they ultimately demonstrated that these technical terms were still under consideration and debate, and that at the time of Nicaea and in the ensuing decades, no universally agreed-upon meaning could be attached to either.

Multiple Trajectories

We have the advantage of knowing which theological formula would ultimately prevail as the orthodox profession of faith regarding the Trinity, the pro-Nicene (neo-?) "one *ousia*, three *hypostaseis*."[82] The great irony, however, was that after the Council of Nicaea, the language of plural *hypostaseis*—or the assertion of separate, distinct identities for the Father and Son (and the Holy Spirit) by recourse to the language of *hypostasis*—characterized the theology of the very people Athanasius attacked as Arian heretics.[83] Arius had proclaimed that "there are three *hypostaseis*, Father, Son, and Holy Spirit," and with respect to *ousia*, he was said to have believed that the "the Father is alien from the Son with respect to *ousia*."[84] The question of Origen's direct influence on Arius has fueled lively modern debate, although Epiphanius himself had no doubt about the answer to that question: "You ought not to praise [Origen] the father of Arius and the root and parent of other heresies."[85] Despite Epiphanius's rather bold proclamation, which reflected his heresiological rhetoric of succession, ultimately Origen and Arius would have held both points of agreement and

---

81. Ath., *decr.* 20.5. Hanson, *Search*, 168; Behr, *Nicene*, 158. On the ambiguity and range of possible interpretations of this phrase (in particular by Athanasius), see Stead, *Substance*, 233–42.
82. Cf. Bas., *ep.* 125.1. See Karmann, *Meletius*, 283–305, 396–411, for an extensive discussion of the origins of the so-called Neo-Nicene theology, both in modern scholarship (and as a modern construct) and in ancient developments.
83. See for example Eus., *d.e.* 5.5.10, for strong language on the Son's subsistence. Also Asterius, in Eus., *de ecclesiastica theologica* 3.4 (Fragment 52, 54, 61 in M. Vinzent, *Asterius von Kappadokien, Die theologischen Fragmente: Einleitung, Kristischer Text, Übersetzung und Kommentar*, Supplements to Vigiliae Christianae 20 [Leiden: Brill, 1993], 116–20) on multiple *hypostaseis*.
      This was in large part the legacy of Origen: "We, however, are persuaded that there are three hypostases, the Father, the Son, and the Holy Spirit, and we believe that only the Father is unbegotten" (Or., *Jo.* 2.75, trans. R. Heine, *Origen: Commentary on the Gospel According to John Books 1–10*, FC 80 [Washington, DC: Catholic University of America Press, 1989], 114). Cf. Or., *princ.* 1.2.2; *commentarii in Jo.* 1.151, 10.246. On Origen's use of *hypostasis*, see Morales, *La théologie*, 22–25.
84. Arius's statement on the *hypostaseis* reproduced in *Pan.* 69.8.1, the letter of Arius to Alexander of Alexandria. Ath., *syn.* 16.4, however, reproduces the same letter but does not reference the Father, Son, or Holy Spirit. On the alien *ousia*, see Ath., *syn.* 15.3.
85. Jer., *Ep.* 51.3.3. For Epiphanius's interplay of "Arianism" and "Origenism" in the fourth century, see Dechow, *Dogma*, 273–95. On the importance of Origen's legacy and the theological points where Arius intersected but also differed from Origen, see Williams, *Arius*, 117–57; Hanson, *Search*, 61–70; Ayres, *Nicaea*, 20–40.

difference. Aspects of Origen's thinking aligned with Arius's own convictions, including the absolute rejection of two first principles, the emphasis on the distinct subsistence of the Father and the Son, and the avoidance of a materialistic understanding of the Son.[86] However, Origen's belief in the eternal generation of the Son certainly would not have resonated with the non-Nicene theology of the fourth century.[87]

Perhaps more than any other creedal statement, the so-called Dedication Creed, one of four documents that resulted from a council in Antioch in 341, best expressed what seems to be the prevailing theological perspective that developed in the Greek East during the 330s.[88] Influenced by the theological views of Eusebius of Nicomedia and Asterius,[89] the creed reiterated the plurality of *hypostaseis* but shunned the language of *ousia* with the statement "that they are three in *hypostasis*, but one in agreement." Furthermore in their conception of the Son's relationship to the Father, the attendees in Antioch focused on the notion of the Son as the "indistinguishable image (*eikōna*) of the divinity and *ousia* and will and power and glory of the Father" as a means to make both the connection and distinction between them more precise.[90] The appeal to image language enabled theologians to simultaneously emphasize the difference between the unbegotten Father and the only-begotten Son, to maintain the similarity between the two via the mediating concept of image, and to distinguish the begotten Son from all other begotten beings.[91] This image language also

---

86. See Behr, *Way*, 200–201.
87. On the eternal Son, cf. Ath., *Ar.* 1.14, 2.35.
88. Ath., *syn.* 23.1–10. Cf. Socr., *h.e.* 2.8.1–7, 2.10.1–21; Soz., *h.e.* 3.5.1–10. On the Dedication Council and creeds, see Hanson, *Search*, 284–92; Ayres, *Nicaea*, 117–22; Gwynn, *Eusebians*, 220–29. Gwynn argues that this creed represented affinity and continuity with the theologies expressed by both Eusebius of Nicomedia and Asterius and a theology acceptable to a "considerable portion of the eastern Church in 341" (224). However, Parvis challenges the view that the Dedication Synod was representative of a moderate and majority Eastern position, and in general her thesis affirms the workings of an Eusebian alliance in the years 325–45. *Marcellus*, 162–77.
89. For the (fragmentary) theology of Asterius, see Hanson, *Search*, 32–41; Vinzent, *Asterius*; Lienhard, *Marcellum*, 89–101. On Asterius and the creed, see Vinzent, *Asterius*, 164–66.
90. Ath., *syn.* 23.3, and 36.6, for the rejection of this phrase. Cf. Eus., *d.e.* 5.1; Philost., *h.e.* 2.15. This is what Williams identifies as the common thread of a loose coalition of theologians affirming a "pluralist '*eikōn* theology'" in opposition to the language of Nicaea. *Arius*, 166. This phrase parallels that of Asterius in Eus., *contra Marcellum* 1.4.33 (Fragment 10 in Vinzent, *Asterius*, 86). However for the signees of this creed, the image language did not necessitate that the Father and Son be of the same substance.
91. However, M. DelCogliano demonstrates that even among the "Eusebians" there was disagreement as to what it meant for the Son to be the image of the Father, although they could accommodate debate and divergence of views among themselves, unlike Athanasius. "Eusebian Theologies of the Son as the Image of God before 341," *JECS* 14, no. 4 (2006): 458–84.

allowed theologians to uphold the divinity of the Son and the Son's ability to convey knowledge of the Father to the extent that the Son is divine either through participation or by his likeness to the Father. Thus they could avoid the materialist implications of *homoousios*.[92] The creed also recognized specifically the standing of the Holy Spirit, who with the Father and Son, "are three in *hypostasis*, but one in agreement." It seems that those gathered at Antioch earnestly attempted to build an acceptable framework of understanding within which a consensus and ecclesiastical harmony could be achieved.

The Dedication Creed was unacceptable to Athanasius, and he framed the council and its pronouncements within his larger polemical narrative of the Arians' inability to establish a firm statement of faith and their conspiracy against him and the orthodox faithful.[93] The traditional scholarly interpretation posits that until the early 360s, Athanasius and his theological allies maintained a one-*hypostasis* theology as their confession of orthodoxy.[94] In fact, a clear statement of a one-*hypostasis* theology in the Athanasian corpus is difficult to find. Perhaps the strongest proof of Athanasius's view is in the *Tomus ad Antiochenos*, in which Athanasius, aligned more closely with Paulinus and the Eustathians of Antioch, seemed to affirm implicitly a one-*hypostasis* theology and required justification of a three-*hypostaseis* theology from the Meletians.[95] Theologians in the West also maintained the one-*hypostasis* position insofar as they could conceptualize, translate, and understand the Greek vocabulary. The statements proffered at the Council of Sardica give a clear expression of their view, in contrast to the Dedication Creed:

> We received and were taught this, holding this catholic and apostolic tradition and faith and confession: there is one *hypostasis* of Father and Son and Holy Spirit, which the heretics themselves call *ousia* . . . . And we have taught that He is true Son, but not as others are called sons do we say that He is Son, because either through this are they gods, on account of regeneration, or they are called

---

92. Again, see DelCogliano, "Eusebian," for the different understandings of "image" by Arius and Asterius, and by Eusebius of Caesarea and his successor Acacius.

93. Ath., *syn.* 22.1–25.5, includes the four statements from the council of 341.

94. On the development of this tradition, see Morales, *La théologie*, 242–67. However, Morales is also careful to point out that Athanasius did not openly profess a one-*hypostasis* theology and that he tried to maintain overall a middle ground between the two theological extremes of the Eusebians and Marcellus of Ancyra.

95. See below for further discussion. However, it was clear from the *Tomus* that the Eustathians also had to justify their position as not Sabellian.

sons because of merit, [but] not because they are one *hypostasis*, which is the case of the Father and the Son.[96]

However, we will examine below how for Athanasius the *Tomus ad Antiochenos* made the pronouncements of the Council of Sardica unnecessary and potentially counterproductive.[97]

The 340s and 350s witnessed more councils and more attempts to generate theological agreement, though at the same time Athanasius's polemic and construction of the Arians was becoming sharper.[98] The theology of Marcellus continued to trouble the majority of eastern theologians, as did that of his onetime disciple Photinus.[99] Several other theological trajectories emerged that further reflected the fluidity and complexities in understanding the nature of the relationship between Father and Son. Aetius and his disciple Eunomius publicly articulated their beliefs that emphasized that the Son was "unlike" the Father in *ousia*.[100] In hostile polemical writings, including those of Epiphanius, proponents of this theology are characterized as Anomoians. However in current scholarship, the appellation Heteroousians has found greater traction to replace the older terms "Neo-Arians" and Eunomians. Notably, a small council gathered at Sirmium in 357 determined that the use of *ousia* language was unscriptural, ambiguous, and unsuitable for describing the relationship between Father and Son and therefore condemned its use. This view represented a step further in rebuffing *ousia* language that began in 351 with the Council of Sirmium, whose creed was derived from the fourth

96. Thdt., *h.e.* 2.8.39, 43. On the Council of Sardica and its problematic documents, see M. Tetz, "Ante omnia de sancta fide et de integritate veritatis. Glaubensfragen auf der Synode von Serdika (342)," *ZNW* 76 (1985): 243–69; Hanson, *Search*, 293–306; S. Hall, "The Creed of Sardica," StPatr 19 (1989): 173–84; Barnes, *Athanasius*, 71–81; Martin, *Athanase*, 422–36; Lienhard, "Settlement," 113–14; Morales, *La théologie*, 259–65.

97. Cf. Ath., *tom.* 5.1.

98. See Hanson, *Search*, 274–314; Ayres, *Nicaea*, 105–30. For the 350s, see Hanson, *Search*, 315–47; Ayres, *Nicaea*, 133–66.

99. Cf. Ath., *syn.* 26.5–6, 27.1. For extended discussions on the theology of Marcellus of Ancyra, see Lienhard, Marcellum; K. Seibt, *Die Theologie des Markell von Ankyra*, Arbeiten zur Kirchengeschichte 59 (Berlin: Walter de Gruyter, 1994), and for his historical context and career, see Parvis, *Marcellus*. See also Simonetti, *La crisi*, 66–71; Hanson, *Search*, 217–35; Ayres, *Nicaea*, 62–69; Morales, *La théologie*, 248–57. *Pan.* 72.2.1–3.5 preserves a copy of Marcellus's statement of faith in his letter to Julius of Rome, written in 341.

100. Cf. Philost., *h.e.* 3.15–16, 4.12 (on Aetius), and 6.1–4 (on Eunomius), and throughout; Thdt., *h.e.*, 2.27.1–29.12. See Kopecek, *History*; Hanson, *Search*, 598–636; R. Lim, *Public Disputation, Power, and Social Order in Late Antiquity*, Transformation of the Classical Heritage 23 (Berkeley: University of California Press, 1995), 109–48; throughout Vaggione, *Eunomius*; Ayres, *Nicaea*, 144–49; Behr, *Nicene*, 267–82.

creed of the Council of Antioch of 341.[101] The "manifesto" of 357 typified a
growing resistance to any use of *ousia* and its derivatives and marked the development of a theological perspective broadly described as Homoian, which
was affirmed at the Council of Ariminum and in a follow-up meeting in Nike
in 359.[102] Acacius of Caesarea was one voice of the Homoian position. He
tried (unsuccessfully) to ratify his view at the Council of Seleucia in 359, but
he eventually found support with Constantius, and his position was sustained
at a synod in Constantinople in 360.[103] This period also saw the consolidation
of the Homoiousians as an identifiable group led by Basil of Ancyra, who
preferred to view the Son as "like the Father in *ousia*."[104] In essence, this theological vector represented a via media element in the ongoing disputes, and
we will now consider how even Athanasius attempted to form an alliance
with its proponents.[105]

The Synod of Alexandria (362) and the *Tomus ad Antiochenos*

Following Julian's decree that allowed bishops exiled under Constantius to retain their posts, Athanasius returned to Alexandria on 21 February 362. The
long-term effect of this recall was significant for the ongoing theological and
ecclesiastical disputes of the fourth century.[106] The Homoians' privileged position at the end of Constantius's reign ended when Julian openly embraced paganism. Furthermore, the other theological and ecclesiastical "parties," the Homoiousian, Heteroousian, and pro-Nicene, all had an opportunity to reconsider
and reset their positions and priorities.[107] The prospects brightened for some
party realignment and coalition building, which was not viable under the prior
regime, and perhaps through a sense of desperation or a carefully considered
strategy, Athanasius opened the door to forming a theological alliance.

---

101. Ath., *syn.* 8.3–7; Hilar., *Syn.* 11; Socr., *h.e.* 2.29.1–30.49; Soz., *h.e.* 4.6.1–16. This was the so-called "Blasphemy of Sirmium." See Hanson, *Search*, 343–47; Ayres, *Nicaea*, 137–38; Morales, *La théologie*, 272–76.
102. Cf. Ath., *syn.* 28.1–30.10, for subsequent creedal statements, and 33.1–40.5, for direct criticisms of their rejection of *ousia* language in its varied forms. See throughout, Brennecke, *Studien*; Williams, *Ambrose*, especially for developments in the Latin west. See Hanson, *Search*, 557–97, who shows how diverse a category this was; also Barnes, *Athanasius*, 144–51.
103. Cf. Ath., *syn.* 28.1–12, for Acacius's statement made at Seleucia. See Brennecke, *Studien*, 46–47. For more on Acacius, see chapter 5.
104. Hanson, *Search*, 348–57; Morales, *La théologie*, 31–39, 276–83.
105. Cf. *Pan.* 73.2.1–22.8. Epiphanius condemned these "heretics" as "Semi-Arians," thus establishing a rhetorically driven characterization of their theology.
106. See Karmann, *Meletius*, 150–56, for a succinct summary of Julian's rise to power and his policies to-ward Christians. See also Bowersock, *Julian*; Brennecke, *Studien*, 96–107.
107. Cf. Socr., *h.e.* 3.25.1–21; Soz., *h.e.* 6.4.1–11.

Shortly after his arrival in Alexandria, Athanasius convened a small but significant council that included Eusebius of Vercelli, who was serving the remainder of his exile in Egypt after his stay in Palestine.[108] This council produced a paper known as the *Tomus ad Antiochenos*.[109] The document was addressed to a five-bishop commission that was involved in the tense situation in Antioch following the deposition of bishop Meletius in 361.[110] In chapter 5, we will discuss the ensuing schism that eventually saw no less than four rival claimants to the episcopal see.[111] For our purposes here, it is enough to note that among the disputants, three could be considered orthodox: Meletius, Paulinus, and Vitalius, although Vitalius ultimately did not pass Epiphanius's standard for orthodoxy. The *Tomus* addressed a number of important theological issues, including an explicit affirmation of the divinity of the Holy Spirit, which must have resulted from Athanasius's prior concerns and correspondence with his friend and colleague Serapion, bishop of Thmuis: "And the Holy Spirit is not a creature, nor a stranger, but is proper and indivisible from the *ousia* of the Son

---

108. Cf. Ruf., *Hist.* 10.28–31; Socr., *h.e.* 3.5.1, 3.7.1–24; Soz., *h.e.* 5.12.1–5; Thdt., *h.e.* 3.4.2–5.2. Lucifer of Cagliari was also among the recalled exiles but did not attend the council and sent two deacons to represent him while he made his way toward Antioch. Eusebius might have been influential in calling this synod; see Karmann, *Meletius*, 186, n. 103.
    On the council in Alexandria, see Simonetti, *La crisi*, 358–72; Hanson, *Search*, 639–53; M. Simonetti, "Il concilio di Alessandria del 362 e l'origine della formula trinitaria," *Augustinianum* 30 (1990): 353–60; Barnes, *Athanasius*, 155–58; Martin, *Athanase*, 542–65; Simonetti, "Eusebio," 162–65; A. Camplani, "Atanasio e Eusebio tra Alessandria e Antiochia (362–363): Osservazioni sul *Tomus ad Antiochenos*, l'*Epistula catholica* e due fogli copti (edizione di *Pap. Berol.* 11948)," in Covolo, Uglione, and Vian, *Eusebio di Vercelli*, 191–246; Morales, *La théologie*, 358–65; Karmann, *Meletius*, 168–92.

109. There is debate about a second letter from the council, the so-called "Catholic Letter" (*epistula catholica*). See M. Tetz, "Ein enzyklisches Schreiben der Synode von Alexandrien (362)," *ZNW* 79 (1988): 262–81; Barnes, *Athanasius*, 156; Ayres, *Nicaea*, 173–74; Behr, *Nicene*, 96–97, although its attribution to Athanasius as such is also disputed; see Fitschen, *Serapion von Thmuis*, 79–84; Camplani, "Atanasio," 219–26; Morales, *La théologie*, 365–74; Karmann, *Meletius*, 182–84.
    On the *Tomus*, see Simonetti, *La crisi*, 367–68; M. Tetz, "Über nikäische Orthodoxie. Der sog. *Tomus ad Antiochenos* des Athanasios von Alexandrien," *ZNW* 66, nos. 3–4 (1975): 194–222; Camplani, "Atanasio"; Ayres, *Nicaea*, 173–75; Behr, *Nicene*, 95–100; P. Gemeinhardt, "Der Tomus ad Antiochenos (362) und die Vielfalt orthodoxer Theologien im 4. Jahrhundert," *ZKG* 117, nos. 2–3 (2006): 169–96; Morales, *La théologie*, 375–89; Karmann, *Meletius*, 193–305.

110. Ath., *tom.*, 1.1–2.3, although Antioch itself is not specifically named. On the deposition, see Brennecke, *Studien*, 66–81; A. Martin, "Les témoignages d'Épiphane de Salamine et de Théodoret à propos de Mélèce d'Antioch," in *Epiphania: Études orientales, grecques et latines offertes à Aline Pourkier*, ed. E. Oudot and F. Poli (Paris: De Boccard, 2008), 147–71; Karmann, *Meletius*, 135–49. On the senders and recipients, see Martin, *Athanase*, 558–65; Camplani, "Atanasio," 199–201; Karmann, *Meletius*, 194, 197–200, especially n. 120. On Athanasius's essential authorship of this document, see Karmann, *Meletius*, 194–95.

111. On the schism, see F. Cavallera, *Le schisme d'Antioche (IVe–Ve siècle)* (Paris: Picard, 1905); K. Spoerl, "The Schism at Antioch since Cavallera," in Barnes and Williams, *Arianism after Arius*, 101–26; Karmann, *Meletius*. For Epiphanius's role in the schism, see Dechow, *Dogma*, 57–91.

and of the Father."[112] The *Tomus* is also a realization of the process Athanasius initiated in the previous decade to make the Council of Nicaea and its creed all-sufficient over all other synods and councils and their resulting creeds.[113]

Also important was the flexible tone of the *Tomus* regarding the question of *hypostaseis*. Modern scholars have understood the document's apparent willingness, albeit qualified, to accept an interpretation of three *hypostaseis* to be an important concession by Athanasius and an attempt at rapprochement and alliance, in particular with the supporters of Meletius in Antioch.[114] In the context of the Antioch situation, the *Tomus*, through an imagined dialogue, addresses two groups and two theological perspectives to find a way to reconcile and join them together.[115] On one side are the one-*hypostasis* theologians led by Paulinus and broadly identified as the Eustathians, named after Eustathius, the former bishop of Antioch who was revered by pro-Nicenes for being an early defender of orthodoxy. On the other side are the three-*hypostaseis* partisans who were collectively the Meletians. The former group apparently held grave concerns that the theology of three-*hypostaseis* necessarily implied either three subsistences that were "alienated and estranged, alien in essence from one another," which was branded as Arian, or "three beginnings and three gods."[116] Furthermore, when the Meletians were asked to explain what they believed the

112. Ath., *tom.* 5.4. On the pneumatology of the *Tomus*, see Morales, *La théologie*, 138–41.

113. Ath., *tom.* 5.1–3. See Karmann, *Meletius*, 212–19. Hence Athanasius's opposition to the pronouncements of the Council of Sardica, even though they seemingly supported his theological perspective. On the problem of Sardica, see Tetz, "Über nikäische," 203–5; Morales, *La théologie*, 259–65.

114. Athanasius had earlier signaled room for compromise with the Homoiousians in Ath., *syn.* 41.1–8: "Toward those accepting all other things prescribed in Nicaea, but only doubting the *homoousion*, it is not necessary to treat them as enemies. For we also do not resist them as Ario-maniacs or as those fighting against the Father, but as brothers toward brothers we converse, having the same mind with us, but hesitating only with regard to the phrase" (41.1). Consider also the tone regarding the clergy in Ath., *epistula ad Rufinianum*. See Kopecek, *History*, 226–27; Barnes, *Athanasius*, 133; Martin, *Athanase*, 529–33; Ayres, *Nicaea*, 171–77; Behr, *Nicene*, 95–100; Morales, *La théologie*, 313–55.

Not all scholars see the *Tomus* as a conciliatory document; see Hanson, *Search*, 639–53; T. Elliot, "Was the *Tomus ad Antiochenos* a Pacific Document?," *JEH* 58, no. 1 (2007): 1–8. On the difficulty of assessing exactly what the Meletian Trinitarian theology was, see Karmann, *Meletius*, 283–305. He makes a convincing argument that the Meletians were the earliest community to initiate the theological developments that ultimately became the phrase "Neo-Nicene" confession.

115. For discussions of the two groups and their theological positions, see Morales, *La théologie*, 380–83; Karmann, *Meletius*, 220–51. Simonetti does not see the three-*hypostaseis* group as specific Meletians present at the council, but rather as an Athanasian construction of a more general anti-Arian view prevalent in the east. "Il concilio." This is also echoed by Camplani, "Atanasio," 204–16, and both in opposition to L. Abramowski, "Trinitarische und christologische Hypostasenformeln," *Theologie und Philosophie* 54 (1979): 38–49, especially 41–47. Camplani suggests that the contents of the theological dialogue constituted a *procedimento prolettico*, a model for the accord to be established in Antioch. "Atanasio," 215.

116. Ath., *tom.* 5.3. See Karmann, *Meletius*, 225–28.

three-*hypostaseis* meant, they replied that "because they believed in one Holy Trinity, not a trinity in name alone, but truly existing and subsisting, both Father, truly existing (ὄντα) and subsisting (ὑφεστῶτα), and Son, truly existing as a substance (ἐνούσιαν ὄντα) and subsisting (ὑφεστῶτα), and Holy Spirit, truly subsisting (ὑφεστηκός) and existing (ὑπάρχον)."[117] Without using the term *hypostasis* in their reply, the Meletians expressed their firm belief in a Triune Godhead with truly existing, subsistent persons, which was a definite foil to any Modalist theology and clearly an expression with echoes of the Origenist tradition.[118] However, they also emphasized that their confession did not imply "three gods or three beginnings," which was certainly one way to interpret a theology of three-*hypostaseis*. Rather, they articulated their orthodox credentials by acknowledging "one Trinity, one divinity and one beginning, and Son, *homoousios* with the Father, as the fathers said, and the Holy Spirit, neither a creature nor an alien, but proper to and indivisible from the *ousia* of the Son and the Father."[119] This reply seems to be an overture toward rapprochement between separated but potentially joinable communities.

The attention of the synod at Antioch then turned to the Eustathians, who confessed a one-*hypostasis* theology and ensured that their beliefs did not lead to modalism.[120] The Eustathians firmly rejected any Sabellian interpretation of their theology (thus implicitly that of Marcellus of Ancyra).[121] They affirmed that like Athanasius, they understood and used *hypostasis* and *ousia* interchangeably, which necessitated for them one *hypostasis*, since Father and Son were *homoousios*, of one *ousia* and of one nature.[122] The unnamed Eustathians then expressed their agreement with the interpretation of three-*hypostaseis* given by the unnamed Meletians, and together they anathematized "Arius as an

---

117. Ath., *tom.* 5.4. Karmann notes that the Meletians here refrained from using *hypostasis*, and that the slight variance in descriptive participles for each of the divine persons is intended to simultaneously express the identity and difference of the three *hypostaseis* but within the confession of a belief in the Trinity. *Meletius*, 229, n. 180. See also Morales, *La théologie*, 67–77, on Athanasius's careful use of derivations of the verb ὑφίστημι.

118. Karmann also insightfully observes a parallel in this expression with Ath., *ep. Serap.* 1.28.1–4. *Meletius*, 230.

119. Ath., *tom.* 5.4. See Karmann, *Meletius*, 220–36, on the three-*hypostaseis* position.

120. Ath., *tom.* 6.1. See Karmann, *Meletius*, 236–41, on the one-*hypostasis* position.

121. This is the Miahypostatic tradition explored by Lienhard, *Marcellum*. Earlier, especially during his foray into the West (second exile), Athanasius was aligned with Marcellus, but Athanasius began to distance himself from Marcellus, although never condemning him outright.

122. Ath., *tom.* 6.2. Cf. Ath., *ep. Afr.* 5. The charge of Sabellianism in fourth-century disputes was a cipher for the theology of Marcellus. See Hanson, *Search*, 444–45, for how the synonymous use of these terms ultimately prevented Athanasius from clearly articulating the distinct subsistence of the divine persons. See also Karmann, *Meletius*, 240–41, n. 201, on how *ousia*, *hypostasis*, and *physis* were essentially synonymous for Athanasius, and 246–48, n. 209, for how the synod in 362 and the *Tomus* did not explicitly differentiate the terms *ousia* and *hypostasis*. See also Morales, *La théologie*, 43–45.

adversary of Christ, Sabellius and Paul of Samosata as impious men, Valentinus and Basilides as aliens from the truth, and Mani as an inventor of wicked things."[123] Therefore, the (imagined) statements and clarifications made by the disputing parties in Antioch implied that all actually shared the same orthodox Nicene faith, thus laying the foundation for rapprochement.[124]

The *Tomus* also included reflections on the Incarnation of Christ, which were driven largely by concerns stemming from disputes over "Arian" theology. But the statements also foreshadowed the debate that would ensue in the 370s, necessitated in particular by the teachings of Apollinarius of Laodicea.[125] We will examine this subject in the next chapter.

The cynical scholar might view Athanasius's theological accommodation at this point in his career as entirely self-serving, politically motivated, and driven purely by difficult personal circumstances. However, one could also see Athanasius moving toward adaptation, compromise, and openness. Whatever the reasons, the theological and ecclesiastical implications of the Synod of Alexandria of 362 and the *Tomus* were not just relevant to Alexandria and Antioch but had potential to impact the entire Mediterranean world.[126] The *Tomus* clearly shows that Athanasius already had an established relationship with Paulinus, the leader of the "Eustathian" party in Antioch. So the synod's efforts to broker a union with Meletius and his supporters signaled a shift in attitude and perhaps a relaxing of doctrinal rigidity so characteristic of Athanasius's rhetoric.[127] Athanasius must have recognized the potential strength in numbers. We are left to wonder which came first, his theological openness that could lead to ecclesiastical union or his desire for rapprochement and hence theological softening. Unfortunately, the events after the synod, initiated by Lucifer of Cagliari's improper ordination of Paulinus as bishop of Antioch in 362, precluded the work

---

123. Ath., *tom.* 6.3. Tetz suggests the anathemas against Sabellius and Paul addressed theological suspicions associated with the Eustathians, while the other three addressed the community of Meletius. "Über nikäische," 201–2.

124. Karmann, *Meletius*, 241–51.

125. Athanasius also dealt with disputes over the Incarnation toward the end of his career in his *epistula ad Adelphium, epistula ad Epictetum,* and *epistula ad Maximum*. Martin, however, argues that the Christology of the *Tomus* was not informed by issues relating to Apollinarius but instead to Arius (*Athanase*, 552–57), while Simonetti suggests that it was ("Eusebio," 164–65). For a thorough discussion, see Karmann, *Meletius*, 251–70, who agrees with Martin that this section of the *Tomus* was by and large not informed by questions over Apollinarian theology. See also Tetz, "Über nikäische," 208–17; Camplani, "Atanasio," 208–10.

126. See Gemeinhardt, "Tomus," 184–96, for a concise summation of theological developments after the Alexandrian synod.

127. *tom.* 3.1. On Eustathius, see Hanson, *Search*, 208–17. On the relationship between Athanasius and Paulinus, see Karmann, *Meletius*, 206, n. 138.

of the five-bishop commission.[128] Unable to come to an agreement with Meletius, Athanasius was compelled to support his old ally Paulinus in his claim to
legitimacy.[129] Not surprisingly, Epiphanius also ultimately sided with Paulinus
and thus his hero Athanasius. But as we will now consider, Epiphanius also
exhibited theological flexibility, as he shifted from a one-*hypostasis* to three-
hypostaseis confession and in this way transitioned to becoming his own man.

The Evolution of Epiphanius

We began this chapter with the Christians in Syedra who turned with a plea for
help to Epiphanius for his orthodox theological expertise. His response was the
Ancoratus, a lengthy letter composed in late 373 or early 374. We know that
Epiphanius dictated his thoughts to his scribe Anatolios; and perhaps due to
haste and the petitioners' desperation, we might forgive the bishop for the
work's seeming lack of organization.[130] However, examining the text with a better understanding of the context in which it was written reveals a broad pattern
of sections that address specific theological themes and issues, such that the
Ancoratus functions in a way as a series of catechetical lessons.[131] Epiphanius
covered several essential subjects, including the correlative divinity of the Son
and the Holy Spirit, the full Incarnation, the real and bodily resurrection, and
the errors of paganism. The *Ancoratus* is also significant because it is the earliest
written testimony of Epiphanius's theology, and it serves as an important point
of comparison with the views he expressed soon after in the *Panarion*. An important observation here is that Epiphanius, known by modern scholarship as
a rigid and intolerant dogmatist, demonstrated an evolution in his theology
and an apparent willingness to adapt and change his positions.

---

128. Cf. Ruf., *Hist.* 10.28–31; Socr., *h.e.* 3.6.1–3, 3.9.1–10; Soz., *h.e.* 5.12.2–13.5; Thdt., *h.e.* 3.4.1–5.4. On
the ordination of Paulinus, see Karmann, *Meletius*, 306–21. On the failure to unify, see Martin, *Athanase*, 578–90.

129. Cf. Bas., *ep.* 89.2; Ruf., *Hist.* 10.31. Athanasius made clear his final break with the Meletians in his
letter to Jovian and "hardened" his theological position, as reflected in the *ep. Afr.* See Martin, *Athanase*, 619–25; Morales, *La théologie*, 392–94, 396–405. For the chronological sequence, see J. Zachhuber, "The Antiochene Synod of AD 363 and the Beginnings of Neo-Nicenism," *ZAC* 4.1 (2000):
83–101, especially 93–98; von Stockhausen, "Antiochien"; Karmann, *Meletius*, 412–25. However,
Zachhuber dismisses the ordination of Paulinus as a factor in the break between Athanasius and
Meletius, while Karmann, *Meletius*, 415–16, especially n. 160, offers a persuasive counterargument.

130. *Anc.* 119.16, closed with a greeting from Anatolios.

131. On the idea of the *Ancoratus* as catechesis, see C. Riggi, "Formule di fede in Sant'Epifanio di Salamina," *Salesianum* 41 (1979): 309–21; idem, "La catéchèse adaptée aux temps chez Epiphane," StPatr
17, no. 1 (1982): 160–68, and explored more recently by Y. Kim, "The Pastoral Care of Epiphanius of
Cyprus," StPatr 67 (2013): 247–55.

Epiphanius's One-*Hypostasis-Homoousios* Theology

In the *Ancoratus*, Epiphanius maintained a one-*hypostasis* theology, which he believed was inextricably connected to the confession of *homoousios*: "To say *homoousios* is the bond of the faith. For if you say *homoousios*, you destroy the power of Sabellius. For whenever [you say] *homoousios*, it is indicative of one *hypostasis*, but it indicates that the Father is enhypostatic, the Son is enhypostatic, and the Holy Spirit is enhypostatic."[132] It appears that in the *Ancoratus*, *homoousios* and one *hypostasis* are theological concepts that necessarily implied each other. The singular being of God, comprising Father, Son, and Holy Spirit, exists as one *hypostasis*, one subsistent, unified being, and thus each is described as "enhypostatic," which seems to signify that each individual divine person together necessarily comprises one hypostatic God.[133] Furthermore, the term *homoousios* functions to underscore the unity of the one Godhead and the existence of only one divinity, especially as an argument against the charge of polytheism: "And whenever someone says *homoousios*, he does not indicate that he is alien from the same divinity, but that the Son is God from God, and the Holy Spirit is God, of the same divinity, not three gods. . . . We do not say gods; [we say] God the Father, God the Son, God the Holy Spirit, and not gods. For there is no polytheism in God. But through the three names, the one divinity of the Father, Son, and Holy Spirit <is indicated>."[134] Epiphanius concluded with the following: "But the Trinity, is always of the same *ousia*, neither another *ousia* besides the divinity, nor another divinity besides the *ousia*, but the same divinity and from the same divinity, the Son and the Holy Spirit."[135] Epiphanius, like his pro-Nicene colleagues, was playing a tricky game of theological wordplay and logic to negotiate one Godhead with three distinct, individual persons, while at the same time trying to avoid the two extremes of Sabellian modalism and polytheism.[136]

Epiphanius was also careful to maintain that there is no gradation of divine

---

132. *Anc.* 6.4–5. See Kösters, *Trinitätslehre*, 135–43; Kim, *Saint Epiphanius*, 67, n. 9. The term "enhypostatic," was ἐνυπόστατος/ν, which I have only transliterated. While the term had a much more complicated history in the next century, Epiphanius used it eighteen times in the *Ancoratus*, and he seemed to use it as a term to indicate the real, essential existence of the persons of the Trinity, in particular as a foil to Sabellian modalism (in opposition to ἀνυπόστατος/ν). But at the same time, by its use Epiphanius maintained a one-*hypostasis* theology and avoided plural *hypostaseis*.

133. *Anc.* 7.3, captured well this idea: "The Trinity is not a coalescence, not something different in itself, from its very own unity, but exists in a *hypostasis* of perfection. Perfect is the Father; perfect is the Son; perfect is the Holy Spirit: Father and Son and Holy Spirit."

134. *Anc.* 6.6, 6.8.

135. *Anc.* 6.10.

136. Cf. Ath., *ep. Serap.* 1.28.1–4. See Morales, *La théologie*, 503–4, for how Athanasius did the same.

substance within the Godhead, which is ensured by the term *homoousios*: "Again would that we not hesitate to indicate, as steadfast and certain in God, our hope, that nothing has been changed in the Father and Son and Holy Spirit, but that the holy Trinity is of the same rank and *homoousios*."[137] Later in the *Ancoratus*, Epiphanius attributed the following statement to an unnamed opponent: "And the heretic says: 'clearly I believe that the Father is Father, and the Son is Son, and the Holy Spirit is Holy Spirit, and I confess three *hypostaseis* in one *ousia*. I say not another *ousia* besides the divinity, not another divinity besides the *ousia*."[138] However, Epiphanius then explained that such a statement shows that the anonymous heretic believes the *ousia* of "divinity" is a broader category of substance that differs qualitatively from that of humanity, and that this divine *ousia* itself could be differentiated or gradated among Father, Son, and Holy Spirit: "But he [the heretic] holds to such a opinion that has been hidden, that from us [humans] having compared the divinity, he says in himself, that as I have a human body and soul and spirit, thus also does the divinity."[139] Epiphanius continued to explain that one must confess that Father, Son, and Holy Spirit are of the same *ousia*, with no hierarchy or differentiation of *ousiai* conceived or allowed, and a singular *hypostasis*: "But in accordance with himself did he [the Holy Spirit] assume the likeness [of a dove], in accordance with himself being a *hypostasis*, not a different kind besides that of the Father and Son, but of the same *ousia*, *hypostasis* from the same *hypostasis* of the Father and of the Son and of the Holy Spirit."[140]

The Three Persons

One of the ongoing challenges faced by theologians like Athanasius and Epiphanius was how to identify and distinguish the three divine persons without succumbing to modalism or polytheism. Eventually, pro-Nicene Christians turned to *hypostasis*—differentiated from *ousia*—as the term of choice to resolve this problem. But in the middle decades of the fourth century, plural *hypostaseis* still belonged within the purview of the non-Nicenes.[141] Epiphanius's solution

---

137. *Anc.* 64.2.
138. *Anc.* 81.4. See Kösters, *Trinitätslehre*, 300–303, on the difficulty of translating these "heretical" expressions, as well as the challenge of determining where the heretic stopped speaking and where Epiphanius expressed his own view (here I follow Kösters's suggestions).
139. *Anc.* 81.5.
140. *Anc.* 81.7. For a thorough discussion of this section, including the possible candidates for the unnamed heretic, see Kösters, *Trinitätslehre*, 298–308. Athanasius was also emphatic about the one common, unique divine nature of Father, Son, and Spirit; see Morales, *La théologie*, 478–80.
141. Hanson examines the challenges Athanasius faced in this regard. *Search*, 444–45. See Zachhuber,

in the *Ancoratus* was recourse to a "Theology of the Name."[142] He understood "Father" and "Son" (and "Holy Spirit") as unique names applicable only to the divine persons and not in the generic or human sense of the words "father" and "son." Furthermore, one simply could not conceive of the Father without conceiving of the Son: "But however much your thinking rises to comprehend and to believe in the Son, at the same time it thinks also about the Father. For the name is significant. For whenever you call on the Son, saying 'Son,' you think about the Father: for from the Son, the Father is thought about. And whenever you call on the Father, you indicate the Son: for the Father is called such in all ways from the Son."[143] In fact, Epiphanius apparently introduced a hapax legomenon to articulate further his concept:[144]

Each of the names is mononymic, not having a duplication.[145] For the Father is Father and has no parallel, nor is he joined together with another father, so that there may not be two gods. (2) And <the?> Son is only-begotten, true God from true God, not having the name of Father, nor being alien from the Father, but

"Basil." Another alternative problematic term was *prosōpon*, used by Marcellus of Ancyra and Apollinarius of Laodicea, not in the Sabellian sense of ἀνυπόστατα πρόσωπα, but referring to the plurality of persons within the Godhead. On Marcellus, see Lienhard, *Marcellum*, and for Apollinarius, throughout K. Spoerl, "A Study of the 'Κατὰ Μέρος Πίστις' by Apollinarius of Laodicea," PhD diss., University of Toronto, Toronto, 1991; P. Gemeinhardt, "Apollinaris of Laodicea: A Neglected Link of Trinitarian Theology between East and West?," *ZAC* 10 (2006): 286–301.

142. This is the appellation given and explored by Kösters, *Trinitätslehre*, 121–62. Basil of Caesarea developed sophisticated arguments about the Trinity via recourse to names, especially in opposition to Heteroousian theology. See M. DelCogliano, *Basil of Caesarea's Anti-Eunomian Theory of Names: Christian Theology and Late-Antique Philosophy in the Fourth-Century Trinitarian Controversy*, Supplements to Vigiliae Christianae 103 (Leiden: Brill, 2010).

143. *Anc.* 5.9. Cf. Ath., *Dion.* 17, 22.

144. The translation, annotation, and discussion drawn from Kim, *Saint Epiphanius*, 72–74. Epiphanius followed the Christian interpretive tradition of viewing Father and Son as Aristotelian relatives, in which the "Father's existence entails the Son's existence, and if the Father is eternal, so too is the Son eternal" (DelCogliano, *Theory*, 228). The belief in the co-eternality of the Son supported by name relativity would have put Epiphanius in continuity with the thinking of Origen and other Alexandrians, although certainly with modifications. See DelCogliano, *Theory*, 228–34.

The recourse to name theory is generally in response to "Neo-Arian" or Heteroousian arguments. See Kim, *Saint Epiphanius*, 71, n. 14.

145. "mononymic" = μονώνυμον, meaning something like "singular, unique name." Kösters argues that it was essentially an invented term (see Lampe, 884, with the only attestation in Epiphanius). *Trinitätslehre*, 152–53. Furthermore, Kösters suggests that Epiphanius eventually replaced this term with a developed theology of the term *hypostasis*. *Trinitätslehre*, 157. Epiphanius's use of the concept "mononymic" bears interesting parallels with Basil's understanding of proper names, which do not disclose actual substance, but distinguishing marks of the named. See Bas., *adversus Eunomium libri tres* 2.5, 28–29; DelCogliano, *Theory*, 190–96. Ath., *ep. Serap.* 1.16.1–7, articulated specific ideas about the distinction of each person of the Trinity in terms of relations (also without recourse to the term *hypostasis*; see Morales, *La théologie*, 217–31). DelCogliano also demonstrates Athanasius's view that all God's names refer to the divine substance, although they do not reveal exactly what God's substance is. *Theory*, 127–33.

existing as Son of the Father. He is only-begotten, that the "Son" may be mononymic; and he is God from God, in order that Father and Son may be called one God. (3) And the Holy Spirit is one-of-a-kind, not having the name of "Son," nor having the naming of "Father," but thus called Holy Spirit, not alien from the Father. (4) For the Only-begotten himself says: "The Spirit of the Father" (Matt 10:20), and "the one proceeding from the Father" (John 15:26), and "he will receive from what is mine" (John 16:14), in order that he may not be believed alien from the Father and of the Son, but of the same *ousia*, the same divinity, divine Spirit, the "Spirit of truth" (John 14:17, 15:26, 16:13), the "Spirit of God" (Rom 8:9), the Spirit "Paraclete" (John 14:16, 14:26, 15:26, 16:7), called mononymically,[146] not having a parallel, not being equated with some other spirit, not called by the name of the Son or being named with the naming of the Father, in order that the mononymic names may not be homonymic, (5) except "God" in the Father, "God" in the Son, in the Holy Spirit, "of God" (Rom 8:9) and "God."[147] (6) For the "Spirit of God" (Rom 8:9), both Spirit of the Father and Spirit of the Son, is not according to some synthesis, as soul and body are in us, but is in the midst of Father and Son, from the Father and the Son, third in naming. (7) "Going forth," for it says, "baptize in the name of Father, Son, and Holy Spirit" (Matt 28:19). And if the Father baptizes in his own name, in the name of God, and the perfect seal in the name of God has been sealed in us, and Christ baptizes in his own name, in the name of God, and the perfect seal in the name of God has been sealed in us, who would dare to wage war against his own soul, saying that the Spirit is alien from the divinity? (8) For if <we seal> in the name of the Father and in the name of the Son and in the name of the Holy Spirit, there is one seal of the Trinity. Therefore, there is one power of the divinity in the Trinity. And if God is the One, but the others are created and not God, by what reason are the two connected to the one in the seal of perfection? (9) Then at any rate, we were sealed in a royal name, the one of the Father (and the others are not royal), but we further have been enslaved to principles and created things. And, the name alone of the Father was not able to save, but the one

---

146. This is the adverb μονωνύμως.

147. Cf. Ath., *ep. Serap.* 1.4.1–4, for a discussion of how in Scripture, references to the Holy Spirit are always qualified to designate him from all other spirits. For a discussion of the philosophical background of the term "homonymic" (ὁμώνυμα), see Kösters *Trinitätslehre*, 154–56. Bas., *Eun.* 2.1–5, 9–10, argued against Eunomius's idea that different names necessarily meant different substances. Thus according to the Heteroousian view, "Father" and "Son," because they are different names, would mean they are of different *ousiai*. See DelCogliano, *Theory*, 38–42, for the implications in Eunomius's thinking of homonymic and synonymic names as applied to simple beings.

who created added to himself two other elements, according to the thinking of those who blaspheme, in order that his divinity might add other powers and might be able to save the one sealed by him, and that the man created by him might gain deliverance through the forgiveness of sins.[148]

In this particular passage, Epiphanius was working through his defense of the divinity of the Holy Spirit, which ultimately for him is inextricably linked to the divinity of the Son. But we can see how he made recourse to the notion that the unique identifying names of "Son" and "Holy Spirit," along with "Father," each constitutes a unique, distinct divine reality (in other words, each is "enhypostatic"), and yet all three necessarily comprise what it means to be God. Thus for Epiphanius, the appeal to the baptismal formula of Matthew 28:19 is an important scriptural proof of the divinity of all three persons, lest baptism be in the name of the divine Father and two creatures.[149]

In the *Ancoratus*, Epiphanius exhibited a degree of theological perspicuity and innovation that generally has been overlooked by modern scholarship. Clearly, he was aware of the theological and philosophical problems that came with the doctrine of the Trinity, and he offered his own attempt to bring clarity and applicable vocabulary to the ongoing debates. However, by the time Epiphanius composed the *Panarion*, his language had shifted away from the concept of "monҩymic" (although names in and of themselves were still important to him), and he accepted the plural use of *hypostasis* to distinguish the divine persons: "But the Trinity was always Trinity, and the Trinity never receives an addition, being one divinity, one sovereignty, one glory, but enumerated as Trinity, Father, Son, and Holy Spirit. And not as one thing called with three names, but the names are perfect, the *hypostaseis* perfect."[150] This statement even includes an echo of Epiphanius's name theory. But in the short time between composing the *Ancoratus* and the *Panarion*, Epiphanius transitioned to the theological formula that would become the well-known orthodox confession.[151] In Basil of Caesarea's response to a letter from Epiphanius, Basil praised Epiphanius for making the transition to a three-*hypostaseis* theology: "And this has exceedingly encouraged my soul, the addition (well and accurately) of pre-

---

148. *Anc.* 8.1–9. Cf. Ath., *Ar.* 2.41, on the necessity of naming the Son in baptism, although without the equal emphasis on the Spirit. See Kösters, *Trinitätslehre*, 151–63, for a thorough discussion.
149. Cf. Ath., *decr.* 31.1–4. See also *Pan.* 62.4.4.
150. *Pan.* 62.3.6. This is in his refutation of Sabellius. Compare also his usage in *Pan.* 25.6.4, 72.1.3, 73.34.2, 78.24.5 (all plural).
151. Cf. Bas., *ep.* 125.1.

cision on your part to remaining theological matters: that it is necessary to confess three *hypostaseis*."[152] Thus Epiphanius, who is so often viewed as a rigid dogmatist in modern scholarship, exhibited a willingness to change his view. Perhaps it is not too far out of the question also to suggest that Athanasius made Epiphanius's shift possible through the accommodation of the *Tomus ad Antiochenos*. Although Athanasius did not openly embrace the three *hypostaseis*, his apparent willingness to accept an interpretation of this theology enabled his admirers and successors, like Epiphanius, to make the transition.[153]

Epiphanius followed Athanasius theologically and rhetorically on a wide range of issues, and we have only briefly discussed two points of intersection. There were many other lines of continuity between the two bishops. For example, when subordinating theologians used scriptural passages that seem to imply that the Son was "created" or "became" (for example, Prov 8:22; Acts 2:36; Heb 3:2–3), Epiphanius reiterated Athanasius's emphatic point that one must distinguish between biblical verses that apply to the eternal Word and those that apply to the Incarnate Christ.[154] Indeed the approach of both theologians to biblical exegesis remains an area of further exploration for modern scholars.[155] However, Epiphanius also found occasion to disagree with Athanasius, in particular on the issue of calculating Easter Sunday and the corresponding fast days leading up to it. So Epiphanius did not merely plagiarize or assume wholesale the thought of Athanasius.[156] The Egyptians had a long-standing custom of calculating the Sunday date of Easter vis-à-vis the vernal equinox, a practice that allegedly was affirmed as the norm at the Council of Nicaea, whereas the churches of Cyprus and Epiphanius continued to follow the tradition prevalent in Antioch of celebrating Easter on the Sunday after the Jewish Passover.[157]

---

152. Bas., *ep.* 258.3.

153. See Gemeinhardt, "Tomus," 191–96, for a discussion on how the Athanasian accommodation impacted the theological debate of the early 370s leading up to the Council of Constantinople.

154. Cf. Ath., *Ar.* 1.53–2.14, 2.44–56; *Anc.* 41.1–44.6; *Pan.* 69.12.1–4, 69.14.1–3, 69.20.1–21.6, 69.37.1–39.5, 69.42.1–11.

155. See Stefaniw, "Straight Reading," for initial theoretical reflections on Epiphanius's mode of exegesis.

156. See Holl, "Bruchstück," but criticized by Lebon, "Sur quelques"; Kösters, *Trinitätslehre*, 36–37, esp. n. 123. On Athanasius's view, see Ath., *syn.* 5.1–3.

157. Eus., *h.e.* 7.20.1, on Egypt's custom; see also Martin, *Athanase*, 156–70. For the dispute over Easter in the second century, see Eus., *h.e.* 5.23.1–25.1. Cf. Socr., *h.e.* 5.22.1–82. For Cyprus and Epiphanius, see Dechow, *Dogma*, 53–55. Epiphanius was vehemently opposed to the practice of the Quartodecimans, whom he refuted in *Pan.* 50. See A. Mosshammer, *The Easter Computus and the Origins of the Christian Era* (Oxford: Oxford University Press, 2008), especially 40–55, 109–246, for a comprehensive study of early Christian calendric calculations and systems.

Athanasius may have written to Epiphanius asking him to cease pressing the issue.[158]

Therefore, while Epiphanius rhetorically situated himself in theological and ecclesiastical continuity with Athanasius, and others viewed him in this respect as well, Epiphanius also innovated, developed, and contributed in own way to pro-Nicene theology. This chapter has argued that Epiphanius was more than a "second-rate theologian standing in the tradition of Athanasius."[159] While Epiphanius was certainly a self-imagined successor to Athanasius, he also made important transitions as a thinker, a theologian, and as we will see in the chapters to come, a bishop who became his own man and who is worthy of deeper appreciation in modern scholarship.

---

158. This is the opinion of Holl, "Bruchstück," 187. The fragment is found in the *Chronicon Paschale*, in Dindorf's edition, page 9, lines 7–20. However, D. Brakke identifies a different Epiphanius (of Skhedia) as the recipient of the letter and suggests that fragment belongs to a dispute internal to Egypt. "Athanasius' *Epistula ad Epiphanium* and Liturgical Reform in Alexandria," StPatr 36 (2001): 482–88.

159. Hanson, *Search*, 658.

PART THREE

Ascents

CHAPTER 5

Arbiter of Orthodoxy

Epiphanius the Bishop

The Way to Cyprus

The circumstances in which Epiphanius became bishop of Cyprus are not entirely clear and are a matter of some disagreement. Perhaps the most perplexing
question is simply, why Cyprus? After all, Epiphanius was a native of Palestine,
educated in Egypt, and was seemingly well situated as the leader of his monastic community in the district of Eleutheropolis. Furthermore, he was born in a
village less than a day's travel from the heart of a reimagined Christian geography, the new *umbilicus* of the world.[1] In addition to Jerusalem, other cities in
Palestine could have used his ecclesiastical leadership. Epiphanius spent up-
wards of three decades in Palestine leading his monastery, yet his career trajectory ultimately took him to the copper island. It is not enough to say that only
chance circumstances displaced him from his homeland. Ecclesiastical and
theological reasons may have made a long-term stay and leadership in Palestine
unpalatable or perhaps even impossible for him.[2]

The problem with Jerusalem and its environs was its theological uncertainty.[3] Granted, the entire Greek East was in a state of constant theological flux

---

1. Cyr. H., *catech.* 13.28.
2. See Perrone, "Rejoice," 161–66, for a succinct summary of theological and political issues in the
   fourth century.
3. It seems that certain Christians in Palestine were sympathetic to Arius and his supporters, although
   Bishop Macarius, who ruled from 312 to 335, was decidedly "orthodox." See Williams, *Arius*, 48–59.

during the mid-fourth century, and shifting loyalties were as much about disagreements over the nature of the Father and the Son as they were about inter-
and intraecclesiastical political rivalries. Nevertheless, disputes within specific
Palestinian locales gradually led to the formation of ecclesiastical factions that
would affect Epiphanius's future there. He had in his homeland three cities in
which he could have risen through the *cursus honorum* of the ecclesiastical hierarchy. He was ordained by Eutychius, so it would seem logical that he would
look to Eleutheropolis.[4] He could have been drawn to Caesarea, although its
strong association with the legacy of Origen, as well as the leadership of Eusebius and his successor Acacius, would have presented formidable obstacles. Finally, Epiphanius could have had an eye toward Jerusalem, the newly imagined
Holy City, but it too would not be the right fit for his particular convictions. We
will "tour" these cities in order to observe why each ultimately could not be
Epiphanius's final destination and why a bishopric in Palestine was not to be for
him. We will then consider the circumstances in which he became lead bishop
of Cyprus. Finally, we will conclude with an analysis of an autobiographical account that elucidates how Epiphanius conceived and executed his role as bishop
and what he understood was the basis of his authority.

Eleutheropolis

In his important biographical entry on Epiphanius, Pierre Nautin suggests that
the questionable theology of Eutychius was one of the root causes of Epiphanius's departure to Cyprus.[5] Epiphanius wrote the following about Eutychius in
his entry against the "Semi-Arians": "For Eutychius of Eleutheropolis, such as
he acquired from the blessed Maximus of Jerusalem, the confessor bishop, the
faith of clear orthodoxy, because of enmity toward Cyril, joined with the faction
of Acacius. On the one hand, up to that time he was orthodox, but dissembled
on account of his [episcopal] throne, as did many others of Palestine."[6] Exactly
when Eutychius was ordained bishop of Eleutheropolis is unclear. But Epiphanius implied that, although he had received the faith from the orthodox Maximus, Eutychius owed his position (either the acquisition or maintenance

---

4. Jer., *Adu. Io. Hier.* 4.
5. Nautin, "Épiphane," c. 619. Nautin, however, changed his view later in P. Nautin, "Eutychius, évêque
    d'Éleuthéropolis en Palestine," in *DHGE* 16 (Paris: Letouzey et Ané 1967), c. 95–97.
6. *Pan.* 73.23.7. The exact reason for the enmity between Eutychius and Cyril is unclear, although it
    may have had to do with Cyril's attempts to assert his authority over Jerusalem and its environs.

thereof) to the support and patronage of Acacius of Caesarea.[7] Eutychius was present at the Council of Seleucia in 359 and was one of the signatories of the profession of faith proposed by Acacius that rejected the use of *homoousios* or *homoiousios*, indeed *ousia* language altogether, on the grounds that none of the terms had a scriptural basis.[8] However, Acacius and his allies constituted a minority of the bishops in attendance, and they were opposed by the Homoiousians, among whom was the deposed Cyril of Jerusalem.[9] The inability of the attendees to agree on anything led one of the presiders, Leonas, to dissolve the council.[10] The majority bishops then met on their own, in particular to resolve the dispute over the deposition of Cyril, and they summoned Acacius and his faction to meet with them.[11] Acacius refused to participate, so the Homoiousians unseated him and several of his Homoian allies, including Eutychius.[12]

A few years later in autumn 363, after the death of Julian and the accession of Jovian, a group of eastern bishops met at a synod in Antioch chaired by Meletius and assented to a qualified interpretation of the Nicene faith, and Eutychius was among the signatories.[13] Thus Eutychius appeared the pragmatist and perhaps a bit of an opportunist, and his party alignment was the result of changing political circumstances and perhaps self-preservation. Still, based on the evidence presented by Epiphanius, it seems Eutychius was counted among the heretics and was thus worthy of condemnation. Hence Nautin suggests that the broken relationship between the two men was a factor in Epiphanius's departure. The picture, however, is not so clear, and Nautin recognizes as much when he later revised his position, arguing instead that Epiphanius maintained

7. *Pan.* 73.23.4–7, 73.27.7. Nautin suggests that Maximus, before his death in 348, made Eutychius bishop of Eleutheropolis. "Eutychius," c. 96–97. Cf. Jer., *Chronicon* a. 348, on the death of Maximus.

8. *Pan.* 73.26.2, with Eutychius's signature. On the proceedings of the council, cf. Ath., *syn.* 12.1–7; Socr., *h.e.* 2.40.1–34. On the council and the events prior to and after it, see Brennecke, *Studien*, 40–56; Barnes, *Athanasius*, 146–48; Martin, *Athanase*, 518–27; Ayres, *Nicaea*, 157–66; Behr, *Nicene*, 83–95.

9. See below on Cyril's deposition.

10. Socr., *h.e.* 2.40.35–36.

11. Socr., *h.e.* 2.40.38–42.

12. Socr., *h.e.* 2.40.45.

13. Socr., *h.e.* 3.25.1–21; Soz., *h.e.* 6.4.1–11. Socrates insinuated that the Acacians believed Meletius had the favor of the emperor. See Karmann, *Meletius*, 341–54. On the theological and political significance of the council, see Simonetti, *La crisi*, 371–77; Brennecke, *Studien*, 173–78; Zachhuber, "Synod," 83–101; Morales, *La théologie*, 390–91; Martin, "Les témoinages," 159–69; Karmann, *Meletius*, 358–411. On Athanasius's apparently positive initial view of the synod, see von Stockhausen, "Antiochien," 94–95. Zachhuber doubts (and Brennecke outright rejects) Acacius's presence at the council and dismisses Socrates's insinuation of opportunism. But the presence of Eutychius and his firm connection to Acacius might indicate otherwise, and Karmann suggests that Acacius had lost influence among the Homoians, who were firmly led by Eudoxius and Euzoius. *Meletius*, 401.

a good relationship with Eutychius and even viewed him in his heart of hearts as orthodox.[14] At the end of the entry on the Semi-Arians, Epiphanius presented brief descriptions of the different factions, and he also described the disputed situation following the death of Acacius sometime after the Council of Lampsacus in 364.[15] Both Cyril of Jerusalem and Eutychius attempted to appoint successors to the see of Caesarea.[16] Cyril tried at first to consecrate Philumen, who was replaced by Eutychius's choice, Cyril the Elder (not Cyril of Jerusalem), who was then replaced by the former Cyril's choice, Gelasius, his nephew.[17] The final "winner" of the contest was a certain Euzoius.[18] Epiphanius then noted the names of Gemellinus, Philip of Scythopolis, and Athanasius of Scythopolis, all of whom he accused of teaching Arianism and persecuting orthodox believers.[19] Nautin sees an underlying implication here that as Euzoius had been the successor of Acacius in Caesarea, so Gemellinus was the direct successor of Eutychius in Eleutheropolis.[20] Furthermore, Nautin suggests the possibility of a direct connection between Epiphanius's departure from Palestine and the consecration of Gemellinus, namely that Epiphanius had put his own name forward as a candidate for the bishopric and upon failure was compelled to leave Palestine as a result of the ill will generated by such a contest.[21]

While Nautin's theory is certainly plausible, it must remain in the realm of speculation. Perhaps a better explanation for why Epiphanius did not climb the ladder of ecclesiastical leadership in Palestine is that because of his firm convictions about what constituted orthodoxy, he refused to play the game of dissembling and shifting alliances necessary to garner the patronage that could lead to higher office. In so many fourth-century cases of clerical succession, personal connections and factional support were pivotal in ascending the ecclesiastical *cursus honorum*. But for Epiphanius, there was no place where an orthodox and a heretic could commingle. Therefore, although Epiphanius was ordained "presbyter of the monastery" and "was listened to by Eutychius," his potential patron's choice to ally himself with the likes of Acacius of Caesarea to secure his

---

14. See Nautin, "Eutychius," c. 97; Kösters, *Trinitätslehre*, 32–33.
15. Cf. Socr., *h.e.* 4.4.1–6; Soz., *h.e.* 6.7.1–10, although Sozomen mistakenly placed Homoousians there. On Lampsacus, see Brennecke, *Studien*, 206–9; Barnes, *Athanasius*, 161; Martin, *Athanase* 591; Karmann, *Meletius*, 453–54.
16. *Pan.* 73.37.1–38.4.
17. *Pan.* 73.37.5.
18. Cf. Jer., *Vir. ill.* 113. Not to be confused with Euzoius, the bishop of Antioch.
19. *Pan.* 73.37.6.
20. Nautin, "Eutychius," c. 97.
21. Nautin, "Eutychius," c. 97.

own position ultimately closed the door to the church in Eleutheropolis for Epiphanius.[22]

Caesarea

Another city where Epiphanius could have been a candidate to serve in the ecclesiastical hierarchy was Caesarea, the provincial capital. For many Christians, Caesarea was doubly significant because of the legacy of Origen, who made the city into an intellectual center with a formidable library.[23] We have partly considered the roots of Epiphanius's eventual vehement opposition to Origen's speculative theology, which for Epiphanius was intimately connected to his understanding of the ascetic life and the necessary realities of the physical and resurrection bodies. When he composed the *Ancoratus* in 373/4, Epiphanius revealed his avowedly anti-Origenist convictions on paper, and in *Panarion* 64, as systematically as Epiphanius was capable, he expressed his unbending hostility toward what he understood to be Origen's theology.[24] But in occasional moments in his corpus of writings, Epiphanius surprisingly reflected on the positive contributions of Origen to the Christian faith, despite his ultimately heretical demise. For example in his later treatise on weights and measures, Epiphanius briefly discussed Origen's compilation of the *Hexapla*, an edition of the Hebrew Scriptures that placed six different versions of the text in parallel columns.[25] Epiphanius described Origen as follows:

> And so, in the *Hexapla* or *Octapla*, which is by him, where the two columns of Hebrew and the six translations he set in order side by side, he has contributed to the lovers of the good a great increment of knowledge. If only in his discourses he had not erred, bringing harm to the world and to himself, when he taught wrongly the things pertaining to the faith and explained most of the Scriptures in an unorthodox manner.[26]

---

22. Jer., *Adu. Io. Hier.* 4.
23. See Irshai, "Oblivion," 130–36, for a description of Origen's relationship to Caesarea. On the library, see Barnes, *Constantine*, 81–105; A. Carriker, *The Library of Eusebius of Caesarea*, Supplements to Vigiliae Christianae 67 (Leiden: Brill, 2003); A. Grafton and M. Williams, *Christianity and the Transformation of the Book: Origen, Eusebius, and the Library of Caesarea* (Cambridge, MA: Harvard University Press, 2006).
24. See throughout Dechow, *Dogma*.
25. Epiphanius also mentioned the *Hexapla* in *Pan.* 64.3.5–8. Cf. Eus., *h.e.* 6.16.1–4.
26. Epiph., *mens.* 7. Translation from J. Dean, *Epiphanius' Treatise on Weights and Measures: The Syriac Version*, Studies in Ancient Oriental Civilization, 11 (Chicago: University of Chicago Press, 1935), 22.

Even in the *Panarion*, Epiphanius (begrudgingly) recognized Origen's abilities:

> And as much as has been said by him in his sermons and through his prefaces on ethics and both the nature of living and other things, being reputed moderately, he often explained things cleverly. But as much as he laid down opinions in dogmatic matters, concerning both the faith and greater speculations, he has been found to be the most harmful of all, of those who came before and after him, except for the shameless conduct in the heresies.[27]

Epiphanius knew that Origen was a scholar. Perhaps Epiphanius wondered if the Alexandrian would have been a formidable contributor to the Christian faith, had it not been for his incredible (secular) learning. Nevertheless, Epiphanius's imagined world had no room to accommodate both orthodox Christianity and *paideia*. So Epiphanius castigated and rejected Origen: "Thus you, Origen, your mind blinded by your Greek education, have vomited poison for your followers and have become noxious food for them, by which you yourself have been harmed while harming more people."[28]

Surely Epiphanius was aware of the connection between Origen and the city of Caesarea. He acknowledged that Origen had lived for a time in Palestine, although he also asserted that afterward Origen spent some twenty-eight years in Tyre.[29] But if Christian Caesarea was not tainted by its affiliation with Origen, it certainly was by its prominent fourth-century leaders. One of the direct beneficiaries of Origen's Caesarean legacy was of course Eusebius, who along with his mentor Pamphilus became one of the Alexandrian's vocal defenders.[30] Origen was a pivotal figure in Eusebius's *Ecclesiastical History*, appearing as an archetype Christian philosopher.[31] Without a doubt, Eusebius was deeply influenced by Origen's legacy, as almost all fourth-century eastern theologians were. Eusebius was also one of the foremost figures in the "Arian" or "Eusebian" con-

---

27. *Pan.* 64.5.6–7.
28. *Pan.* 64.72.9.
29. *Pan.* 64.2.6, 64.3.3.
30. See E. Junod, "L'Apologie pour Origène de Pamphile et la naissance de l'origénisme," StPatr 26, no. 2 (1993): 267–86; R. Amacker and E. Junod, *Pamphile et Eusèbe de Césarée: Apologie pour Origène suivi de Rufin d'Aquilée: Sur la falsification des livres d'Origène*, SC 464, 465 (Paris: Les Éditions du Cerf, 2002).
31. Much of Book 6 is dedicated to life and work of Origen. See Barnes, *Constantine*, 99–101; P. Cox (Miller), *Biography in Late Antiquity: A Quest for the Holy Man*, Transformation of the Classical Heritage 5 (Berkeley: University of California Press, 1983), especially 69–101; Kannengiesser, "Eusebius."

spiracy that dogged Athanasius and orthodox Christians, of which Epiphanius was surely aware when he wrote about the confrontation between the confessor Potamon and Eusebius at the Council of Tyre.[32] But similarly to Origen, Epiphanius must have occasionally felt a sense of regret over Eusebius and what he could have been had he adhered to the correct faith. As we considered in chapter 2, Eusebius's literary influence, although obscured, was present through much of the *Panarion*. Although earlier scholars have criticized Eusebius for being unoriginal, much should be said in praise of his innovation as a *Christian* writer.[33] Nevertheless, like Origen, Eusebius was tainted with heresy, and Epiphanius's black-and-white world could not allow the great ecclesiastical historian to walk alongside the likes of Athanasius. Of course Eusebius was also bishop of Caesarea, beginning circa 313 until his death on 30 May 339. This meant that for Epiphanius's earliest years of monastic foundation in his homeland, Eusebius was the metropolitan bishop, and undoubtedly for Epiphanius, Caesarea would have belonged to heretics and was off-limits for any orthodox Christian.

Acacius, who succeeded Eusebius as bishop, would have left no doubt in Epiphanius's mind that Caesarea was infected with the disease of heresy.[34] Acacius was much involved in the theological disputes of the ensuing decades, and he was a regular participant in councils and synods that Epiphanius would have deemed heretical.[35] Acacius eventually was counted among the Homoians in hostile sources, but his theological and political commitments were apparently ambiguous and relative to the political circumstances in which he found himself.[36] He was not a theological extremist but a pragmatist and perhaps an opportunist. Epiphanius, however, portrayed him in a somewhat different light. In his entry against the "Semi-Arians," Epiphanius described the fractious nature of all of the Arian heretics in great detail, and their inability to agree with one another testified to how far they were from the singular truth that Epiphanius defended.[37] Acacius appears in this entry as a factional leader, although

---

32. *Pan.* 68.8.4.
33. See L. Perrone, "Eusebius of Caesarea as a Christian Writer," in *Caesarea*, eds. Raban and Holum, 515–30.
34. Socr., *h.e.* 2.4.1. For the "heretical" actions of Acacius and his connection to Eusebius, see Ath., *syn.* 12.1–13.5. On Acacius's other activities, see Philost., *h.e.* 5.1. For broader examination of the impact of Acacius, see Simonetti, *La crisi*, 326–41; Kopecek, *History*, 414–18.
35. For examples, see Hanson, *Search*, 284–306, 362–80, 579–83.
36. Cf. Ath., *syn.* 38.1.
37. *Pan.* 73.23.2–4. Epiphanius identified the Homoiousians (Basil of Ancyra, George of Laodicea, Silvanus of Tarsus), the Homoians (Eudoxius of Constantinople, George of Alexandria, Euzoius of An-

Epiphanius emphasized that all of the different divisions ultimately constituted the same Arian heresy:

> For although being the same [as the others], Acacius and those with him nei-
> ther confessed the *homoousion* nor [that the Son is] a creature, <like> one of the
> created things. On the one hand, because of the times, they remained silent
> about <the word> "creature"; on the other hand, they were all just like the Ari-
> ans. But in that time they concealed [the fact] that they believed no different
> than these, because with them had been mixed in those who were orthodox in
> nature, but who were as hypocrites and practiced hypocrisy, fearing the right
> hand of the emperor.[38]

This passage is particularly telling because it directly precedes the quotation above regarding Eutychius, and it seems to insinuate that despite being ortho-dox, Eutychius mingled among Acacius's party for the sake of maintaining his position; whereas Acacius himself was an "Arian," even if because of his circum-stances he was reticent about what he specifically believed.[39] Nevertheless, Epiphanius made it abundantly clear in what follows that Acacius was Ho-moian, and he included the creedal statement that was authored by Acacius himself and presented at the highly contentious Council of Seleucia.[40] Un-doubtedly, Acacius was to be counted among the heretics, and Caesarea would not have been any sort of place where Epiphanius could have found patronage or an opportunity to serve within the ecclesiastical hierarchy.

Jerusalem

From the vantage point of his monastery in Eleutheropolis, Epiphanius wit-nessed the transformation of Jerusalem into a Christian capital. He must have felt the intense historical and theological draw of the city with the very stones upon which Jesus walked and the locales where the most important moments

---

tioch), and a third faction that included Acacius, Meletius, and Eutychius.

38. *Pan.* 73.23.6.

39. Another historical problem associated with Acacius was his participation in the Synod of Antioch in 363, under the leadership of Meletius, which promulgated a return to the Nicene Creed in light of the continued threat of Heteroousian theology. See Brennecke, *Studien*, 173–78; Zachhuber, "Synod," 84–86; Martin, "Les témoinages," 164, n. 107.

40. *Pan.* 73.23.8–27.9. Cf. Ath., *syn.* 29.1–9; Socr., *h.e.* 2.40.1–48. See Brennecke, *Studien*, 40–56; Barnes, *Athanasius*, 144–51. Athanasius also condemned Acacius as an opportunist heretic; see Martin, *Athanase*, 581–82.

in the history of salvation had occurred. During the early years of Epiphanius's life and time in Egypt, Jerusalem was shepherded by the reliable and orthodox bishop, Macarius, who was known to be an anti-Arian stalwart.[41] At least according to later tradition, Macarius was also involved in helping the empress Helena recover and verify the true Cross. Thus he was a catalyst in the transformation of Jerusalem in the early fourth century.[42] Macarius was succeeded by Maximus, who was handpicked by the elder bishop and enjoyed the full confidence of his predecessor in his orthodoxy.[43] Although Maximus had participated in the condemnation of Athanasius at the Council of Tyre, he claimed that he had been deceived and later made amends by joining the bishops in support of Athanasius at the Council of Sardica.[44] Furthermore, Maximus convened a synod in Jerusalem of bishops from Syria and Palestine that publicly acknowledged communion with Athanasius and affirmed him as the rightful bishop of Alexandria.[45] It seems that during this early period of transformation, Jerusalem was in good hands, and perhaps Epiphanius imagined that he might some day join the ranks of the clergy in the holy city.

This hope would have changed, however, with the accession of Cyril to the bishopric of Jerusalem.[46] The fifth-century ecclesiastical historians Socrates and Sozomen gave the distinct view that Maximus was ejected from his see by a conspiracy perpetrated by Acacius of Caesarea and Patrophilus of Scythopolis, two figures with whom we have become quite familiar, and that they installed Cyril as replacement.[47] Both Jerome and Rufinus offered the impression that Cyril's orthodoxy was questionable at best, and because both were personally familiar with the Holy Land, their reports merit consideration.[48] Cyril's own

---

41. Cf. Arius, *epistula ad Eusebium Nicomediensem* 3 (*Urk.* 1).
42. Soz., *h.e.* 2.1.1–10. See Drijvers, *Cyril*, 36, 172–73.
43. Soz., *h.e.* 2.20.1-1-3.
44. Socr., *h.e.* 2.8.3. On Sardica, cf. Ath., *apol. sec.* 51.3.
45. Ath., *apol sec.* 57.1–7; *h. Ar.* 25.1–5; Socr., *h.e.* 2.24.1–3. This happened on Athanasius's return journey from his second exile, and Maximus's convocation was likely against ecclesiastical custom, because he was not the metropolitan. This action was thus doubly provocative. See Martin, *Athanase*, 445–46.
46. For examinations of Cyril's life and career, see Hanson, *Search*, 398–413; Ayres, *Nicaea*, 153–57; Drijvers, *Cyril*, 31–63; P. Van Nuffelen, "The Career of Cyril of Jerusalem (*c.* 348–87): A Reassessment," *JTS* 58, no. 1 (2007): 134–46. The date of his ordination as bishop of Jerusalem is contested between 348 and 351.
47. Socr., *h.e.* 2.38.2; Soz., *h.e.* 4.20.1. Their report is countered by Thdt., *h.e.* 2.26.6. See Drijvers, *Cyril*, 32–34.
48. Jer., *Chron.* a. 348, described the circumstances in which Cyril became bishop: "Although he had been ordained as presbyter by Maximus, after his death thus was the bishopric promised to him [Cyril] by Acacius, bishop of Caesarea, and certain other Arians, if he would repudiate his ordination by Maximus." On the questionable orthodoxy of Cyril, cf. Ruf., *h.e.* 10.24; Socr., *h.e.* 5.8.3; Soz., *h.e.* 7.7.3.

writings, however, do not reveal any particular "Arian" doctrine or leanings, and perhaps it remains best to suggest that Cyril, apparently like other churchmen in Palestine, was a moderate and a pragmatist.[49] His initial "alliance" with Acacius secured the patronage Cyril needed to ascend to an episcopal see. But once his position was secured, Cyril immediately pursued his own agenda, in particular the elevation of the status of Jerusalem and thus his own office.[50] This led to increasing tensions and ultimately a falling out with Acacius, whose own bishopric was threatened by Jerusalem's growing prominence. Cyril claimed "metropolitan rights . . . as leader of an apostolic see," which was a direct challenge to the authority of Acacius, and both men accused each other of harboring heretical doctrines: Acacius for "declaring the doctrines of Arius" and Cyril for "being in accord with those who teach the *homoousion* of the Son with the Father."[51] Sozomen reported that Cyril had maintained the *homoousion*, but he also indicated that he received Basil of Ancyra and George of Laodicea into communion, even though both had been deposed at the behest of Acacius.[52] These bishops were of course well known Homoiousian leaders.

Acacius was finally able to depose Cyril in 357 on the pretext that Cyril misappropriated church property by selling a robe and sacred vessels to secure funds to purchase food during a famine in Palestine.[53] Based on a comment by Jerome in his *Chronicle*, some scholars maintain that a certain Eutychius replaced Cyril temporarily as bishop of Jerusalem.[54] However, the identity of this Eutychius is disputed and may have been the result of some confusion on the part of Jerome.[55] Furthermore, if Epiphanius's documentation of the Council of Seleucia is accurate, our familiar Eutychius subscribed as bishop of Eleutheropolis in 359. Thus, if Eutychius was installed as Cyril's replacement sometime in 357, by 359 he was no longer bishop of Jerusalem.[56] According to Socrates, Cyril

---

49. On his "Arianism," see Lyman, "Mapping," 48–53; Drijvers, *Cyril*, 181–86.
50. Rubin, "Caesarea," 561, on Cyril's opportunism. See Drijvers, *Cyril*, 153–76, on the attempt to promote Jerusalem.
51. Soz., *h.e.* 4.25.2.
52. Soz., *h.e.* 4.24.1–25.1.
53. Soz., *h.e.* 4.25.3–4; Thdt., *h.e.* 2.26.7. Soz., *h.e.* 4.25.1–2, also mentioned that Cyril was deposed for having admitted Eustathius and Elpidius into communion, which further fueled Acacius's animosity.
54. Jer., *Chron.* a. 348: "Maximus, bishop of Jerusalem after Macarius, died. After him the Arians fell upon the church, that is, Cyril, Eutychius, again Cyril, Irenaeus, Cyril for a third time, Hilarius, Cyril for a fourth time." Drijvers, *Cyril*, 39, assumes Eutychius of Eleutheropolis.
55. Nautin, "Eutychius," c. 96–97.
56. *Pan.* 73.26.2. Van Nuffelen demonstrates the impossibility (contra Drijvers) that the Eutychius who became bishop of Jerusalem was the same as the Eutychius of Eleutheropolis, so this Eutychius must be an otherwise unknown figure. "Career," 137.

evaded any occasion to answer the charges directly for two years, despite repeated summons by Acacius, and Cyril made the rather unusual move of appealing to the emperor and the secular judicial system to plead his case and request a new conciliar hearing.[57] During this time, Cyril solidified his connections with Homoiousian partisans, especially Silvanus of Tarsus, and at Seleucia Cyril was counted among the followers of Basil of Ancyra, Eustathius of Sebaste, and Silvanus.[58] The council was his opportunity to make a defense. But as we examined above, Acacius refused to participate in the proceedings, and the Homoiousian majority deposed Cyril's opponents en masse, including Eutychius and Eudoxius of Antioch, and presumably reinstalled Cyril to the see of Jerusalem.[59] Acacius then went to Constantinople to appeal directly to Constantius, and there he told the emperor of Cyril's alleged financial improprieties.[60] Cyril was deposed once again through the machinations of Acacius at the Council of Constantinople in 360 and replaced by the Acacian Irenaeus (Herrenius in Socrates), according to Jerome's reckoning.[61] In the ensuing years, Cyril was able to retain his see, only to be deposed again under Valens, and then finally restored.[62]

With all of the troubles and ecclesiastical challenges Cyril faced, one would think Epiphanius would have admired him for the trials he suffered at the hands of Acacius and his heretic allies. However, when Epiphanius composed the *Panarion*, he had no doubt Cyril belonged "together with Basil of Galatia, Anianus, ordained bishop in Antioch, and George of Laodicea."[63] In other words, Cyril was counted among the "Semi-Arian" heretics according to Epiphanius's standard of orthodoxy. Thus Cyril's position and authority as bishop of Jerusalem would have been illegitimate, and any opportunities Epiphanius might have had to serve in the ecclesiastical hierarchy would not have been acceptable.

57. Socr., *h.e.* 2.40.38–42; Soz., *h.e.* 4.22.2–4, 4.22.25, although Socrates was unaware of the charges leveled against Cyril, and Sozomen was dependent on Socrates.
58. Thdt., *h.e.* 2.26.9.
59. Socr., *h.e.* 2.40.43–45.
60. Thdt., *h.e.* 2.27.1–2.
61. Jer., *Chron.* a. 348; Socr., *h.e.* 2.14.17. Cf. Socr., *h.e.* 2.42.1–6, Soz., *h.e.* 4.25.1–5 on the council at Constantinople. See Van Nuffelen, "Career," 137–38, on Irenaeus and Herrenius as the same individual.
62. For these years, see Drijvers, *Cyril*, 42–44, but more importantly Van Nuffelen, "Career," 137–41, on the confusion in later sources over Cyril's deposition(s).
63. *Pan.* 73.27.8.

Finally, to Cyprus

In the provincial system of the Roman Empire, Cyprus was not among the most important locales.[64] In fact in the high imperial period, it was little more than a minor administrative post and not the envy of any Roman politician aspiring toward bigger and better things.[65] Overall, the island experienced little in the way of political or military turmoil, with the exception of the Jewish revolt beginning in 115, which allegedly resulted in the deaths of 240,000 people.[66] The fate of Cyprus, however, changed dramatically with the provincial reorganization under Diocletian in 293.[67] He placed the island under the supervision of a *consularis* (or *praeses*), who answered to the *praefectus praetorio Orientis*. This later changed to oversight by the *vicarius Orientis*, and later still, around 331, to the *comes Orientis* who resided in Antioch.[68] In the fourth century (332/3 and 342), the city of Salamis and the island in general were ravaged by earthquakes and tidal waves, but in 346, Salamis was refounded as Constantia in honor of Constantius, who helped to rebuild it, and it regained its status as the capital of the island.[69]

As a Christian locale, Cyprus boasted an Apostolic pedigree by claiming

64. For Cyprus in the Roman period, see T. Mitford, "Roman Cyprus," *Aufstieg und Niedergang der römischen Welt* 7, no. 2 (1980): 1285–384, but more comprehensive is D. Potter, "Η ΚΥΠΡΟΣ ΕΠΑΡΧΙΑ ΤΗΣ ΡΩΜΑΪΚΗΣ ΑΥΤΟΚΡΑΤΟΡΙΑΣ," in *ΙΣΤΟΡΙΑ ΤΗΣ ΚΥΠΡΟΥ, ΤΟΜΟΣ Β': ΑΡΧΑΙΑ ΚΥΠΡΟΣ, ΜΕΡΟΣ Β'* (ΛΕΥΚΩΣΙΑ: ΙΔΡΥΜΑ ΑΡΧΙΕΠΙΣΚΟΠΟΥ ΜΑΚΑΡΙΟΥ Γ', 2000), 763–864 (I am grateful to the author for a copy of the English version); T. Davis, "Earthquakes and the Crises of Faith: Social Transformation in Late Antique Cyprus," *Buried History* 46 (2010): 5–16. For reflections on Cyprus in late antiquity, see G. Bowersock, "The International Role of Late Antique Cyprus," 14th Annual Lecture on the History and Archaeology of Cyprus (Nicosia: Bank of Cyprus Cultural Foundation, 2000).
For more general histories of (ancient) Cyprus, see G. Hill, *A History of Cyprus*, 4 vols. (Cambridge: Cambridge University Press, 1940–72); V. Karageorghis, *Cyprus: From the Stone Age to the Romans* (London: Thames and Hudson, 1982); C. Kyrris, *History of Cyprus* (Nicosia: Nicocles Publishing House, 1985).
65. Potter, "ΚΥΠΡΟΣ," 788–96, with some exceptions.
66. Dio Cassius, 75.32, but greatly exaggerated. See Potter, "ΚΥΠΡΟΣ," 809–11.
67. On Cyprus in the late Roman and Byzantine periods, see the excellent collection of articles in Bryer and Georghallides, *"The Sweet Land of Cyprus,"* especially E. Chrysos, "Cyprus in Early Byzantine Times," 3–14, and A. Papageorghiou, "Cities and Countryside at the End of Antiquity and the Beginning of the Middle Ages in Cyprus," 27–51. Also see D. Metcalf, *Byzantine Cyprus 491–1191*, Cyprus Research Centre Texts and Studies in the History of Cyprus 62 (Nicosia: Cyprus Research Centre, 2009).
68. Hill, *History*, Vol. 1, 230; Mitford, "Cyprus," 1375–80; Potter, "ΚΥΠΡΟΣ," 856.
69. On the natural disasters, see Mitford, "Cyprus," 1376, and for the cultural effect of these quakes, see Davis, "Earthquakes." For ancient Salamis, see V. Karageorghis, *Salamis in Cyprus: Homeric, Hellenistic, and Roman* (London: Thames and Hudson, 1969). The struggle for primacy between Salamis and Paphos extended back into the Hellenistic period, and Salamis lost its standing as capital sometime in the second century BCE; see Mitford, "Cyprus," 1309.

Barnabas as a native son and being an important stop during Paul's first missionary journey.[70] According to Acts 13:4–12, the pair landed at Salamis and crossed the island to Paphos, the seat of the proconsul Sergius Paulus, whom they converted to the faith.[71] Cyprus and its denizens sporadically appear in other parts of the Acts narrative, for example Mnason, a Cypriot Christian living in Jerusalem (Acts 21:16). Cyprus was apparently where persecuted Christians fled following the martyrdom of Stephen, although some, including Cypriots and men from Cyrene, went to Antioch to preach the Gospel (Acts 11:19–20). Barnabas in particular played an important role in affirming the island's apostolic claim. The apocryphal fifth-century *Acts of Barnabas* provides a first-person account of a traveling companion of Barnabas named John, who described Barnabas's journeys and efforts to convert the Cypriot people. Thus the island could claim as old a connection to earliest Christianity as any other place in the Roman world. Little, however, is known about Christian Cyprus in the subsequent two centuries.

As mentioned, Diocletian's restructuring of the empire in the late third century had a direct effect on Cyprus, as the island was subordinated to Antioch, and around 367, the division of the diocese of Oriens into two, Oriens and Aegyptus, put the island even more firmly in the sphere of Antioch.[72] Although the imperial reorganization of the provinces did not necessarily translate directly into the ecclesiastical hierarchy, the augmented status of Antioch and its close proximity to Cyprus must have influenced the political situation.[73] The gravitational pull eastward would become important in Cypriot Christianity in the fourth and well into the fifth centuries, and the looming presence of Antioch and its theological and ecclesiastical turmoil throughout much of the

---

70. Cyprus also later (c. eighth century) claimed that Lazarus came to the island and was first bishop of the city of Citium (modern Larnaca) and that he died his "second" death there.

    For Christian Cyprus, see Hill, *History,* Vol. *1,* 247–51; Mitford, "Cyprus," 1381–83; B. Englezakis, *Studies on the History of the Church of Cyprus, 4th–20th Centuries,* trans. N. Russell (Brookfield, VT: Variorum, 1995). Quite dated now is J. Hackett, *A History of the Orthodox Church of Cyprus. From the Coming of the Apostles Paul and Barnabas to the Commencement of the British Occupation (A.D. 45–A.D. 1878). Together with Some Account of the Latin and Other Churches Existing on the Island* (Oxford: Methuen, 1901).

71. See T. Davis, "Saint Paul on Cyprus: The Transformation of an Apostle," in *Do Historical Matters Matter to Faith: A Critical Appraisal of Modern and Postmodern Approaches to Scripture,* ed. J. Hoffmeier and D. Magary (Wheaton: Crossway, 2012), 405–23.

72. Dechow, *Dogma,* 47. As Davis, "Earthquakes," 9–10, points out, the refounding of Salamis as Constantia and its elevation as metropolitan rendered it even closer under the watchful eye of Antioch and the praetorian prefect.

73. Dechow, *Dogma,* 47, suggests that Cyprus remained ecclesiastically independent despite its political subservience to Antioch.

154 EPIPHANIUS OF CYPRUS

fourth century may in part have influenced the selection of the decidedly pro-Nicene Epiphanius as head bishop of the island.

Theologically speaking, Cyprus went against the prevailing winds of the Greek East. Rather than adhering to the majority theological views espoused by the "Eusebians," the bishops of Cyprus were decidedly "Athanasian," even before the accession of Epiphanius. While little can be concluded based on participation alone, we are certain that at least two Cypriot bishops were present at the Council of Nicaea, Cyril of Paphos and Gelasius of Salamis, and that Spyridon, bishop of Tremithus and famed miracle-worker, was also there, although he was not among the signatories.[74] In subsequent decades we find more hints of the ecclesiastical and theological orientation of Cyprus. For example, the bishops of Cyprus (including Spyridon) signed the encyclical letter sent from the Council of Sardica in 343 that exonerated Athanasius of all the charges made against him.[75] Athanasius listed the bishops of Cyprus as unwavering and unanimous supporters, and he also later affirmed that churches on Cyprus had always maintained the faith of Nicaea.[76] From these scant details, perhaps we can tentatively conclude that throughout the "Arian" controversy, the bishops of Cyprus sided with Athanasius and the minority pro-Nicenes.

As we examined in the previous chapter, the deposition of Meletius as bishop of Antioch in 360/1 led to a schism in the regional capital with eventually four different candidates claiming the bishopric.[77] Meletius was immediately replaced by Euzoius, who had been closely allied with Arius and even deposed with him. Euzoius was endorsed by Constantius and therefore would have been the "official" bishop until his death in 376.[78] Thus the imperial territory of Cyprus was technically under the political oversight of Antioch, which was led ecclesiastically by a "heretic" bishop.[79] This is not to say, however, that the Antiochene church was able to impose its ecclesiastical or theological will upon Cyprus. But the circumstances point to what could have been a source of tension and fear for the bishops of Cyprus, that a heretic bishop would assert

74. Dechow, *Dogma*, 45. On Spyridon, cf. Socr., *h.e.* 1.12.1–8; Soz., *h.e.* 1.11.1–11.
75. Ath., *apol. sec.* 50.2. There were twelve signatories, unfortunately without the names of their respective sees. On the council, see Hill, *History*, 250–51; Barnes, *Athanasius*, 71–81.
76. Ath., *h. Ar.* 28.2; *ep. Jov.* 2.
77. Socr., *h.e.* 2.44.1–7; Soz., *h.e.* 4.28.1–11; Thdt., *h.e.* 2.31.1–13. For the situation in 360/1, see Brennecke, *Studien*, 66–81; Spoerl, "Schism"; Karmann, *Meletius*, 135–49.
78. Euzoius was then replaced by Dorotheus; cf. Philost., *h.e.* 9.14; Socr., *h.e.* 4.35.4; Soz., *h.e.* 6.37.24.
79. Certainly by the fifth century, Antioch had made direct claims of authority over Cyprus; see G. Downey, "The Claim of Antioch to Ecclesiastical Jurisdiction over Cyprus," *Proceedings of the American Philosophical Society* 102, no. 3 (1958): 224–28.

some kind of influence on the island, backed by imperial sanction.[80] If indeed
Athanasius's testimony is right, then the theological orientation of Cyprus
would not have been aligned with the powers that be either at the imperial
court or in the capital of the region. Thus the choice of Epiphanius, a non-
Cypriot, as metropolitan was probably not accidental but a deliberate and potentially provocative selection.[81]

The *Vita* of Epiphanius offers a rather elaborate story of how Epiphanius
became the leader of the church in Cyprus, which may reflect the relative uncertainty of the actual circumstances in which he ascended to the see.[82] The
hagiography is a composite work compiled sometime in the fifth or sixth century and attributed to John and Polybius, two of Epiphanius's disciples. Although the *Vita* has been relegated to the status of hagiographic fiction since
the seventeenth century, a simple dismissal is not entirely warranted.[83] The *Vita*
narrates a story in which Epiphanius decided to visit Hilarion in the city of
Paphos on Cyprus, where he was told by his teacher that he ought to make his
way to Salamis to avoid a storm at sea on his return journey. Epiphanius, however, boarded a ship bound for Askalon and ended up being shipwrecked and
washed up in Salamis. Meanwhile the bishops of Cyprus had convened to elect
a new bishop for Salamis, and among them was a venerable confessor bishop
named Pappos. Before Epiphanius was to depart for Palestine, he went to the
market in Salamis where he was spotted by Pappos and his associates. They
invited Epiphanius to pray with them in the church. Epiphanius demurred that
he was unqualified to lead prayers at church, at which point Pappos ordained
Epiphanius against his will as deacon, presbyter, then bishop. Pappos explained
that God had revealed to him that he would find the next bishop of Salamis in
the marketplace. Thus the selection of Epiphanius was miraculous and divinely
sanctioned.[84]

The story, of course, contains several hagiographical tropes that should
cause modern readers some suspicion. Nevertheless, a few details on Epiphanius's selection as bishop of Cyprus merit further consideration. The most important of these is the connection to Hilarion. As we observed in chapter 1, Jerome reported that Epiphanius knew Hilarion intimately, and the *Apophthegmata*

---

80. See Nautin, "Épiphane," c. 619.
81. Davis suggests that the Cypriots had a strong desire for links to Palestine and Apostolic Christianity
at the expense of Antioch, and thus the choice of Epiphanius as their bishop. "Earthquakes," 14–15.
82. See Rapp, "*Vita*," 141–42.
83. See throughout, Rapp, "*Vita*."
84. *v. Epiph.* 55–62.

tradition also highlights the connection between the two. According to Jerome and Sozomen, Hilarion was born in a small village near Gaza but studied grammar in Alexandria, where he entered the Egyptian desert, found Antony, and embraced the monastic way of life.[85] He eventually returned to his homeland, sold all of his patrimony, and practiced asceticism in a tiny cell.[86] In the same account, Sozomen related how Hilarion died and was buried while he was on Cyprus, but his disciple Hesychas stole the body and interred it in Palestine, where it became a cult site known for miraculous healing.[87] However, later in his narrative, Sozomen explained the circumstances in which Hilarion departed Gaza during a period of civil unrest and persecution of Christians by local pagans, about which Julian apparently did nothing.[88] As the people of Gaza sought him out, Hilarion fled, first traveling to Sicily and then settling in Cyprus.[89] He initially arrived in Paphos and remained there for two years. But according to Jerome, Hilarion then made his way further inland to a retreat in the mountains and dwelt there for another five years before he passed away.[90]

In the sequence of Sozomen's narrative, the rioting in Gaza occurred sometime after the death of George of Cappadocia at the hands of rioters in November 361, following his return to Alexandria as Athanasius's replacement.[91] Jerome reported that when Antony died (356), Hilarion was sixty-five years old and died when he was eighty (371).[92] Thus we can date his arrival and the beginning of his seven-year stay on Cyprus to sometime in 364. If we entertain Nautin's theory that Epiphanius failed in a bid to succeed Eutychius as bishop of Eleutheropolis sometime after the Council of Lampsacus in 364/5, then Epiphanius could have departed Palestine and gone to Cyprus, perhaps to visit his old teacher.[93] Epiphanius also may have decided to leave Palestine because of the generally anti-Nicene stance of Valens, who was baptized by Eudoxius of Constantinople in 366.[94] Thus we have a great deal of circumstantial evidence, but

85. Jer., *Vit. Hil.* 1–2; Soz., *h.e.* 3.14.21–22. Sozomen's account exhibits some differences with that of Jerome.
86. Soz., *h.e.* 3.14.-23–24.
87. Soz., *h.e.* 3.14.26–27. Cf. Jer., *Vit. Hil.* 46, on the stolen body.
88. Soz., *h.e.* 5.9.1–13. On Gaza, see R. Van Dam, "From Paganism to Christianity at Late Antique Gaza," *Viator* 16 (1985): 1–20.
89. Soz., *h.e.* 5.10.1–4. Cf. Jer., *Vit. Hil.* 37–41.
90. Jer., *Vit. Hil.* 43. Doubts remain, however, about the reliability of Jerome's account.
91. Soz., *h.e.* 5.9.1–13.
92. Jer., *Vit. Hil.* 29, 44.
93. Nautin emphasizes that the bishops of Cyprus would not have searched for a candidate outside of Cyprus, and thus Epiphanius must have been on the island. "Épiphane," 619.
94. See Lenski, *Failure*, 211–63. When Valens became emperor over the eastern half of the Roman Em-

perhaps enough to suggest some conclusions as to how Epiphanius became the leader of the church on Cyprus: (1) the bishops of Cyprus were markedly Athanasian in their theology and ecclesiastical allegiance; (2) Antioch, the city with oversight of Cyprus's political (and ecclesiastical?) affairs, was led by an "Arian" heretic; (3) Hilarion, the famed ascetic, spent his final years in Cyprus; (4) Epiphanius left his monastery and native Palestine but under uncertain circumstances, perhaps due to a failed attempt to succeed Eutychius; (5) Epiphanius came to Cyprus where his old ascetic teacher had established himself; (6) the bishops of Cyprus, aware of the presence of Epiphanius and his reputation for asceticism and orthodoxy, elected him as their metropolitan. That Hilarion had a hand in this is not inconceivable. Perhaps Epiphanius finally found the patronage he needed to ascend the ecclesiastical hierarchy that he was lacking in his native land and thus became the lead bishop of Cyprus in 367 (see chapter 7 for the date of his election).

The Bishop's Early Agenda

The *Vita* describes how Epiphanius's election as bishop was almost immediately contested by certain individuals in Cyprus, including a deacon within his own church, an extortionist local notable, and active Valentinian heretics who actually maintained their own ecclesiastical hierarchy.[95] Apparently, the main points of contention against the bishop were his non-Cypriot origin and his commitment to a life of poverty and simplicity. But the *Vita* reports that Epiphanius prevailed over his opponents through the miraculous intervention of God, another clear sign of divine favor.[96] The *Vita* also underscores the presence and threat of "heretics" on the island, including Ophites, Sabellians, Nicolaitans, Simonians, Basilideans, Carpocratians, and the aforementioned Valentinians. In the *Panarion*, Epiphanius also identified the historic presence of the Ebionites and Marcionites in Cyprus.[97] The *Vita* emphasizes that once Epiphanius

---

pire, he was generally indifferent to matters of orthodoxy and heresy, but after his baptism, he openly favored the Homoian position and deposed bishops who did not conform. Contrast with R. Errington, *Roman Imperial Policy from Julian to Theodosius* (Chapel Hill: University of North Carolina Press, 2006), 175–88, who views Valens more as a pragmatist in religious matters. Brennecke, *Studien*, 183–242, views Valens (and Valentinian) as part of the "imperial church" and thus Homoian, but concerned overall with continuity with the policy of Constantius and with harmony and peace in the church and empire.

95. *v. Epiph.* 63–67, 93–105.
96. Rapp, "*Vita*," 151–54.
97. Cf. *Pan.* 30.18.1, 42.1.2; *v. Epiph.* 106.

had silenced their Bishop Aetius, the numerous Valentinians on the island all became orthodox Christians.[98] Despite the hagiographical tropes, we can probably still assume that Epiphanius spent the earlier years of his administration consolidating his authority over Cyprus and ensuring that the island was "free" of heretics and orthodox in its confession.

In more practical matters, the *Vita* includes several anecdotes about Epiphanius's care for the poor, dealings with local notables, administration of justice, and construction projects.[99] Sozomen reported that Epiphanius was a capable administrator: "For dedicating himself to both the population and the great, coastal city, he served with such virtue, involving himself in civic affairs, that in a short while he became known to all manner of citizens and foreigners alike."[100] Epiphanius's reputation for asceticism apparently attracted numerous followers to the island, and by the early 380s, Jerome implied that several monasteries on the island either grew or were established by virtue of the bishop's presence:

> After Rhodes and Lycia, at last she [Paula] arrived on Cyprus, where falling at the knees of the venerable Epiphanius, she was retained by him for ten days not in refreshment, as he had thought, but in the work of God, as the affairs have demonstrated. Visiting all of the monasteries of that region, as she was able to do in proportion, she left relief of expenses for the brothers *whom love for the holy man had gathered there from all over the world.*[101]

Sozomen's account was composed after the death of Epiphanius, and the *Vita* was outright hagiography. But the overall impression that the bishop managed and cared for his own flock and adopted island home is consonant with Epiphanius's pastoral concerns as they are evident in his own writings.[102]

The surviving material remains also may attest to Epiphanius's effective management of the overall community of Constantia during his tenure as bishop. The city of Salamis, before its rededication as Constantia, had a long history dating back well into the Bronze Age. In the Roman period, the city bore all the trappings of a proper Greek/Roman city, with an enormous gymnasium and bath

---

98. *v. Epiph.* 105. The *Vita* (130), however, also later betrays this exaggeration when it identifies Valentinian deacons who opposed the burial of Epiphanius within the city.

99. See Rapp, "*Vita*," 158–68.

100. Soz., *h.e.* 6.32.4.

101. Jer., *Ep.* 108.7.3 (emphasis mine)

102. See Kim, "Pastoral," 247–56. For a preliminary examination of the nature of and activities related to pastoral care in late antiquity, see P. Allen and W. Mayer, "Through a Bishop's Eyes: Towards a Definition of Pastoral Care in Late Antiquity," *Augustinianum* 40 (2000): 345–98.

complex, stadium, theater, marketplaces, and forums.[103] The city was also known for its pagan temple dedicated to Zeus. After the earthquakes that destroyed many communities in Cyprus, Salamis became the beneficiary of Constantius, who funded much of the city's rebuilding; hence the renaming to Constantia. The *Vita* provides important building details that have been affirmed by some of the archaeological remains.[104] In particular, it describes how God informed Epiphanius that he should build a larger church to replace the older, smaller one, and he apparently hired sixty foremen to facilitate this construction project.[105] The ruins of the massive five-aisle church remain today. However the dating of the eponymous building is disputed by scholars and situated chronologically sometime either in the fourth or fifth century.[106] If the former is the case, then Epiphanius's involvement in its construction was quite possible. But if the latter date is correct, it testifies to the popular reception of Epiphanius, for it suggests that the bishop was greatly admired by the citizens of Constantia well after his death.[107] Epiphanius also may have facilitated the "Christianization" of the city of Constantia, as its pagan sculptures were mutilated and public buildings began to bear Christian symbols.[108] The erection of the elegant "Cambanopetra" basilica in the fifth century is further proof of the city's firm Christian identity well into the Byzantine period, and much is owed to Epiphanius in this regard.[109]

The Problem of Apollinarius

Epiphanius likely spent the early years of his tenure as bishop consolidating the Christian orthodox identity of Cyprus, but he soon became involved in theo-

103. See Karageorghis, *Salamis*, 165–96.
104. See Rapp, "*Vita*," 163–68.
105. *v. Epiph.* 72.
106. A. Megaw, "Byzantine Architecture and Decoration in Cyprus: Metropolitan or Provincial?," *Dumbarton Oaks Papers* 28 (1974): 57–88; C. Delvoye, "La place des grand basiliques de Salamine de Chypre dans l'architecture paléochrétienne," in *Salamine de Chypre, Histoire et Archéologie: État des recherches*, Colloques Internationaux du Centre National de la Recherche Scientifique 578 (Paris: Éditions du Centre National de la Recherche Scientifique, 1980), 314–27; A. Papageorghiou, "Foreign Influences on the Early Christian Architecture of Cyprus," in *Acts of the International Archaeological Symposium "Cyprus between the Orient and the Occident,"* Nicosia, 8–14 September 1985, ed. V. Karageorghis (Nicosia: Department of Antiquities, Cyprus, 1986), 490–503.
107. *v. Epiph.* 83, implies that even around the time of Epiphanius's death, the building was not yet finished.
108. Karageorghis, *Salamis*, 190–92.
109. See G. Roux, *Salamine de Chypre XV: La basilique de la campanopétra* (Paris: De Boccard, 1998). See also Englezakis, "Epiphanius of Salamis, the Father of Cypriot Autocephaly," in *Studies*, 29–40, for his legacy and its role in the fifth-century dispute between Cyprus and Antioch.

logical and ecclesiastical affairs beyond his island environs. Although Syedra in Pamphylia was only a short distance away, the request by its orthodox denizens for Epiphanius's theological instruction was a significant recognition of his reputation and authority, especially as a successor to Athanasius. As we examined in the previous chapter, when Epiphanius wrote the *Ancoratus*, he spent a great deal of time explicating and defending the doctrine of the Trinity, with a particular emphasis on the divinity of the Holy Spirit. However, the *Ancoratus* also includes substantial reflections on other theological issues, including the views of Origen on biblical exegesis and the resurrection body and the theology of Apollinarius of Laodicea on the Incarnation.

Like certain other formerly admirable Christians who had succumbed to heresy, Apollinarius must have elicited mixed feelings among pro-Nicene Christians.[110] On the one hand, Apollinarius and his father of the same name were respected for their written achievements, especially their "rewritings" of Scripture into genres that mirrored the literature of the classical tradition. Because of Julian's decree that Christians were forbidden to teach classical texts, the Apollinarii rendered the Pentateuch into heroic verse, some of the historical books of the Hebrew Bible into verse and tragic form, and the Gospels into Platonic dialogues.[111] Athanasius regarded the younger Apollinarius with some esteem, as he had visited and befriended the then priest in Laodicea on the return journey from his second exile. Basil of Caesarea had considered Apollinarius a trusted teacher.[112] Jerome also had spent time listening to Apollinarius lecture and even regarded him as a teacher, but he was also careful to emphasize later that he had never embraced Apollinarius's doctrines and only learned exegetical matters from him.[113] Epiphanius considered Apollinarius "ever beloved among the orthodox and ordered among the best."[114]

But by the early 370s, whatever positive contributions Apollinarius had made with regard to Christian literature or his Trinitarian doctrine were compromised by his teaching on the Incarnation of Christ.[115] However, as in the

110. For introductions to Apollinarius and his thought, see H. Lietzmann, *Apollinaris von Laodicea und seine Schule: Texte und Untersuchungen* (Tübingen: Verlag von J.C.B. Mohr [Paul Siebeck], 1904); C. Raven, *Apollinarianism: An Essay on the Christology of the Early Church* (Cambridge: University Press, Cambridge, 1923); E. Mühlenberg, *Apollinaris von Laodicea*, Forschungen zu Kirchen- und Dogmengeschichte 23 (Göttingen: Vandenhoeck & Ruprecht, 1969); Spoerl, "Study."
111. Socr., *h.e.* 3.16.1–6.
112. Soz., *h.e.* 6.25.7; Bas., *ep.* 361. See Barnes, *Athanasius*, 92.
113. Jer., *Ep.* 84.2.
114. *Pan.* 77.24.8. Cf. *Pan.* 77.19.5–7.
115. Kim, *Saint Epiphanius*, 36, n. 125. See also Gemeinhardt, "Apollinaris," for an examination of Apol-

case of Marcellus, modern scholars often find it challenging to discern exactly what Apollinarius believed and taught versus what was attributed to him by his opponents. The theology of Apollinarius manifests itself in several different (mis)represented ideas, some of which certainly originated with the theologian but were distorted and amplified over time.[116] Nevertheless, one core accusation against Apollinarius that seems to "stick" throughout the controversy is his denial that the incarnate Christ had assumed a human mind (νοῦς), that is, a human intellectual soul: "Some people wish to make lacking the incarnate *parousia* of Christ and the perfect economy in him. I do not know why they, who do not think rightly, were saying that Christ has not assumed a mind."[117] According to Epiphanius, the root of the Apollinarian conviction is the apparent belief that the human mind, fickle and subject to passion, is the seat of human sin.[118] Thus only the presence of the *Logos* as the "mind" of Christ in place of the human mind could safeguard the sinless Savior in the salvific economy.[119] To the contrary, Epiphanius argued that it is precisely and only through the presence of the *Logos* in the assumption of full humanity, including the mind, that Christ's humanity did not succumb to sin:

> For possessing the mind in truth, just as he was possessing the entire Incarnation in truth, [the mind] was not being directed toward irrational desires nor was he doing or reckoning the things of the flesh like us. But as God, who came to be in true flesh from the virgin Mary, he was acting with flesh and with soul

linarius's trinitarian thought. In *Anc.* 75–80, Epiphanius addressed the theological issues associated with Apollinarius without explicitly naming him. Furthermore in the *Pan.*, he expressed some hesitation and remorse that Apollinarius had become a heretic, and some uncertainty remains as to what doctrines Apollinarius actually taught and what were later distortions.

For specific examinations of Apollinarius's Christological doctrine, see R. Greer, "The Man from Heaven: Paul's Last Adam and Apollinaris' Christ," in *Paul and the Legacies of Paul*, ed. W. Babcock (Dallas: Southern Methodist University Press, 1990), 165–82; Spoerl, "Study"; eadem, "Apollinarius and the Response to Early Arian Christology," StPatr 26 (1993): 421–27; eadem, "Apollinarian Christology and the Anti-Marcellan Tradition," JTS 45, no. 2 (1994): 545–68; B. Daley, "Divine Transcendence and Human Transformation: Gregory of Nyssa's Anti-Apollinarian Christology," StPatr 32 (1997), 87–95; idem, "'Heavenly Man' and 'Eternal Christ': Apollinarius and Gregory of Nyssa on the Personal Identity of the Savior," JECS 10, no. 4 (2002): 469–88.

116. On Epiphanius and Marcellus, Lienhard observes: "Epiphanius listed Marcellus in his catalogue of heresies, but had a hard time saying just what his heresy was." Marcellum, 9. See also C. Riggi, "La διαλογή des Marcelliens dans le Panarion, 72," StPatr 15, no. 1 (1984): 368–73. On some distortions of Apollinarius's views, see E. Moutsoulas, "La lettre d'Athanase d'Alexandrie a Épictète," in Kannengiesser, *Politique*, 313–33, at 319–25.

117. *Anc.* 77.3.

118. Cf. *Anc.* 79; *Pan.* 77.26.1–27.9; Apollinarius, *epistula ad Diocaesarienses* 2.256.5–7.

119. *Anc.* 80.1–8.

and with mind and with the entire vessel, he who dwelt with the race of men, from on high from the Father, enhypostatic God-*Logos*.[120]

In the *Panarion*, Epiphanius echoed this idea: "So as the *Logos* who came was <not> defective in the flesh, although possessing human flesh; neither has he conceived in his mind things not suitable to his divinity. But the Lord who came accomplished these things that were rational for the flesh and soul and human mind, in order that he might not disturb the ordering of the true incarnate *parousia*."[121]

When Epiphanius addressed these issues in the *Ancoratus*, he used the polemical appellation "Dimoirites," "those who wage war" (against the mind of Christ), and he mentioned the name of the Apollinarians only once, and never the person of Apollinarius.[122] However, by the time Epiphanius sat down to pen his entry against the Apollinarians in the *Panarion*, he had clearly resigned himself to the fact that Apollinarius was the originator of this heretical teaching and thus begrudgingly made the bishop of Laodicea an outright heresiarch:

> The senior and venerable Apollinarius of Laodicea, who was always beloved by us and by the blessed Pope Athanasius and by all the orthodox, this man was the one who at the beginning conceived of and advanced this saying. And when first I was informed by some of those who had been taught by him, I did not believe it, that one who happened to be such a man could introduce this saying into the world. Still, in hopeful expectation I waited patiently until I could learn the facts, for we were saying that the pupils who came to us from him had not understood the profound <proclamations> of the learned man and intelligent teacher, and that they fabricated these things themselves and had not learned them from him.[123]

But alas, Epiphanius's hopes were disappointed, and he described how it became necessary to convene a council to address these issues.[124] The minutes of the gathering were forwarded to Athanasius himself, who wrote a letter re-

---

120. *Anc.* 79.4. See Kösters, *Trinitätslehre*, 294–98.
121. *Pan.* 77.26.6. For fuller discussions of Epiphanius and Apollinarian Christology, see Kösters, *Trinitätslehre*, 280–98; Kim, *Saint Epiphanius*, 34–42.
122. *Anc.* 13.8. See Kösters, *Trinitätslehre*, 51–62.
123. *Pan.* 77.2.1–3.
124. *Pan.* 77.2.6. It is unclear to which synod Epiphanius was referring.

sponding to these issues that Epiphanius included in the *Panarion*.[125] Thus between the time Epiphanius composed the *Ancoratus* and the *Panarion*, he had learned enough about the alleged teachings of Apollinarius to name the venerable bishop outright as the originator of the heretical doctrines.

Continuing Contention

In the meantime, western involvement in the ongoing dispute over the Trinity also intensified in the early 370s, especially through the theological writings of Hilary of Poitiers and the ecclesiastical efforts of Damasus, who succeeded Liberius as bishop of Rome in 366.[126] A contentious dialogue and deeper interaction between East and West emerged as a result, and the once loose efforts of the exiled Athanasius to connect the "halves" of the Roman Mediterranean world found greater traction in the years leading up to the Council of Constantinople. On the eastern side, Basil of Caesarea exerted considerable effort in this conversation, although he faced an uphill struggle because of his unwavering support of Meletius as the legitimate bishop of Antioch.[127] Basil tried (but failed) to garner the support of Athanasius to resolve the schism in Antioch and to broker an agreement with the West, including an outright condemnation of Marcellus of Ancyra.[128] Meanwhile, Damasus had convened a council in Rome that affirmed the Nicene faith, and the resulting letter, the so-called *Confidimus quidem*, invited the bishops of the East to unite with Rome in common theological cause.[129] Basil responded with more letters, again trying to bring Athanasius and Meletius together to unite with the bishops of the West, and he sent the Meletian deacon Dorotheus to the West with a letter expressing his own response and confession of faith.[130] The response came to Caesarea around Eas-

---

125. This is the letter addressed to Epictetus, in which Athanasius mentioned "various synods" in Gaul, Spain, and Rome that condemned the thinking of Arius. Athanasius also referred to the "minutes" sent to him by Epictetus. For a discussion of this letter, along with those addressed to Adelphios and Maximus, see Martin, *Athanase*, 626–35. See also Moutsoulas, "La lettre."
126. For an examination of Hilary's work, see Ayres, *Nicaea*, 179–85. For interactions between West and East in the early 370s, see Hanson, *Search*, 795–802; Martin, *Athanase*, 604–35, 789–817. On key developments in the mid- and late 360s, see Karmann, *Meletius*, 453–62.
127. For example, cf. Bas., *ep.* 214.2, 258.3, 266.2. See Hanson, *Search*, 797–800; Rousseau, *Basil*, 270–317; Martin, *Athanase*, 604–13; Karmann, *Meletius*, 456.
128. Cf. Bas., *ep.* 66–70. Furthermore, Basil maintained suspicions about the orthodoxy of Paulinus and his alleged proclivity for the theology of Marcellus of Ancyra; cf. Bas., *ep.* 263.5. See Lienhard, "Cappadocian," 118–19; Behr, *Nicene*, 107–8.
129. The dating of the council is disputed, as early as 368 and as late as 372.
130. Cf. Bas., *ep.* 82, 89–90, 92.

ter 373 in the person of Evagrius, a Eustathian presbyter who brought a letter expressing the inadequacy of Basil's confession and demanding an envoy of more repute to be sent to the West.[131] Basil refused, citing bad weather and his own physical maladies as excuses.[132]

Athanasius died on 2 May 373 and was succeeded by Peter, whose assumption of the see of Alexandria was disrupted by Lucius, the non-Nicene who was dispatched by Valens to claim the bishopric. Peter was imprisoned but escaped and fled to Rome, where presumably he maintained the Athanasian line on all things ecclesiastical and theological, including support for Paulinus as bishop of Antioch.[133] The situation at Antioch had become increasingly complicated after the failure of Athanasius's attempt at rapprochement through the *Tomus ad Antiochenos* and the synod led by Meletius in Antioch in 363. After Lucifer of Cagliari had ordained Paulinus as the "orthodox" bishop of Antioch, there were three claimants to the see, including the Homoian Euzoius, who had been chosen after the deposition of Meletius.[134] A sort of stalemate ensued, and the favored leader of the Antiochene church was in part dependent upon the ecclesiastical proclivities of the emperor of the East, namely Valens. Furthermore, Basil's failure to bring Athanasius to his side in support of Meletius as legitimate bishop was indicative of the continued divisiveness that characterized the situation in Antioch. In the mid-370s, however, matters became even more complicated. Meletius had been exiled by the emperor Valens in 370, and in his stead the Meletian community was led by his presbyters Diodore and Flavian.[135] In 375, Paulinus subscribed to the profession of faith sent by Damasus and thus established communion with the bishop of Rome.[136] Vitalius, who was originally ordained by Meletius and served as one of his partisans, came under the influence of Apollinarius and embraced his theological views.[137] Apparently, Vitalius had a falling out with the Meletian community due to some mistreatment by the presbyter Flavian, who had hindered Vitalius from meeting with

---

131. Bas., *ep.* 138.2.
132. Bas., *ep.* 156.
133. Socr., *h.e.* 4.22.1–6.
134. Philost., *h.e.* 5.5; Socr., *h.e.* 2.44.5; Soz., *h.e.* 4.28.10; Thdt., *h.e.* 2.31.10.
135. Cf. Socr., *h.e.* 4.2.4–7; Soz., *h.e.* 6.7.10; Thdt., *h.e.* 4.25.1–6. After a period of tolerance, Meletius was sent into exile in 370, with the intensification of Valens's Homoian religious policy, although it is unclear exactly what Meletius's status was between 365 and this exile. Valens also apparently left Paulinus alone. Karmann, *Meletius*, 454–55.
136. Insinuated by Bas., *ep.* 129.3. For the sequence of events, see Martin, *Athanase*, 801–2.
137. Soz., *h.e.* 6.25.1–5.

Meletius.[138] However in 375, Vitalius tried to align himself with the party of Paulinus, and later that year, the presbyter Vitalius made his way to Rome to secure communion with Damasus and was apparently successful. He then returned to Antioch with a letter for Paulinus from Damasus, which is unfortunately not extant. But soon thereafter, two more letters followed. The third letter, called *Per filium meum* and addressed to Paulinus, affirmed the communion between Damasus and Paulinus, recognized the growing suspicion over the theology of Apollinarius, and outlined the conditions in which Vitalius could be accepted. Vitalius demurred and rejected communion with Paulinus, and he was subsequently ordained as bishop of Antioch by Apollinarius sometime in late 376 or early 377.[139] Thus a fourth contender for the bishopric of Antioch further muddied an already dysfunctional ecclesiastical situation, and in this context Epiphanius traveled to Antioch to attempt to mediate between the parties of Paulinus and Vitalius.[140]

Intervention and Arbitration in Antioch (*Panarion* 77.20.1–24.5)

Thus far, we have unpacked the circumstances in Palestine during the middle decades of the fourth century that created the environment that ultimately precluded Epiphanius from ascending to the higher offices of the church hierarchy. We also examined how Cyprus was a locale certainly rich in its own cultural importance but of minimal importance in the grand scheme of the Roman Empire. Perhaps in some way the island's insignificance contributed to a headstrong attitude among its Christian inhabitants that gave rise to a sense of firm conviction and independence. Since the reign of Diocletian, the political shadow of Antioch loomed over Cyprus. We have suggested that the city's ecclesiastical turmoil and theological uncertainty galvanized the Cypriot Christian leaders, who already exhibited loyalty and orientation toward the Athanasian line, to find a new leader, even an outsider, to continue to steer their ship in the right direction. Epiphanius was their man, and after several years presumably spent taking care of internal matters, he set foot on the "international" stage both as a writer and as a bishop. So we come now to another autobiographical episode that he included in the pages of the *Panarion*, and our task

---

138. Soz., *h.e.* 6.25.3. Exactly when this took place is not clear.
139. Thdt., *h.e.* 5.4.1. See Mühlenberg, *Apollinaris*, 50–53; Dechow, *Dogma*, 66–70; Hanson, *Search*, 658–59; Kösters, *Trinitätslehre*, 55, n. 228, 61, n. 267; Behr, *Nicene*, 112.
140. See Karmann, *Meletius*, 278–81, especially n. 263, on Epiphanius's attempt at arbitration.

will be to sift through both the historical possibilities, that Epiphanius really was involved in a type of ecclesiastical arbitration, and the imagined realities, what Epiphanius wanted his readers to see in him and his actions.

20.1 For when you ask some of them, they all report differently. Some say that the Lord did not assume a perfect incarnation, nor did he become a perfect man. (2) But since for many this had become something to be shunned, afterward they finally used deception, as I later learned accurately from their very mouths. (3) For I arrived in Antioch and met with their leaders, among whom was Vitalius the bishop, a most reverent man in life, character, and lifestyle. (4) And advising and exhorting them, I was saying that they should be in agreement with the faith of the holy church and dismiss the contentious saying. (5) But Vitalius was saying, "For what difference is there between us?" For he was maintaining some disagreement against the venerable and notable man, Paulinus the bishop, and Paulinus against the mentioned Vitalius, who had been summoned by me. (6) Therefore I wanted to bring both together into peace, for both seemed to declare the orthodox faith, and each was maintaining disagreement on account of some accusation. (7) For Vitalius was imputing to Paulinus the name of Sabellius. On which account when I came <to Antioch?>, I withheld full communion with Paulinus, until he persuaded me with a written explanation, <through> which he already earlier had established agreement with the blessed father Athanasius, for the sake of an apology. (8) For he presented and gave freely to me a copy of this with his signature. It maintained wisely concerning the Trinity and likewise concerning the *nous* of the incarnate Christ, [composed] by the very hand of our father Athanasius. I have appended the explanation, and it is as follows:[141]

Copy, <by> the hand of Paulinus the bishop

21.1 I Paulinus, bishop, thus think just as I received from the Fathers, that there exists the perfect subsistent Father, perfect subsistent Son, and perfect subsistent Holy Spirit. (2) On account of which also I receive the above written interpretation concerning the three subsistences and the one *hypostasis* or *ousia*, and [I receive] those who think thus.[142] For it is pious to think and to

141. Ath., *tom.* 11.2.
142. Paulinus here was assenting to the contents of the *Tomus.*

confess the Trinity in one divinity. (3) And concerning the Incarnation of the *Logos* of the Father, which came to be on our account, thus I think just as has been written above, that according to John, "the *Logos* became flesh." (4) For [I believe] not according to the impious, who say that he has suffered a change, but that for our sake he became a man, born from the holy Virgin and the Holy Spirit. (5) For thus the Savior was not having a soulless body, either without sensation or without a *nous*. (6) For in no way was the body of the Lord himself, who became man for our sake, without a *nous*. (7) Wherefore I anathematize those who deny the faith confessed in Nicaea and those who do not confess that the Son is from the *ousia* of or *homoousios* with the Father. (8) I anathematize those who say that the Holy Spirit is a creature who has come to be through the Son. (9) And still I anathematize Sabellius and Photinus and all heresy, as I agree with the faith according to Nicaea and all that has been written above. The end.

22.1 And I was saying to brother Vitalius and those with him: "And what do you say? If there is some disagreement between us, set it right." And he said, "Let them say." (2) They [Paulinus et al.] said that they [Vitalius et al.] do not say that Christ had become a perfect man. But he [Vitalius] defended himself immediately that, "Yes, we confess that Christ assumed a perfect man." And this was wonderful for those listening, and they were filled with joy. (3) <But> knowing the thinking of those who win over the minds of their own brothers <through> pretenses, I persisted, asking accurately, "Do you confess that Christ truly assumed flesh?" And he concluded, "Yes." (4) [I asked], "From Mary the holy Virgin without the seed of man and through the Holy Spirit?" And he confessed this. (5) [I asked], did the God-*Logos*, the Son of God, when he came, truly take up flesh from the Virgin?" And he concluded with emphasis. And already I was made joyful, since I had heard from some, the aforementioned pupils who had come to me in Cyprus, that the flesh from Mary was not wholly confessed. (6) And when the most reverent man confessed that our Lord Jesus Christ took up the flesh from Mary, again it was asked by me if also he had assumed a soul (ψυχήν). And he also concluded this with similar emphasis, that it was not necessary to say otherwise, but he spoke truth concerning everything. (7) For it is necessary for the one who writes to men concerning the truth to disclose his whole mind, to have before his eyes the fear of God, and to compose nothing that has been falsified against the good news of Scripture.

23.1 So Vitalius confessed also that he [Christ] assumed a human soul: for this man was the one was saying, "Yes, Christ was a perfect man." Then after I asked concerning soul and flesh, accordingly I asked: "Did Christ who came assume a *nous*?" And speaking at once he answered, "No." (2) Then I [said] to him: "So how do you say that he became a perfect man?" And he revealed his own reasoning of his thought: "I say he was a perfect man, if I make the divinity in place of the *nous*, and the flesh and the soul, so that he was a perfect man from flesh and soul and divinity in place of the *nous*." (3) So with his contentiousness known, we argued many things about this and offered proof from Scripture, that it is necessary to confess that the God-*Logos* assumed all things perfectly: that he perfectly dispensed the economy in the incarnate *parousia*; and that he also unified this in perfection after the resurrection from the dead; and that he possessed it, spiritual and whole and not other, with his own divinity, united in himself; that the whole perfection completed one divinity and is seated in heaven at the right hand of the Father, on the throne of glory of his eternal lordship and kingdom. Finally, I rose up, without persuading both sides on account of the preceding contention.

(4) I perceived from this that the argument for them was not on account of the *nous*, but in the case of the *nous* was another thought. For sometimes they did not confess that he [Christ] assumed a soul. (5) When I suggested and said, "For what is the *nous*? Do you believe it is a *hypostasis* in a man? Thus is not a man composite?" Then by some it was believed that the spirit in man is always celebrated in the divine Scripture. (6) But when we demonstrated that the *nous* is not the spirit, since the Apostle [Paul] wisely said, "I sing with my *nous*, not with my spirit" (1 Cor 14:15), thereupon their arguments were many.[143] We were not able to persuade those who love contention.

24.1 Then again I was saying to some of them, "What? Do you say that the *nous* is a *hypostasis*?" With some of them saying that it is not, I persuaded them by it, that it is not necessary to think that it [*nous*] is what is called the "spirit of a man," because of the saying, "I will sing with my mind; I will sing also with my spirit." Since they did not have something to say to this, I was saying: (2) "Therefore the *nous* is not a *hypostasis*, but a movement of our entire *hypostasis*. But you in turn say that Christ is the *nous*, so then do you imagine that Christ is non-hypostatic (ἀνυπόστατον) and that he had made the presence of his incarnate *parousia* only in pretense and appearance? Just so they were not able to yield their argument. (3) And then the state of my life was in much distress, because among the aforementioned brothers, and worthy of praise, contentions

---

143. Cf. *Anc.* 76.1–6.

foolishly where thrown, in order that the aforementioned devil, the enemy of men, might contrive dissensions among us. (4) The hurt with regard to the thinking, brothers, is much, from such a cause. For it would have been simplest, if from the beginning concerning this no argument had been set in motion. For what did this innovation benefit the world or aid the church? Or rather, did it not damage, working hatred and discord? But since the argument was put forward, it has become frightful. (5) For it is not for the betterment of our salvation; for it is a denial not only on the part of the one who does not confess in this [point], but also in the smallest [point]. For it is necessary that in whatever happens, one does not go aside from the path of truth.

The Arbiter

At the beginning of the entry, Epiphanius recalled how certain pupils of Apollinarius had visited Cyprus, and he was appalled when he had heard the ideas they espoused and assumed that they had misconstrued their teacher.[144] His first course of action was to wait patiently with the hope that the issue would be clarified in due time, especially because he admired and revered Apollinarius as an orthodox Christian bishop. But matters only grew worse, bringing the "east into great turmoil," such that a synod had to be called.[145] Epiphanius claimed that the minutes of this uncertain synod were forwarded to Athanasius, who wrote a letter in response to Epictetus of Corinth.[146] Epiphanius included the entire letter in the entry which had the rhetorical effect of reinforcing the sense of continuity from Athanasius to Epiphanius.

After quoting Athanasius's letter, Epiphanius added his own reflections on the humanity of Christ and his criticisms of those who doubted it, and he ridiculed the questions they asked in regard to the bathroom habits of figures from the Hebrew Bible and Jesus himself.[147] He then inserted the account translated above, about halfway through the entry. The most notable aspect of this episode is the fact that Epiphanius had traveled to Antioch in late 376 or early 377 to

144. *Pan.* 77.2.2–4.
145. *Pan.* 77.2.5–6.
146. Scholars debate the date of Athanasius's letter and whether he was dealing specifically with the theology of Apollinarius himself and/or his followers or some other (earlier) groups. See Lietzmann, *Apollinaris*, 11–12; Raven, *Apollinarianism*, 103–10; Moutsoulas, "La lettre." For an analysis of this letter and its place in the larger debate about the person of Christ, see Jacobs, *Circumcised*, 85–88.
147. *Pan.* 77.15.1–19.10.

arbitrate the dispute between the parties of Vitalius and Paulinus. While there might appear to be some room for doubt that this episode had transpired at all, several factors support its overall authenticity, including an oblique complaint from Apollinarius himself.[148] The ongoing dispute over the bishopric of Antioch that lasted for another two decades after Epiphanius's account, the condemnation of Apollinarius and by association Vitalius, who was never recognized as bishop, and the sustained support for Paulinus, particularly by western and pro-Nicene interests, all align with the picture Epiphanius painted of the outcome of his arbitration efforts. Epiphanius believed that he had the clout to intervene in matters beyond Cyprus and indeed in the metropolitan capital of Antioch. Furthermore, that Vitalius and Paulinus both participated in the proceedings also seems to indicate that they also perceived Epiphanius to have some degree of authority. This was no small action on the part of the metropolitan bishop of Cyprus, but his deeds should not come as a surprise. By now, Epiphanius the bishop was experienced in dealing with heresy, in Cyprus just as he had in Egypt and Palestine, and he was not one to sit idly while the threat of heresy persisted, even if attacking it meant encroaching on an ecclesiastical jurisdiction beyond his own.

Athanasian Authority

Epiphanius withheld full communion from Paulinus because of Vitalius's charge of Sabellianism, a charge that was of course not surprising since Paulinus was the leader of the Eustathian faction in Antioch that maintained a strict one-*hypostasis* theology.[149] But Paulinus was able to demonstrate his orthodoxy by providing Epiphanius with a signed copy of the *Tomus* with Paulinus's personal explanation and subscription appended.[150] Epiphanius twice invoked the name of Athanasius in his description of the transaction with Paulinus, and there is little doubt that for Epiphanius, the legitimacy of Paulinus's claim to orthodoxy was rooted in the authority of the famed bishop of Alexandria and his personal authorship of the *Tomus*.[151]

Paulinus also made it clear in his explanation that he espoused a one-*hypostasis* doctrine but at the same time affirmed the subsistence of each of the

148. Cf. Facundius of Hermianae, *Ad Iustinianum* 4.2.47–51. Rapp, "*Vita*," 20.
149. *Pan.* 77.20.7.
150. *Pan.* 77.20.7–8.
151. *Pan.* 77.20.7–8.

persons of the Trinity. That Epiphanius accepted this documentation as orthodox is also noteworthy, because it implies that at the time of this intervention in Antioch, a one-*hypostasis* theology as espoused by the Eustathians was orthodox, even as he made the transition to a three-*hypostaseis* doctrine during his composition of the *Panarion*. Again this is very much in line with the accommodation expressed in the *Tomus*, even if the synod in Alexandria had not taken a decisive theological position in this regard.[152] What was apparently more important for Epiphanius was Paulinus's clear attribution of a human mind to the Incarnate Christ, a recognition of the orthodoxy of the faith and creed of Nicaea, and an affirmation of the divinity of the Holy Spirit.[153]

Heresy-Hunting

The remainder of the episode provides a sort of transcript of Epiphanius's interview with and investigation of Vitalius. Here we gain the distinct sense that we have moved past the recollection of the real moments of arbitration into the imagination of Epiphanius himself. With a certain degree of literary flair and suspicious construction, he set up the proceedings with what appear to be positive shared affirmations regarding the Incarnation of Christ. Epiphanius and Vitalius agreed that Christ had assumed a "perfect man," which was initially cause for joy among the brethren gathered.[154] However, as Epiphanius pressed his investigation further, the seams of unity began to split as the question of Christ's assumption of a human mind took center stage. Try as he did, using Scripture to substantiate his convictions, Epiphanius was unable to persuade Vitalius of the necessity of Christ's assumption of a *nous*, and thus his efforts at brokering a peace between the contending parties resulted in failure.

The entry continues with further questioning, not of Vitalius himself but presumably of his followers, and again there remains a lingering sense that Epiphanius inflated the original dialogue to serve his rhetorical self-presentation. Epiphanius disputed with the followers over their erroneous understanding of the *nous* as a *hypostasis*, a subject he already refuted in the *Ancoratus*, and their apparent confounding of the human *nous* and *pneuma*.[155] He

---

152. Cf. Ath., *tom.* 5.1–6.4.

153. *Pan.* 77.21.4–7. On Paulinus's appendix to the *Tomus* and his theological explanation, see P. Amidon, "Paulinus' Subscription to the *Tomus ad Antiochenos*," *JTS* 53, no. 1 (2002): 53–74; Karmann, *Meletius*, 278–81.

154. *Pan.* 77.22.2–5.

155. Cf. *Anc.* 77.1–7. See Kim, *Saint Epiphanius*, 171–72.

lamented the destructive and divisive nature of theological contentions as he rhetorically suggested that his own beliefs were simple and easy to understand. As the interlocutor in the dialogue, he appeared the reasoned thinker whose arguments were firmly rooted in Scripture, while he portrayed his opponents as confused, inconsistent, contentious, but easily swayed.

The end result of this episode is that Epiphanius had affirmed the orthodoxy of Paulinus and established communion with him, thus recognizing him as the legitimate bishop of Antioch. As we will see in the final chapter, Epiphanius even went so far as to travel to Rome to defend Paulinus's claim before Pope Damasus. It is not difficult to imagine that some of Apollinarius's followers had come to Cyprus, an island that under the administration of Epiphanius was becoming known as a monastic haven, and that these visitors communicated the teachings they had heard to the metropolitan. Epiphanius was thus informed of the development of a Christological threat that he was already familiar with when he composed the *Ancoratus*. Despite reluctance due to his admiration for the once orthodox Apollinarius, Epiphanius's patience could only last for so long, and he was spurred to action. The most important step he took was journeying to Antioch, the city that had cast its political and ecclesiastical shadow over Cyprus, where he engaged in a heresiological investigation in which he acted as arbitrator. Thus Epiphanius, who as abbot of his monastery had confronted a local heretical problem not so long before, now went on the offensive as the lead bishop of Cyprus, ascending to the role of heresy-hunter that would characterize the remainder of his life and legacy. As we will see in the next chapter, Epiphanius was also a clever polemicist, and he innovated and raised the genre of heresiology to new heights of rhetorical sophistication.

CHAPTER 6

Reimagining the Wilderness

Epiphanius the Naturalist

In both Egypt and in his native Palestine, Epiphanius encountered and confronted different heretical groups, and his experiences with them led to the maturation and solidification of his convictions about how to deal with them. In his youth, his interactions with women of a Gnostic heresy profoundly shocked him, especially their presence *within* the congregation of his church community and perhaps because of how close he came to joining them. According to his recollection, he was able to resist them by God's grace and was delivered from the temptation of the attractive women. His next action was to report them to the local bishops, who in turn expelled them. The bishops' response underscored Epiphanius's view that the problem of heresy should be remedied by the structures of church leadership. In Palestine, the encounters with the hermit Peter represented yet another step in Epiphanius's formation as a heresy-hunter. As an ordained leader of a monastic community, he took it upon himself to confront, refute, and anathematize Peter. As a bishop in Cyprus and self-styled arbiter of orthodoxy, Epiphanius continued to develop as a heresy-hunter and took on the role of both judge and jury in the Meletian schism in Antioch. Once he had ascertained that Vitalius was not a viable candidate because of his heretical beliefs, Epiphanius supported Paulinus as the rightful bishop of Antioch. Also noteworthy is that Epiphanius accepted Paulinus's signing of the *Tomus ad Antiochenos* as a standard of orthodoxy, a document that was of course connected directly with the efforts of Athanasius.

In all of these cases, however, the orthodox Epiphanius was limited in what he could do to his heretical opponents. On his own as an ordained abbot or even as a metropolitan bishop, Epiphanius could not enforce his will and judgment. Certainly to identify, name, and gather a body of knowledge to refute heretical beliefs and practices were direct steps that heresiologists could take against their enemies, and underlying all of these actions was a totalizing rhetorical discourse that created a dichotomy of insider and outsider, self and other.[1] When Epiphanius composed the *Panarion*, his world was certainly becoming Christian in its political and social orientation, although the emperor of the eastern half of the Roman Empire at that time, Valens, could be counted among the heretics by the standards of pro-Nicene Christians.[2] Neither Epiphanius nor his allies were in a position to impose any forced measures upon their heretical opponents, and they did not possess any real authority to command a soldier or to permanently silence any heresy. As we saw in the Peter the Archontic episode, the best Epiphanius was able to do was categorize and marginalize. Thus heresiology itself, even in the increasingly Christianized world of the late fourth century, certainly facilitated the imagination of a neatly ordered world divided between those who were right and those who were not. But it could hardly move beyond polemic, and the use of real sticks and stones was not in the purview of the likes of Epiphanius. Thus the *Panarion* was the literary embodiment of an imagined violence against a rhetorically constructed enemy.

This discursive violence permeated the thematic framework of the *Panarion* as a "medicine chest" of preventatives, antidotes, and cures against the bites and stings of noxious creatures.[3] Epiphanius equated heretics with deadly and harmful beasts that threatened innocent Christians with venomous doctrines and practices, and he developed a new taxonomy to stigmatize the heretical "other" with these known and feared creatures.[4] In order to protect believers

---

1. On classification of heresies as a rhetorical strategy, see Lyman, "Topography." The development of Christian discourse in its varied forms was a long and complicated process that became even more acute in the post-Constantinian world. For a broad examination, see Cameron, *Rhetoric*. The process of naming was an extremely important step in the development of heresiology, as it functioned as a means to distinguish and differentiate the various heretical sects from true Christianity. Justin Martyr was fundamental in this; see Le Boulluec, *La notion*, 36–91. Furthermore, the growth of a Christian language to articulate self and difference emerged hand in hand with the Christianization of knowledge and ultimately society and culture. For this process, Inglebert, *Interpretatio*, is indispensable.
2. On Valens's religious position and political maneuvering, see Lenski, *Failure*, 211–63, although contrast with Errington, *Policy*, 175–88.
3. See Pourkier, *L'hérésiologie*, 77–84.
4. On his sources, see J. Dummer, "Ein naturwissenschaftliches Handbuch als Quelle für Epiphanius von Constantia," *Klio* 55 (1978): 289–99; J. Verheyden, "Epiphanius of Salamis on Beasts and Heretics: Some Introductory Comments," *Journal of Eastern Christian Studies* 60, nos. 1–4 (2008): 143–73. On the taxonomy of heresiology and the ordering of knowledge, see R. Flower, "Genealogies of

from the bites of such harmful manifestations of nature, Epiphanius provided his readers with the knowledge to identify and refute dangerous heretics and to apply suitable preventatives, remedies, and antidotes. By and large, the creatures Epiphanius identified were to be found in the wilderness, away from the urban context of daily life. The wilderness was associated with the unbridled freedom and potential savagery of nature and was in many ways a place to be feared and avoided.[5] But it was also the locus in which ascetic exemplars like Antony waged spiritual and physical warfare against demons that often appeared in the guise of wild animals.[6] Even Jesus himself had entered the wilderness both as a place for purification and preparation and for testing and temptation. Dangerous animals populated this landscape; and as poisonous creatures lurked about and threatened human well-being, Epiphanius imagined that wild heretics also set their traps and endangered the believer's theological health. Thus orthodoxy is preserved only in the safe and orderly confines of the church and its caretakers. If a believer dared to move beyond the security of the church (and the city?), he or she could become the victim of predatory heretics.[7] However, at times the animals of the wilderness would penetrate the city and the ordered structures of human life, and they had to be removed or eliminated. Likewise, heretics infiltrated the holy church, and it was up to its guardians to identify and expel them from the community. Thus the Gnostic women of Epiphanius's youth were found among the congregations of the city, and the young monk reported them to the local bishops, who in turn banished them. The abbot Epiphanius confronted Peter, a heretic within the midst of his community, and the heresy-hunter expelled the harmful "creature" and isolated him in his cave. Thus heretics invaded and breached the imagined boundaries established by the orthodox Epiphanius.

Knowledge was the key to keeping the church pure, and Epiphanius

---

Unbelief: Epiphanius of Salamis and Heresiological Authority," in *Unclassical Traditions, Vol. II: Perspectives from East and West in Late Antiquity*, Cambridge Classical Journal, Proceedings of the Cambridge Philological Society, Supplementary Vol. 35, ed. C. Kelly, R. Flower, M. Williams (Cambridge: Cambridge Philological Society, 2011), 70–87. On comparisons with animals as part of the larger phenomenon of physiognomy in antiquity, see Barton, *Power*, 122–28. See also Henderson, *Construction*, 120–57, for the schematization of heresy in different religious traditions.

5.   But see Goehring, "Encroaching," on the constructed dichotomy between city and desert in the monastic (and modern) literary imagination.

6.   See I. Gilhus, *Animals, Gods and Humans: Changing Attitudes to Animals in Greek, Roman and Early Christian Ideas* (New York: Routledge, 2006), 220–24.

7.   Again, Goehring discusses how the "desert" in the monastic ethos was the locus of truth and true monastic withdrawal, while the city was associated with falsehood and worldliness. In this way, Epiphanius's imagined dichotomy represented a reversal that was consonant with his affirmation of the structure of the urban ecclesiastical hierarchy. Indeed, Goehring argues that ascetics occupied both city and desert and all the spaces in-between. "Encroaching."

equipped his readers with the tools necessary to identify heretics in order to refute and expel them. He likened himself to ancient naturalists who imparted knowledge about the nature of wild animals, and he said that he would similarly attempt "to reveal the roots and beliefs of the heresies."[8] He added that these naturalists wrote about wild animals in particular "to frighten men and ensure their safety, so that they would recognize terrible and deadly beasts, be safe, and escape them," and they also "prescribed medicines made from roots and plants to cure the sickness caused by these serpents."[9] Similarly Epiphanius said that his purpose was

> to expose the appearance of the terrible reptiles and beasts, and their poisons and deadly bites. And to correspond with them, I shall provide an antidote to counteract their poison as much as I am able, in brief with one or two arguments, in order to save any who so desire <to be saved?> with the Lord, who whether knowingly or not, have fallen into the snake-like teachings of these sects.[10]

The comparison of wicked men and heretics to wild animals, especially serpents, was by no means novel among Jews or Christians, and even Jesus himself did not shy away from identifying certain men with a brood of vipers (cf. Matt 12:34, 23:33) and empowering his followers to "tread on snakes and scorpions" (Luke 10:19).[11] Even Epiphanius's hero Athanasius used snake imagery to disparage heretics: "Eusebius and Arius, like snakes coming out of a hole, vomited out the poison of this impiety."[12] Epiphanius, however, did not settle merely for stock associations and attacks. He escalated his rhetorical attacks by equating specific creatures and their unique behaviors with particular heretics and their distinctive errors.[13] Perhaps the simplest motive for these comparisons was

---

8. *Pan.*, Proem 2, 3.2.
9. *Pan.*, Proem 2, 3.3
10. *Pan.*, Proem 2, 3.4–5.
11. However, Dummer does not see Epiphanius influenced by the biblical precedent ("Handbuch," 292), although Verheyden challenges this assertion ("Epiphanius," 145). For early heresiological reference to serpents, see for example Iren., *haer.* 1.30.15; Hipp., *haer.* 5.11.1, who mentioned a hydra, a mythological serpent. Iren., *haer.* 3.2.3, also referred to his heretical enemies as "snakes trying in a slippery way to escape from all points."
12. Ath., *h. Ar.* 66.2.
13. In other words, he was the first to systematize this knowledge into a rhetorical trope. See Pourkier, *L'Hérésiologie*, 79–81. See also P. Mena, "Insatiable Appetites: Epiphanius of Salamis and the Making of the Heretical Villain," StPatr (2013): 257–63, for Epiphanius's rhetorical use of disease and deviant sexuality, combined with existing tropes to invoke "effeminacy as disease" to construct a heretical villain.

similar to that of the naturalists: to warn and to engender fear in the hearts of readers who also might have been familiar with the dangerous animals of the eastern Mediterranean basin. But as we shall see, Epiphanius had more sophisticated ideas in mind.

Closely related to ancient naturalist knowledge is that of ancient medicine.[14] As already evident in Epiphanius's own words, the line between these two types of knowledge was rather blurry; and even as the bulk of the imagery in the *Panarion* relates to wild and dangerous animals, the overall theme of the work is that of a medicine chest. Epiphanius's heresiology can and does have a prescriptive, healing, and restorative function, and Epiphanius clearly envisioned it as such:

> And thus, most beloved, my work <has been composed?> for the sake of prevention of the aforementioned [heresies] and your <safety?>, in order to reveal the forms of the terrible snakes and beasts, and their poisons and deadly bites. And in opposition to these, as much as we are able in short, we will provide anyway one or two statements, in the manner of antidotes, in order to check their poison and to save the one who so desires in pursuit of the Lord and the one who has fallen in accordance with willing or unwilling knowledge into the snake-like bites of the heresies.[15]

According to Epiphanius, the ancient naturalists also recognized the twofold function of the knowledge they provided. Through their information, they both struck fear in their readers and "caring for the same things, they prescribed remedies from roots and plants to counteract the evil of the aforementioned serpents."[16]

In ancient understandings of medicine and the body, two etiologies relating to health and infection are operative: imbalance and invasion.[17] In the former, represented by the theories of Hippocrates and later Galen, the body maintains its well-being and health by a proper balance of internal bodily factors, among them the humors, temperature, and moisture, while in the latter, the body is understood to be a closed system but vulnerable to external attack. In early Christian concepts of health and medicine, the second of the two models seems

---

14. For a broad study of ancient medicine, see V. Nutton, *Ancient Medicine* (New York: Routledge, 2004).
15. *Pan.* Proem 2, 3.4–5.
16. *Pan.* Proem 2, 3.3.
17. See Martin, *Corinthian*, 139–62. I am also grateful to Thomas Whitley for his insights in "Ancient Antidotes: Pollution, Sexual Slander, and the Body in Epiphanius' *Panarion*" (paper delivered at the 2013 annual meeting of the North American Patristics Society).

to hold sway, and this is certainly the perspective in the *Panarion*.[18] The ancients did not have a firm understanding of pathogens and microbiology, but they definitely understood that bites and stings from harmful creatures could adversely affect the body. In other words, external agents that either attack or invade the body are the cause of sickness. Epiphanius exploited the healthy fear his readers must have had of certain animals in the natural world and the potential damage they could inflict on the human body, and he extended the physical imagery to a metaphor about an individual's spiritual health. Thus the false teachings of the heretics and the heretical doctrines that penetrated the minds and souls of Christians are imagined to be the same as the bites of snakes and the venom they injected into the body.[19] Heretics are aggressive predators, intent on attacking, invading, and infecting the Body of Christ. Thus the rhetorical "naturalist" and "medicinal" knowledge found in the *Panarion* is essential to the physical and spiritual well-being of the orthodox church.[20]

Epiphanius's approach to heresiology reflects a broader late antique phenomenon: a burgeoning confidence and a deepening sophistication in the rhetorical tone and language of accusation and attack. Furthermore, as we have seen, he was part of an ongoing process in which Christian thinkers and writers were appropriating and reframing *paideia*, even as some like Epiphanius openly eschewed it, to reflect their own understandings of the world over and against their pagan predecessors.[21] Systematizing this knowledge is also very much a feature of late antique literary culture, and the antiquarian and encyclopedic impulse also reflects a rich engagement with and ordering of older traditions.[22]

---

18. See Martin, *Corinthian*, 163–97. On Christian attitudes toward medicine, see G. Ferngren, *Medicine and Health Care in Early Christianity* (Baltimore: Johns Hopkins University Press, 2009), who argues overall that early Christian views on medicine and health were consistent with those of their Greco-Roman context and not driven primarily by a demonic etiology of disease and promises of miraculous healing.

19. Gilhus: "Epiphanius' point is that animals infect the body of the Church with their poison." *Animals*, 240.

20. Barton makes the important argument that medical knowledge and prognosis were in and of themselves exercises in rhetoric. *Power*, 133–68.

21. For example, Inglebert studied in great depth the Christian reinterpretation of cosmography, geography, and history. *Interpretatio*.

22. On the ordering of knowledge, see the introduction and essays in J. König and T. Whitmarsh, eds., *Ordering Knowledge in the Roman Empire* (Cambridge: Cambridge University Press, 2007). See V. Nutton, "From Galen to Alexander: Aspects of Medicine and Medical Practice in Late Antiquity," *Dumbarton Oaks Papers* 38, Symposium on Byzantine Medicine, ed. J. Scarborough (1984): 1–14, on the compiling and selecting of medical knowledge, as well as on conflicting attitudes among Christians between dependence on secular or "spiritual" medicine for healing. See also more recently, P. van der Eijk, "Principles and Practices of Compilation and Abbreviation in the Medical 'Encyclopedias' of Late Antiquity," in *Condensing Texts: Condensed Texts*, Palingenesia 98, ed. M. Horster and C. Reitz (Stuttgart: Franz Steiner Verlag, 2010), 520–54.

  Many ancient thinkers were deeply interested in understanding and ordering the animal world,

Epiphanius desired to provide for his readers a guide to the venomous heretics that lived in this terrifying wilderness. Thus he imagined and presented the *Panarion* as a sort of Christian version of an ancient naturalist and medical text.[23] He imagined and presented himself as a "naturalist" and as a "physician" (which ultimately were one and the same), and the knowledge he provided functioned to persuade his readers that he was the scientific authority. But the *Panarion* is also more than just knowledge for its own sake; through his use of metaphorical imagery, Epiphanius also implied and perhaps subtly advocated violence and action against heretical creatures. The knowledge he provided was meant to empower Christians and not to paralyze them with fear, to the extent that he might train the orthodox hunted to even become the hunter. For Epiphanius, merely safeguarding the innocent and remaining on the defensive was not enough; Christians should go on the offensive.

Toward a New Taxonomy of Heresy

In the second preface to the *Panarion*, Epiphanius cited an impressive list of ancient naturalists from whom the reader would presume he drew information about harmful animals and natural preventatives and cures.[24] He wrote:

> And Nicander, the investigator of beasts and creeping creatures, provided the knowledge of their natures. And others, having studied roots and plants, wrote about their matter, such as Dioscorides the Wood Cutter, Pamphilos, King Mithridates, Callisthenes, Philon, Iolaos of Bithynia, Heracleidas of Taranto, Crateuas the Root Cutter, Andreas, Bassos the Tulian, Niceratos, Petronios, Niger, Diodotos, and certain others.[25]

---

and the philosophic study of the natural world was already of some interest to the pre-Socratic philosophers. Aristotle, however, really was the first Greek thinker to produce serious studies of all things relating to the animal world, a tradition that developed fully in the Hellenistic and Roman periods. See R. French, *Ancient Natural History: Histories of Nature* (New York: Routledge, 1994). For a broad examination of Greco-Roman and early Christian attitudes and understandings of the relationship between humans and animals, see R. Grant, *Early Christians and Animals* (New York: Routledge, 1999); Gilhus, *Animals*, with some discussion of Epiphanius in 238–42.

On Epiphanius's antiquarian tendencies, see Jacobs, "Epiphanius." On his encyclopedic efforts, see Flower, "Genealogies."

23. Perhaps this helps to explain why Epiphanius was mistakenly identified as the author of the *Physiologus*; cf. Nautin, "Épiphane," c. 629. On the *Physiologus*, see briefly Grant, *Animals*, 52–72.

24. Dummer argues that Epiphanius's naturalist knowledge was largely derived from an epitomized source. "Handbuch," 295. See also Verheyden, "Epiphanius," 146–48, on this list of authors and the unlikelihood that Epiphanius had consulted them directly.

25. *Pan.*, Proem 2, 3.1–2. Dioscorides was a first-century CE author of a medical book; Pamphilos was

At the head of this list is Nicander of Colophon, a second-century BCE poet who wrote at least two didactic poems on poisonous animals and natural remedies.[26] The first is the *Theriaca*, which primarily describes a variety of venomous animals and their behaviors, and the second is the *Alexipharmaca*, which elaborates on a variety of natural poisons, cures, and concoctions.[27] Although the poems appear to demonstrate his extensive knowledge of harmful creatures and natural cures, Nicander not only drew heavily from the writings of the ancient naturalist Apollodorus but also frequently manipulated and mangled the information in the composition of the two poems.[28] Nevertheless, despite Nicander's shortcomings, the poems were well known and became important sources in the transmission of zoological and pharmacological information to later Hellenistic and Roman writers, and they contained the kind of useful knowledge that would have been popular fodder for guidebooks. Epiphanius was likely not directly engaging the texts of Nicander or any of the authors he cited, but rather was using a compilation of naturalist knowledge derived from other texts that were part of a larger tradition of ancient biological and pharmacological knowledge.[29] In the hands of the heresiologist, however, this knowledge, which presumably served a practical, prophylactic purpose, was appropriated and adapted to produce a hybridized literary product put to rhetorical and polemical use in his imagined world, divided between orthodoxy and heresy.

---

possibly from Amphipolis and wrote a botanical work cited by Galen; King Mithridates VI of Pontus legendarily built up an immunity to poisons; Philon could refer to any number of known physicians cited by Galen; Iolaos of Bithynia was a third-century BCE author of a medical text; Heracleidas of Tarentum was a first-century BCE physician of the Empiricist school; Crateuas was a second-/first-century BCE physician and botanist and was personal physician to Mithridates VI; Andreas was a third-century BCE physician at the court of Ptolemy IV and wrote a pharmacopoeia; Bassos was author of a botanical work cited by Pliny; Niceratos was a first-century BCE author on plants; Petronius was a first-century CE author on pharmacy; Niger was a first-century CE Latin author on medicine; Diodotos was a first-century BCE author on botany.

26. For an introduction, text, and translation, see A. Gow and A. Scholfield, *Nicander: The Poems and Poetical Fragments* (Cambridge: Cambridge University Press, 1953).

27. See. J. Scarborough, "Nicander's Toxicology I: Snakes," *Pharmacy in History* 19, no. 1 (1977): 3–23; idem, "Nicander's Toxicology II: Spiders, Scorpions, Insects and Myriapods," *Pharmacy in History* 21, no. 1 (1979): 3–34, 73–92. Both are available in J. Scarborough, *Pharmacy and Drug Lore in Antiquity: Greece Rome, Byzantium* (Burlington, VT: Ashgate, 2010).

28. Scarborough, "Toxicology I," 3–5.

29. See Dummer, "Handbuch," and this is in direct contrast with R. Zionts, who argues that Epiphanius's use of Nicander reflects an intimate knowledge with the classical literary tradition. "A Critical Examination of Epiphanius' 'Panarion' in Terms of Jewish-Christian Groups and Nicander of Colophon," PhD diss., Pennsylvania State University, University Park, 2002. I disagree with his overstated argument that Epiphanius was well versed in *paideia* and that he conscientiously modeled the *Panarion* on the didactic poems of Nicander. Rather, like Dummer argues, Epiphanius, despite his anti-intellectual rhetoric, used knowledge from the classical tradition (in this case in handbook form) when it suited his purposes. "Handbuch," 299.

Heresiology as Ophiology

The most frequent and detailed associations Epiphanius made between heretics and harmful animals were serpents. Again, this link would have invoked for his readers the biblical image of the serpent in Eden, but it also would have stirred up common fears about snakes that resulted from daily experience and folk culture.[30]

The "Viper with No Birth Pangs"

We find the first example of this heresiological image in *Panarion* 26, on those familiar "Gnostics" or "Borborites." They allegedly were hypersexualized libertines who engaged in all manner of unseemly behavior including cannibalism, consumption of bodily substances, and frequent orgies.[31] Epiphanius was especially disturbed by the "licentiousness and fornication" of this heresy, manifest in their practice of ritual sex.[32] The adherents of this heresy purportedly forbade insemination, and the men carrying out their rituals were said to withdraw and climax instead into their hands. The heretics would then eat the semen as a type of Eucharistic host. Furthermore, if a woman happened to become pregnant, she would abort and remove the fetus, grind it with various spices, and ritually consume the mixture.[33]

Whatever the veracity of such details, certainly the descriptions would have elicited a visceral response of disgust from the readers. As if the account was not enough to turn his readers away from such a heresy, Epiphanius likened these heretics to what he called a "viper with no birth pangs."[34] When a male and female of this breed of viper copulate, they intertwine, and then the male thrusts its head into the open jaws of the female, which bites off the male's head. The poison that the female consumes then grows into a pair of snakes that mature in her belly and then tear themselves out, killing the mother in the process. Because the female does not actually give birth to its brood, it is known as a

---

30. On the symbolic meaning of the serpent in ancient thought, see Grant, *Animals*, 4–5; Gilhus, *Animals*, 162–63, 213–15, and especially J. Charlesworth, *The Good and Evil Serpent: How a Universal Symbol Became Christianized*, Anchor Yale Bible Reference Library (New Haven: Yale University Press, 2010).
31. *Pan.* 24.4.1–5.8. See Mena, "Epiphanius," on the trope of the heretic marked by an uncontrollable sexual appetite.
32. *Pan.* 26.19.2.
33. *Pan.* 26.5.4–6.
34. *Pan.* 26.19.2. Charlesworth, *Serpent*, 452–60, provides a useful appendix of ancient Greek words for serpent, many of which are found in the *Panarion*.

"viper with no birth pangs."[35] Epiphanius took this creature and its gruesome matricidal reproductive behavior and compared it to a Gnostic sect that allegedly engaged in frequent copulation but forbade insemination. He tried to provoke alarm and disgust through this image as he said: "It happens to be the most dreadful and fearsome of all the snakes, since it achieves its own destruction in itself and receives its filth through its mouth, and this deranged sect is like it."[36] Thus the serpents and the heretics became one and the same.

The *Dipsas*

Panarion 34 described a sect known as the Marcosians, named after its founder Marcos, whom Epiphanius identified as a successor to Valentinus. Irenaeus was the first heresiologist to discuss this heresy in detail, and both Hippolytus and Epiphanius drew on his account and as his successors, included the Marcosians in their respective works. This inclusion of the Marcosians by all three authors presents us with a useful basis of comparison, specifically with regard to how Epiphanius intensified his antiheretical rhetoric through his use of natural imagery.[37] In his account, Epiphanius described how Marcos apparently combined Gnostic teachings with magical chicanery and regularly performed a sort of sleight of hand show to attract followers. At the heart of his spectacle was the manipulation of the physical and chemical properties of certain liquids that appeared to the audience as magical. In one rite, the Marcosians would prepare three chalices filled with white wine, and Marcos would utter an incantation after which the liquid in the chalices magically changed color.[38] Epiphanius then quoted an extensive excerpt from Irenaeus that described another trick with different liquids.[39] Marcos focused his manipulative attention on women, usually the best dressed, highest ranking, and wealthiest, convincing them that he had the power to bestow upon them the gift of prophecy, and he used aphrodisiac potions and liquid concoctions to seduce his prey.[40]

In *Against Heresies*, Irenaeus broadly structured his attack against the Marcosians by identifying and naming the heresiarch, describing their particular

---

35. *Pan.* 26.19.3–5. Cf. Herodotus 3.109; Nicander, *Theriaca* 128–37; Pliny the Elder, *Naturalis Historia* 10.82; Aelian, *De Natura Animalium* 1.24. Nicander did not assign the same name to this breed of viper, although he did write about the same reproductive behavior and added the extra detail that the young snakes gnaw through the mother in vengeance for the death of the sire.
36. *Pan.* 26.19.6.
37. Iren., *haer.* 1.13.1–22.1; Hipp., *haer.* 6.39.1–55.3.
38. *Pan.* 34.1.1–7.
39. *Pan.* 34.2.1–20.12; cf. Iren., *haer.* 1.13.1–21.5.
40. *Pan.* 34.2.6–11.

practices and beliefs, and finally refuting their cosmology and theology with an emphasis on their flawed exegesis of Scripture.[41] He then punctuated the discussion by reaffirming what true Christians believe about the nature of God the Father and the Son. Irenaeus regularly infused his heresiology with invective, berating heretics for their blasphemy, foolishness, impiety, deception, and demonic inspiration, among other things. At the end of his discussion of the Marcosians, Irenaeus wrote:

> Therefore, holding this "Rule," notwithstanding that they [heretics] very much say various and many things, we make clear easily that they have deviated from the truth. For almost all that are heretics say that there is one God, but through their wicked thinking they alter it [the truth], being ingrates to him who made them, just as also the heathen through their idolatry. Moreover, they despise the creative work of God, speaking against their own salvation, and being their own bitterest accusers and false witnesses. Indeed, they will rise again in the flesh (although they may not wish it), that they may acknowledge the greatness of the one raising them from the dead. Moreover, on account of their disbelief, they will not be numbered among the just.[42]

Irenaeus established a clear line of demarcation between orthodox and heretic, those who possessed the truth and those who maintain manifold heretical opinions. The Apostles had received the truth from Christ and handed it down to subsequent generations, and it was safeguarded by the succession of orthodox bishops. This truth could be formulated and expressed in a core confession of faith called the "Rule of Truth."[43] For Irenaeus, orthodoxy is characterized by oneness, that is, by the simplicity and singularity of the truth it proclaims, whereas heresy is marked by plurality and a diversity of conflicting opinions.[44] But heresy is also deceptive, at times having the veneer of truth. Thus Irenaeus's work was absolutely necessary to safeguard the truth and protect the faithful. Epiphanius's extensive quotation from Irenaeus is

---

41. For Irenaeus's innovations in heresiology, see Le Boulluec, *La notion*, 113–88, especially 114–21, 127–28, on the Marcosians. On Irenaeus's understanding of biblical exegesis, formed in large part in reaction to "heretical" interpretations, see Le Boulluec, *La notion*, 215–53.

42. Iren., *haer.* 1.22.1.

43. Iren., *haer.* 1.22.1, 4.33.8, 5.20.1–2.

44. Cf. Iren. *haer.* 1.preface 1–2. See Le Boulluec, *La notion*, 148–62, on Irenaeus's appeal to "simplicity" in opposition to heretical obscurity and incomprehensibility and on heretical diversity and multiplicity.

itself notable because it underscores the sense in which he affirmed Irenaeus's heresiological authority:

> The blessed elder Irenaeus made this precise inquiry, exposing comprehensively, in order, all of their falsified teaching. Wherefore indeed, as has already been made clear by me, because I am satisfied with what has been studied by him, I have provided everything, word for word, as has been recounted in his work. They will be refuted by the very things that have been said by the holy man against their wickedness.[45]

Epiphanius understood himself to be part of a succession of orthodox Christians who defend the truth and battle against heresy, and he was happy to draw on the work of his predecessors, if not quote them wholesale.

Hippolytus escalated his anti-Marcosian rhetoric by emphasizing that the heresiarch drew his ideas specifically from astrology and Pythagorean philosophy: "So I hope that these things are clear to those who possess a sound mind, that they [Marcosian ideas] are without authority and far from the knowledge according to right religion. They are part of astrological invention and the arithmetic art of Pythagoras."[46] The connection between Christian heresy and pagan religion and philosophy is certainly manifest in the earliest heresiological rhetoric. But for Hippolytus, it is a driving force in his entire composition. His heresiology is unique in that it systematically outlines the different beliefs professed by various philosophical schools and identifies which heretical doctrines were influenced by them. For Hippolytus, nothing new was to be found among the heretics' doctrines, for they had derived every single idea from the pagans of bygone eras.[47]

Throughout the *Panarion*, Epiphanius also maintained the Irenaean dichotomy of truth and error and the Hippolytan emphasis on the link between pagan religion/philosophy and heresy. But he also developed his own unique antiheresiological rhetoric. He compared the Marcosians with a breed of viper known as the *dipsas*, which he said was known to drink from pools of water formed in rock depressions.[48] The serpent would secrete its poison into these puddles, and when an animal drank from them, it would die. Epiphanius also

---

45. *Pan.* 34.21.1–2.
46. Hipp., *haer.* 6.52.1. Cf. Iren., *haer.* 1.1.1.
47. See Vallée, *Study*, 41–62. Cf. Iren., *haer.* 2.14.1–9.
48. *Pan.* 34.22.3.

wrote that when a *dipsas* struck a victim, he or she would feel a burning sensation and severe thirst. The victim would drink and drink until vomiting, at which point Epiphanius said the body expelled not only the consumed liquid but also the very life of the afflicted.[49] Again the invasive medical etiology is at work here. The snake/heretic uses its poison/heresy to pollute water that is consumed by the victim, both resulting in death: one physical, the other spiritual. Something as essential to life as water could thus become deadly. Epiphanius cleverly paralleled the unique practices of a heretical sect that was derided for its use of potions and liquids with the fearful effects of the poison of a terrifying breed of snake, and he concluded his refutation by saying that Marcos "causes the death of his dupes with a drink."[50] Again, serpent and heretic, venom and heresy, have become one and the same.

The "Blood-Letting Viper"

Epiphanius dedicated *Panarion* 48 to the Phrygians, Montanists, and Tascodrugians, heresies known for an emphasis on prophecy and revelation.[51] He described the beliefs and practices of the Montanists for most of the entry, but toward the end he discussed the Tascodrugians, which he thought were either part of the broader prophetic movement or one that emerged from it.[52] The name of the sect derives either from its alleged practice of ritual nose-pegging or the posture its members took while praying. Epiphanius reported rumors of another rather shocking practice: "In this heresy or one related to it, so called of the Quintillianists or Priscillianists or Pepuzians, they say that something terrible and a wicked deed happens. For at a certain festival, with bronze needles they prick the entire body of a child, that is, of just a baby, and procure for themselves its blood, verily for the sake of a sacrifice."[53]

Based on this practice, or at least rumors of it, Epiphanius then compared this heresy with a breed of snake called the "blood-letting viper," "whose mis-

---

49. *Pan.* 34.22.3–5. Cf. Nic., *Ther.* 335–42. Nicander related a similar account of the *dipsas*, whose bite caused an inflammation of the heart and an intense thirst. The victim would drink until "his belly bursts his navel, spilling the too heavy load" (Gow and Scholfield, *Nicander*, 51). See Scarborough, "Toxicology I." 6. Others who wrote about the *dipsas* include Philumenus, *de Venantis Animalibus* 20.1—3; Lucan, *Bellum Civile* 9.718, 737–60; Lucian, *Dipsades*. See Dummer, "Handbuch," 297.
50. *Pan.* 34.22.6.
51. See throughout Trevett, *Montanism.*
52. *Pan.* 48.14.3–6. See C. Trevett, "Fingers up Noses and Pricking with Needles: Possible Reminiscences of Revelation in Later Montanism," *VC* 49, no. 3 (1995): 258–69; S. Elm, "'Pierced by Bronze Needles': Anti-Montanist Charges of Ritual Stigmatization in Their Fourth-Century Context," *JECS* 4, no. 4 (1996): 409–39.
53. *Pan.* 48.14.5–6.

chief drains the blood of the whole body of those who have been bitten and thus causes death."[54] Again, Epiphanius cleverly linked heretics and their specific beliefs or practices with image of a harmful creature from the natural world, thus blurring the lines between human and animal, heretic and serpent: "For it [the heresy] pricks the body of an innocent child and its blood procured for partaking, verily <pretending?> that this is a rite in the name of Christ, deceiving those who have been beguiled."[55]

Origen the Viper

By the time Epiphanius sat down to compose the *Panarion*, his anti-Origenist convictions were firmly in place. As we examined in chapter 1, the Egypt in which Epiphanius received his training as a young monk was pervaded by Origen's influence and ideas, and Oliver Kösters argues that Epiphanius was neither born an anti-Origenist nor was he early on as staunchly opposed to Origen's theology as his later writings and reputation would have us believe.[56] His opposition must have had a period of incubation and development. Epiphanius's practice of the ascetic life, training his real, physical body, must have played a role in his belief that the body of this life on earth is very much a part of God's larger economy of human salvation and thus must be resurrected in its consummation.[57] Origen's alleged assertion that the resurrection body would be of a different nature and his ideas about the origin of the body and the fall of the human soul were problematic for Epiphanius.

Epiphanius's understanding and exegesis of Scripture were also central to his belief that Origen had it all wrong. Early in the *Panarion*, Epiphanius insinuated that the learned Origen's prideful attempt to interpret all of Scripture led to his downfall: "For from this goal, wishing to leave none of the holy Scriptures un-interpreted, he wrapped himself in the allure of sin and expounded deadly words."[58] After a lengthy exposition on all of Origen's allegedly flawed interpretations and resulting doctrines, Epiphanius concluded his entry by again attacking Origen the man and his admirers. At the heart of Epiphanius's criticism is the total corruption resulting from Origen's education: "For this is what happened to him and all those persuaded by him, to suffer, on account of

---

54. *Pan.* 48.15.6. Cf. Nic., *Ther.* 283–308; Philum., *Ven.* 21. Cyr. H., *catech.* 16.8 also mentioned Montanist ritual practices, but that they slit the throats of little children and chopped the bodies into pieces for a ritualistic meal.

55. *Pan.* 48.15.7.

56. See the important discussion in Kösters, *Trinitätslehre*, 20–33.

57. Cf. *Anc.* 87.

58. *Pan.* 64.3.9.

which I also mourn for him, because alas, how you have been hurt and have hurt many others, as though bitten by a fearful viper, I mean, by worldly education, and you have become noxious to others."[59] Using the thematic polemic of the *Panarion*, Epiphanius equated *paideia* with a poisonous serpent. Thus heresy, secular learning, and deadly animals are all one and the same.

The entry concludes with yet another image from the natural world:

> For the naturalists say that the dormouse dwells in its lair and bears its young, many at a time, up to five and still more, and vipers hunt these. And if the viper finds the den full, not being able to eat its entirety, it eats to its satisfaction with one or two. Having stabbed their eyes, it brings food and feeds them, having been blinded, until when it wishes to take each of them and eat. But if it happens that some ignorant people chance upon them and take them for food, they take something noxious, that which was fed by the poison of the viper.[60]

The story suggests that Origen was the viper. But it also introduces the added twist that not only was the serpent dangerous, so were the young mice it poisoned. Thus Epiphanius blurred the differences between snake, venom, and victim, implying that any and all of them could harm the orthodox believer. Origen and his doctrines were to be feared and avoided, but so were those who had been persuaded and corrupted by them. Epiphanius finished with a telling indictment: "Thus you, Origen, your mind blinded by your Greek education, have vomited poison for your followers and have become noxious food for them, by which you yourself have been harmed while harming more people."[61]

The *Dryinas*

In *Panarion* 65 on Paul of Samosata, Epiphanius provided a few details from the heresiarch's biography. Although Paul had become bishop of Antioch, "having been puffed up in his thought, he fell away from the truth and revived the heresy of Artemon, who was once alive in the beginning [of it] many years before and has [since] died."[62] The entry then focuses on refuting Paul's adoptionist notions, and Epiphanius essentially accused him of teaching Jewish doctrine because Paul denied that Christ, the only-begotten Son and the Word, is God

---

59. *Pan.* 64.72.5.
60. *Pan.* 64.72.7–8.
61. *Pan.* 64.72.9.
62. *Pan.* 65.1.4. Cf. Eus., *h.e.* 5.28.1.

and a subsistent being.[63] Epiphanius also said that Paul of Samosata and his followers were not truly Jews because they did not practice circumcision or observe the Sabbath, so they instead became "second-rate Jews."[64] Furthermore,
Paul asserted that Jesus was a mere man upon whom the one God/Word descended; thus by claiming that Jesus was only a man, Paul had revived the error
of the Jews.[65] Epiphanius was furious that Paul and his followers deceived others by calling themselves Christians despite promulgating tawdry Jewish doctrines. So he compared them to a breed of viper called the *dryinas*.[66] This snake
generally inhabits tall grasses around oak trees, camouflaging itself in the fallen
leaves and waiting for its victims.[67] Although the snake does not have a particularly painful bite, it causes death nevertheless.[68] The key detail about this snake
is its effective use of camouflage, which parallels Paul's deception of "being
clothed with the name of Christ."[69] Again, Epiphanius coordinated the particular characteristics of a heresy with those of a venomous creature.

Mani the *Kenchritis*

Among the lengthiest entries is one dedicated to Mani, the Persian heresiarch
vilified for plagiarizing and bastardizing a new religion.[70] Epiphanius drew
heavily on the *Acta Archelai*, attributed to Hegemonius, for his material on
Manichaeism, including a substantial biography and doctrinal information.[71]
However, because of its vehemently anti-Manichean polemic and the subsequent discovery of Manichaean texts, scholars question the reliability of the
Acta Archelai as a source on Mani and Manichaeism.[72] But it perfectly suited
the needs of the heresiologist Epiphanius, although he may also have had access
to supplementary anti-Manichaean writings.[73] The entry painstakingly mean-

63. *Pan.* 65.2.1–5.10.
64. *Pan.* 65.2.4.
65. *Pan.* 65.7.1–8.12.
66. *Pan.* 65.9.4.
67. The name of the snake was derived from the adjective "oaken." See Liddel and Scott, *Lexicon*, 450.
68. *Pan.* 65.9.5. Cf. Nic., *Ther.* 424–37; Philum., *Ven.* 25.
69. *Pan.* 65.9.6.
70. See C. Riggi, *Epifanio Contro Mani: Revisone Critica, Traduzione Italiana e Commento Storico del
    Panarion di Epifanio, Haer. LXVI* (Rome: Pontificium Institutum Altioris Latinitatis, 1967).
71. Cf. Cyr. H., *catech.* 6.22–31, for another use of the *Acta.* See Riggi, *Mani*, xxi–xxvii. Both Epiphanius
    and Jerome, *Vir. ill.* 72, believed the text was written by Archelaus himself, while Heraclianus, bishop
    of Chalcedon (as cited in Photius, *Bibliotecha*, Cod. 85) attributed it to Hegemonius. See the recent
    collection of essays by J. BeDuhn and P. Mirecki, eds., *Frontiers of Faith: The Christian Encounter with
    Manichaeism in the Acts of Archelaus*, Nag Hammadi and Manichaean Studies 61 (Leiden: Brill,
    2007).
72. See S. Lieu, *Manichaeism in Mesopotamia and the Roman East*, Religions in the Graeco-Roman
    World 118 (Leiden: Brill, 1994), 132–52.
73. *Pan.* 66.21.3: "Refutations have already been composed wonderfully by great men against the dis-

ders through a variety of teachings and corresponding refutations, but it is also noteworthy for including a lengthy biographical narrative of Mani's life.

At the heart of Epiphanius's account is the idea that Mani's belief system was derived from other sources; in other words, Mani was a plagiarist and theological thief.[74] Furthermore, Mani was originally a slave who changed his name from Cubricus (Corbicius in the Latin *Acta*), which in Babylonian apparently means "vessel."[75] Cubricus was owned by a widow who died childless and left him a substantial inheritance. The woman had received the wealth from Terbinthus, who in turn was a slave of Scythianus, a Saracen.[76] Scythianus "had been taught the language and literature of the Greeks there [in Egypt] and had become proficient in their futile worldly doctrines."[77] Epiphanius described the twofold source of Scythianus's teachings: first, "the wantonness of his luxury" led him to "think of something new, in keeping with his taste, to offer the world," and second, "he took his pretenses from Pythagoras."[78] Scythianus began to develop a dualistic view of the universe. After hearing about the Mosaic Law, he took his ideas to Jerusalem and began to debate with the teachers of the Law, but to no avail. He was also "a sorcerer, importing the terrible and pernicious arts of magic from the heathen wisdom of the Indians and Egyptians," but attempting to practice his dark arts on the roof of a house, he fell and died.[79] His slave Terbinthus inherited his possessions and fled to Persia, curiously changing his name to "Buddha" to avoid being recognized.[80] Terbinthus also "engaged in magic and conjuring, for he was educated as well."[81] He found lodging with an elderly widow and carried on his master's dualistic thinking, engaging in debate with followers of Mithras. But when he failed to persuade them, he too went to a rooftop to perform magic, fell, and died.[82]

After Terbinthus perished, the woman with whom he had lodged acquired Scythianus's wealth and purchased Mani sometime later. Mani mastered the

graced man, by the bishop Archelaus as has been said, but as I have heard, by Origen, Eusebius of Caesarea, Eusebius of Emesa, Serapion of Thmuis, Athanasius the Alexandrian, George the Laodicean, Apollinarius the Laodicean, Titus, and many others who spoke against him."

74. And a successor to the ur-heresiarch Simon Magus. See E. Spät, "The 'Teachers' of Mani in the *Acta Archelai* and Simon Magus," *VC*, no. 1 (2004): 1–23.

75. *Pan.* 66.1.4–5. Epiphanius ridiculed Mani's name, which in Greek means "mad." Cf. Eus., *h.e.* 7.31.1; Cyr. H., *catech.* 6.20.

76. *Pan.* 66.1.7. Cf. *Acta Archelai* 62.4.

77. *Pan.* 66.1.8.

78. *Pan.* 66.2.5, 66.2.9. The *Act. Archel.*, 42.5, 52.3, attributed Scythianus's education to the Egyptians and his dualistic teaching to Pythagoras.

79. *Pan.* 66.3.1–8.

80. Cf. *Act. Archel.* 63.2.

81. *Pan.* 66.3.12.

82. *Pan.* 66.3.12–14. Cf. *Act. Archel.* 63.5–6.

doctrines of Scythianus and continued to teach the dualistic worldview he had inherited. The *Acta Archelai* includes a story about Mani's attempt to heal the son of the Persian king, and Epiphanius repeated the story, stating that Mani, "blinded by his own wickedness, thought he might be able to work some cure for the son of the king somehow from what he had discovered in the books of his master, Terbinthus, that is Buddha, the successor of Scythianus."[83] He gave the boy drugs to no avail. The prince died, and Mani was imprisoned as a result. Many of his disciples visited him, and he sent three of them to Judaea to find Jewish and Christian books. Mani was "determined to deceive his dupes with the name of the Christian religion."[84] Although the emphasis of Epiphanius's reimagining of Mani's biography is on the dubious origins of Mani's teachings, at this point he confirmed that Mani's achievement was mingling the dualistic worldview originally taught by Scythianus with Christianity. Therefore Mani had committed a troubling heretical crime by introducing a false Christian veneer to an already condemnable dualistic worldview: "Taking and examining them [the books], he cultivated error, connecting his own falsehood with the truth."[85] The entry then proceeds at length to explicate and refute Manichaean teachings.

Epiphanius's biographical narrative highlights the various sources of Mani's doctrines, a poisonous amalgam of eastern religions, astrology, magic, dualism, Greek philosophy, Judaism, and Christianity. Concluding his discussion, Epiphanius claimed that his refutation has crushed the heads of the *amphisbaina*, a two-headed viper, and the *kenchritis*, a snake that "hides its poison and deceives through its varied colors, being in the middle of much forest brush and becoming like its surroundings."[86] Mani, who derived his erroneous doctrines from a variety of sources and adorned his belief system with all these "colors," only "sets himself up in the name of Christ." Thus the comparison with the deceptive serpent was a natural fit.[87]

Other Serpents

The serpent imagery prevails throughout the *Panarion* as Epiphanius made several more connections between serpents and heretics. In his concluding re-

---

83. *Pan.* 66.4.4. Cf. *Act. Archel.* 64.8–9.
84. *Pan.* 66.5.4–6.
85. *Pan.* 66.8.8.
86. *Pan.* 66.88.3. For the *amphisbaina*, cf. Nic., *Ther.* 373–84; Philum., *Ven.* 27, and for the *cenchritis* cf. Nic., *Ther.* 463–83; Philu., *Ven.* 26.
87. *Pan.* 66.88.3.

marks about Simon Magus, Epiphanius wrote: "For there is caprice and uncertainty in him, since he is a deceiver who has clothed himself in the form of the name of Christ, just like the snake-ish death of the abortions conceived from the wind eggs of asps and other vipers."[88] This characterization is certainly unpleasant and grotesque, but to great rhetorical effect. Simon's successor was Menander, to whom Epiphanius dedicated a brief entry, and at its conclusion, he related a story of asps collected into earthen jars and buried in the four corners of an Egyptian temple.[89] The stronger snakes would consume the weaker until the last, strongest snake "turning on itself and beginning to eat from its tail up to a certain part, it consumes its entire body. Thus it remained no longer whole, but became half a snake, on account of which they call it an *aspidogorgon*."[90] The polemical point is that just as the snake having consumed itself no longer existed, so the heresy of Menander had been wiped out.[91]

Continuing on the theme of succession, Epiphanius connected Satornilus and Basilides and accused them of borrowing their heretical ideas from one another, which reminded Epiphanius of an old proverb: "An asp borrowing poison from a viper."[92] He wrote how the deceptive and dangerous heresiarch Basilides, "just as in the manner of a *kerastes*, having buried itself in the sandy ground, pokes up to the air with its horn and works death to those who chance upon it."[93] Epiphanius applied the same serpent connection with the Pneumatomachoi.[94] The heresy of Cerinthus is like a "rotting viper," whose body is apparently covered with long red hair, appears to be like a goat or sheep, and has a harmful bite.[95]

More generically, Epiphanius likened Colorbasus to the *phalaggios*, a snake with four heads, and the *amphisbaina*, a two-headed viper. The Sethians' teaching was like the poison of an asp.[96] Epiphanius applied the common word for a

---

88. *Pan.* 21.7.2. On Simon, cf. Just., *1 Apol.* 26.1–3, 56.1–4; Iren., *haer.* 1.23.1–5; Hipp., *haer.* 6.7.1–20.4; Eus., *h.e.* 2.13.1–6.

89. *Pan.* 22.2.2. On Menander, cf. Iren., *haer.* 1.23.5; Hipp., *haer.* 7.28.1. On the heresiological importance of the master-disciple succession of Simon and Menander, see Le Boulluec, *La notion* 80–82.

90. A neologism, but also applied to the Ebionites at *Pan.* 30.26.5–6. See Verheyden, "Epiphanius," 155–56.

91. Cf. *Pan.* 30.26.6. Epiphanius applied the same comparison to the Ebionites, with the idea that their doctrines and practices were self-destructive.

92. *Pan.* 23.7.2. Tert., *Marc.* 3.8, cited the same proverb. On Satornilus, cf. Iren., *haer.* 1.24.1–7; Hipp., *haer.* 7.28.1–7.

93. *Pan.* 24.10.6. Cf. Nic., *Ther.* 258–82; Philum., *Ven.* 17. On Basilides, cf. Iren., *haer.* 1.24.1–7; Hipp., *haer.* 7.14.1–27.13.

94. *Pan.* 74.14.3.

95. *Pan.* 28.8.4. Cf. Nic., *Ther.* 320–33. On Cerinthus, cf. Iren., *haer.* 1.26.1; Hipp., *haer.* 7.33.1–2.

96. *Pan.* 35.3.9, 39.10.7. On the *phalaggios*, cf. Nic., *Ther.* 752–58; Philum., *Ven.* 15. According to Liddel

"snake" in his dismissal of the heresiarch Lucian, while he claimed to have thrashed the heresiarch Theodotus like a "still wriggling snake," as he did the head of Bardesanes.[97] The Apostolics' heresy is like a viper and the "quick-darting serpent" or "blind snake" or "mouser."[98] These snakes have little venom but are nuisances nonetheless and ought to be eradicated. Similarly, Epiphanius mentioned the Sabellian *libus*, *molouros*, and *elops*, which are harmless breeds of snakes easily exterminated by his refutation.[99] The Semi-Arians were likened to a "dreadful serpent," as were the Antidicomarians.[100] All of these examples further reinforce the rhetorical effect of Epiphanius's encyclopedic heresiological taxonomy and the blurring of the line between heretic and serpent.

Heresiology as *Historia Animalium*

Arachnids and Insects

Epiphanius occasionally turned to the arachnid and insect world to conjure up additional skin-crawling comparisons to great effect. As much as venomous snakes were a terrifying threat for people in the ancient world, ubiquitous scorpions, spiders, and a host of insects were equally troublesome, annoying, and at times deadly. The most interesting application of this natural imagery is in the entry against Valentinus, who according to the heresiological tradition was a notorious heresiarch with widespread ideas and influence.[101] After a lengthy explication and refutation of the Valentinian Gnostic system, Epiphanius equated the heresiarch with a scorpion.[102] He drew on folk knowledge about scorpion behavior in an interesting comparison:

For sowing his [Valentinus's] dream into many, calling himself a Gnostic, he linked many scorpions into one chain, as it says in the old and famous parable.

---

and Scott, it refers to the malmignatte, a type of venomous spider. *Lexicon*, 1913. On Colorbasus, cf. Iren., *haer*. 1.14.1.; Hipp., *haer*. 4.13.1.

97. *Pan*. 43.2.8., 54.6.5, 56.3.7.

98. *Pan*. 61.8.5. *Pan*. 32.7.9, also likened the Secundian heresy to the "mouser." On the "quick-darting serpent," cf. Nic., *Ther*. 491; Philum., *Ven*. 26; "blind snake," cf. Nic., *Ther*. 491; Philum., *Ven*. 29; "mouser," cf. Nic., *Ther*. 490; Philum., *Ven*. 22.

99. *Pan*. 62.8.5. On the *libus*, cf. Nic., *Ther*. 490; *molouros*, cf. Nic., *Ther*. 491; *elops*, cf. Nic., *Ther*. 490; Philum., *Ven*. 28.

100. *Pan*. 73.38.5, 78.24.7.

101. Iren., *haer*. 1.1–11.5, was an important starting point in his attack of the Valentinians, but much of Books 1 and 2 was dedicated to refuting Valentinus's system as well as the variations developed by his "successors." See also Hipp., *haer*. 6.21.1–37.9.

102. Cf. Nic., *Ther*. 770–804.

They say that scorpions linking up one after the other like a chain, up to ten or even more, will let themselves down from a roof or housetop, and thus with cunning inflict their harm on men. So this man and those derived from him called Gnostics have become authors of error; and taking their false ideas from him, each man has become pupil to the other, produced additional error after his teacher, and introduced another heresy clinging to its predecessor. And thus in a succession those called Gnostics have been divided into different heresies, having taken their pretenses, as I have said, from Valentinus and those who preceded him.[103]

The comparison with scorpions and the tale about their linking behavior uniquely underscores the common heresiological rhetoric of succession.[104] According to the heresiologists, in the *diadochē* of heretics, which began with the ur-heresiarch Simon Magus, each successive generation results in deeper corruption and further deviation from the truth, and Epiphanius drove this point home by conjuring up a clever image from the natural world.[105]

Epiphanius also used two different types of beetles in the *Panarion*. The first is known as the *bouprēstis* (literally "cow-swelling") beetle, which apparently when eaten by cattle causes them to swell up and die, and is like the heresy of the Cainites, which revered the biblical murderer because its members "yearn for what is worse."[106] Epiphanius applied the same parallel to the heresy of Aerius, and in addition compared them to the "blister beetle."[107] He also introduced several types of wasps into his heresiological taxonomy.[108] For example, he likened the heresiarch Apelles, who was both a student of Marcion and a fellow disciple of the heresiarch Lucian, to a certain wasp known as a "stinging" wasp.[109] This breed has a short, poisonous stinger, and it builds its nest among bushy weeds. If someone upsets or destroys the wasps' lair, they fly out in a rage and attack whatever is nearby, even a rock or tree. If they happen to find the

103. *Pan.* 31.36.4–6. Clem., *str.* 1.21 (143.4), mentioned a similar anecdote of scorpions linking together to achieve their goal.
104. Again, on succession see Le Boulluec, *La notion*, 40, 80–91, 162–73; Pourkier, *L'hérésiologie*, 53–63; Kim, "Reading," 393–400. Contrast this imagery, for example, with the language of procreation and kinship deployed by Clement in the *Stromateis*, as observed by Buell, *Making*, 50–68.
105. This rhetorical theme is found in other heresiological traditions; see Henderson, *Construction*, 134–36.
106. *Pan.* 38.8.7. Cf. Nic., *Alexipharmaca* 335–47.
107. *Pan.* 75.8.4. Cf. Nic., *Ther.* 755; *Alex.* 115–28. The Collyridians were also likened to them; cf. *Pan.* 79.9.5.
108. The Nazoraeans (29.9.5) were like a "small wasp" (cf. Nic., *Ther.* 739–47, 811; Philu., *Ven.* 11), and the Cerdonians (41.3.5) the *bembix* (cf. Nic., *Ther.* 806).
109. *Pan.* 44.1.1.

person, their sting brings some pain. But when these wasps sting a rock, their stingers break and they die. Thus Epiphanius compared the rock with the "truth"; heretics attack it but ultimately die.[110] Epiphanius made several generic comparisons between heretics and other arachnids and insects. He claimed to have crushed the Severians like a scorpion, the Valesians like a "double-sting scorpion," and Hieracas like a "winged scorpion."[111] Epiphanius destroyed the Alogoi like a millipede or wood louse, and did the same to the Anomoians.[112] Epiphanius did not have as many unique comparisons with arachnids and insects based on their behavior as he did with snakes. Nevertheless, the rhetorical effect and reaction produced by this imagery are the same: revulsion.

Amphibians, Fish, and Lizards

In his entry against the Nicolaitans, Epiphanius criticized the heresiarch's capricious approach to sexual continence. He followed the biblical and heresiological tradition in identifying Nicolaus as one of the original seven deacons chosen by the Apostles who for a time was numbered among the righteous (cf. Acts 6:1–6).[113] Unfortunately, "the devil later dove into this man and beguiled his heart," and he promulgated heretical ideas:[114]

> For this man, having a beautiful wife and practicing continence from his wife, as in imitation of those he saw who were devoting themselves to God, was continent up to a certain point. He could not bear to master his self-control, but wishing like a dog to return to its own vomit, seeking after some bad pretexts he contrived an excuse for his own intemperate passion. It would have been more beneficial for him <to feel shame and to repent?>. So departing from his goal, he simply came together with his wife.[115]

Nicolaus was ashamed of his failure at celibacy, so he began to teach that one had to have sex to inherit eternal life.[116] He then promulgated Gnostic teachings to justify his immoral behavior, which in turned spawned several other li-

---

110. *Pan.* 44.7.2–6.
111. *Pan.* 45.4.10, 58.4.17, 67.8.1.
112. *Pan.* 51.35.4, 76.54.38. Cf. Nic., *Ther.* 811–12.
113. Cf. Iren., *haer* 1.26.3; Clem., *str.* 3.4 (25.5–26.3); Hipp., *haer.* 7.36.2–3.
114. *Pan.* 25.1.3.
115. *Pan.* 25.1.4.
116. *Pan.* 25.1.5.

centious heresies, including the familiar "Borborites." Because Nicolaus made a vow but could not remain true to it, Epiphanius likened him to a *hydrops* that, "having come out of the water onto land, returns back again into the water."[117]

The Archontics exhibited the dangerous characteristics of many harmful animals and possessed the "treachery of a toad," and the teachings of the Quartodecimans were dismissed like the "swollenness of the *baion* or toad."[118] Epiphanius concluded the entry against the Ebionites by invoking a beach scene upon which "a casting up of fish occurs, and it causes injury to the feet of those who are crossing the elevated areas (from among the fish, some are poisonous, I mean sting ray, *drakaina*, shark, and eels, as I have already said)."[119] A similar list of harmful sea creatures follows the refutation of the Ophites.[120]

The heresiarch Heracleon was like a *sēps*, which can refer to a type of serpent. But here Epiphanius was explicitly referring to a four-footed gecko-like lizard.[121] Although its bite is considered harmless, "its spittle hurled upon either food or drink causes immediate death to the partaker."[122] This gecko was equated with the Quintillianists, a Montanist offshoot.[123] Epiphanius briefly discussed the heretics known as Sampsaeans, a Jewish-Christian group he compared to a "solar lizard," apparently based on the Hebrew word for "sun."[124] However, he deemed these heretics worse than the solar lizard because at least the latter, although it has poor sight, can still see with the aid of the sun, while the former is always blind. Finally, the Messalians were likened to a "many-footed chameleon."[125]

Mammals

Although reptiles and insects dominate Epiphanius's new taxonomy, he occasionally equated heretics with mammals, for example comparing the Adamians with the common mole:

---

117. *Pan.* 25.7.3. Lampe attests to this creature only in Epiphanius, identifying it as "an amphibious reptile." *Lexicon*, 1423. In older usage, the term referred to dropsy, a medical condition characterized by the buildup of excess bodily fluids; cf. Liddel and Scott, *Lexicon*, 1845.

118. *Pan.* 40.8.8, 50.3.5.

119. *Pan.* 30.34.9. Cf. Nic., *Ther.* 822–36.

120. *Pan.* 37.9.3.

121. Nic., *Ther.* 147–58, described the *sēps* as a snake, but 817–18 more like a lizard; Philu., *Ven.* 23; Luc., *Bellum Civile* 9.761–65. On the gecko, cf. Nic., *Ther.* 483–84.

122. *Pan.* 36.6.7.

123. *Pan.* 49.3.4.

124. *Pan.* 53.2.2–4. Cf. Philu., *Ven.* 34.

125. *Pan.* 80.11.7.

It is a devastating thing, an animal that roots out from below the crops of men, especially cucumber beds and pungent plants, onions and garlic, purse-tassels and such as these, lilies and other things. But if breaking forth from its burrow it happens to appear on the surface out in the open air or is caught, hunted by men, it produces something laughable to all who hunt this animal. Thus also I am attempting to say concerning the heresy at hand, that it is blind at heart and ignorant, working devastation for itself, and cuts down from below its own standing, and finishes the damage of the roots of all, <I mean>, of all men who have fallen upon it.[126]

Perhaps Epiphanius drew on his own gardening experience to explain the food preferences of moles, but the point is clear. As the blind mole wreaked destruction yet appeared an utterly laughable creature when caught, so too did the blind Adamian heretics work ruin for themselves and those who fell among them.

Epiphanius used the diminutive form for the "shrew mouse" in his invective against the Melchizedekians. Common in Egypt, this tiny mammal inflicts an apparently harmless bite but infects its victims with leprosy that slowly destroys the body. In the same way, the seemingly harmless teachings of these heretics infiltrate the minds of those who hear them, and without a proper cure cause destruction.[127] Epiphanius's readers would have known this rodent, and the effect of comparing it to the Melchizedekian heresy would have elicited caution even in the face of a seemingly harmless creature.

Mythical Creatures

Epiphanius also equated heretics with well-known mythical or semimythical creatures.[128] He mentioned the basilisk in a number of entries and may have been referring to a real breed of snake, such as the Egyptian cobra, or to the mythological serpent with a petrifying gaze.[129] He likened the arch-heresiarch Simon Magus, the "Gnostics," and the Cathari to this creature.[130] Epiphanius vilified the Archontics for "possessing the arrogance of a dragon," and he

126. *Pan.* 52.1.2–4.
127. *Pan.* 55.9.16–17.
128. See Grant, *Animals*, 34–43.
129. Cf. Nic., *Ther.* 396–411, describing a poisonous snake; Philu., *Ven.* 31. See Liddel and Scott, *Lexicon*, 310. On a number of occasions, Epiphanius's term could refer to multiple animals. See Verheyden, "Epiphanius," 155.
130. *Pan.* 21. 7.3, 26.3.9, 59.13.4.

"maimed" Noetus and his followers like an "earthen dragon," which "cannot turn itself neither to the right nor left in pursuing a man."[131] He also compared the Manichaeans and Arians to dragons.[132] However at the end of his entry against the Arians, Epiphanius conflated this "dragon" with the hydra, another mythological beast: "Having left behind this slain hydra, with its seven heads and segmented body, we proceed as usual to what remains, my beloved, as ever calling upon the aid of God to have the same care for us and for any who desire to read this book, for the healing of those who have been bitten and for the correction of those already proven to be among the wicked."[133] In his entries against the Arians, Semi-Arians, and Anomoians, Epiphanius went to great lengths to demonstrate their diversity and factionalism in contrast to the unity of the orthodox.[134] This is a common heresiological trope, and hence the hydra with manifold heads.

Perhaps the most interesting mythological creature Epiphanius cited is in *Panarion* 36 against the Gnostic Heracleon, "successor" of Colorbasus:

> For all of them [Heracleonites], having molded themselves into a one-hundred-headed or one-hundred-handed body, they mimicked the *Kottos* or *Briareus*, which they also call *Aigaion* or *Gyes* or the so-called many-eyed *Argos*, mythologized once upon a time by the poets of the Greeks. Those sorts of people talk marvels in their recitations, composing and saying that one had one hundred hands, and at one time fifty heads and at another one hundred, and another had one hundred eyes—and because of this, they say that Hermes is called "Argeiphontes," as he had slain the many-eyed Argos—and thus each of these people [heretics], wishing to establish authority for himself, named himself a head, secretly introducing other things besides the wasted labor and insane teaching of his own teachers.[135]

Equating heresy with pagan mythology is another well-established heresiological tactic that enabled Christians to add the stain of idolatry, and Epiphanius

---

131. *Pan.* 40.8.8, 57.10.8. Cf. Nic., *Ther.* 438–57; Philu., *Ven.* 30. Again, the "dragon" here is possibly another generic word for a serpent; cf. Liddel and Scott, *Lexicon*, 448; Lampe, *Lexicon*, 386.
132. *Pan.* 66.88.4, 69.81.6
133. *Pan.* 69.81.7. On the heresiological theme of contrast between the manifold expressions of heresy and the unity of orthodoxy, see Henderson, *Construction*, 120–23.
134. Henderson, *Construction*, 95–98.
135. *Pan.* 36.1.3–5.

here clearly departed from the naturalist guidebooks that served as the basis for much of his discussion.[136] But to underscore his notion that heretics always breed other heretics and that their multifarious variations always contrast with the singular unity of the orthodox truth, he turned to a comparison with a rather fantastic mythological creature.

All of the examples discussed above, some specific and others more generic, are characteristic of Epiphanius's rather clever use of natural imagery to escalate his heresiological rhetoric.[137] In particular, the negative biblical and theological pedigree of snakes matches well Epiphanius's attempts to demonize heretics and heresiarchs. In late ancient Christian thought, animals were frequently metaphors for bestial human habits and stand-ins for demonic obstacles that hindered progress in the ascetic enterprise and ultimately in the salvation of the soul.[138] Thus by drawing on fear of the dangerous side of the natural world and of the manifold threats to the Christian body, Epiphanius augmented the soteriological fears of his readers. He appropriated the classical encyclopedic knowledge of naturalists, much of which would have been at least anecdotally familiar to his readers, and he merged it with the dangerous theology and practices of heretics, thus blurring the difference between human and animal and creating a new heresiological taxonomy. This is Epiphanius at his heresiological and rhetorical best.

Heresiology as Healing

Not all in the *Panarion*, however, is intended to elicit adverse reactions. Epiphanius's heresiology systematically presents knowledge of the poisonous beliefs and practices of heresies in the most negative ways possible, but it also contains knowledge of the truth, that is, the orthodox doctrines of the Christian faith. Thus the *Panarion* simultaneously and paradoxically embodies both knowl-

---

136. On the heresiological connection between pagan myth and heresy, see Le Boulluec, *La notion*, 119–35.

137. The examples cover most but not all of Epiphanius's references to harmful creatures, and several were repeated or used generically. See Verheyden, "Epiphanius," 150–54.

138. Gilhus, *Animals*, 205–26. See also French, *History*, 225–34, for an examination of the *Physiologus*, a second-century CE text that for a long time was mistakenly attributed to Epiphanius, and how the author of the text utilized allegorical interpretations of animal behaviors to connect them with human morality.

edge to destroy the soul and to restore and save it. For Epiphanius, the truth derived from a proper exegesis of Scripture is the antidote to all heretical poisons, and he incorporated lengthy exegetical discussions in many entries throughout the *Panarion*.[139] He believed his theological explications and refutations were the medicines his fellow Christians could use to heal themselves and to cure victims of heresy, and at times he used medical and pharmacological imagery to describe his cures. He also exhibited a sense of trepidation and hesitation because he was well aware that the comprehensive knowledge he was providing in the *Panarion* was both helpful and potentially dangerous:

> I accurately recount everything concerning each heresy, as I said, revealing horrible things for the sake of treatment for those who have fallen. And for the sake of refutation, I prepare a medicinal drug made from the divine Scriptures and right reasonings, as I said, providing <it> in the Lord according to a twofold manner: for the sake of recovery for those going through sickness and great pain, and <for the sake of> a preventative remedy, as I said, for those who have not ever been infected. Giving the drug of the truth to the wise, may we also be called a disciple of the disciples of our Lord and Savior, who is the help of bodies and souls.[140]

Furthermore, Epiphanius did not limit the access to his medicines to just orthodox Christians; rather, he envisioned his cures as available and efficacious for patients across the spectrum of belief. In the conclusion of his entry against the Encratites, he wrote:

> Again, having mutilated with the mighty hand of the truth the harmful beast, deprived of its teeth, let us proceed to what remains. As usual we call upon the God of all as our guide and defender from horrible things, aid of our judgment and the one who is giver of wisdom, in order that when we learn from him that which is true, we might be able to make known their <silly talk?> and that we might provide a medicinal antidote against them, made from many sorts of unguents, from the word of the truth. May the physician's fee of God be given

---

139. Biblical exegesis was an important locus in the early development of heresiological discourse, and in many cases, particular methods of reading Scripture were in part reactions to what were understood to be heretical interpretations. See Le Boulluec, *La notion*, 189–253.
140. *Pan.* 48.15.3–5.

ungrudgingly for the sake of healing to those already stricken, and for the sake of treatment for those who chance upon it [heresy], and for the sake of a preventative from suffering for those about to learn things they did not know, and for the sake of our salvation.[141]

Epiphanius's rhetorical construction also reflects a complex development in Christian attitudes toward medicine and healing in late antiquity when the lines between practical and spiritual cures became blurred, especially in relation to the physical body and human suffering.[142] Epiphanius's information on medicine and drugs was also largely derivative and generic, and he clearly drew on source material from naturalists, medical writings, and perhaps even common folkloric knowledge. For example, in his entry on Paul of Samosata, Epiphanius described a metaphorical medical procedure in which he "with the surgeon's scalpel of the Gospel, has scratched [the bites] of those who have been bit and has drawn out the poison from them."[143] Epiphanius frequently mentioned nameless oils and salves with healing properties, but he did not describe any specific substance or remedy. Rather, he linked the nonspecific medicines with some theological modifier, as in the "oil of the loving-kindness of God" used against the bites of the Tatianists and the "preventative draught of the Lord's Resurrection" against the poison of Origen.[144] In a slightly different but related way, Epiphanius mentioned a specific folk practice in his entry against the Alogoi, a heresy that rejected the Gospel of John and Revelation.[145] He described them "as a feeble snake, unable to

141. *Pan.* 47.3.4–5.
142. See D. Amundsen, "Medicine and Faith in Early Christianity," *Bulletin of the History of Medicine* 56 (1982): 326–50; Nutton, "Galen," 5–10; G. Ferngren, "Early Christianity as a Religion of Healing," *Bulletin of the History of Medicine* 66, no. 1 (1992): 1–15. As Martin has demonstrated, Christian attitudes toward and understandings of the body, its pollution, preservation, and resurrection, were from the beginning varied, confused, complicated, and contextually informed. *Corinthian.* See especially 186–94, for an examination of ancient understandings of the relationship between the body and drugs and medicines, both at the folk and professional level. On ancient drugs, see also V. Nutton, "The Drug Trade in Antiquity," *Journal of the Royal Society of Medicine* 78 (1985): 138–45.
    For the relationship between monasticism and Christian attitudes and practices toward sickness and healthcare, see A. Crislip, *From Monastery to Hospital: Christian Monasticism and the Transformation of Health Care in Late Antiquity* (Ann Arbor: University of Michigan Press, 2005); idem, *Thorns in the Flesh: Illness and Sanctity in Late Ancient Christianity,* Divinations: Rereading Late Ancient Religion (Philadelphia: University of Pennsylvania Press, 2013).
143. *Pan.* 65.9.7.
144. *Pan.* 46.5.11, 64.72.4.
145. See S. Manor, "Epiphanius' *Alogi* and the Question of Early Ecclesiastical Opposition to the Johannine Corpus," PhD diss., University of Edinburgh, 2011; idem, "Epiphanius' Account of the *Alogi*: Historical Fact or Heretical Fiction?" StPatr 52 (2012): 161–70. Epiphanius well may have invented heresies to suit his heresiological purposes.

withstand the smell of dittany, also storax, or of frankincense or of southern-wood, or the smell of pitch, or incense, or lignite stone, or hartshorn."[146] Just as those to the harmful animals, Epiphanius's references to the various cures and preventatives come at the end of each entry. But the real substance of these meta-phorical medicines was prepared in Epiphanius's exegetical refutations. Like a spiritual pharmacist, Epiphanius prepared the scriptural ingredients for the rem-edies needed to cure the maladies of heresy, and thus the *Panarion* embodied the meaning of its title, the "medicine chest."

Implied Violence

Despite the thematic layer of healing and restoration, the overwhelming tone in the *Panarion* is deleterious. Epiphanius's reimagined taxonomy ordered here-siarchs and heretics according to a schema of the dangerous side of the natural world, which blurred the line between human and animal, heretic and noxious creature. He exploited the fear of venomous and harmful creatures, and many of his descriptions, which cleverly equated the beliefs and practices of heretics with wild animals, must have been intended to elicit disgust and dread. The snakes, insects, and other creatures in the *Panarion* would have been familiar to many of Epiphanius's readers, and the rhythms of daily life, both within and beyond the city, would have reminded them of the ever-present and lurking threat of harmful animals. Epiphanius provided the essential knowledge his readers needed to avoid such "creatures" and to treat those who were afflicted by them. However, fear, reactive caution, and first aid constituted only part of the intended responses to any encounter with these dangerous heretical beasts. Indeed, another overwhelming thematic idea, constantly reiterated by Epipha-nius, undergirded the pages of the *Panarion*: violence.

The late ancient Mediterranean world was certainly no stranger to violence, and the ascendancy of Christianity had little ameliorating effect on its ubiqui-ty.[147] At least according to much of the literary evidence that survives, Chris-

---

146. *Pan.* 51.1.1. Epiphanius also mentioned the effect of the odor of storax against snakes in *Pan.* 78.24.7. Nic., *Ther.* 35–56, explained the effects of fumigation by burning these substances, among others. Cf. Herodotus 3.107.

147. See the manifold expressions and examples of late antique violence, with varied attempts to explain their causes, in the collection of essays in Drake, *Violence in Late Antiquity*; Gaddis, *No Crime*; T. Sizgorich, *Violence and Belief in Late Antiquity: Militant Devotion in Christianity and Islam* (Philadel-phia: University of Pennsylvania Press, 2009); Drake, "Curious Case."

tians became quite adept at meting out violence upon *each other*; and while the theological controversies and conflicts of the fourth century were predominantly expressed in literary form and voiced at conciliar meetings, there were moments when these disputes spilled into the realm of the physical.[148] The pagan historian Ammianus Marcellinus famously wrote that the emperor Julian recognized that "no hostile beasts are as deadly to men, as are most Christians to each other."[149] Heresiology, especially in its Christian iteration, was at its heart characterized by polemic and violence, because it tried in no uncertain terms to define and demarcate insider and outsider. And as we have examined already thus far, the *Panarion* was no exception to this project. Epiphanius's novel taxonomy was a unique expression of this Christian reimagining and redefining of society and culture, and it served to dehumanize the object of his polemical attack.[150] Indeed, Epiphanius may have been inspired by the very words of Jesus: "See, I have given you authority to tread on snakes and scorpions, and over all the power of the enemy; and nothing will hurt you" (Luke 10:19, NRSV). Although the original context of this Gospel text was referring to the demons cast out by the followers of Jesus, Epiphanius found little trouble in blurring the distinctions between demons, heretics, and venomous creatures, as he invoked the same words in his entry against the "asp" that was Marcion.[151] And while he certainly wanted his readers to be scared and disgusted, he also sought to make them proactive, to take the initiative against heretics.

At the conclusion of almost every entry in the *Panarion* beginning with that dedicated to Simon Magus, Epiphanius articulated the success of his heresiological efforts by referencing some sort of violent action against one the noxious animals he connected to the heretic(s). About Simon, Epiphanius claimed that he "has struck this man with the words of the truth," and this after his reference to aborted snake fetuses, and with respect to Basilides he "has crushed this

---

148. Gaddis, *No Crime*, 70. However, recent scholarship has reconsidered the nature of religious conflict, including its manifestation in physical and discursive violence, and with respect to late antiquity, has started to challenge the fundamental assumption (operative in the books referenced above) that the post-Constantinian world was characterized by coercion while the period preceding by nonviolent competition. See W. Mayer, "Religious Conflict: Definitions, Problems and Theoretical Approaches," in *Religious Conflict from Early Christianity to Early Islam*, Arbeiten zur Kirchengeschichte 121, ed. W. Mayer and B. Neil (Berlin: Walter de Gruyter, 2013), 1–14, who introduces the most recent scholarship and provides ample references.

149. Amm., *Res gestae* 22.5.4.

150. Here I take Epiphanius's polemic a step further than Verheyden, "Epiphanius," 172: "Likening the heretic to a creepy beast is the ultimate insult."

151. *Pan.* 42.16.14.

man with the teaching of the truth."[152] Epiphanius often connected these violent acts with a particular offensive weapon or implement, be it a club or a sandal, which was often endowed with the power of the truth, the Gospel, or some other modifier. For example, Epiphanius used a reed against the *hydrops* Nicolaus, the "wood of life" against the "viper with no birth pangs," that is, the Gnostics, a "cudgel of the faith and the truth" against Carpocrates, and the "sandal of the Gospel" against Secundus.[153] Against Hieracas, Epiphanius claimed that he "tore to pieces his wings and broke his head with the club of life.[154] Most often in his references to beating or killing various heretical creatures, Epiphanius assaulted their heads, and this image surely mirrored the scene of God's judgment against the serpent in Genesis 3:15.

Epiphanius never encouraged his readers to physically attack any of the heretics he refuted in the *Panarion*. Rather, through his clever rhetoric, manifest in a novel heresiological taxonomy, which had the effect of blurring the difference between man and beast, Epiphanius implied a violent reaction and response to heresy. Thus the pages of his heresiology contained a literary, discursive violence, which left the door open to physical action. He had "armed" his readers with essential knowledge, frequently embodied in some form of weapon, and thereby empowered the orthodox to take the initiative, to go on the offensive, to crush, smash, bash, split open, maim, and trample heresy and heretics.[155] Epiphanius was not afraid of taking action when he perceived that the orthodox church was under threat, and the years following the composition of his magnum opus reflected this mindset. He ultimately spent the final years of his life fighting what he thought was a war for the sake of true Christianity. In the final chapter, we will examine Epiphanius's life after the *Panarion* and how he embodied the rhetoric of his heresiology.

---

152. *Pan.* 20.7.3, 24.10.8.
153. *Pan.* 25.7.3, 26.19.6, 27.8.4, 32.7.9.
154. *Pan.* 67.8.4.
155. See the list of actions in Verheyden, "Epiphanius," 164.

CHAPTER 7

To Infamy and Beyond

Epiphanius after the Panarion

When Epiphanius finished writing the *Panarion*, he was by ancient standards a very old man of about sixty. Had he passed away soon thereafter, his legacy as a notable ascetic and a defender of orthodoxy would have remained secure. Perhaps it is also safe to suggest that his reputation and reception in the modern world would have engendered less scholarly indignation. But when evaluating historical subjects, words go hand in hand with deeds, and there is a living afterlife that we must consider before completing our study of Epiphanius. Remarkably, the heresiologist lived for almost twenty-five more years after completing his magnum opus. When Jerome described Epiphanius in 393 as "still alive up to this day and presently in extreme old age," the venerable bishop still had another ten years of life left in him.[1] Epiphanius did much in these years, moved throughout the empire, and in a real sense became the living embodiment of the *Panarion*. Like an actor following a script, Epiphanius spent the rest of his life putting his words into action. Orthodoxy became orthopraxy.

The Journey to Rome

After the death of Valens at the Battle of Adrianople in 9 August 378, which briefly left Gratian as the sole ruler of the Roman Empire, Meletius once again returned

---

1. Jer., *Vir. ill.* 114.

204

from exile and reasserted his claim as bishop of Antioch, although Dorotheus, the successor to Euzoius, held the see.[2] The city continued to be divided as the stalwart Paulinus, whom Valens had essentially left alone, still claimed leadership of the Antiochene church. The continued disagreement among the pro-Nicene Christians almost erupted in violence before a sort of compromise solution was reached that in the end would prove futile but for the time being secured peace. The partisans of each claimant essentially agreed that while both Paulinus and Meletius were alive, no potential successor of either man would seek or accept ordination as bishop of the city, and that if one of the two died, the remaining bishop would claim sole leadership of the see.[3] Based on ensuing events, however, Meletius clearly held the position of greater authority.

Theodosius, who was Gratian's choice as the new Augustus of the East, assumed power in the eastern half of the Roman Empire on 19 January 379. On 28 February of the next year, he issued a decree addressed to the people of Constantinople, the so-called *Cunctos populos*, which affirmed the faith according to Damasus of Rome and Peter of Alexandria.[4] The emperor entered the city of Constantinople on 24 November 380, and with hopes of unifying the church, interviewed Demophilus, the Homoian bishop of Constantinople, and asked if he was willing to accept the Nicene Creed, to which Demophilus replied in the negative, abdicated, and left the city.[5] A few days later, Gregory of Nazianzus was chosen by the pro-Nicenes to become the bishop of Constantinople.[6] Sometime in early 381, Theodosius called for a council in Constantinople that apparently was not intended to be the ecumenical council it would become in the memory of later Christians, but more local in character.[7] The council was

2.   Euzoius died in 376. Cf. Philost., *h.e.* 9.14; Socr., *h.e.* 4.35.4, 5.3.2; Soz., *h.e.* 6.37.17. The timing of Meletius's return, and under whose decree it was made possible, is complicated by R. Errington, "Church and State in the First Years of Theodosius," *Chiron* 27 (1997): 21–72, especially 21–33.

3.   Socr., *h.e.* 5.5.1–8; Soz., *h.e.* 7.3.1–5. This arrangement was disputed by some, identified as "Luciferi-ans," who uncompromisingly rejected Meletius, who in their eyes had been ordained by Arian heretics. Thdt., *h.e.* 5.3.1–16, in his usual hagiographical way, gave a different account in which the saintly Meletius beseeched Paulinus to end their strife and unite the churches in Antioch, but Paulinus steadfastly refused and continued the schism.

4.   On Theodosius in general, see S. Williams and G. Friell, *Theodosius: The Empire at Bay* (New Haven: Yale University Press, 1995), but critiqued by Errington, *Policy*, 212–59. On the circumstances of his accession, see R. Errington, "The Accession of Theodosius I," *Klio* 78, no. 2 (1996): 438–53. On Theodosius's religious policies (and their limits), see Errington, "Church," especially 36–41 on the *Cunctos populos*; idem, "Christian Accounts of the Religious Legislation of Theodosius I," *Klio* 79, no. 2 (1997): 398–443.

5.   Socr., *h.e.* 5.7.1–11; Soz., *h.e.* 7.5.1–7. See Errington, "Church," 39–40; idem, *Policy*, 219–21.

6.   Gregory had come earlier to the city at the request of the pro-Nicenes to organize and mobilize them; see Errington, "Church," 33–36.

7.   The classic study on the council is A. Ritter, *Das Konzil von Konstantinopel und sein Symbols: Studien*

chaired by Meletius, which attests to the recognition of his standing as leader of the Antiochene Christians. But before much ecclesiastical business was actually transacted, the aged bishop died.[8] Gregory then assumed leadership of the council, and at the same time, the "local" flavor of the gathering suddenly changed with the arrival of a delegation of Egyptian bishops led by Timothy, Peter's successor in Alexandria.[9]

One of the first items on the agenda was replacing Meletius. Gregory apparently pushed for Paulinus, which would have fulfilled the conditions of the agreement made two years prior.[10] However, rather than honoring the pact made by the divided pro-Nicene factions before Meletius left for the council, those loyal to Meletius refused to subject themselves to Paulinus and instead chose Flavian, who was consecrated at the council, to be their bishop, thus prolonging the Antiochene schism.[11] Sozomen described a church divided over the issue of succession: "And the Egyptians, Arabians, and Cypriots were vexed at the wrong done to Paulinus. But the Syrians and Palestinians and Phoenicians, and the majorities of those in Armenia and Cappadocia and Galatia and in Pontus, were in agreement with Flavian."[12] But Damasus and the bishops of the West sided with Paulinus, and, with the western emperor Gratian, they called for a synod to settle the issue.[13]

In 382, Jerome, Paulinus, and Epiphanius traveled to Rome to attend this synod, and in the old imperial capital, both Paulinus and Epiphanius were personally welcomed by Paula:

And when on account of certain dissensions imperial letters had summoned to Rome bishops from the east and west, she provided for the admirable men and

zur Geschichte und Theologie des II Ökumenischen Konzils, Forschungen zur Kirchen- und Dogmengeschichte 15 (Göttingen: Vandenhoeck & Ruprecht, 1965), but for important criticisms, see Errington, "Church," 41–47, 54–66.

8. Gr. Naz., de vita sua 1507–83. This may also suggest why Epiphanius was not in attendance. See Ritter, Konzil, 53–68.

9. Timothy succeeded Peter on 14 February 381. See below for a discussion of the dispute over the elevation of Gregory as bishop of Constantinople. Hanson makes the important observation that the bishop of Alexandria would not have attended a council chaired by Meletius, and thus his arrival after the death of the bishop of Antioch implied that Theodosius invited the bishops of Egypt and Illyricum with the hopes of expanding the scope and impact of the originally local council. Search, 808–9.

10. Gr. Naz., de vita sua 1583–679.

11. Socr., h.e. 5.9.3–5; Soz., h.e. 7.11.1–4; Thdt., h.e. 5.9.16. The exact sequence and circumstances in which Flavian was chosen are unclear; see Hanson, Search, 810; Errington, "Church," 54–60.

12. Soz., h.e. 7.11.2.

13. Soz., h.e. 7.11.3–4.

pontiffs of Christ, Paulinus bishop of the city of Antioch, and Epiphanius, of Salamis in Cyprus, which is now called Constantia, of whom she even had Epiphanius as a guest. While Paulinus was remaining in another home, she held him as if with the kindness of her own home.[14]

Beyond this, we are uncertain about Epiphanius's activities in Rome, although clearly he was there to advocate for Paulinus's rightful claim to the see of Antioch. Nevertheless, the connection with Paula is important, and Epiphanius and the notable patroness must have enjoyed each other's company and forged a new friendship.

The "Quiet" Years

After the events of 382, we have fewer details of Epiphanius's life for the next decade. Once he returned to Cyprus, he presumably resumed his episcopal duties. Meanwhile, after Jerome came back to Rome in 382, he forged a reputation as a biblical scholar and theologian and enjoyed the patronage of Pope Damasus.[15] He also established lasting (and potentially controversial) relationships with certain aristocratic women for whom he became a sort of biblical guru.[16] But in the late summer of 385, Jerome rather suddenly departed Rome (under a cloud of suspicion): "Moreover in the month of August, with the annual winds blowing, with the holy presbyter Vincentius, and with other monks who now live in Jerusalem, untroubled I boarded a ship at the Roman port, with a very large crowd of saints following me."[17] Sometime thereafter, his friend, patroness, and companion Paula and her daughter Eustochium left for the East, and during the journey, the women enjoyed the hospitality of Epiphanius in Cyprus. But instead of resting in the comforts of Constantia, Paula made it a point

---

14. Jer., *Ep.* 108.6.1. Cf. Jer., *Ep.* 127.7.1.
15. See Kelly, 80–90; S. Rebenich, *Hieronymus und sein Kreis: Prosopographische und sozialgeschichtliche Untersuchungen* (Stuttgart: Franz Steiner Verlag, 1992), 141–53; M. Vessey, "Jerome's Origen: The Making of a Christian Literary *Persona*," StPatr 28 (1993): 135–45.
16. Kelly, *Jerome*, 91–103.
17. Jer., *Adversus Rufinum libri III* 3.22. On the departure from Rome and its circumstances, see Kelly, *Jerome*, 111–15; S. Rebenich, *Jerome*, The Early Church Fathers (New York: Routledge, 2002), 31–40; M. Williams, *The Monk and the Book: Jerome and the Making of Christian Scholarship* (Chicago: University of Chicago Press, 2006), 49–62, 277–80; A. Cain, *The Letters of Jerome: Asceticism, Biblical Exegesis, and the Construction of Christian Authority in Late Antiquity* (Oxford: Oxford University Press, 2009), 99–128.

to visit all of the monasteries on the island to encourage the brethren and provide extra funds for them.[18] She eventually reunited with Jerome in Antioch, and together they settled in the "Holy Land" and established twin monastic communities in Bethlehem.[19] On another occasion when Epiphanius was visiting Palestine, Paula had fallen ill, and Jerome tried to use the venerable bishop to convince her to drink some wine. She was, however, on to Jerome's stratagem, and she gently refused Epiphanius's entreaties.[20] This western connection and Epiphanius's personal relationship with Paula (and Jerome) would prove pivotal in the 390s when Epiphanius began his final heresiological struggle against Origenism.

Before examining the final battles of Epiphanius's life, we shall digress for a moment to consider two other details we can date with some certainty, his composition of the *De mensuris et ponderibus* and *De xii gemmis*. Scholars have known about these two texts for quite some time but have relegated them to the status of handbooks of esoteric biblical knowledge, and both need updated editions and translations and scholarly reconsideration.[21]

On Weights and Measures

Pierre Nautin describes this text as "a sort of manual for the study of the Bible," and it includes a hodgepodge of different subjects: the different *sigla* and punctuation used by several translators of the Hebrew Bible, the story of the production of the Septuagint and Epiphanius's belief in its absolute authority, the various biblical weights and measures and their contemporary equivalents, and several observations relating to biblical geography.[22] It survives primarily in a Syriac translation, although portions exist in Greek, Armenian, and Georgian.[23] The information on weights and measures has been of particular interest

18. Jer., *Ep.* 108.7.3.
19. Jer., *Ep.* 108.20.1–7. See Kelly, *Jerome*, 116–40.
20. Jer., *Ep.* 108.21.1–5.
21. Fortunately Andrew Jacobs's recent examinations have given them some new life. See throughout Jacobs, "Matters"; idem, "Epiphanius," 451–64.
22. Nautin, "Épiphane," c. 627–28. See also Jacobs, "Epiphanius," 452–57.
23. See throughout Dean, *Treatise*; E. Moutsoulas, ΤΟ 'ΠΕΡΙ ΜΕΤΡΩΝ ΚΑΙ ΣΤΑΘΜΩΝ' ΕΡΓΟΝ ΕΠΙΦΑΝΙΟΥ ΤΟΥ ΣΑΛΑΜΙΝΟΣ, ΘΕΟΛΟΓΙΑ 44.1–2 (1973): 157–98; idem, "L'oeuvre d'Epiphane de Salamine 'De mensuris et ponderibus' et son unité littéraire," StPatr 12 (1975): 119–22; M. Stone, "Concerning the Seventy-Two Translators: Armenian Fragments of Epiphanius, *On Weights and Measures*," HTR 73, no. 1 (1980): 331–36; M. van Esbroeck, *Les versions géorgiennes d'Épiphane de Chypre, Traité des poids et des mesures*, CSCO 460–461, Scriptores Iberici 19–20 (Leuven: Peeters, 1984); E. Moutsoulas, "La tradition manuscrite de l'oeuvre d'Epiphane de Salamine *De mensuris et*

to papyrologists who have compared Epiphanius's account with other extant material.[24]

However, for our purposes, we make only a few observations: (1) Epiphanius completed the final version of the treatise in 392, and according to the Syriac preface, at the behest of "Bardion," a Persian priest living in Constantinople, "a learned man, eager to learn (whatever is of) value in the divine Scriptures."[25] Epiphanius continued to enjoy a reputation as a biblical scholar and was again asked to compose something. (2) The treatise's subject matter suggests that in the "quiet" decade, Epiphanius was very much engaged in study of the Scriptures, and he was apparently well informed about problems in translating the Hebrew Bible. As we have seen, he even recognized the contribution of Origen and his *Hexapla* in this regard.[26] Again, Epiphanius's knowledge and exegesis of the Bible remain open for further research. (3) Epiphanius did not shy away from using the work of those he condemned or suspected of heresy, as his comments on Origen suggest. He also made an oblique reference to using Eusebius's *Onomasticon* and even made a comparison on a particular point using Josephus.[27] Throughout the treatise, however, Epiphanius demonstrated that heresy was still very much on his mind, especially that of Origen. Not surprisingly, soon after he wrote this text he reengaged in heresy-hunting activities. (4) Finally, the survival of this treatise in a variety of languages suggests that Epiphanius's later reception was perhaps wider than one would expect compared to perceptions of him in modern scholarship. In particular, the Armenian medieval tradition valued this treatise, and the attribution of numerous other works to him attests to Epiphanius's lasting legacy.[28]

---

ponderibus," in *Texte und Textkritik: Eine Aufsatzsammlung,* Texte und Untersuchungen zur Geschichte der altchristlichen Literatur 133 (1987), 429–40; M. Stone and R. Ervine, *The Armenian Texts of Epiphanius of Salamis: De Mensuris et Ponderibus,* CSCO 583, Subsidia 105 (Leuven: Peeters, 2000).

24. See, for example, P. Mayerson, "Epiphanius' *Sabitha* in Egypt: Σάμβαθον/cάμφαθον/cάμαθον," *BASP* 35 (1998): 215–18; idem, "A Note on Syriac *Sabitha* and *Kollathon* in the Papyri," *BASP* 36 (1999): 83–86; idem, "Kα(μ)ψάκηc in the Papyri, LXX and *TLG*," *BASP* 36 (1999): 93–97; idem, "Measures (μετρηταί) and Donkeyloads of Oil in *P. Wisc.* II.80," *Zeitschrift für Papyrologie und Epigraphik* 127 (1999): 189–92; R. Bagnall and K. Worp, "ΤΕΤΡΑΧΡΥΣΟΝ," *Tyche* 15 (2000): 3–6; N. Kruit and K. Worp, "The Spathion Jar in the Papyri," *BASP:* 38 (2001): 79–87.

25. Epiph., *mens.* 20, provided information to extrapolate a certain date. Dean, *Treatise,* 11. The description of Bardion comes from a Syriac preface to the treatise. See also Moutsoulas, "L'oeuvre," for a discussion of the various stages of composition and an analysis of its literary cohesion.

26. Epiph., *mens.* 7.

27. Epiph., *mens.* 74.

28. See Stone and Ervine, *Texts,* 109–25.

On the Twelve Stones

Yet another example of Epiphanius's serious, if not eccentric, engagement with Scripture is his treatise interpreting the stones of the breastplate of the high priest (cf. Exod 28:15–21).[29] While some fragments and passages survive in several languages, the main text is extant in Georgian.[30] Epiphanius likely composed this curious treatise sometime before 394, and he even presented a copy of it to Jerome.[31] However, the treatise is dedicated to a certain Diodore and again was written in response to a request.[32] Epiphanius cycled through discussions of each of the twelve stones. In the first sequence, he gave descriptions of the color, origins and locations, and potential medicinal properties of the stones. In the next cycle, he assigned each stone to a name of the sons of Jacob and provided spiritual interpretations for each gem.[33] Epiphanius probably drew on some kind of handbook of lapidary information as he had the naturalist information of the *Panarion*, and he included all manner of esoteric knowledge and anecdotes related to particular stones.[34] Epiphanius's interpretation of the stones is at times a bewildering display of intertextual connections, as he linked Old Testament, New Testament, geographic, mineralogical, medical, historical, and ethnographic images and knowledge with a seemingly virtuoso command of the Bible.[35]

---

29. Jacobs states: "Epiphanius' treatise *On Gems* is his most antiquarian and his most thoroughly scriptural—indeed, we see how fully the two impulses are intertwined in Epiphanius's interpretive process." "Epiphanius," 457.
30. Namely Greek, Latin, Coptic, Arabic, Armenian, and Ethiopic. There is also an Armenian epitome. See R. Blake, *Epiphanius De Gemmis: The Old Georgian Version and the Fragments of the Armenian Version* and H. de Vis, *The Coptic-Sahidic Fragments*, Studies and Documents 2 (London: Christophers, 1934); B. Weischer, "Ein arabisches und äthiopisches Fragment der Schrift 'De XII gemmis' des Epiphanios von Salamis," *Oriens Christianus* 63 (1979): 103–7; M. Stone, "An Armenian Epitome of Epiphanius's *De gemmis*," *HTR* 82, no. 4 (1989): 467–76. Although see now F. Albrecht and A. Manukyan, *Epiphanius von Salamis: Über die zwölf Steine in hohepriesterlichen Brustschild (De duodecim gemmis rationalis) nach dem Codex Vaticanus Borgianus Armenus 31*, Gorgias Eastern Christian Studies 37 (Piscataway, NJ: Gorgias Press, 2014).
31. Cf. Jer., *Commentariorum in Hiezechielem libri XIV* 9.28.305–7; *Ep.* 64.21.1; *Commentariorum in Esaiam libri XVIII* 15.54.109–12. Blake suggests that the likely date when Epiphanius presented the copy was in 394 in the midst of the controversy with John of Jerusalem (on which, see below). *De Gemmis*, xiii. But Nautin has doubts because this was not necessarily the only time Epiphanius traveled to Palestine. "Épiphane," c. 628.
32. Nautin states this was Diodore of Tyre ("Épiphane," c. 628), while Quasten suggests Diodore of Tarsus (*Patrology, Vol. 3*, 389).
33. See Jacobs, "Epiphanius," 457–63, for analysis of this treatise.
34. Blake, *De Gemmis*, xc–xcvii; Jacobs, "Epiphanius," 457, n. 106.
35. Jacobs, "Epiphanius," 459–63.

The Origenist Controversy Phase I:
Heresy-Hunting John of Jerusalem

The "quiet years" abruptly ended in 393 when Epiphanius again emerged on the public scene and directly involved himself in the ecclesiastical politics of the Greek East.[36] From this point until his death, Epiphanius exerted all of his remaining energy to battle against what he understood to be the heresy of Origenism. At the beginning of 393, an anti-Origenist monk named Atarbius was in Palestine trying to secure public condemnations of Origen, including from Jerome and Rufinus, both of whom had established monastic settlements with funding from their wealthy aristocratic patronesses.[37] Jerome was willing to concede to Atarbius's demand, but his friend Rufinus refused to even meet with the monk.[38] Although no explicit link is mentioned in any sources, this Atarbius may very well have been working at the behest of Epiphanius.[39] Most telling about Atarbius's anti-Origenist efforts in 393 is the corresponding return of Epiphanius to his heresy-hunting activities, which suggests an association between the two.

Passive-Aggressive Verbal Confrontations

Epiphanius began a campaign against Origenist heresy, and the target of his inquisition was John, the bishop of Jerusalem, who had succeeded Cyril in 387.[40] As we examined in chapter 5, Epiphanius did not afford much respect for Cyril and his allegedly "Semi-Arian" ways. Perhaps it is no surprise that his

---

36. Most of the contents of this section (with modifications) was previously published in Y. Kim, "Epiphanius of Cyprus vs. John of Jerusalem: An Improper Ordination and the Escalation of the Origenist Controversy," in *Episcopal Elections in Late Antiquity*, Arbeiten zur Kirchengeschichte 119, ed. J. Leemans, P. Van Nuffelen, S. Keough, C. Nicolaye (Berlin: Walter de Gruyter, 2011), 411–22. See now F. Fatti, "*Pontifex tantus*. Giovanni, Epifanio e le origini della prima controversia origenista," *Adamantius* 19 (2013): 30–49.

37. Jer., *Ruf.* 3.33.

38. Why Jerome, who was a devotee and translator of Origen, turned against the Alexandrian has perplexed modern scholars. Kelly argues that Jerome wanted to appease Epiphanius and to start with a "clean conscience" with respect to his work on Origen, since he claimed that he admired only the exegetical work and not the heretical doctrines. *Jerome*, 198. Perhaps concern over his own public persona, especially following his somewhat mysterious but scandalous departure from Rome in 385, and his need to initiate some "damage control" over his seeming devotion to Origen influenced his change of heart. See Vessey, "Jerome's Origen." Brown suggests that Jerome's convictions about the body and human sexuality also affected his changed attitude toward Origen. *Body*, 379–85.

39. Nautin, "Épiphane," c. 622–23; Kelly, *Jerome*, 198, n. 12.

40. Socr., *h.e.* 5.15.9. Nautin, "La date," 33–35.

suspicions against Cyril would shift to his successor, although the "resolution" of the Trinitarian controversy had given way to a new (but actually old) heretical threat. Most likely during near the end of Lent 393, Epiphanius traveled to Palestine and was in Jerusalem as the guest of Bishop John.[41] A war of words ensued between the two bishops, with public sermons and passive aggression as the weapons of choice. The exact sequence of events, based on Jerome's recollection some three years after the fact, is murky, although we can discern at least four different verbal confrontations.[42] The first melee occurred when Epiphanius preached a sermon specifically against Origenism in John's presence. Jerome recognized that although the sermon's ostensible target was Origen, the actual attack was directed at John. Jerome described how "you [John] and your posse, with canine smiles and wrinkled noses, scratching your heads, with nods, were talking about the 'crazy old man.'"[43] John then sent one of his archdeacons to tell Epiphanius to stop talking, which Jerome characterized as an insult to the bishop. The second confrontation unfolded during a procession from one church building to another during which crowds of people surged to meet Epiphanius and present their children for a blessing. The throng was apparently so dense that he could hardly take a step forward. Jerome then chided John, who was apparently displeased by Epiphanius's popularity: "Were you not so twisted with jealousy that you yelled at the 'vainglorious old man'? Were you not ashamed to say to his face that he was willingly and deliberately delayed?"[44]

The third skirmish happened on a day when gathered congregants had waited until the seventh hour of the day for a chance to hear Epiphanius preach. John preached first, delivering a harsh sermon against the Anthropomorphites, and through his gestures, he insinuated that Epiphanius was to be counted among their number.[45] Once John finished his lengthy sermon, Epiphanius rose and said: "All that has been said by my brother and colleague, my son in age, has been said well and faithfully. What has been condemned, I also do with my voice. But equally in the manner in which we have condemned this heresy,

41. Jer., *Adu. Io. Hier.* 10–14. The exact occasion for the following events is disputed, either during Easter celebrations or the Encaenia in September, the annual commemoration of the dedication of the Holy Sepulchre basilica. However, based on Jerome's overall account and in particular the content of the sermons delivered by Epiphanius and John, the Paschal season is likely. For Epiphanius in Jerusalem during Lent and Easter, see Dechow, *Dogma*, 397–403, and during the Encaenia, see P. Nautin, "Études de chronologie hiéronymienne (393–397)," *Revue des études augustinennes* 19, nos. 1–2 (1973): 69–86; Kelly, *Jerome*, 199.

42. On the date of the *Adu. Io. Hier*, see P. Nautin, "Études de chronologie hiéronymienne (393–397)," *Revue des études augustiniennes* 18, nos. 3–4 (1972): 209–18.

43. Jer., *Adu. Io. Hier.* 11.

44. Jer., *Adu. Io. Hier.* 11.

45. On the Anthropomorphites, see below.

we ought also to condemn the perverse doctrines of Origen."[46] Jerome then "reminded" John how the audience burst forth with laughter and applause. The final verbal scuffle occurred when John delivered a sermon summarizing his forty-day catechetical instruction, after which he invited Epiphanius to speak, a request that was considered to be a great honor. Although Epiphanius affirmed what John had preached, he was troubled that John had attempted to convey the faith of all doctrines of the church in a single sermon. Epiphanius then departed John's company and fled to Jerome's monastery in Bethlehem, where he lamented John's preaching. The monks persuaded Epiphanius to return to the city, which he apparently did, only to leave the same night, presumably back to Cyprus.[47] These verbal confrontations exhibit the growing rift between the two bishops that was widened by Epiphanius's blatant attempts to pin some allegation of Origenism on John, who seems to have avoided the subject altogether, and they set the stage for what would transpire in the next year.

An Improper Ordination

Sometime after Pentecost in 394, Epiphanius journeyed to his homeland monastery. A delegation of monks from Jerome's monastery at Bethlehem visited him, and Epiphanius, in a letter of self-defense written to John (translated into Latin by Jerome), described what happened during a worship service:

> While therefore the Collect was being celebrated in the church of the villa that is next to our monastery, I ordered him, though unaware and bearing no suspicion, to be "seized" by a number of deacons and his voice silenced, lest in his desire to free himself he might adjure me in the name of Christ. And I ordained him first as a deacon, pressing upon him the fear of God and compelling him, so that he might minister. He resisted mightily, contesting that he was unworthy. Thus hardly was I able to compel him, and we were able to persuade him with the testimonies of the Scriptures and with a presentation of the commandments of God. And when he had ministered the holy sacraments, again with great difficulty and with his mouth silenced, I ordained him presbyter. And with the same words with which I had previously persuaded him, I pressed him to sit in the row of presbyters.[48]

---

46. Jer., *Adu. Io. Hier.* 11. Epiphanius also condemned human characterizations of God, as in *Pan.* 70.2.1–8.11.
47. Jer., *Adu. Io. Hier.* 14.
48. Jer., *Ep.* 51.1.5–6.

The "seized" monk was none other than Jerome's younger brother Paulinian.[49] Epiphanius explained that the pretext for this ordination was that the monastic community at Bethlehem did not have someone who was either able or willing to administer the sacraments, so he took the initiative to ordain Paulinian.[50]

When Epiphanius wrote this letter to John months after the event, he knew exactly what he had done. John apparently had made public and written complaints concerning Epiphanius's actions, but in his defense Epiphanius maintained that he "had done him no harm, caused him no injury, nor extorted anything violently. In a monastery of brothers—and brothers who were foreigners, under no obligation to your jurisdiction, and because of our own insignificance and letters, which we frequently directed to them, they also began to have a sense of disunity with your communion."[51] Furthermore, Epiphanius audaciously declared that John ought to have been grateful and emphasized that John had already tried unsuccessfully on numerous occasions to ordain Paulinian.[52] In other words, John knew Paulinian's status as a desirable candidate for ordination, and Epiphanius must have recognized that Paulinian was a coveted asset. Thus this act of ordination was doubly provocative because it was improperly conducted for a monastery within John's oversight and it thwarted John's previous attempts to ordain Paulinian. Epiphanius veiled his entire discussion and justification of this act with a rather disingenuous veneer of Christian love, and he even explained how pleased he had been at the news of his own episcopal colleagues ordaining presbyters and other clerics: "For many bishops in communion with me have both ordained presbyters in our own jurisdiction, whom we were not able to 'capture,' and have sent to us deacons and subdeacons, whom we have received with gratitude."[53] Here Epiphanius betrayed his own duplicity, because he implied that he recognized something improper in his ordination of Paulinian, although he tried to claim otherwise, "since there is no difference in the priesthood of God when it is provided for the benefit of the church."[54] That this was an overstepping of ecclesiastical authority

---

49. On Paulinian, see Fatti, "*Pontifex*," 41–44; Y. Kim, "Jerome and Paulinian, Brothers," *VC* 67, no. 5 (2013): 517–30.
50. Jer., *Ep.* 51.1.7.
51. Jer., *Ep.* 51.1.2–3.
52. Although John later complained that Paulinian was also too young to be ordained presbyter; cf. Jer., *Ep.* 82.8.1–5.
53. Jer., *Ep.* 51.2.1. Fatti, "*Pontifex*," 43–44, suggests that because Jerome and his brethren were foreigners, their monastery was independent of the authority of Jerusalem and that perhaps it was John who was overstepping his authority.
54. Jer., *Ep.* 51.1.3.

is unmistakable, and in many ways this kind of behavior has rendered Epiphanius's reputation quite distasteful to modern sensibilities. The taint of self-righteousness in his personality is indeed difficult to deny.

Epiphanius's Ingenious Plan

What is perhaps most telling about this letter is the fact that although Epiphanius addressed the ordination issue in the opening paragraphs, the vast majority of the correspondence is dedicated to condemning Origen and accusing John of Origenism. Epiphanius also engaged in a letter-writing campaign against John and apparently wrote to other bishops of Palestine and to Pope Siricius concerning his dispute with John.[55] By deliberately violating episcopal practice, Epiphanius provoked a quarrel and shifted the attention to his intended target all along, John the alleged Origenist. The improper ordination was a calculated move that accomplished two goals. First, John was put into a position to which he had to respond. He simply could not overlook such a blatant disregard of his authority, so he took action. As bishop of Jerusalem, John had jurisdiction over the Church of the Nativity in Bethlehem, which was closely linked to Jerome's monastic community. So John excommunicated Jerome and his brethren, effectively barring them from entering the Cave and Church of the Nativity, as well as churches in the see of Jerusalem, and he essentially denied them administration of and participation in the Eucharist.[56] John also was able to add the seal of the imperial court to this ecclesiastical sentence when he secured an official banishment of Jerome and his monks from Palestine from Flavius Rufinus, the praetorian prefect of the East.[57] The penalty, however, was not carried out due to the assassination of the prefect on 27 November 395.[58] Because of Epiphanius's provocations, John was forced to alienate and exclude Jerome's Bethlehem monastic community from communion.

Epiphanius's second goal was to make Jerome an anti-Origenist ally. Jerome seemed eager to avoid any charge of heresy and acceded readily to the demands

55. Jer., *Adu. Io. Hier.* 44.
56. Jer., *Adu. Io. Hier.* 42. On the excommunication, see P. Nautin, "L'excommunication de saint Jérôme," *Annuaire de l'école pratique des hautes études Ve section—sciences religieuses* 80–81 (1972–73): 7–37.
57. Jer., *Adu. Io. Hier.* 43.
58. John also later lifted the ecclesiastical punishment on Holy Thursday, 2 April 397. On Rufinus, see J. Liebeschuetz, *Barbarians and Bishops: Army, Church and State in the Age of Arcadius and Chrysostom* (Oxford: Oxford University Press, 1990), 89–92.

of Atarbius, but this was not enough for Epiphanius. The ordination of Paulinian was no accident, and by using Jerome's brother as leverage, Epiphanius forced Jerome's hand in the simmering dispute. They already had a well-established relationship, as they had traveled together over a decade earlier to Rome in support of Paulinus of Antioch. Surely they must have had some interesting conversations, especially because during the 380s, Jerome was an avowed admirer and translator of Origen, while Epiphanius had made his sentiments regarding the Alexandrian quite clear in *Panarion* 64. Jerome's early translation projects included Origen's homilies on Jeremiah, Ezekiel, Isaiah, Song of Songs, and Luke, which for the first time introduced some of Origen's works to the Latin West.[59] Even up to 393, Jerome was clearly a devotee of Origen. That year, he published his *On Illustrious Men* in which he extolled Origen's "immortal genius."[60] But in the same work, Jerome included Epiphanius among the renowned: "Epiphanius, bishop of Salamis on Cyprus, wrote books *Against All Heresies* and many other things, which are read by the educated on account of their matter, by the simpler folk as well on account of the words."[61] So it seems that Jerome could admire both men. Ironically, prior to the outbreak of the Origenist controversy, Jerome had carefully crafted a public persona as the Latin West's version of Origen, that is, Jerome the biblical scholar and exegete.[62] But whatever feelings Jerome may have had about aspects of Origen's thoughts, the events of 394 moved him firmly into the anti-Origenist camp, and he had Epiphanius to "thank" for this.[63]

The end of this first phase of active heresy-hunting yielded several results, some of which must have been most pleasing to Epiphanius. First, Paulinian moved to Cyprus to serve as a cleric under Epiphanius's authority, although he continued to maintain contact with and visit his older brother.[64] Second, Jerome waged an all-out war of words for the next several years with his one-time friend and fellow translator Rufinus (with a brief truce in 397) that sadly

59. Jerome translated Origen's homilies on Jeremiah, Ezekiel, and Isaiah from 380 to 381 and on the Song of Songs from 383 to 384. For Jerome's literary activities during this period, see F. Cavallera, *Saint Jérôme: Sa vie et son oeuvre, Tome I–II* (Louvain: "Spicilegium Sacrum Lovaniense" Bureaux, 1922), vol. 2, 153–65; P. Nautin, "L'activité littéraire de Jérôme de 387 à 392," *Revue de théologie et de philosophie* 115 (1983): 247–59; Williams, *Monk*, 267–301.
60. Jer., *Vir. ill.* 54.8. For the dating of *De viris illustribus*, see P. Nautin, "La date."
61. Jer., *Vir. ill.* 114.
62. See Vessey, "Jerome's Origen"; S. Rebenich, "Jerome: The 'Vir Trilinguis' and the 'Hebraica Veritas,'" *VC* 47, no. 1 (1993): 50–77; Williams, *Monk*, 45–62; Cain, *Letters*, 43–67.
63. Cf. Jer., *Ep.* 84.2, where he claimed that he had always opposed Origen's doctrines.
64. Jer., *Adu. Io. Hier.* 41.

left their friendship in tatters and the question of Origenism unresolved for the time being.[65] This conflict set the stage for an even larger clash with new powerbrokers and players that ultimately consumed the remainder of Epiphanius's life.

The Origenist Controversy Phase II: Heresy-Hunting John Chrysostom

The Origenist controversy has been studied by Elizabeth Clark and with a focus on Epiphanius by Jon Dechow.[66] Both scholars have provided considerable insight into the underlying theological, ascetic, and philosophical issues at the heart of this dispute over the theology and writings of the famed Alexandrian. Our focus here will be on the historical and political developments that unfolded in the late 390s up to Epiphanius's fateful final voyage home in 403 to demonstrate how all of his life experiences, actions and writings as a church leader, and convictions regarding orthodoxy and heresy culminated in this last, deeply flawed, but characteristically Epiphanian confrontation with John Chrysostom.

The Life and Times of Bishop Theophilus

Sometime before the Council of Constantinople in 381, Peter the bishop of Alexandria had tried to elevate Maximus the "Cynic" to the see of the imperial capital, a move that was neither ratified by Theodosius nor accepted by the Council of Constantinople.[67] This attempt by the bishop of Alexandria to handpick the bishop of Constantinople was one step in what would become a protracted conflict between Alexandria and Constantinople over ecclesiastical primacy that unfolded over the next century, and one catalyst that escalated this epic clash between metropolitans was the recognition by the Council of Con-

65. For their relationship, see F. Murphy, *Rufinus of Aquileia (345–411): His Life and Works*, Catholic University of America Studies in Mediaeval History, New Series 6 (Washington, DC, 1945), 59–81, 138–57; Kelly, *Jerome*, 195–258.

66. See throughout Clark, *Controversy*, and Dechow, *Dogma*. See also E. Prinzivalli, "The Controversy about Origen before Epiphanius," in *Origeniana Septima*, 195–213, and now the reassessments in the recent collection of essays in *Adamantius* 19.

67. Soz., *h.e.* 7.9.4; Thdt., *h.e.* 5.8.3. See Errington, "Church," 37–39, 67–72, including an analysis of the role of Ambrose of Milan in the affair. Theodoret identified Timothy, Peter's successor, as initiating the consecration of Maximus.

stantinople of New Rome's status and claim to primacy, second only to Old Rome.[68] The attempts of the Egyptian bishops to influence affairs in the East are also evident in the council proceedings when they raised grave concerns over the illegal ordination of Gregory. He was already bishop of Nazianzus; thus his transfer of bishoprics was against ecclesiastical order.[69] Gregory subsequently and abruptly resigned, which left the capital without a bishop, whereupon the council selected Nectarius, who, according to Sozomen, was chosen in rather miraculous circumstances.[70]

The real drama began with Theophilus, who became bishop of Alexandria on 20 July 385 and was in his own right one of the most controversial and contentious figures in the ecclesiastical political world of the late fourth century.[71] Theophilus tirelessly labored to augment the authority of the see of Alexandria, and he became deeply involved in ecclesiastical politics and conflicts both within Egypt and in the broader eastern Mediterranean. He also famously waged an antipagan campaign that resulted in the destruction of pagan temples and shrines, including the famed Serapeum.[72] Based on what has survived of his writings, he was less interested in theology per se and focused on practical concerns such as maintaining his power and elevating his influence abroad. One of the earliest affairs that drew him into the international scene was the dispute at Jerusalem examined above. At the request of John of Jerusalem in 396, Theophilus intervened in the rift between John and Rufinus on one side and Epiphanius and Jerome on the other.[73] Theophilus had directed his trusted agent Isidore to negotiate a reconciliation, but the decision resulted in utter failure. Three months prior to his arrival in June 396, Isidore had sent letters to John in which he promised that the opposition would be defeated.[74] This letter fell into the hands of Vincentius, Jerome's friend who had left Rome with him

68. Socr., *h.e.* 5.8.13; Soz., *h.e.* 7.9.2–3.
69. Socr., *h.e.* 5.7.2, 5.8.11; Soz., *h.e.* 7.7.6–9. According to Thdt, *h.e.* 5.8.1–2, Meletius himself took the initiative and ordained Gregory. See Hanson, *Search*, 809–10; Errington, *Policy*, 224–26.
70. Soz., *h.e.* 7.8.1–8; cf. Socr. *h.e.* 5.8.12. On the election of Nectarius, see Errington, "Church," 58–59; idem, *Policy*, 226–30.
71. For the life and work of Theophilus, see A. Favale, *Teofilo d'Alessandria (345c.–412): Scritti, Vita e Dottrina*, Biblioteca del "Salesianum" 41 (Turin: Società Editrice Internazionale, 1958); N. Russell, *Theophilus of Alexandria*, Early Church Fathers (London: Routledge, 2007), 3–41.
72. Socr., *h.e.* 5.16.1–14; Thdt., *h.e.* 5.22.1–6. See Errington, *Policy*, 249–51.
73. See Murphy, *Rufinus*, 76–81; Agostino, *Teofilo*, 88–93; Kelly, *Jerome*, 204; Russell, *Theophilus*, 15–17. Prior to Theophilus, "count Archelaus," tried but failed to broker peace; cf. Jer., *Adu. Io. Hier.* 39. See Fatti, "Pontifex," 37.
74. Cf. Jer., *Adu. Io. Hier.* 37. See Murphy, *Rufinus*, 76; Kelly, *Jerome*, 205. On Isidore and Theophilus, see F. Fatti, "Eretico, condanna Origene!" Conflitti di potere ad Alessandria nella tarda antichità," *Annali di Storia dell'Esegesi* 20, no. 2 (2003): 383–435, and 399–403, on this episode.

in 385; thus, Isidore's subsequent attempts to reconcile the parties was marred from the start and predictably faltered. Isidore returned to Alexandria with a letter from John to Theophilus and reported negatively about Jerome, who soon thereafter wrote a letter of self-defense and a scathing attack against John of Jerusalem.[75] Theophilus took matters into his own hands and began to correspond with Jerome and was able to secure peace between the warring factions.[76] Around the same time in 397, Jerome also reconciled momentarily with Rufinus, who returned to the West to visit his parents.[77] Thus Theophilus was able to temporarily calm the storm, although to what extent Origenist theology really had to do with the tensions is unclear.

Further abroad, Nectarius died on 26 September 397, and John, at that time presbyter in Antioch and already becoming famous for his golden eloquence, was selected to succeed and summoned to the imperial capital.[78] Emperor Arcadius wished to add prestige to John's ordination as the new bishop, so he sent requests for other prominent bishops to be present, including Theophilus.[79] The Egyptian archbishop wanted his own candidate, Isidore, to succeed, so he denounced and discredited John as much as he was able.[80] However with a little blackmail and the threat of charges for misconduct, Theophilus was forced to accept John Chrysostom, who became bishop of Constantinople on 26 February 398.[81] This was a slight that Theophilus would not soon forget.[82]

But for the time being, Theophilus buried his grudge and was inclined to play nice with the new bishop, as is evident in the final resolution of the Me-

75. Jer., *Adu. Io. Hier.*, which responded in large part to an apology written by John, which is no longer extant, but circulated as far as Rome. See Murphy, *Rufinus*, 77; Kelly, *Jerome*, 205–7.
76. Cf. Jer., *Ep.* 82.
77. Jer., *Ruf.* 2.1. On Rufinus's journey west, see Murphy, *Rufinus*, 111–37. On their reconciliation, see Murphy, *Rufinus*, 81; Kelly, *Jerome*, 207–9.
78. On John's selection as bishop of Constantinople, see J. Kelly, *Golden Mouth: The Story of John Chrysostom: Ascetic, Preacher, Bishop* (Duckworth: London, 1995), 104–14; W. Mayer, "John Chrysostom as Bishop: The View from Antioch," *JEH* 55, no. 3 (2004): 455–66.
79. Socr., *h.e.* 6.2.1–4; Soz., *h.e.* 8.2.1–4.
80. Socr., *h.e.* 6.2.5–9; Soz., *h.e.* 8.2.16–18.
81. Socr., *h.e.* 6.2.10; Soz., *h.e.* 8.2.19. For Chrysostom's life and work, see Kelly, *Golden Mouth*; C. Tiersch, *Johannes Chrysostomus in Konstantinopel (398–404): Weltsicht und Wirken eines Bischofs in der Hauptstadt des Oströmischen Reiches*, Studien und Texte zu Antike und Christentum 6 (Tübingen: Mohr Siebeck, 2000); W. Mayer and P. Allen, *John Chrysostom*, The Early Church Fathers (London and New York: Routledge, 2000). On the problems presented by the sources, see W. Mayer, "The Making of a Saint: John Chrysostom in Early Historiography," in *Chrysostomosbilder in 1600 Jahren: Facetten der Wirkungsgeschichte eines Kirchenvaters*, Arbeiten zur Kirchengeschichte 105, ed. M. Walraff and R. Brändle (Berlin: Walter de Gruyter, 2008): 39–59. Socrates, as an earlier and more critical source, is worthy of greater consideration, especially as a contrast to Palladius and the funeral oration of Pseudo-Martyrius.
82. Socr., *h.e.* 6.5.10–11. See Agostino, *Teofilo*, 81–83; Russell, *Theophilus*, 17.

letian schism, which had dragged on for decades. The sources are conflicted regarding how and by whom the schism was brought to an end.[83] Paulinus, that Eustathian stalwart, finally passed away in 388, and according to Socrates's account, Paulinus's followers refused to recognize Flavian as bishop of Antioch and instead chose Evagrius.[84] Flavian was of course already the recognized bishop following the Council of Constantinople. Socrates then made the ambiguous statement that Evagrius "did not live for a very long time, and no other was established in his place."[85] So Flavian allegedly made overtures to both Theophilus and Damasus, who together would have maintained a complaint against him for assuming the episcopacy of Antioch in opposition to Paulinus. But ultimately Flavian appeased Theophilus, who in turn sent his presbyter Isidore to Rome to broker a peace, and the Meletian schism finally came to an end.[86] However, Socrates's account (or his source) contains some problems. Damasus of Rome died in the winter of 384 and Evagrius died in 393 or 394; thus Flavian's reconciliation activity had to take place before the end of 384. In other words, Flavian was able to broker a peace with both Alexandria and Rome before Paulinus died in 388, which makes little sense.

We know that in 391/2, at the request of Ambrose of Milan to Theodosius, a council was convened in Capua to resolve the schism at Antioch.[87] Flavian refused to attend and obtained imperial permission to be absent, so the western bishops turned to Theophilus to mediate the dispute. But again, as Theophilus related to Ambrose, Flavian was successful in avoiding judgment in a conciliar setting, and the schism remained at an impasse.[88] A subsequent council held in Caesarea in Palestine in 393 affirmed Flavian's right to the see, and Evagrius's illegal ordination precluded any legitimate claim. The Egyptian church must have softened its anti-Meletian stance at this point, and Theophilus found an

83. Socr., *h.e.* 5.15.4–7, identified Flavian as the initiator of reconciliation, while Soz., *h.e.* 8.3.3–5, was explicit that John Chrysostom appealed to Theophilus to become involved. Furthermore, Thdt., *h.e.* 5.23.5–12, emphasized the role of Theodosius in the recognition of Flavian's rightful claim. See Agostino, *Teofilo*, 72–76; Russell, *Theophilus*, 13–14; Karmann, *Meletius*, 461–62. On John's role and initiative, see Kelly, *Golden Mouth*, 116–18. I recogize, however, that Sozomen's account is nearly hagiographic with regard to John; Mayer, "Making."
84. Socr., *h.e.* 5.15.1. Or Paulinus could have chosen Evagrius to succeed him; cf. Thdt., *h.e.* 5.23.1–4, which would have been irregular.
85. Socr., *h.e.* 5.15.2.
86. Socr., *h.e.* 5.15.3–8.
87. Cf. Ambrose, *Epistulae* 56. See N. McLynn, *Ambrose of Milan: Church and Court in a Christian Capital*, Transformation of the Classical Heritage 22 (Berkeley: University of California Press, 1994), 334–35.
88. Ambr., *Ep.* 56.2.

opportunity to augment his prestige by becoming more directly involved in the affair. In Sozomen's account, the final resolution of the schism took place after John Chrysostom became bishop of Constantinople and mainly at his initiative, whereas Socrates largely ignored the importance of the relationship between John and Flavian. John apparently appealed to Theophilus for assistance in brokering a reconciliation between Flavian and "the bishop of Rome," who by this time was Siricius.[89] John, of course, had a vested interest in the ecclesiastical well-being of Antioch, the city where he was born and rose up the ranks of the church hierarchy. As a young man, he was mentored by none other than Meletius, so John's position on the rightful bishop of the city undoubtedly eschewed the claim of Paulinus.[90] After serving as Meletius's personal aide, John was made a reader in 371. He spent some years dodging ordination and living the ascetic lifestyle, but eventually became a deacon.[91] After Meletius's death in 381, Bishop Flavian ordained John as priest, in which capacity he preached regularly and served the city of Antioch in many ways as a stand-in bishop for Flavian during his absences.[92] Thus when John acceded to the see of Constantinople, it was in his interest to ensure the stability and support of Antioch, and one major obstacle that stood in the way of a healthy Syrian capital was the bishop of Rome. So by asking Theophilus for help with Rome, John in some ways killed two birds with one stone by temporarily appeasing the spite of the Egyptian bishop whose candidate did not succeed at Constantinople and brokering Roman support for Flavian. Acacius of Beroea and Theophilus's trusted Isidore led the successful envoy to Rome, and the Antiochene schism was finally brought to an end.[93]

This was a singular victory for John as he asserted his own leadership over the churches of the East, mollified the tense relationship with Theophilus, and secured recognition for Flavian (and thus the Meletian succession) by the bishop of Rome. However, one lingering question remains: why did Theophilus, who opposed the election of John to the see of Constantinople, agree to

---

89. Soz., *h.e.* 8.3.3–5.
90. Kelly, *Golden Mouth*, 16–18. This is complicated a bit by the fact that Socr., *h.e.*. 6.3.11, reported that John broke ties with the Meletians and was ordained presbyter by Evagrius, the illegitimate successor of Paulinus. However, we have already observed that Socrates's account is problematic, and John's long-standing relationship with Meletius would seem to contradict a recognition of and ordination by a schismatic bishop.
91. Kelly, *Golden Mouth*, 24–38.
92. On John's sermons and leadership in the city, see Kelly, *Golden Mouth*, 55–103.
93. Soz., *h.e.* 8.3.3–5. The old supporters of Paulinus apparently maintained their opposition but had no bishop since the death of Evagrius. See Kelly, *Golden Mouth*, 116–18.

help Chrysostom? In his study of Theophilus, Russell follows the suggestion of Favale that Theophilus "could not afford to spurn his [Flavian's] friendship because he needed the support against the growing supremacy of Constantinople."[94] But this does not make sense in light of the close relationship between John and Flavian. Kelly suggests that "Theophilos' readiness to co-operate with John is not really surprising, for, although he had not taken part in the council of Caesarea, he was fully aware that Flavian's legitimacy was now generally acknowledged in the east; but it shows him in an unexpectedly attractive light, since he is unlikely at this time to have been personally well-disposed to John."[95] This perspective is more plausible than the suggestion that Theophilus sought to partner with Flavian in opposition to Constantinople. Theophilus certainly benefitted from the situation by acting as a power broker, but as we will see below, he was also pragmatic and calculating. Theophilus's "partnership" with John was by no means recognition of the latter's status and authority, especially over Alexandria. This was but a momentary and deliberate delay in what would be a vicious reprisal for the affront that Theophilus experienced over the selection of the successor to Nectarius.

Problems in the Egyptian Desert

While Theophilus was involved in international affairs with Jerusalem, Constantinople, Antioch, and Rome, he experienced trouble on the domestic front when he came into conflict first with a group of monks (the so-called "Anthropomorphites")[96] who maintained that God existed in corporeal form, then with the community of monks in the desert of Nitria led by the so-called Tall Brothers, whom Theophilus had esteemed, and Isidore, his one-time con-

---

94. Russell, *Theophilus*, 14.
95. Kelly, *Golden Mouth*, 117.
96. On the Anthropomorphites, see G. Florovsky, "The Anthropomorphites in the Egyptian Desert," in *Akten des XI. Internationalen Byzantinistenkongresses, München 1958*, ed. F. Dölger, H.-G. Beck (Munich: C.H. Beck, 1960), 154–59; idem, "Theophilus of Alexandria and Apa Aphou of Pemdje," in *Harry Aufstryn Wolfson Jubilee Volume: On the Occasion of His Seventy-Fifth Birthday, English Section*, ed. S. Lieberman (Jerusalem: American Academy for Jewish Research, 1965), 275–310; A. Golitzin, "The Vision of God and the Form of Glory: More Reflections on the Anthropomorphite Controversy of AD 399," in *Abba: The Tradition of Orthodoxy in the West. Festschrift for Bishop Kallistos (Ware) of Diokleia*, ed. J. Behr, A. Louth, D. Conomos (Crestwood, NY: St. Vladimir's Seminary Press, 2003), 273–97; G. Gould, "The Image of God and the Anthropomorphite Controversy in Fourth Century Monasticism," in *Origeniana Quinta*, 549–57; Clark, *Controversy*, 43–84; D. Bumazhnov, "Einige Aspekte der Nachwirkung des *Ancoratus* und des *Panarion* des hl. Epiphanius von Salamis in der früheren monastischen Tradition," *Adamantius* 11 (2005): 158–78; Russell, *Theophilus*, 22–23.

fidant and agent.[97] The sources that describe this conflict vary in their accounts depending on the party to which the authors were sympathetic. But Theophilus claimed that the taint of Origenist heresy was what prompted his hostility.[98] However, personal enmity, especially against Isidore, who refused to be a yes-man to Theophilus's machinations, fueled the dispute. Isidore apparently declined to tell the bishop about a donation made to the church lest Theophilus use the fund inappropriately. Thus Theophilus's turn against him was motivated less by theology than by anger against the insubordination of a former confidant.[99] Ironically, Theophilus was at one point aligned with Origen and his thought, but apparently his desire to maintain his authoritative position trumped any theological convictions he may have held.[100] Consistent with an Origenist perspective, Theophilus railed against the beliefs of the Anthropomorphites in his festal letter for 399. But when monks of this persuasion left their monasteries, came to Alexandria, and threatened the bishop, he had a sudden change of heart and appeased them by proclaiming: "Thus seeing you, so do I see the face of God."[101]

Theophilus tried to discredit Isidore by falsely accusing him of sodomy, even bribing a young man to substantiate the charges. But the alleged victim's mother refused to participate in this lie and reported what had transpired to Isidore.[102] The bishop then decided to excommunicate Isidore, who fled to the monastic community in Nitria, whereupon Theophilus sent letters to various bishops and monks in Egypt ordering the expulsion of the Origenist monks.[103]

---

97. See Agostino, *Teofilo*, 96–104; Kelly, *Golden Mouth*, 191–202; Russell, *Theophilus*, 18–27. The "Tall Brothers" were Dioscorus, Ammonius, Eusebius, and Euthymius, and Theophilus had consecrated Dioscorus as bishop of Hermopolis.

98. Jer., *Ep.* 92; Socr., *h.e.* 6.7.4–10. Socrates attributed the enmity between Theophilus and the Tall Brothers to the former's greed and jealousy. Russell offers a useful reconstruction, drawing on the different accounts. *Theophilus*, 18–22.

99. Socr., *h.e.* 6.9.1–10, gave another reason for the falling out between Theophilus and Isidore. Theophilus was apparently irritated with Peter, an arch-presbyter, and attempted to depose him by accusing him of allowing a Manichaean woman to partake in the sacraments. Peter claimed this woman had renounced her heresy and that even Theophilus had affirmed her decision. Peter summoned Isidore to corroborate his testimony, which he did, causing Theophilus to become enraged and to eject both men from the church. See Fatti, "Eretico," 403–19, on Theophilus's fallout with Isidore and the relevant source problems.

100. Socr., *h.e.* 6.7.1–10; Soz., *h.e.* 8.11.1–5. See Dechow, *Dogma*, 403–8; Rubenson, "Origen," 333–36; Russell, *Theophilus*, 18–34.

101. Soz., *h.e.* 8.11.1–5, discussed Theophilus's festal letter that attacked any anthropomorphic conception of God. Cf. Socr., *h.e.* 6.7.7. Russell offers a translation of fragments of a letter written by Theophilus in 403 in which the bishop recounted his condemnation of Origenism and Anthropomorphite ideas. *Theophilus*, 139–43. See also Agostino, *Teofilo*, 93–95; Haas, *Alexandria*, 263–65.

102. Pall., *v. Chrys.* 6.76–117.

103. Pall., *v. Chrys.* 6.118–22.

Palladius, in his hostile account of Theophilus's behavior, described how a delegation of the threatened monks came to the bishop, who in a fit of rage assaulted Ammonius and shouted, "Heretic! Anathematize Origen!" The battered and bruised monks returned to their cells and continued to pursue their ascetic ideals.[104] But Theophilus was not content with this situation. So he convened a synod at Nitria in late 399 or early 400 to anathematize Origen's works and excommunicate the Tall Brothers and their supporters, although a faction of pro-Origenist monks refused to do so and occupied a monastery church in Nitria.[105] Apparently one of the victims of the synodal action, a Bishop Paul, made his way to Bethlehem, where he found shelter with Jerome.[106] Theophilus wrote a letter to Jerome rebuking him for receiving this fugitive and reminding him of the Nicene canon that forbade harboring the excommunicated, to which Jerome coolly expressed his "gratitude" and the frustration that many had felt at Theophilus's slow move to action against Origenism.[107]

In the spring of 400 with government sanction and troops, Theophilus began a purge of all the allegedly Origenist monks in the Egyptian desert, complete with conflagrations of monastic cells and books, and deposed Dioscorus, the eldest of the Tall Brothers.[108] Some persecuted monks survived by hiding in a cistern, and after Theophilus's attempted pogrom, they fled to Palestine with three hundred of their brethren.[109] When Theophilus heard that the refugees had made their way to the Holy Land, he dispatched a circular letter to the bishops there that explained his dealings with the monks and offered a justification of his behavior, which he couched in explicit anti-Origenist terms.[110] He also included details about how the Origenist monks at Nitria allegedly en-

104. Pall., v. Chrys. 6.118–39. Compare with Soz., h.e. 8.12.1–12, who gave an elaborate story of Theophilus momentarily acquiescing to Isidore and his circle, delaying, throwing monks into prison, but finally condemning them for being Origenists. On Palladius, see D. Katos, *Palladius of Helenopolis: The Origenist Advocate* (Oxford: Oxford University Press, 2011), especially 33-97, on his defense of Chrysostom.

105. Jer., *Ep.* 92, is the synodal letter to the bishops of Palestine (and later to Cyprus), sent after the Tall Brothers and their brethren had left Egypt. Russell, *Theophilus*, 21.

106. Jer., *Ruf.* 3.17. Based on his later apology against Rufinus, the person at issue was apparently this Bishop Paul, who had lost his position under the condemnation of Theophilus. On these developments, see Kelly, *Jerome*, 243–46.

107. Jer., *Ep.* 63, which was Jerome's response.

108. Jer., *Ep.* 92; Pall., v. *Chrys.* 7.1–44; Socr., h.e. 6.7.11–29.

109. On the four different accounts of these events, see Russell, *Theophilus*, 18–21. Pall., v. *Chrys.* 7.48.51. Soz., h.e. 8.13.1, has eighty monks with whom the Tall Brothers first went to Jerusalem, then to Scythopolis.

110. For a complete translation, see Russell, *Theophilus*, 93–99.

gaged in self-mutilation to outwardly exhibit their inward piety.[111] Theophilus sought sanction for his actions from Anastasius, bishop of Rome, and he sent as his agent the monk Theodore, who traveled first to Palestine to report to Jerome.[112] By now Theophilus must have been aware of Jerome's hostility toward Origenist doctrines and his acerbic pen, as just a few years earlier Theophilus had intervened as mediator in the dispute with John of Jerusalem. Jerome replied with enthusiasm for being "summoned to my accustomed duty," and he regretted his earlier criticism of Theophilus's reluctance to take action, which he now realized was a momentary delay in a strike that was even fiercer than expected.[113] Thus Theophilus successfully recruited Jerome as an ally and supporter, with perhaps far less strategy and effort than Epiphanius had needed a few years earlier.[114]

In Constantinople

Meanwhile, as Theophilus dealt with affairs in Egypt, John Chrysostom was struggling through the full range of challenges that came with being bishop of Constantinople. His strong ascetic—perhaps countercultural—moral and practical convictions, especially against elite and aristocratic sensibilities and contrary to the more comfortable lifestyles of certain clerics and the undisciplined behavior of wandering monks in the imperial capital, led to increased friction with the powers that be, both at court and in the church.[115] John also became deeply involved in secular matters, and on several occasions he acted as mediator, negotiator, or advocate in imperial dealings with the court eunuch Eutropius, the Gothic general Gainas, the praetorian prefect Aurelianus, and the former consul and general Severianus.[116] These affairs occupied the bishop from the summer of 399 through the summer of the next year.

Toward the end of this period, John was also drawn into a dispute among

---

111. Jer., *Ep.* 92.1.
112. Jer., *Ep.* 89.
113. Jer., *Ep.* 86.1–2.
114. Jer., *Ep.* 87, 88.
115. For John's criticisms and reforms, see Kelly, *Golden Mouth*, 115–27, 134–37; Tiersch, *Chrysostomus*, 135–82. On the wandering monks, see Caner, *Monks*, 169–77. On the friends and enemies he made as a result of his lifestyle and convictions, see W. Liebeschuetz, "Friends and Enemies of John Chrysostom," in *Maistor: Classical, Byzantine and Renaissance Studies for Robert Browning*, Byzantina Australiensia 5, ed. A. Moffatt (Canberra: Australian Association for Byzantine Studies, 1984), 85–111.
116. See Liebeschuetz, *Barbarians*, 96–125; Kelly, *Golden Mouth*, 145–62; Tiersch, *Chrysostomus*, 265–308. But also Mayer, "Making," for how sources favorable to John credited him with greater involvement in these affairs than was warranted.

various bishops in Asia Minor, and while he initially planned to travel to the disputing cities to sort out the conflict, he was needed by Emperor Arcadius to negotiate with the renegade Gainas.[117] Thus John was compelled to delay travel and send an envoy in his stead, which apparently was not very effective,[118] and John eventually had to intervene.[119] Based on the chronology argued by Kelly, who rejects the older argument that John left the capital shortly after Epiphany 401 and triumphantly returned sometime after Easter of the same year, Chrysostom did not fully resolve the conflict until after Easter 402.[120] An earthquake shook Constantinople in 400, which Chrysostom mentioned in one of his exegetical sermons on Acts, and strong internal evidence from the collection of these sermons suggests that this homily in particular was delivered in the city in early 401, thus making any trip to Asia Minor during that time unlikely.[121] Rather, John departed soon after 6 January 402, the feast of Epiphany and the date on which Empress Eudoxia's infant son was baptized.[122]

The date of John's departure and return to Constantinople is important for our purposes because it has a direct bearing on when his confrontation with Epiphanius occurred, as several significant developments took place in 402. Furthermore based on Palladius's remark that Epiphanius had served as bishop for thirty-six years, the date of Epiphanius's fateful voyage home from the imperial capital, 403, informs us that he assumed leadership of the Christians of Cyprus in 367. However, before we move to the conflict that consumed Epiphanius's final days, we must examine the sequence of events that further escalated this phase of the Origenist controversy.

Old Wounds, New Alliances

Sometime before John Chrysostom left to mediate the ecclesiastical dispute in Ephesus, probably in the late fall of 401, the Tall Brothers along with fifty or so

---

117. Liebeschuetz, *Barbarians*, 189–94.
118. Pall., *v. Chrys.* 13.1–14.128. Kelly, *Golden Mouth*, 163–66.
119. Pall., *v. Chrys.* 14.128–15.41. Kelly, *Golden Mouth*, 172–80.
120. Pall., *v. Chrys.* 15.6–9, 15.42–44, implied that the conflict, which began in April 400, lasted two years. Chrysostom would have departed for Ephesus in early November 401. Kelly bases his argument on the testimony of Palladius and on internal evidence from John's sermons on Acts that suggest his presence in Constantinople in the early months of 401. *Golden Mouth*, 165–66. Kelly also drew on the persuasive argument made by A. Cameron, "Earthquake 400," *Chiron* 17 (1987): 343–60.
121. John Chrysostom, *homiliae in Ac.* 41. See the careful argument laid out by Cameron, "Earthquake," 344–51; Kelly, *Golden Mouth*, 166–68.
122. Kelly, *Golden Mouth*, 172. For the trip to Asia, see Kelly, *Golden Mouth*, 163–80; Tiersch, *Chrysostomus*, 309–26.

of their monastic brethren came to Constantinople with the hope of presenting their case before the emperor and before John.[123] According to Sozomen, the decision to travel to the imperial capital was spurred by news that Theophilus had sent messengers to Constantinople to lodge complaints about these monks and to bar any petitions from reaching the emperor.[124] John, perhaps wary of the specter of the bishop of Alexandria, was cautious in how he dealt with the refugees, apparently receiving them hospitably but not allowing them to participate in the Eucharist.[125] Palladius added a bit more detail about how John first related to the refugees. Apparently some of Theophilus's clergy were in the capital city to curry favor from imperial officials on behalf of their bishop.[126] John summoned and questioned them about the exiled monks. They affirmed that the refugees were indeed maltreated and encouraged John not to extend communion to them but nevertheless to treat them with kindness.[127] John surely recognized that these excommunicated monks fell under the ecclesiastical authority of Theophilus, so he had to tread very carefully lest he offend even more. John wrote a letter to Theophilus requesting the restoration of those excommunicated or that someone be sent to make formal accusations against them.[128] Sozomen reported that no reply came from Egypt, whereas Palladius wrote how Theophilus sent representatives to lay accusations against the monks.[129] That John would deign to compel anything from Theophilus must have sparked the nascent rage that stirred a plan in the bishop of Alexandria's mind that targeted the bishop of Constantinople. Not to be forgotten was the insulting and embarrassing affair of just a few years before when Theophilus failed in his attempt to install Isidore as bishop of the capital.

In the meantime, Theophilus, not one to stay idle or passive, was busy securing support throughout the years 400–402, but not in a way that suggested this was a conflict between two bishops over political and ecclesiastical authority. Rather, Theophilus claimed that all of his actions were motivated by a desire

---

123. Pall., *v. Chrys.* 7.61–83. Cf. Soz., *h.e.* 8.13.3, who identified eighty monks. See Russell, *Theophilus*, 27–30, for a summary of the events that followed the arrival of the Tall Brothers to Constantinople.

124. Soz., *h.e.* 8.13.2.

125. Soz., *h.e.* 8.13.3.

126. These must have been the aforementioned messengers.

127. Pall., *v. Chrys.* 7.92–102.

128. Pall., *v. Chrys.* 7.104–6; Soz., *h.e.*. 8.13.4.

129. Pall., *v. Chrys.* 7.106–14. According to Kelly, this would have been the second envoy sent from Alexandria. *Golden Mouth*, 198, n. 43. The first, however, came not because Theophilus learned that the monks had left for Constantinople. Rather, Theophilus had written first to Constantinople to preclude any chance the monks to plead their case, and they thus departed for the capital when they heard that Theophilus had sent messengers to inform against them.

to root out Origenist heresy. As he had already recruited Jerome to his camp, the next item on his to-do list was to enlist the most notorious anti-Origenist of all, Epiphanius. Theophilus wrote a personal letter to the revered bishop in Cyprus:

> The Lord, who said to his prophet: "Behold, today I have set you over the nations and kingdoms to root out and to sap and to destroy and build up again and to plant" (Jer 1:10), bestows the same grace in every age upon his church, in order that through forbearance his body (cf. Eph 1:23) might be kept unharmed and that in no way at all might the poisons of the doctrines of heretics prevail. Because indeed now we see it has been fulfilled. For the church of Christ, which has "no spot or wrinkle or anything of this sort" (Eph 5:27), with the Gospel sword, has cut down the serpents of Origen, emerging from their caves, and has freed the holy flock of the monks of Nitria from the pestilent contagion.
>
> (2) Thus I have recounted a few of the things that have been accomplished in a general letter, which I laid out for all in common, accordingly as was allowed by the constraint of time. It is of a worthy thing for you, as one who often has contended before us in struggles of this sort, both to encourage those put in the fray and to gather the bishops of the entire island, and to send letters both to us and to the holy bishop of the city of Constantinople, if also to any others you will have considered, in order that with the consent of all, both Origen himself and his nefarious heresy might be condemned.
>
> (3) In fact I have learned that the calumniators of the true faith, Ammonius, Eusebius, and Euthymius, reveling with newfound passion for their heresy, have set sail for Constantinople, in order that they may ensnare new men, those whom they will have been able to overcome, and that they may be joined with the old allies of their impiety. Therefore let it be of your concern, that you relate the course of things to all of the bishops throughout Isauria and Pamphylia and of other provinces that are in the vicinity, and if you consider it worthy, to append our letter, in order that all gathered in spirit with the virtue of our Lord Jesus Christ might deliver those men into the destruction of the impiety of Satan, who is master over them.
>
> (4) And in order that our writings may arrive more swiftly to Constantinople, send an industrious man and someone from among the clergy, just as we have sent fathers of the monks from the very monasteries of Nitria with other holy and most continent men, who might be able to teach everything at hand that has been done. (5) And above all we ask that you utter devoted prayers to

our Lord, by which we might be able then to pursue victory in this battle. In fact no small joy both in Alexandria and throughout Egypt has spread through the hearts of the people, where a few men have been ejected, in order that the pure body of the church might remain. Greet the brothers who are with you. The people who are with us greet you in the Lord.

Epiphanius must have been thrilled when he received this letter. Not only had he reconnected with the ecclesiastical leader of Alexandria, one of Athanasius's successors and bishop of the land that was so formative in his youth, but Epiphanius also must have felt vindicated for his uncompromising anti-Origenist convictions and his confrontation with John of Jerusalem just a few years before. Indeed, the results of that conflict were mediocre at best. Epiphanius certainly succeeded in molding Jerome into an anti-Origenist, but John was still bishop of Jerusalem and "Origenism" was still alive and well. Surely Epiphanius must have known that Theophilus had reviled him for his behavior in Jerusalem, and now the very man who mediated a settlement between Jerome and John (and Rufinus) was seeking a partnership with him.[130]

Of all the people in the ecclesiastical hierarchy of the Greek East, Epiphanius was a strategic and calculated choice on the part of Theophilus, who was continuing to set in motion his plan for revenge against the Tall Brothers, and ultimately John Chrysostom. However, it is important to note that in this letter, Theophilus did not yet attack John the "holy bishop" as an Origenist.[131] Theophilus's carefully chosen words, in particular his identification and "mutilation" of the Origenists as serpents, must have pushed all the right buttons and almost betrayed a knowledge of the *Panarion*.[132] We are fortunate to have a letter that Epiphanius wrote to his friend Jerome regarding these recent developments, and his excitement is palpable:

> To my most beloved lord, son, and brother Jerome, presbyter, and to all the brothers who live with you in the monastery, Epiphanius greets in the Lord.
> The general letter, which has been written to all Catholics, belongs particu-

130. Pall., *v. Chrys.* 16.205–8, for Theophilus's criticism of Epiphanius. Socr., *h.e.* 6.10.2, was more specific about how Theophilus criticized Epiphanius for his alleged Anthropomorphite views. For the letter above, *Jer., Ep.* 90.
131. Socr., *h.e.* 6.10.8, explicitly identified Dioscorus, one of the Tall Brothers, as the object of Theophilus's scorn. While this is certainly true, the machinations of Theophilus soon shifted and focused almost exclusively on the condemnation of Chrysostom.
132. Socr., *h.e.* 6.10.4: "Epiphanius, on account of his exceeding piety and way of life, being a simple man, was easily led on by the writings of Theophilus." Cf. Soz., *h.e.* 8.15.1–2.

larly to you, who having a zeal for the faith against all heresies, spurn the disciples especially of Origen and Apollinarius, whose venomous roots and deeply
planted impiety the Almighty God has pulled out into our midst, in order that
they, made known in Alexandria, might wither in the entire world. (2) In fact I
know, my dearest son, that Amalek has been destroyed to the root and on
Mount Rephidim the trophy of the cross has been erected (cf. Exod 17:8–16).
And, in the way that Israel was victorious with the hands of Moses raised high,
so also the Lord has much strengthened his servant Theophilus, in order that he
might place his banner above the altar of the church of Alexandria against Origen and that it might be fulfilled in him, that which says, "Write this sign, because I will destroy utterly the heresy of Origen from the face of the earth,
Amalek with him."

(3) Lest I appear to repeat again the same things and to produce a longer letter, I have sent to you the very writing, in order that you might be able to know
what he has written to us and how much blessing the Lord has granted to me in
my final days, so that, what I always was proclaiming, might be approved by the
testimony of such a pontiff. Now, moreover, I also think that you have produced
some work; and according to my prior letter with which I encouraged you with
regard to the matter above, that you have finished books, which men of your
own language read. (4) In fact I hear also that certain shipwrecked men have
arrived in the West who not content with their own perdition want to have
more sharers in their death, as if the multitude of sinners may lessen the crime
and the flames of Gehenna may not grow with a greater number of logs. We
heartily greet with you and through you the holy brothers, who serve the Lord
with you in the monastery.[133]

The stars had aligned perfectly in Epiphanius's imagined orthodox world:
Theophilus, the metropolitan of Egypt, the land of his youth and education, was
waging a war against the Origenist monks; the monk Jerome and his brethren in
Bethlehem were battling the forces of heresy in the land where Epiphanius lived
and led his own monastic community some thirty years before; and finally in
Cyprus, under his own leadership he convened a synod that condemned Origen's
life and prohibited the reading of his writings.[134] After this local council, Epiphanius apparently sent a letter to John Chrysostom asking him also to assemble a

133. Jer., *Ep.* 91.
134. Socr., *h.e.* 6.10.5; Soz., *h.e.* 8.14.3, for the synod in Cyprus.

synod with a similar purpose, and the emboldened Theophilus convened a council of his own in Egypt to explicitly condemn the writings of Origen.[135]

The Final Confrontation

Theophilus's chess game was going exactly according to plan. He was using his Cypriot bishop to prepare an attack on the opposing bishop, who had made himself vulnerable by protecting the refugees from Egypt, and Theophilus could now wage a campaign on two fronts: the Tall Brothers and John Chrysostom. Rumors had reached Alexandria that John had in fact received the Tall Brothers and their companions into full communion, an act that would have been a clear affront to Theophilus, and now there seemed to be an undeniable violation of ecclesiastical order and a pretext for retaliation.[136] The refugees, however, did not remain passive petitioners but defended themselves in a letter to Theophilus, affirming that they "anathematize all false doctrine." They also presented a formal petition to John, lodging their complaints against Theophilus and his atrocious behavior.[137] John again pursued a conciliatory route and marshaled other bishops to persuade the Tall Brothers to drop their petition against Theophilus, to whom John also wrote informing him of the accusations made against him: "The men were driven to such a plight, that they accuse you in writing. It remains for you to respond as seems best, for I am not able to keep them from the court."[138] Theophilus was enraged by this letter and wrote a scathing response to John, reported by Palladius: "Utterly inflamed by these things, Theophilus barred from his church the brother of the monks, Dioscorus the bishop, who had grown old in service to the church. To bishop John he wrote, 'I know that you are not unaware of the ordinances of the canons of Nicaea that declare a bishop should not adjudicate beyond his boundaries. But if you are unaware, having learned them, leave the petitions to me. For if even there should be a need for me to be judged, it should be by the Egyptians, and not by you, away by a seventy-five days' journey.'"[139]

Once John received this reply from Theophilus, he tried again to mediate between the exiled monks and the agents of Theophilus, but to no avail. So he

---

135. Socr., *h.e.* 6.10.6–8; Soz., *h.e.* 8.14.3–4.
136. Soz., *h.e.* 8.13.6.
137. Pall., *v. Chrys.* 7.117–22. The charges were so appalling that Palladius refused to repeat them, lest he cause his readers to stumble. See Kelly, *Golden Mouth*, 198–99.
138. Pall., *v. Chrys.* 7.122–28.
139. Pall., *v. Chrys.* 7.129–36.

decided that the matter was at an impasse and no longer worthy of further consideration: "Thus John, conceding to them, dismissed the matter from his thought."[140] This must have come as a great disappointment for the Tall Brothers and their brethren, as they had hoped that John would be their advocate. They turned their attention instead to the royal court and composed a petition outlining their grievances against Theophilus's agents in the city and against the bishop himself and presented it on the feast of John the Baptist, 24 June 402.[141] Sozomen's account elaborates further: "After much time passed, those with Ammonius approached the wife of the emperor when she was out in public, complaining about all the machinations of Theophilus against them. She was aware of the designs against them, and honoring them she stood up. And bending forward from her royal carriage, she nodded her head and, "Bless," she said, "and pray for the emperor and me and our children and our rule. I have set my thoughts on a synod and on the arrival of Theophilus [to it]."[142] Although the two sources present slightly different versions of how the Tall Brothers presented their petition, they both stress the role of the royal family, and by implication that of the empress Eudoxia.[143] An imperial order was issued, demanding that Theophilus come to Constantinople to stand trial in a court presided over by John and that the bishop of Alexandria's agents in the city should substantiate the charges that were made against the refugee monks.[144] A certain Elaphios, a former *princeps agentum in rebus*, traveled to Egypt to summon Theophilus, while imperial officials in Constantinople carried out an investigation of Theophilus's representatives.[145]

Perhaps at this point Theophilus recognized that he had overplayed his hand and feared the coming storm.[146] He had put himself into a difficult situation and was compelled to travel to the capital. He was not, however, totally without options, and as he undertook the journey with delay and by a circuitous land route, he mounted a counteroffensive.[147] One of the key stratagems

---

140. Pall., *v. Chrys.* 8.7–8.
141. Pall., *v. Chrys.* 8.9–11. See Kelly, *Golden Mouth*, 200–201.
142. Soz., *h.e.* 8.13.5.
143. Kelly, *Golden Mouth*, 201. On Eudoxia, see K. Holum, *Theodosian Empresses: Women and Imperial Dominion in Late Antiquity*, Transformation of the Classical Heritage 3 (Berkeley: University of California Press, 1982), 48–78.
144. Pall., *v. Chrys.* 8.17–22.
145. Pall., *v. Chrys.* 8.23–36. On the identity and position of Elaphios, see A.-M. Malingrey and P. Leclercq, *Palladios: Dialogue sur la vie de Jean Chrysostome, Tome I*, SC 341 (Paris: Les Éditions du Cerf, 1988), 158, n. 2.
146. Kelly, *Golden Mouth*, 203.
147. Kelly, *Golden Mouth*, 204–5.

in this plan was deploying Epiphanius on an anti-Origenist mission to Constantinople to discredit the would-be judge John.[148] Although the letter that Theophilus sent to Epiphanius to set him on this course does not survive, by implication the contents must have explicitly identified John as an Origenist heretic, as Epiphanius's subsequent actions in the capital confirm.[149] There was, of course, scant proof that John was in any way an Origenist. But the circumstantial evidence, at least as Theophilus must have presented it to Epiphanius, was enough to put a cloud of suspicion over John. Epiphanius could not help but take action, and sometime after Easter 403 he set sail for Constantinople.

Rather than disembarking in the city center, Epiphanius landed some seven miles away in the suburb of Hebdomon, where the martyrium of Saint John was located, and he "celebrated a service and ordained a deacon" before finally entering into the city.[150] These actions echo what we saw in Epiphanius's conflict with John of Jerusalem. Epiphanius was well aware that the ordination of a cleric outside of his jurisdiction was an improper and provocative act, and again he clearly acted in such a way as to set up a confrontation with the bishop of Constantinople. John, however, must have sent an invitation for the bishop of Cyprus to stay in the episcopal residence and enjoy his hospitality, which Epiphanius, following the (premeditated) advice of Theophilus, refused to do.[151] Epiphanius then made yet another provocative action when he convened a gathering of bishops in the city and presented to them his copy of the synodal decree condemning the writings of Origen. Some of those present subscribed to the decree out of respect for the bishop, but Theotimus, a bishop of Scythia, refused: "'I,' he said, 'O Epiphanius, neither choose to insult those who have passed away long ago, nor dare to attempt a blasphemous act, casting aside what those who came before us did not reject, especially since I do not find any wicked teaching in the books of Origen.'"[152] This Theotimus then produced a copy of one of Origen's writings, read some passages aloud, found nothing against orthodox belief, and criticized those who would dishonor such sacred books.[153]

---

148. Nautin argues that Epiphanius had traveled in 402 after the synod in Cyprus on his own initiative to confront John. "Épiphane," c. 624. But Socr., *h.e.* 6.12.1, made clear that Epiphanius acted at the suggestion of Theophilus.
149. Kelly, *Golden Mouth*, 205.
150. Socr., *h.e.* 6.12.2; Soz., *h.e.* 8.14.6.
151. Socr., *h.e.* 6.12.3; Soz., *h.e.* 8.14.6–7.
152. Socr., *h.e.* 6.12.3–5; Soz., *h.e.* 8.14.8.
153. Socr., *h.e.* 6.12.6.

According to Socrates, John took the high road, refusing to be insulted by the illicit ordination and gathering of bishops. Again he invited Epiphanius to stay at the episcopal residence, to which Epiphanius replied that he would only do so if John expelled Dioscorus and his brethren from the city and subscribed to the condemnation of Origen's writings.[154] John then decided to delay until more "universal" decisions were made, but his adversaries persuaded Epiphanius to make yet another provocative move. Their plan was that at a gathering at the Church of the Holy Apostles, "Epiphanius come forward and in the presence of all the people reject the books of Origen, excommunicate those with Dioscorus, and disparage John as one who even accounted himself for those men."[155] The plot was reported to John, who sent a message through his deacon Serapion: "You do many things contrary to the canons, O Epiphanius. First, you made an ordination in the churches that are under me, then seeing that you were not appointed by me still held services in them, using your own authority. Just now you were urged to come but refused and now again you leave it to yourself to do so. So beware, lest with a tumult happening among the people, you yourself also suffer danger from it."[156] In Socrates's version of the events, this warning was enough for Epiphanius to cease and desist, and with some parting shots directed at John, he left for Cyprus. The last words exchanged by the two men has Epiphanius saying to John, "I hope that you do not die a bishop," while John replied, "I hope that you do not set foot in your country."[157] In a rather sad twist of providence, both prophecies would (and had to) come true.[158]

Sozomen's version provides more details and further nuance on the final confrontation between Epiphanius and John. Drawing on Socrates, Sozomen included similar information on Epiphanius's arrival to the city, John's offers of hospitality, the gathering of bishops to condemn the writings of Origen, the resistance of Theotimus, and the confrontation regarding the plot at the Church of the Apostles.[159] While Socrates had Epiphanius depart for Cyprus after he relented in his planned attack against John, Sozomen added two important episodes:

154. Socr., *h.e.* 6.14.1–2; Soz., *h.e.* 8.14.9.
155. Socr., *h.e.* 6.14.4.
156. Socr., *h.e.* 6.14.6.
157. Socr., *h.e.* 6.14.9–10; Soz., *h.e.* 8.15.7.
158. Gaddis, *No Crime*, 225, observes that since both were holy men, their declarations had to come true.
159. Soz., *h.e.* 8.14.6–11.

In the meantime, it happened that the son of the emperor was ill. Being fearful lest he suffer death, the mother, having sent for Epiphanius, was begging him to pray for the boy. He promised that the ailing child would live, if she would turn away from those heretics around Disocorus. (2) The empress said: "My son, if at least it seems good for God to take him, let this be done. For the Lord who gave him, may take him back. If indeed you are such a one to raise the dead, your archdeacon would not have died." For it happened that not long before, Chrispion died, who was brother of Fuscon and Salamanus (monks discussed [in my work] during the reign of Valens). He [Epiphanius], having him as a cohabitant, ordained him as his archdeacon.

(3) Those with Ammonius (for this seemed good to the empress herself) came to Epiphanius. When he inquired who they were, Ammonius replied and said, "We are the Tall Brothers, O father. But if ever you have met with our disciples or our books, we gladly would like to know." When he [Epiphanius] said no, again he asked, "So how is it that you have considered us to be heretics, having no proof of our thought?" (4) When Epiphanius said by what he had heard, he [Ammonius] said, "But we have come to a mind in quite the opposite way. For we often have met with your disciples and your writings, of which one has the title *Ancoratus*. When many people wish to revile you and to calumniate you as a heretic, we fought for and defended you as a father. Therefore was it necessary to pass judgment from hearsay on an undefended action, of whom you, not trusting, condemned, or to give back such recompense to those who speak well of you?"

(5) Epiphanius then, convinced in a more measured way, dismissed the men. Not long later, he sailed off to Cyprus, either because he condemned his arrival to Constantinople, or because God proclaimed and, as is likely, foretold his death to him. For when he was at sea, before arriving in Cyprus, he died. (6) It is said at any rate that to those who came with him to the marina he said, as he was about to embark on the ship: "I leave to you the city and the palaces and the stage, and I am departing. For I make haste, indeed I make haste." (7) And yet now from many people I heard that report, that John foretold to Epiphanius his death on the sea, and the latter to the former the deposition from his episcopacy. For when they were quarrelling, he [Epiphanius] declared to John: "I hope that you will not die a bishop." And John declared in response: "And I that you will not set foot in your city."[160]

---

160. Soz., *h.e.* 8.15.1–7.

Sozomen's account, although certainly suspect for its dependence on hearsay and its rhetorical flair, offers some insight into what may have been the final words and deeds of Epiphanius's long and illustrious life and career.[161] Eudoxia's appeal for prayer speaks to his reputation as a holy man, even if his reply was not a little insulting, and her indignant response seems to intimate a wider knowledge of Epiphanius and his associates.[162] His encounter with Ammonius is also rather telling. For Epiphanius, who in his own estimation wrote the *Panarion* after conducting much research in both written and oral sources, his conversation with the Nitrian monks is an embarrassing exposure of his perhaps overzealous heresy-hunting mind-set. Presumably based on what he had heard from Theophilus, Epiphanius assumed that the Tall Brothers were without a doubt Origenist heretics, as was John Chrysostom for harboring them. But Epiphanius quickly found in Ammonius a voice of reason, seasoned with a bit of flattery. Perhaps at this point, Epiphanius came to realize that what he thought was a heresy-hunting mission, in which he could readily and dutifully live out the convictions he had written in the *Panarion*, was more the result of Theophilus's sinister machinations than an undertaking for orthodox Christianity. His final words at the dock in Constantinople, if Sozomen is indeed reliable, betray Epiphanius's sense of resignation at his failed efforts. As the subsequent proceedings of the Synod of the Oak demonstrate, the real clash between John Chrysostom and Theophilus was personal, political, and perhaps a little theological.[163] Epiphanius was used and abused by someone he had trusted and believed was a partner in the defense of orthodoxy.

On a ship sailing back to Cyprus in the late spring of 403, Epiphanius breathed his last, and thus ended the life of a late antique giant.

---

161. Nautin is highly critical of Sozomen and his "amplification postérieure" ("Épiphane," c. 625), but Kelly is less skeptical (*Golden Mouth*, 209).

162. Soz., *h.e.* 6.32.5, mentioned Salamanus, Fuscon, Malachion, and Chrispion, monks who lived in Gaza and were instructed by Hilarion. Sozomen's report of Eudoxia's negative exchange with Epiphanius contrasts with Socr., *h.e.* 6.15.1, who suggested that Eudoxia had tried to stir Epiphanius against John.

163. Socr., *h.e.* 6.15.1–20. On the Synod of the Oak, see Kelly, *Golden Mouth*, 211–27; S. Elm, "The Dog That Did Not Bark: Doctrine and Patriarchal Authority in the Conflict between Theophilus of Alexandria and John Chrysostom of Constantinople," in *Christian Origins: Theology, Rhetoric and Community*, ed. L. Ayres and G. Jones (New York: Routledge, 1998), 68–93; Tiersch, *Chrysostomus*, 327–53; Russell, *Theophilus*, 30–34; Katos, *Palladius*, 62–97; P. Van Nuffelen, "Theophilus against John Chrysostom: The Fragments of a Lost Liber and the Reasons for John's Deposition," *Adamantius* 19 (2013): 139–55.

Epilogue

What must have been going through Epiphanius' mind on that sad and fateful journey home? Did he look back on his life and experiences—his ascetic training in Egypt, his monastic leadership in Palestine, his episcopal administration in Cyprus, his literary achievements, his travels in pursuit of heretics and in defense of the truth—and feel content that he had done all he could for Christ and Christendom? Did he think back with satisfaction on how he helped expunge the heretical Gnostic women in Egypt, or how he confronted the Archontic Peter, or his mediation in Antioch, or his clash with John of Jerusalem? Or did he come to realize that he was and always was a small fish swimming in the rather large Mediterranean sea, with its other much larger and more powerful ecclesiastical colleagues and currents that were beyond his control or influence? His attempt to combat Origenist heresy in Constantinople was for all intents and purposes a complete failure, but did it invalidate what he had accomplished up to that point? Whatever shortcomings Epiphanius had in the eyes of both ancient and modern critics, he was undoubtedly a product of his times, an era of intense theological, political, and ecclesiastical competition and instability. But he was also deeply sure of his own convictions and spent most of his life unwaveringly committed to the defense of what he understood to be orthodox Christianity, and in that sense, he was a stabilizing force. It has been too easy to dismiss him as representative of a fanatical, fundamentalist strain of late ancient Christianity, and scholars have done much to disparage his lack of polish and intellectual depth and at times despicable behavior. Without a doubt, he had his shortcomings and deficiencies in character, and he behaved at times in less than honorable ways. But this book has also shown that Epiphanius (and the *Panarion*) was much more complicated, insightful, and imaginative than we thought him to be, and he deserves to be considered among the most important figures of late antiquity.

Bibliography

Editions and Translations

Acta Archelai

Beeson, Charles. *Hegemonius: Acta Archelai.* GCS 16. Leipzig: J.C. Hinrichs, 1906.

Vermes, Mark. *Hegemonius: Acta Archelai (The Acts of Archelaus).* Manichaean Studies 4. Turnhout: Brepols, 2001.

Ambrose of Milan

Zelzer, Michaela. *Sancti Ambrosii Opera, Pars 10, Epistulae et Acta, Tome 3.* CSEL 82. Vienna: Hoelder-Pichler-Tempsky, 1982.

Apophthegmata Patrum

Ward, Benedicta. *The Sayings of the Desert Fathers: The Alphabetical Collection.* Kalamazoo: Cistercian Publications, 1975.

Athanasius of Alexandria

DelCogliano, Mark, Andrew Radde-Gallwitz, and Lewis Ayres. *Works on the Spirit: Athanasius's "Letters to Serapion on the Holy Spirit" and Didymus's "On the Holy Spirit."* Popular Patristics Series 43. Crestwood, NY: St. Vladimir's Seminary Press, 2011.

Gregg, Robert. *Athanasius: "The Life of Antony" and "The Letter to Marcellinus."* The Classics of Western Spirituality. Mahwah, NJ: Paulist Press, 1980.

Lebon, Joseph. *Athanase d'Alexandrie: Lettres à Sérapion sur la divinité du Saint-Esprit.* SC 15. Paris: Éditions du Cerf, 1947.

Opitz, Hans-Georg. *Athanasius Werke II.1, Vol. 3, Die Apologien: 1. De Decretis Nicaeanae Synodi.* Berlin: Walter de Gruyter, 1935.

Opitz, Hans-Georg. *Athanasius Werke II.1, Vol. 4, Die Apologien: 2. De Sententia Dionysii, 3. Apologia De Fuga Sua (1–18).* Berlin: Walter de Gruyter, 1936.

Opitz, Hans-Georg. *Athanasius Werke II.1, Vol. 8, Die Apologien: 8. Historia Arianorum (32–Schluß)*, 9. *De Synodis (1–13)*. Berlin: Walter de Gruyter, 1940.

Opitz, Hans-Georg. *Athanasius Werke II.1, Vol. 9, Die Apologien: 9. De Synodis (13–55)*, 10. *Apologia ad Constantium (1–3)*. Berlin: Walter de Gruyter, 1941.

Opitz, Hans-Georg. *Athanasius Werke III.1, Urkunden zur Geschichte des arianischen Streites 318–328*. Berlin: Walter de Gruyter, 1934.

Shapland, C.R.B. *The Letters of Saint Athanasius Concerning the Holy Spirit*. London: Epworth Press, 1951.

Szymusiak, Jan. *Athanase d'Alexandrie: Deux apologies à l'empereur Constance pour sa fuite*. SC 56. Paris: Les Éditions du Cerf, 1987.

Tetz, Martin. *Athanasius Werke 1.1, Vol. 2, Die dogmatischen Schriften: Orationes I et II Contra Arianos*. New York: Walter de Gruyter, 1998.

Tetz, Martin and Dietmar Wyrwa. *Athanasius Werke 1.1, Vol. 3, Die dogmatischen Schriften: Oratio III Contra Arianos*. New York: Walter de Gruyter, 2000.

Wyrwa, Dietmar and Kyriakos Savvidis. *Athanasius Werke 1.1, Vol. 4: Die dogmatischen Schriften: Epistulae I–IV ad Serapionem*. Berlin: Walter de Gruyter, 2010.

Basil of Caesarea

Courtonne, Yves. *Saint Basile: Lettres, Tome I*. Paris: Société d'Édition "Les Belles Lettres," 1957.

Courtonne, Yves. *Saint Basile: Lettres, Tome II*. Paris: Société d'Édition "Les Belles Lettres," 1961.

Courtonne, Yves. *Saint Basile: Lettres, Tome III*. Paris: Société d'Édition "Les Belles Lettres," 1966.

DelCogliano, Mark and Andrew Radde-Gallwitz. *St. Basil of Caesarea: Against Eunomius*. FC 122. Washington, DC: Catholic University of America Press, 2011.

Sesboüé, Bernard. *Basile de Césarée: Contre Eunome, Tome I*. SC 299. Paris: Les Éditions du Cerf, 1982.

Sesboüé, Bernard. *Basile de Césarée: Contre Eunome, Tome II*. SC 305. Paris: Les Éditions du Cerf, 1983.

Berossus

Burstein, Stanley. *The Babyloniaca of Berossus*. Sources and Monographs. Sources from the Ancient Near East 1.5. Malibu: Undena Publications, 1978.

Verbrugghe, Gerald and John Wickersham. *Berossus and Manetho: Introduced and Translated; Native Traditions in Ancient Mesopotamia and Egypt*. Ann Arbor: University of Michigan Press, 1996.

Clement of Alexandria

Stählin, Otto. *Clemens Alexandrinus, zweiter Band, Stromata Buch I–VI*. GCS 52. neu Herausgegeben von L. Früchtel, 4. Auflage mit Nachträgen von U. Treu. Berlin: Akademie-Verlag, 1985.

Cyril of Jerusalem

McCauley, Leo. *The Works of Saint Cyril of Jerusalem*. Vol. 1. FC 61. Washington, DC: Catholic University of America Press, 1968.

McCauley, Leo. *The Works of Saint Cyril of Jerusalem*. Vol. 2. FC 64. Washington, DC: Catholic University of America Press, 1970.

Dio Cassius

Cary, Earnest. *Dio's Roman History*. LCL 176. Cambridge, MA: Harvard University Press, 1925.

Epiphanius

Albrecht, Fleix and Arthur Manukyan. *Epiphanius von Salamis: Über die zwölf Steine im hohepriesterlichen Brustschild (De duodecim gemmis rationalis) nach dem Codex Vaticanus Borgianus Armenus 31*. Gorgias Eastern Christian Studies 37. Piscataway, NJ: Gorgias Press, 2014.

Amidon, Philip. *The "Panarion" of St. Epiphanius, Bishop of Salamis: Selected Passages*. Oxford: Oxford University Press, 1990.

Blake, Robert. *Epiphanius De Gemmis: The Old Georgian Version and the Fragments of the Armenian Version* and Henry de Vis, *The Coptic-Sahidic Fragments*. Studies and Documents II. London: Christophers, 1934.

Dean, James. *Epiphanius' Treatise on Weights and Measures: The Syriac Version*. Studies in Ancient Oriental Civilization 11. Chicago: University of Chicago Press, 1935.

Holl, Karl. *Epiphanius (Ancoratus und Panarion)*. GCS 25, 31, 37. Leipzig: J.C. Hinrichs Buchhandlung, 1915, 1922, 1933, with revised editing by C.-F. Collatz and M. Bergermann, Vol. 1 and J. Dummer, Vol. 2 and 3. New York: Akademie Verlag/Walter de Gruyter, 1980, 1985, 2013.

Kim, Young Richard. *Saint Epiphanius: Ancoratus*. FC 128. Washington, DC: Catholic University of America Press, 2014.

Moutsoulas, Elias. ΤΟ "ΠΕΡΙ ΜΕΤΡΩΝ ΚΑΙ ΣΤΑΘΜΩΝ" ΕΡΓΟΝ ΕΠΙΦΑΝΙΟΥ ΤΟΥ ΣΑΛΑΜΙΝΟΣ. ΘΕΟΛΟΓΙΑ 44.1–2 (1973): 157–98.

Pini, Giovanni. *Epifanio di Salamina: Panarion, Libro primo*. Letteratura Cristiana Antica, Nuova serie 21. Brescia: Morcelliana, 2010.

Riggi, Calogero. *Epifano Contro Mani: Revisione Critica, Traduzione Italiana e Commento Storico del Panarion di Epifanio, Haer. LXVI*. Rome: Pontificium Institutum Altioris Latinitatis, 1967.

Riggi, Calogero. *Epifanio: L'ancora della fede*. Collana di Testi Patristici 9. Rome, Città Nuova Editrice, 1977.

Stone, Michael and Roberta Ervine. *The Armenian Texts of Epiphanius of Salamis: De Mensuris et Ponderibus*. CSCO 583, Subsidia 105. Leuven: Peeters, 2000.

van Esbroeck, Michel. *Les versions géorgiennes d'Épiphane de Chypre: Traité des poids et des mesures*. CSCO 460–461, Scriptores Iberici 19–20. Leuven: Peeters, 1984.

Williams, Frank. *The Panarion of Epiphanius of Salamis*. 2 volumes (with revised volumes). Nag Hammadi and Manichaean Studies 35, 36, 63, 79. Leiden: Brill, 1987, 1994, 2009, 2012.

Eusebius

Amacker, René and Éric Junod. *Pamphile et Eusèbe de Césarée: Apologie pour Origène suivi de Rufin d'Aquilée, Sur la falsification des livres d'Origène*. SC 464–465. Paris: Les Éditions du Cerf, 2002.

Heikel, Ivar. *Eusebius Werke VI, Die Demonstratio Evangelica*. GCS 23. Berlin: Akademie-Verlag, 1913.

Karst, Josef. *Eusebius Werke V, Die Chronik*. GCS 20. Leipzig: J.C. Heinrichs'sche Buchhandlung, 1911.

Mras, Karl. *Eusebius Werke VIII, Die Praeparatio Evangelica, Teil I*. GCS 43. Berlin: Akademie-Verlag, 1954.

Places, Édouard des. *Eusèbe de Césarée: La Préparation évangélique, Livres II–III*. SC 228. Paris: Les Éditions du Cerf, 1976.

Places, Édouard des. *Eusèbe de Césarée: La Préparation évangélique, Livres V,18–36–VI*. SC 266. Paris: Les Éditions du Cerf, 1980.

Schroeder, Guy. *Eusèbe de Césarée: La Préparation évangélique, Livre VII*. SC 215. Paris: Les Éditions du Cerf, 1975.

Schroeder, Guy and Édouard des Places. *Eusèbe de Césarée: La Préparation évangélique, Livres VIII-IX-X*. SC 369. Paris: Les Éditions du Cerf, 1991.

Sirinelli, Jean and Édouard des Places. *Eusèbe de Césarée: La Préparation évangélique, Livre I*. SC 206. Paris: Les Éditions du Cerf, 1974.

Zink, Odile. *Eusèbe de Césarée: La Préparation évangélique, Livres IV–V,1–17*. SC 262. Paris: Les Éditions du Cerf, 1979.

Gregory of Nazianzus

Gallay, Paul. *Grégoire de Nazianze: Discours 27–31 (Discours théologiques)*. SC 250. Paris: Les Éditions du Cerf, 1978.

Hippolytus

Marcovich, Miroslav. *Hippolytus: Refutatio omnium haeresium*. Patristische Texte und Studien 25. Berlin: Walter de Gruyter, 1986.

Historia Acephala

Martin, Annick and Micheline Albert. *Histoire "acéphale" et Index syriaque des Lettres festales d'Athanase d'Alexandrie*. SC 317. Paris: Les Éditions du Cerf, 1985.

Irenaeus of Lyons

Rousseau, Adelin and Louis Doutreleau. *Irénée de Lyon: Contre les hérésies, Livre I, Tome I–II*. SC 263–264. Paris: Les Éditions du Cerf, 1979.

Rousseau, Adelin and Louis Doutreleau. *Irénée de Lyon: Contre les hérésies, Livre II, Tome I–II.* SC 293–294. Paris: Les Éditions du Cerf, 1982.

Rousseau, Adelin, et al. *Irénée de Lyon: Contre les hérésies, Livre IV, Tome I–II.* SC 100. Paris: Les Éditions du Cerf, 1965.

Rousseau, Adelin, et al. *Irénée de Lyon: Contre les hérésies, Livre V, Tome II.* SC 153. Paris: Les Éditions du Cerf, 1969.

Jerome

Ceresa-Gastaldo, Aldo. *Gerolamo: Gli Uomini Illustri. De viris illustribus.* Biblioteca Patristica 12. Florence: Nardini Editore, 1988.

Deferarri, Roy. *Early Christian Biographies.* FC 15. Washington, DC: Catholic University of America Press, 1952.

Feiertag, Jean Louis. *S. Hieronymi Presbyteri Opera, Opera III, Opera Polemica II.* CCSL 79A. Turnhout: Brepols, 1999.

Helm, Rudolf. *Eusebius Werke, siebenter Band: Die Chronik des Hieronymus, Hieronymi Chronicon, 3. unveränderte Auflage mit einer Vorbemerkung von Ursula Treu.* GCS 24. Berlin: Akademie Verlag, 1956.

Hilberg, Isidor. *Sancti Hieronymi Epistulae Pars I: Epistulae I–LXX.* CSEL 54. 2nd ed. Vienna: Verlag der Österreichischen Akademie der Wissenschaften, 1996.

Hilberg, Isidor. *Sancti Hieronymi Epistulae Pars II: Epistulae LXXI–CXX.* CSEL 55. 2nd ed. Vienna: Verlag der Österreichischen Akademie der Wissenschaften, 1996.

Hilberg, Isidor. *Sancti Hieronymi Epistulae Pars III: Epistulae CXXI–CLIV.* CSEL 56/1. 2nd ed. Vienna: Verlag der Österreichischen Akademie der Wissenschaften, 1996.

Lardet, Pierre. *S. Hieronymi Presbyteri Opera, Pars III, Opera Polemica I.* CCSL 79. Turnhout: Brepols, 1982.

Jubilees

Charles, Robert. *The Book of Jubilees or The Little Genesis.* Translations of Early Documents Series 1. Palestinian Jewish Texts (Pre-Rabbinic). New York: Macmillan, 1917.

Wintermute, Orval. "Jubilees: A New Translation and Introduction." In *The Old Testament Pseudepigrapha, Vol. 2.* The Anchor Bible Reference Library, edited by J. Charlesworth. New York: Doubleday, 1985.

Julius Africanus

Wallraff, Martin. *Iulius Africanus: Chronographiae; The Extant Fragments.* GCS Neue Folge 15. Translated by W. Adler. Berlin: Walter de Gruyter, 2007.

Justin Martyr

Falls, Thomas. *St. Justin Martyr: Dialogue with Trypho.* Selections from the Fathers of the Church 3. Washington, DC: Catholic University of America Press, 2003.

Manetho

Verbrugghe, Gerald and John Wickersham. *Berossus and Manetho, Introduced and Translated: Native Traditions in Ancient Mesopotamia and Egypt.* Ann Arbor: University of Michigan Press, 1996.

Nicander

Gow, Andrew and Alwyn Scholfield. *Nicander: The Poems and Poetical Fragments.* Cambridge: Cambridge University Press, 1953.

Origen

Barkley, Gary. *Origen: Homilies on Leviticus 1–16.* FC 83. Washington, DC: Catholic University of America Press, 1990.

Bruce, Barbara. *Origen: Homilies on Joshua.* FC 105. Washington, DC: Catholic University of America Press, 2002.

Butterworth, George. *Origen: On First Principles.* New York: Harper and Row, 1966. Reprint. Gloucester, MA: Peter Smith, 1973.

Heine, Ronald. *Origen: Commentary on the Gospel According to John Books 1–10.* FC 80. Washington, DC: Catholic University of America Press, 1989.

Heine, Ronald. *Origen: Commentary on the Gospel According to John Books 13–32.* FC 89. Washington, DC: Catholic University of America Press, 1993.

Jaubert, Annie. *Origène: Homélies sur Josué.* SC 71. Paris: Les Éditions du Cerf, 1960.

Palladius

Malingrey, Anne-Marie. *Palladios: Dialogue sur la vie de Jean Chrysostome, Tome II,* SC 342. Paris: Les Éditions du Cerf, 1988.

Malingrey, Anne-Marie and Philippe Leclercq. *Palladios: Dialogue sur la vie de Jean Chrysostome, Tome I.* SC 341. Paris: Les Éditions du Cerf, 1988.

Meyer, Robert. *Palladius: Dialogue on the Life of St. John Chrysostom.* ACW 45. New York: Newman Press, 1985.

Philipp Melanchthon

Bretschneider, Karl. *Philippi Melanthonis Opera Quae Supersunt Omnia.* Corpus Reformatorum 1. Halle: C.A. Schwetschke et Filium, 1834.

Philostorgius

Amidon, Philip. *Philostorgius: Church History.* Writings from the Greco-Roman World 23. Leiden: Brill, 2007.

Bidez, Joseph. *Philostorgius: Kirchengeschichte, 3, bearbeite Auflage von F. Winkelmann.* GCS 21. Berlin: Akademie-Verlag, 1981.

Photius

Henry, René. *Bibliothèque, Tome II*. Paris: Société d'Édition "Les Belles lettres," 1960.

Pseudo-Clement

Rehm, Bernhard. *Die Pseudoklementinen I: Homilien*. GCS 42. Berlin: Akademie-Verlag, 1953.

Rehm, Bernhard. *Die Pseudoklementinen II: Rekognitionen in Rufins Übersetzung*. GCS 51. Berlin: Akademie-Verlag, 1965.

Socrates

Hansen, Günther and Manjan Sirinjan. *Socrates Scholasticus: Kirchengeschichte*. GCS Neue Folge 1. Berlin: Akademie Verlag, 1995.

Périchon, Pierre and Pierre Maraval. *Socrate de Constantinople: Histoire ecclésiastique, Livre I*. SC 477. Paris: Les Éditions du Cerf, 2004.

Périchon, Pierre and Pierre Maraval. *Socrate de Constantinople: Histoire ecclésiastique, Livres II–III*. SC 493. Paris: Les Éditions du Cerf, 2005.

Périchon, Pierre and Pierre Maraval. *Socrate de Constantinople: Histoire ecclésiastique, Livres IV–VI*. SC 505. Paris: Les Éditions du Cerf, 2006.

Périchon, Pierre and Pierre Maraval. *Socrate de Constantinople: Histoire ecclésiastique, Livre VII*. SC 506. Paris: Les Éditions du Cerf, 2007.

Sozomen

Angliviel de la Beaumelle, Laurent, André-Jean Festugière, Bernard Grillet, and Guy Sabbah. *Sozomène: Histoire ecclésiastique, Livres VII–IX*. SC 516. Paris: Les Éditions du Cerf, 2008.

Festugière, André-Jean, Bernard Grillet, and Guy Sabbah. *Sozomène: Histoire ecclésiastique, Livres I–II*. SC 306. Paris: Les Éditions du Cerf, 1983.

Festugière, André-Jean, Bernard Grillet, and Guy Sabbah. *Sozomène: Histoire ecclésiastique, Livres III–IV*. SC 418. Paris: Les Éditions du Cerf, 1996.

Festugière, André-Jean, Bernard Grillet, and Guy Sabbah. *Sozomène: Histoire ecclésiastique, Livres V–VI*. SC 495. Paris: Les Éditions du Cerf, 2005.

Hansen, Günther. *Sozomen: Kirchengeschichte*. GCS Neue Folge 4. Berlin: Akademie Verlag, 1995.

Theodoret

Hansen, Günther. *Theodoret: Kirchengeschichte*. GCS Neue Folge 5. Berlin: Akademie Verlag, 1998.

Secondary Scholarship

Abramowski, Luise. "Trinitarische und christologische Hypostasenformeln." *Theologie und Philosophie* 54 (1979): 38–49.

Abramowski, Luise. "Die Anakephalaiosis zum Panarion des Epiphanius in der Handschrift Brit. Mus. Add. 12156." *Le Muséon* 96, nos. 3–4 (1983): 217–30.

Adler, William. "'Berossus, Manetho,' and '1 Enoch' in the World Chronicle of Panodorus." *HTR* 76, no. 4 (1983): 419–42.

Adler, William. *Time Immemorial: Archaic History and Its Sources in Christian Chronography from Julius Africanus to George Syncellus.* Dumbarton Oaks Studies 26. Washington, DC: Dumbarton Oaks Research Library and Collection, 1989.

Adler, William. "The Origins of the Proto-Heresies: Fragments from a Chronicle in the First Book of Epiphanius' *Panarion*." *JTS* 41, no. 2 (1990): 472–501.

Adler, William. "Sextus Julius Africanus and the Roman Near East in the Third Century." *JTS* 55, no. 2 (2004): 520–50.

Adler, William. "The *Chronographiae* of Julius Africanus and Its Jewish Antecedents." *ZAC* 14, no. 3 (2011): 496–524.

Allen, Pauline and Wendy Mayer. "Through a Bishop's Eyes: Towards a Definition of Pastoral Care in Late Antiquity." *Augustinianum* 40 (2000): 345–98.

Altaner, Berthold. *Patrologie: Leben, Schriften, und Lehre der Kirchenväter.* Freiburg: Herder, 1950.

Amidon, Philip. "Paulinus' Subscription to the *Tomus ad Antiochenos*." *JTS* 53, no. 1 (2002): 53–74.

Amundsen, Darrel. "Medicine and Faith in Early Christianity." *Bulletin of the History of Medicine* 56 (1982): 326–50.

Anatolios, Khaled. *Athanasius: The Coherence of His Thought.* New York: Routledge, 1998.

Anatolios, Khaled. *Retrieving Nicaea: The Development and Meaning of Trinitarian Doctrine.* Grand Rapids: Baker Academic, 2011.

Aragione, Gabriella. "Una 'storia' universale dell'eresia: Il Panarion di Epifanio," in Pini, *Epifanio*, 5–75.

Arnold, Duane. *The Early Episcopal Career of Athanasius of Alexandria.* Christianity and Judaism in Antiquity 6. Notre Dame, IN: University of Notre Dame Press, 1999.

Attridge, Harold and Gohei Hata, eds. *Eusebius, Christianity, and Judaism.* Detroit: Wayne State University Press, 1992.

Ayres, Lewis. *Nicaea and Its Legacy: An Approach to Fourth-Century Trinitarian Theology.* Oxford: Oxford University Press, 2004.

Ayres, Lewis. "Athanasius' Initial Defense of the Term Ὁμοούσιος: Rereading the *De decretis*." *JECS* 12, no. 3 (2004): 337–59.

Ayres, Lewis. "Innovation and *Ressourcement* in Pro-Nicene Pneumatology." *Augustinian Studies* 39, no. 2 (2008): 187–206.

Bagnall, Roger. *Egypt in Late Antiquity.* Princeton: Princeton University Press, 1993.

Bagnall, Roger and Klaas Worp. "ΤΕΤΡΑΧΡΥΣΟΝ." *Tyche* 15 (2000): 3–6.

Barnard, Leslie. "Athanasius and the Meletian Schism in Egypt." *Journal of Egyptian Archaeology* 59 (1973): 181–89.

Barnard, Leslie. "Some Notes on the Meletian Schism in Egypt." StPatr 15 (1975): 399–405.

Barnes, Michel. "The Beginning and End of Early Christian Pneumatology." *Augustinian Studies* 39, no. 2 (2008): 169–86.

Barnes, Michel and Daniel Williams, eds. *Arianism after Arius: Essays on the Development of the Fourth Century Trinitarian Conflicts.* Edinburgh: T&T Clark, 1993.

Barnes, Timothy. *Tertullian: A Historical and Literary Study.* Oxford: Oxford University Press, 1971.

Barnes, Timothy. *Constantine and Eusebius.* Cambridge, MA: Harvard University Press, 1981.

Barnes, Timothy. "Angel of Light or Mystic Initiate? The Problem of the *Life of Antony.*" *JTS* 37, no. 2 (1986): 353–68.

Barnes, Timothy. *Athanasius and Constantius: Theology and Politics in the Constantinian Empire.* Cambridge, MA: Harvard University Press, 1993.

Barton, Tamsyn. *Power and Knowledge: Astrology, Physiognomics, and Medicine under the Roman Empire.* The Body, in Theory. Ann Arbor: University of Michigan Press, 1994.

Bauer, Walter. *Rechtgläubigkeit und Ketzerei im ältesten Christentum.* Tübingen: Mohr, 1934.

Beatrice, Pier Franco. "The Word '*Homoousios*' from Hellenism to Christianity." *Church History* 71, no. 2 (2002): 243–72.

Becker, Adam and Annette Yoshiko Reed, eds. *The Ways That Never Parted: Jews and Christians in Late Antiquity and the Early Middle Ages.* Texts and Studies in Ancient Judaism 95. Tübingen: Mohr Siebeck, 2003.

BeDuhn, Jason and Paul Mirecki, eds. *Frontiers of Faith: The Christian Encounter with Manichaeism in the Acts of Archelaus.* Nag Hammadi and Manichaean Studies 61. Leiden: Brill, 2007.

Behr, John. *The Way to Nicaea.* Formation of Christian Theology 1. Crestwood, NY: St Vladimir's Seminary Press, 2001.

Behr, John. *The Nicene Faith.* Formation of Christian Theology 2. Crestwood, NY: St Vladimir's Seminary Press, 2004.

Benko, Stephen. "The Libertine Gnostic Sect of the Phibionites According to Epiphanius." *VC* 21 (1967): 103–19.

Bienert, Wolfgang and Uwe Kühneweg, eds. *Origeniana Septima: Origenes in den Auseinandersetzungen des 4. Jahrhunderts.* Bibliotheca Ephemeridum Theologicarum Lovaniensium 137. Leuven: Peeters, 1999.

Bigham, Steven. *Epiphanius of Salamis, Doctor of Iconoclasm? Deconstruction of a Myth.* Patristic Theological Library 3. Rollinsford, NH: Orthodox Research Institute, 2008.

Binns, John. *Ascetics and Ambassadors of Christ: The Monasteries of Palestine 314–631.* Oxford: Oxford University Press, 1994.

Bitton-Ashkelony, Brouria. "The Attitudes of Church Fathers toward Pilgrimage to Jerusalem in the Fourth and Fifth Centuries." In *Jerusalem: Its Sanctity and Centrality to Judaism, Christianity, and Islam*, edited by L. Levine, 188–203. New York: Continuum, 1999.

Bitton-Ashkelony, Brouria. *Encountering the Sacred: The Debate on Christian Pilgrimage in Late Antiquity.* Transformation of the Classical Heritage 38. Berkeley: University of California Press, 2005.

Bitton-Ashkelony, Brouria and Aryeh Kofsky. "Monasticism in the Holy Land." In Limor and Stroumsa, *Christians and Christianity*, 257–91.

Bowersock, Glen. *Julian the Apostate.* Cambridge, MA: Harvard University Press, 1978.

Bowersock, Glen. *Hellenism in Late Antiquity.* Ann Arbor: University of Michigan Press, 1990.

Bowersock, Glen. "The International Role of Late Antique Cyprus." 14th Annual Lecture on the History and Archaeology of Cyprus. Nicosia: Bank of Cyprus Cultural Foundation, 2000.

Boyarin, Daniel. *Dying for God: Martyrdom and the Making of Christianity and Judaism.* Figurae: Reading Medieval Culture. Stanford: Stanford University Press, 1999.

Boyarin, Daniel. *Border Lines: The Partition of Judaeo-Christianity.* Philadelphia: University of Pennsylvania Press, 2004.

Boyarin, Daniel. "Rethinking Jewish Christianity: An Argument for Dismantling a Dubious Category (to which is Appended a Correction of My *Border Lines*)." *Jewish Quarterly Review* 99, no. 1 (2009): 7–36.

Brakke, David. "The Authenticity of the Ascetic Athanasiana." *Orientalia* 64 (1994): 17–56.

Brakke, David. "The Greek and Syriac Versions of the *Life of Antony*." *Le Muséon* 107 (1994): 29–53.

Brakke, David. *Athanasius and Asceticism.* Baltimore: Johns Hopkins University Press, 1995.

Brakke, David. "Athanasius' *Epistula ad Epiphanium* and Liturgical Reform in Alexandria." StPatr 36 (2001): 482–88.

Brakke, David. The Early Church in North America: Late Antiquity, Theory, and the History of Christianity." *Church History* 71, no. 3 (2002): 473–91.

Brakke, David. *The Gnostics: Myth, Ritual, and Diversity in Early Christianity.* Cambridge, MA: Harvard University Press, 2010.

Brennecke, Hanns. *Studien zur Geschichte der Homöer: Der Osten bis zum Ende der homöischen Reichskirche.* Beiträge zur historischen Theologie 73. Tübingen: J.C.B. Mohr (Paul Siebeck), 1988.

Brent, Allen. *Hippolytus and the Roman Church in the Third Century: Communities in Tension before the Emergence of a Monarch-Bishop.* Supplements to Vigiliae Christianae 31. Leiden: Brill, 1995.

Brown, Peter. "The Rise and Function of the Holy Man in Late Antiquity." *Journal of Roman Studies* 61 (1971): 80–101.

Brown, Peter. *The Body and Society: Men, Women, and Sexual Renunciation in Early Christianity.* Lectures on the History of Religions 13. New York: Columbia University Press, 1988.

Brown, Peter. *Power and Persuasion in Late Antiquity: Towards a Christian Empire.* Madison: University of Wisconsin Press, 1992.

Bryer, Anthony and George Georghallides, eds. *"The Sweet Land of Cyprus": Papers Given at the Twenty-Fifth Jubilee Spring Symposium of Byzantine Studies, Birmingham, March 1991.* Nicosia: Cyprus Research Centre for the Society for the Promotion of Byzantine Studies, 1993.

Buckley, Jorunn. "Libertines or Not: Fruit, Bread, Semen and Other Body Fluids in Gnosticism." *JECS* 2, no. 1 (1994): 15–31.

Buell, Denise Kimber. *Making Christians: Clement of Alexandria and the Rhetoric of Legitimacy.* Princeton: Princeton University Press, 1999.

Buell, Denise Kimber. *Why This New Race: Ethnic Reasoning in Early Christianity.* New York: Columbia University Press, 2005.

Bugár, István. "Epiphanius of Salamis as Monastic Author? The So-Called *Testamentum Epiphanii* in the Context of Fourth-Century Spiritual Trends." StPatr 42 (2006): 73–81.

Bumazhnov, Dmitrij. "Einige Aspekte der Nachwirkung des *Ancoratus* und des *Panarion* des hl. Epiphanius von Salamis in der früheren monastischen Tradition." *Adamantius* 11 (2005): 158–78.

Burgess, Richard. "The Dates and Editions of Eusebius' *Chronici Canones* and *Historia Ecclesiastica*." *JTS* 48, no. 2 (1997): 471–504.

Burrus, Virginia. "The Heretical Woman as Symbol in Alexander, Athanasius, Epiphanius, and Jerome." *HTR* 84, no. 3 (1991): 229–48.

Burton-Christie, Douglas. *The Word in the Desert: Scripture and the Quest for Holiness in Early Christian Monasticism.* Oxford: Oxford University Press, 1993.

Cain, Andrew. *The Letters of Jerome: Asceticism, Biblical Exegesis, and the Construction of Christian Authority in Late Antiquity.* Oxford: Oxford University Press, 2009.

Cameron, Alan. "Earthquake 400." *Chiron* 17 (1987): 343–60.

Cameron, Averil. *Christianity and the Rhetoric of Empire: The Development of Christian Discourse.* Sather Classical Lectures 55. Berkeley: University of California Press, 1991.

Cameron, Averil. "Apologetics in the Roman Empire—a Genre of Intolerance?" In *"Humana Sapit": Études d'antiquité tardive offerts à Lellia Cracco Ruggini.* Bibliothèque de l'Antiquité Tardive 3, edited by J.-M. Carrié and R. Testa, 219–27. Turnhout: Brepols, 2002.

Cameron, Averil. "How to Read Heresiology." *Journal of Medieval and Early Modern Studies* 33, no. 3 (2003): 471–92.

Cameron, Averil. "Jews and Heretics—a Category Error?" In Becker and Reed, *The Ways*, 345–60.

Camplani, Alberto. "Atanasio e Eusebio tra Alessandria e Antiochia (362–363): Osservazioni sul *Tomus ad Antiochenos*, l'*Epistula catholica* e due fogli copti (edizione di *Pap. Berol.* 11948)." In Covolo, Uglione, and Vian, *Eusebio*, 191–246.

Caner, Daniel. *Wandering, Begging Monks: Spiritual Authority and the Promotion of Monasticism in Late Antiquity*. Transformation of the Classical Heritage 33. Berkeley: University of California Press, 2002.

Carriker, Andrew. *The Library of Eusebius of Caesarea*. Supplements to Vigiliae Christianae 67. Leiden: Brill, 2003.

Cavallera, Ferdinand. *Le schisme d'Antioche (IVe–Ve siècle)*. Paris: Picard, 1905.

Cavallera, Ferdinand. *Saint Jérôme: Sa vie et son oeuvre, Tome I–II*. Louvain: "Spicilegium Sacrum Lovaniense" Bureaux, 1922.

Chadwick, Henry. *Origen: Contra Celsum, Translated with an Introduction and Notes*. Cambridge: Cambridge University Press, 1953.

Chadwick, Henry. "Bishops and Monks." StPatr 24 (1993): 45–61.

Charlesworth, James, ed. *The Old Testament Pseudepigrapha, Vol. 2*. New York: Doubleday, 1985.

Charlesworth, James. *The Good and Evil Serpent: How a Universal Symbol Became Christianized*. Anchor Yale Bible Reference Library. New Haven: Yale University Press, 2010.

Chitty, Derwas. *The Desert a City: An Introduction to the Study of Egyptian and Palestinian Monasticism under the Christian Empire*. Oxford: Blackwell, 1966.

Chrysos, Evangelos. "Cyprus in Early Byzantine Times." In Bryer and Georghallides, "*The Sweet Land of Cyprus*," 3–14.

Clark, Elizabeth. "Devil's Gateway and Bride of Christ: Women in the Early Christian World." In *Ascetic Piety and Women's Faith: Essays on Late Ancient Christianity*. Studies in Women and Religion 20, edited by E. Clark, 23–60. Lewiston: Edwin Mellen Press, 1986.

Clark, Elizabeth. "New Perspectives on the Origenist Controversy: Human Embodiment and Ascetic Strategies." *Church History* 59, no. 2 (1990): 145–62.

Clark, Elizabeth. *The Origenist Controversy: The Cultural Construction of an Early Christian Debate*. Princeton: Princeton University Press, 1992.

Clark, Elizabeth. "Ideology, History, and the Construction of 'Woman' in Late Ancient Christianity." *JECS* 2, no. 2 (1994): 155–84.

Clark, Elizabeth. *History, Theory, Text: Historians and the Linguistic Turn*. Cambridge, MA: Harvard University Press, 2004.

Clark, Gillian. "Philosophic Lives and the Philosophic Life: Porphyry and Iamblichus." In Hägg and Rousseau, *Greek Biography*, 29–51.

Coakley, Sarah. "Disputed Questions in Patristic Trinitarianism." *HTR* 100, no. 2 (2007): 125–38.

Cohen, Shaye. "A Virgin Defiled: Some Rabbinic and Christian Views on the Origins of Heresy." *Union Seminary Quarterly Review* 36, no. 1 (1980): 1–11.

Collatz, Christian-Friedrich and Arnd Rattmann. *Epiphanius IV: Register zu den Bänden I–III (Ancoratus, Panarion haer. 1–80 und De fide) nach den Materialen von Karl Holl*. GCS Neue Folge 13. Berlin: Walter de Gruyter, 2006.

Condamin, Albert. "St. Épiphane a-ti-il admis la légitimité du divorce pour adultère?" *Bulletin de littérature ecclésiastique* 1 (1900): 16–21.

Cooper, Kate. *The Virgin and the Bride: Idealized Womanhood in Late Antiquity*. Cambridge, MA: Harvard University Press, 1996.

Covolo, Enrico dal, Renato Uglione, and Giovanni Maria Vian, eds. *Eusebio di Vercelli e il suo tempo*. Biblioteca di Scienze Religiose 133. Rome: LAS, 1997.

Cox Miller, Patricia. *Biography in Late Antiquity: A Quest for the Holy Man*. Transformation of the Classical Heritage 5. Berkeley: University of California Press, 1983.

Crislip, Andrew. *From Monastery to Hospital: Christian Monasticism and the Transformation of Health Care in Late Antiquity*. Ann Arbor: University of Michigan Press, 2005.

Crislip, Andrew. *Thorns in the Flesh: Illness and Sanctity in Late Ancient Christianity*. Divinations: Rereading Late Ancient Religions. Philadelphia: University of Pennsylvania Press, 2013.

Croke, Brian. "The Originality of Eusebius' *Chronicle*." *American Journal of Philology* 103 (1982): 195–200.

Croke, Brian. "Porphyry's Anti-Christian Chronology." *JTS* 34, no. 1 (1983): 168–85.

Croke, Brian. "The Origins of the Christian World Chronicle." In *History and Historians in Late Antiquity*, edited by B. Croke and A. Emmett, 116–31. Oxford: Pergamon Press, 1983.

Crouzel, Henri. "Les Pères de l'Église ont-ils permis le remariage après separation?" *Bulletin de littérature ecclésiastique* 70 (1969): 3–43.

Crouzel, Henri. "Encore sur Divorce et Remariage selon Épiphane." *VC* 38 (1984): 271–80.

Daley, Brian. "Divine Transcendence and Human Transformation: Gregory of Nyssa's Anti-Apollinarian Christology." *StPatr* 32 (1997), 87–95.

Daley, Brian. "'Heavenly Man' and 'Eternal Christ': Apollinarius and Gregory of Nyssa on the Personal Identity of the Savior." *JECS* 10, no. 4 (2002): 469–88.

Daly, Robert, ed. *Origeniana Quinta: Papers of the 5th International Congress, Boston College, 14–18 August 1989*. Bibliotheca Ephemeridum Theologicarum Lovaniensium 105. Leuven: Leuven University Press, 1992.

Davis, Thomas. "Earthquakes and the Crises of Faith: Social Transformation in Late Antique Cyprus." *Buried History* 46 (2010): 5–16.

Davis, Thomas. "Saint Paul on Cyprus: The Transformation of an Apostle." In *Do Historical Matters Matter to Faith: A Critical Appraisal of Modern and Postmodern Approaches to Scripture*, edited by J. Hoffmeier and D. Magary, 405–23. Wheaton: Crossway, 2012.

Dechow, Jon. *Dogma and Mysticism in Early Christianity: Epiphanius of Cyprus and the Legacy of Origen*. Patristic Monograph Series 13. Macon, GA: Mercer University Press, 1988.

Dechow, Jon. "Origen and Corporeality: The Case of Methodius' *On the Resurrection.*" In Daly, *Origeniana Quinta*, 509–18.

Dechow, Jon. "From Methodius to Epiphanius in Anti-Origenist Polemic," *Adamantius* 19 (2013): 10–29.

De Clercq, Victor. "Eusèbe de Verceil." In *DHGE* 15, c. 1477–83. Paris: Letouzey et Ané, 1963.

DelCogliano, Mark. "Eusebian Theologies of the Son as the Image of God before 341." *JECS* 14, no. 4 (2006): 458–84.

DelCogliano, Mark. "Basil of Caesarea, Didymus the Blind, and the Anti-Pneumatomachian Exegesis of Amos 4:13 and John 1:3." *JTS* 61, no. 2 (2010): 644–58.

DelCogliano, Mark. *Basil of Caesarea's Anti-Eunomian Theory of Names: Christian Theology and Late-Antique Philosophy in the Fourth-Century Trinitarian Controversy.* Supplements to Vigiliae Christianae 103. Leiden: Brill, 2010.

Delvoye, Charles. "La place des grand basiliques de Salamine de Chypre dans l'architecture paléochrétienne." In *Salamine de Chypre, Histoire et Archéologie: État des recherches*, 314–27. Colloques Internationaux du Centre National de la Recherche Scientifique 578. Paris: Éditions du Centre National de la Recherche Scientifique, 1980.

Devos, Paul. "ΜΕΓΑ ΣΑΒΒΑΤΟΝ chez saint Épiphane." *Analecta Bollandiana* 108, nos. 3–4 (1990): 293–306.

Donaldson, Terence, ed. *Religious Rivalries and the Struggle for Success in Caesarea Maritima.* Studies in Christianity and Judaism 8. Waterloo, ON: Wilfrid Laurier University Press, 2000.

Dörries, Hermann. "Die Vita Antonii als Geschichtsquelle." *Nachrichten von der Akademie der Wissenschaften in Göttingen, Philologisch-Historisch Klasse* 14 (1949): 359–410.

Desjardins, Michel. "Bauer and Beyond: On Recent Scholarly Discussions of Αἵρεσις in the Early Christian Era." *Second Century* 8, no. 2 (1991): 65–82.

Douglass, Laurie. "A New Look at the *Itinerarium Burdigalense.*" *JECS* 4, no. 3 (1996): 313–33.

Downey, Glanville. "The Claim of Antioch to Ecclesiastical Jurisdiction over Cyprus." *Proceedings of the American Philosophical Society* 102, no. 3 (1958): 224–28.

Drake, Harold. "Eusebius on the True Cross." *JEH* 36, no. 1 (1985): 1–22.

Drake, Harold, ed. *Violence in Late Antiquity: Perceptions and Practices.* Burlington: Ashgate, 2006.

Drake, Harold. "The Curious Case of George and the Camel." In *Studies of Religion and Politics in the Early Christian Centuries.* Early Christian Studies 13, edited by D. Luckensmeyer and P. Allen, 173–93. Strathfield, NSW: St Pauls Publications, 2010.

Drecoll, Volker. *Die Entwicklung der Trinitätslehre des Basilius von Cäsarea: Sein Weg vom Homöusianer zum Neonizäner.* Forschungen zur Kirchen- und Dogmengeschichte 66. Göttingen: Vandenhoeck & Ruprecht, 1996.

Drijvers, Jan Willem. *Helena Augusta: The Mother of Constantine the Great and the Legend of Her Finding of the True Cross*. Brill's Studies in Intellectual History 27. Leiden: Brill, 1992.

Drijvers, Jan Willem. *Cyril of Jerusalem: Bishop and City*. Supplements to Vigiliae Christianae 72. Leiden: Brill, 2004.

Drobner, Hubertus. *The Fathers of the Church: A Comprehensive Introduction*. Translated by S. Schatzmann. Peabody, MA: Hendrickson Publishers, 2007.

Droge, Arthur. *Homer or Moses? Early Christian Interpretations of the History of Culture*. Hermeneutische Untersuchungen zur Theologie 26. Tübingen: J.C.B. Mohr (Paul Siebeck) Verlag, 1989.

Dummer, Jürgen. "Epiphanius, Ancor. 102,7 und die Sapientia Salomonis." *Klio* 43–45 (1965): 344–50.

Dummer, Jürgen. "Die Angaben über die gnostische Literatur bei Epiphanius, Pan. Haer. 26." In *Koptologische Studien in der DDR*, 191–219. Halle: Wissenschaftliche Zeitschrift der Martin-Luther-Universität, 1965.

Dummer, Jürgen. "Die Sprachkenntnisse des Epiphanius." In *Die Araber in der alten Welt* 5.1, edited by F. Altheim and R. Stiehl, 392–435. Berlin: Walter de Gruyter, 1968.

Dummer, Jürgen. "Epiphanius von Constantia und Homer." *Philologus* 119, no. 1 (1975): 84–91.

Dummer, Jürgen. "Ein naturwissenschaftliches Handbuch als Quelle für Epiphanius von Constantia." *Klio* 55 (1978): 289–99.

Dummer, Jürgen. "Zur Epiphanius-Ausgabe der 'Griechischen Christlichen Schriftsteller.'" In *Texte und Textkritik: Eine Aufsatzsammlung*, 119–25. Texte und Untersuchungen zur Geschichte der altchristlichen Literatur 133. Berlin: Akademie Verlag, 1987.

Dummer, Jürgen. "Epiphanius von Constantia und die Apologie des Aristides." *Philologus* 138, no. 2 (1994): 267–87.

Edwards, Mark. "Did Origen Apply the Word *Homoousios* to the Son?" *JTS* 49, no. 2 (1998): 658–70.

Edwards, Mark. "Birth, Death, and Divinity in Porphyry's *Life of Plotinus*." In Hägg and Rousseau, *Greek Biography*, 52–71.

Edwards, Mark. "Alexander of Alexandria and the *Homoousion*." *VC* 66, no. 5 (2012): 482–502.

Edwards, Mark, Martin Goodman, Simon Price, eds. *Apologetics in the Roman Empire: Pagans, Jews, and Christians*. Oxford: Oxford University Press, 1999.

Elliot, Tom. "Was the *Tomus ad Antiochenos* a Pacific Document?" *JEH* 58, no. 1 (2007): 1–8.

Elm, Susanna. *"Virgins of God": The Making of Asceticism in Late Antiquity*. Oxford: Oxford University Press, 1994.

Elm, Susanna. "'Pierced by Bronze Needles': Anti-Montanist Charges of Ritual Stigmatization in Their Fourth-Century Context." *JECS* 4, no. 4 (1996): 409–39.

Elm, Susanna. "The Dog That Did Not Bark: Doctrine and Patriarchal Authority in the

Conflict between Theophilus of Alexandria and John Chrysostom of Constantinople." In *Christian Origins: Theology, Rhetoric and Community*, edited by L. Ayres and G. Jones, 68–93. New York: Routledge, 1998.

Elsner, Jaś. "The *Itinerarium Burdigalense*: Politics and Salvation in the Geography of Constantine's Empire." *Journal of Roman Studies* 90 (2000): 181–95.

Englezakis, Benedict. "Epiphanius of Salamis, the Father of Cypriot Autocephaly." In *Studies on the History of the Church of Cyprus, 4th–20th Centuries*, translated by N. Russell, 29–40. Brookfield, VT: Variorum, 1995.

Errington, R. Malcolm. "The Accession of Theodosius I." *Klio* 78, no. 2 (1996): 438–53.

Errington, R. Malcolm. "Church and State in the First Years of Theodosius." *Chiron* 27 (1997): 21–72.

Errington, R. Malcolm. "Christian Accounts of the Religious Legislation of Theodosius I." *Klio* 79, no. 2 (1997): 398–443.

Errington, R. Malcolm. *Roman Imperial Policy from Julian to Theodosius*. Chapel Hill: University of North Carolina Press, 2006.

Fatti, Federico. "Eretico, condanna Origene!" Conflitti di potere ad Alessandria nella tarda antichità." *Annali di Storia dell'Esegesi* 20, no. 2 (2003): 383–435.

Fatti, Federico. "Pontifex tantus. Giovanni, Epifanio e le origini della prima controversia origenista." *Adamantius* 19 (2013): 30–49.

Favale, Agostino. *Teofilo d'Alessandria (345c.–412): Scritti, Vita e Dottrina*. Biblioteca del "Salesianum" 41. Turin: Società Editrice Internazionale, 1958.

Ferngren, Gary. "Early Christianity as a Religion of Healing." *Bulletin of the History of Medicine* 66, no. 1 (1992): 1–15.

Ferngren, Gary. *Medicine and Health Care in Early Christianity*. Baltimore: Johns Hopkins University Press, 2009.

Fitschen, Klaus. *Serapion von Thmuis: Echte und unechte Schriften sowie die Zeugnisse des Athanasius und anderer*. Patristische Texte und Studien 37. Berlin: Walter de Gruyter, 1992.

Florovsky, Georges. "The Anthropomorphites in the Egyptian Desert." In *Akten des XI. Internationalen Byzantinistenkongresses, München 1958*, edited by F. Dölger and H.-G. Beck, 154–59. Munich: C.H. Beck, 1960.

Florovsky, Georges. "Theophilus of Alexandria and Apa Aphou of Pemjde." In *Harry Aufstryn Wolfson Jubilee Volume: On the Occasion of His Seventy-Fifth Birthday, English Section*, edited by S. Lieberman, 275–310. Jerusalem: American Academy for Jewish Research, 1965.

Flower, Richard. "Genealogies of Unbelief: Epiphanius of Salamis and Heresiological Authority." In *Unclassical Traditions, Volume 2: Perspectives from East and West in Late Antiquity*. Cambridge Classical Journal, Proceedings of the Cambridge Philological Society, Supplementary Vol. 35, edited by C. Kelly, R. Flower, and M. Williams, 70–87. Cambridge: Cambridge Philological Society, 2011.

Fotiou, Stavros. "Orthodoxia as Orthopraxia According to Saint Epiphanius of Salamis." *Phronema* 24 (2009): 51–63.

Fraenkel, Pierre. "Histoire sainte et hérésie chez Saint Épiphane de Salamine, d'après le tome I du *Panarion.*" *Revue de théologie et de philosophie* 12 (1962): 175–91.

Frank, Georgia. *The Memory of the Eyes: Pilgrims to Living Saints in Christian Late Antiquity.* Transformation of the Classical Heritage 30. Berkeley: University of California Press, 2000.

Frede, Michael. "Celsus' Attack on the Christians." In *Philosophia Togata II: Plato and Aristotle at Rome*, edited by J. Barnes and M. Griffin, 218–40. Oxford: Oxford University Press, 1997.

Frede, Michael. "Origen's Treatise *Against Celsus.*" In Edwards, Goodman, and Price, *Apologetics in the Roman Empire*, 131–55.

Frede, Michael. "Eusebius' Apologetic Writings." In Edwards, Goodman, and Price, *Apologetics in the Roman Empire,* 223–50.

French, Roger. *Ancient Natural History: Histories of Nature.* New York: Routledge, 1994.

Gaddis, Michael. *There Is No Crime for Those Who Have Christ: Religious Violence in the Christian Roman Empire.* Transformation of the Classical Heritage 39. Berkeley: University of California Press, 2005.

Gallagher, Eugene. "Eusebius the Apologist: The Evidence of the *Preparation* and the *Proof.*" StPatr 26 (1993): 251–60.

Gemeinhardt, Peter. "Der Tomus ad Antiochenos (362) und die Vielfalt orthodoxer Theologien im 4. Jahrhundert." *ZKG* 117, nos. 2–3 (2006): 169–96.

Gemeinhardt, Peter. "Apollinaris of Laodicea: A Neglected Link of Trinitarian Theology between East and West?" *ZAC* 10 (2006): 286–301.

Gero, Stephen. "With Walter Bauer on the Tigris: Encratite Orthodoxy and Libertine Heresy in Syro-Mesopotamian Christianity." In *Nag Hammadi, Gnosticism, and Early Christianity*, edited by C. Hedrick and R. Hodgson, 287–307. Peabody, MA: Hendrickson, 1986.

Giagkou, Theodoros and Chrysostomos Nassis, eds., *ΑΓΙΟΣ ΕΠΙΦΑΝΙΟΣ ΚΩΝΣΤΑΝΤΙΑΣ ΠΑΤΗΡ ΚΑΙ ΔΙΔΑΣΚΑΛΟΣ ΤΗΣ ΟΡΘΟΔΟΞΟΥ ΚΑΘΟΛΙΚΗΣ ΕΚΚΛΗΣΙΑΣ: ΠΡΑΚΤΙΚΑ ΣΥΝΕΔΡΙΟΥ* (Thessaloniki: Ekdoseis Mygdonia, 2012)

Gilhus, Ingvild. *Animals, Gods and Humans: Changing Attitudes to Animals in Greek, Roman and Early Christian Ideas.* New York: Routledge, 2006.

Goehring, James. "Pachomius' Vision of Heresy: The Development of a Pachomian Tradition." *Le Muséon* 95 (1982): 241–62.

Goehring, James. "Libertine or Liberated: Women in the So-Called Libertine Gnostic Communities." In *Images of the Feminine in Gnosticism*, edited by K. King, 329–44. Studies in Antiquity and Christianity. Philadelphia: Fortress Press, 1988.

Goehring, James. "The World Engaged: The Social and Economic World of Early Egyptian Monasticism." In *Gnosticism & the Early Christian World: In Honor of James M. Robinson*, edited by J. Goehring, C. Hedrick, and J. Sanders, with H. Betz, 134–44. Sonoma, CA: Polebridge Press, 1990.

Goehring, James. "The Origins of Monasticism." In Attridge and Hata, *Eusebius*, 235–55.

Goehring, James. "The Encroaching Desert: Literary Production and Ascetic Space in Early Christian Egypt." *JECS* 1, no. 3 (1993): 281–96.

Goehring, James. "Melitian Monastic Organization: A Challenge to Pachomian Originality." StPatr 25 (1993): 388–95.

Goehring, James. "Monastic Diversity and Ideological Boundaries in Fourth-Century Egypt." *JECS* 5, no. 1 (1997): 61–84.

Goehring, James. *Ascetics, Society, and the Desert: Studies in Early Egyptian Monasticism.* Studies in Antiquity and Christianity. Harrisburg, PA: Trinity Press International, 1999.

Goehring, James. "Hieracas of Leontopolis: The Making of a Desert Ascetic." In Goehring, *Ascetics*, 110–33.

Golitzin, Alexander. "The Vision of God and the Form of Glory: More Reflections on the Anthropomorphite Controversy of AD 399." In *Abba: The Tradition of Orthodoxy in the West. Festschrift for Bishop Kallistos (Ware) of Diokleia*, edited by J. Behr, A. Louth, and D. Conomos, 273–97. Crestwood, NY: St. Vladimir's Seminary Press, 2003.

Goranson, Stephen. "The Joseph of Tiberias Episode in Epiphanius: Studies in Jewish and Christian Relations." PhD diss., Duke University, Durham, NC, 1990.

Goranson, Stephen. "Joseph of Tiberias Revisited: Orthodoxies and Heresies in Fourth-Century Galilee." In *Galilee through the Centuries: A Confluence of Cultures.* Duke Judaic Studies 1, edited by E. Meyers, 335–43. Winona Lake, IN: Eisenbrauns, 1999.

Gould, Graham. "The Image of God and the Anthropomorphite Controversy in Fourth Century Monasticism." In Daly, *Origeniana Quinta*, 549–57.

Gould, Graham. *The Desert Fathers on Monastic Community.* Oxford: Oxford University Press, 1993.

Grafton, Anthony and Megan Williams. *Christianity and the Transformation of the Book: Origen, Eusebius, and the Library of Caesarea.* Cambridge, MA: Harvard University Press, 2006.

Grant, Robert. *Eusebius as Church Historian.* Oxford: Oxford University Press, 1980.

Grant, Robert. *Early Christians and Animals.* New York: Routledge, 1999.

Greer, Rowan. "The Man from Heaven: Paul's Last Adam and Apollinaris' Christ." In *Paul and the Legacies of Paul*, edited by W. Babcock, 165–82. Dallas: Southern Methodist University Press, 1990.

Gregg, Robert and Dennis Groh. *Early Arianism: A View of Salvation.* Philadelphia: Fortress Press, 1981.

Gribomont, Jean. "Eustathe de Sébaste." In *Dictionnaire de spiritualité: Ascétique et mystique, doctrine et histoire* vol. 4, no. 2, 1708–12. Paris: Beauchesne, 1961.

Gribomont, Jean. "Eustathe de Sébaste." In *DHGE* 16, 26–33. Paris: Letouzey et Ané, 1967.

Griggs, C. Wilfred. *Early Egyptian Christianity, from Its Origins to 451 C.E.* Coptic Studies 2. Leiden: Brill, 1990.

Groh, Dennis. "The *Onomasticon* of Eusebius and the Rise of Christian Palestine." StPatr 18 (1983): 23–31.

Groh, Dennis. "Jews and Christians in Late Roman Palestine: Towards a New Chronology." *Biblical Archaeologist* 51, no. 2 (1988): 80–96.

Gwynn, David. *The Eusebians: The Polemic of Athanasius of Alexandria and the Construction of the "Arian Controversy."* Oxford: Oxford University Press, 2007.

Haas, Christopher. "The Alexandrian Riots of 356 and George of Cappadocia." *Greek, Roman, and Byzantine Studies* 32, no. 3 (1991): 281–301.

Haas, Christopher. *Alexandria in Late Antiquity: Topography and Social Conflict.* Baltimore: Johns Hopkins University Press, 1997.

Hackett, John. *A History of the Orthodox Church of Cyprus. From the Coming of the Apostles Paul and Barnabas to the Commencement of the British Occupation (A.D. 45–A.D. 1878). Together with Some Account of the Latin and Other Churches Existing on the Island.* Oxford: Methuen, 1901.

Hägg, Tomas and Philip Rousseau, eds. *Greek Biography and Panegyric in Late Antiquity.* Transformation of the Classical Heritage 31. Berkeley: University of California Press, 2000.

Hall, Stuart. "The Creed of Sardica." StPatr 19 (1989): 173–84.

Harmless, William. *Desert Christians: An Introduction to the Literature of Early Monasticism.* Oxford: Oxford University Press, 2004.

Hanson, Richard. *The Search for the Christian Doctrine of God: The Arian Controversy, 318–381.* Edinburgh: T&T Clark, 1988.

Harrington, Daniel. "The Reception of Walter Bauer's 'Orthodoxy and Heresy in Earliest Christianity' during the Last Decade." *HTR* 73, nos. 1–2 (1980): 289–98.

Hauschild, Wolf-Dieter. "Die Pneumatomachen: Eine Untersuchung zur Dogmengeschichte des vierten Jahrhunderts." Dissertation zur Evang.–Theologischen Fakultät der Universität, Hamburg, 1967.

Hauben, Hans. "The Melitian 'Church of the Martyrs' Christian Dissenters in Ancient Egypt." In *Ancient History in a Modern University, Vol. 2. Early Christianity, Late Antiquity and Beyond*, edited by T. Hillard, R. Kearsley, C. Nixon, and A. Nobbs, 329–49. Grand Rapids, MI: Eerdmans, 1998.

Hauben, Hans. "Épiphane de Salamine sur le schisme mélitien." *Salesianum* 67, no. 4 (2005): 737–70.

Hauben, Hans. *Studies on the Melitian Schism in Egypt (AD 306–335)*, edited by P. Van Nuffelen. Burlington, VT: Ashgate, 2012.

Haykin, Michael. *The Spirit of God: The Exegesis of 1 and 2 Corinthians in the Pneumatomachian Controversy of the Fourth Century.* Supplements to Vigiliae Christianae 27. Leiden: Brill, 1994.

Henderson, John B. *The Construction of Orthodoxy and Heresy: Neo-Confucian, Islamic, Jewish, and Early Christian Patterns.* Albany: State University of New York Press, 1998.

Hill, George. *A History of Cyprus*, 4 vols. Cambridge: Cambridge University Press, 1940–72.

Hoffman, R. Joseph. *Celsus on the True Doctrine: A Discourse against the Christians.* Oxford: Oxford University Press, 1987.

Holl, Karl. *Die Handschriftliche Überlieferung des Epiphanius (Ancoratus und Panarion)*. Texte und Untersuchungen zur Geschichte der altchristlichen Literatur 36, no. 2. Leipzig: J.C. Hinrichs, 1910.

Holl, Karl. "Ein Bruchstück aus einem bisher unbekannten Brief des Epiphanius." In *Festgabe für Adolf Jülicher zum 70. Geburtstag 26. Januar 1927*, 159–89. Tübingen: J.C.B. Mohr 1927. Reprinted in K. Holl, *Gesammelte Aufsätze zur Kirchengeschichte*, T. 2, 204–24. Tübingen: J.C.B. Mohr (Paul Siebeck) 1928.

Holum, Kenneth. *Theodosian Empresses: Women and Imperial Dominion in Late Antiquity*. Transformation of the Classical Heritage 3. Berkeley: University of California Press, 1982.

Holum, Kenneth, et al. *King Herod's Dream: Caesarea on the Sea*. New York: W.W. Norton, 1988.

Hunt, E. David. *Holy Land Pilgrimage in the Later Roman Empire, AD 312–460*. Oxford: Oxford University Press, 1982.

Hunt, E. David. "Constantine and Jerusalem." *JEH* 48, no. 3 (1997): 405–24.

Hunt, E. David. "Were There Christian Pilgrims before Constantine?" In *Pilgrimage Explored*, edited by J. Stopford, 25–40. Woodbridge, Suffolk: York University Press, 1999.

Hunt, E. David. "The Itinerary of Egeria: Reliving the Bible in Fourth-Century Palestine." In *The Holy Land, Holy Lands, and Christian History: Papers Read at the 1998 Summer Meeting and the 1999 Winter Meeting of the Ecclesiastical History Society*. Studies in Church History 36, edited by R. Swanson, 34–54. Suffolk: Boydell Press, 2000.

Inglebert, Hervé. *Interpretatio Christiana: Les mutations des saviors (cosmographie, géographie, ethnographie, histoire) dans l'Antiquité chrétienne (30–630 après J.-C.)*. Collection des Études Augustiniennes, Série Antiquité 166. Paris: Institut d'Études Augustiniennes, 2001.

Iricinschi, Eduard and Holger Zellentin, eds. *Heresy and Identity in Late Antiquity*. Texts and Studies in Ancient Judaism 119. Tübingen: Mohr Siebeck, 2008.

Irmscher, Johannes. "Die Epiphaniosausgabe der 'Griechischen Christlichen Schriftsteller.'" *Helikon* 22–27 (1982–87): 535–41.

Irmscher, Johannes. "L'edizione di Epifanio nei GCS." *Augustinianum* 24 (1984): 573–79.

Irshai, Oded. "From Oblivion to Fame: The History of the Palestinian Church (135–303 CE)." In Limor and Stroumsa, *Christians and Christianity*, 91–139.

Jacobs, Andrew. *Remains of the Jews: The Holy Land and Christian Empire in Late Antiquity*. Divinations: Rereading Late Ancient Religion. Stanford: Stanford University Press, 2004.

Jacobs, Andrew. *Christ Circumcised: A Study in Early Christian History and Difference*. Divinations: Rereading Late Ancient Religion. Philadelphia: University of Pennsylvania Press, 2012.

Jacobs, Andrew. "Matters (Un-)Becoming: Conversions in Epiphanius of Salamis." *Church History* 81, no. 1 (2012): 27–47.

Jacobs, Andrew. "Epiphanius of Salamis and the Antiquarian's Bible." *JECS* 21, no. 3 (2013): 437–64.

Johnson, Aaron. "Identity, Descent, and Polemic: Ethnic Argumentation in Eusebius' *Praeparatio Evangelica.*" *JECS* 12, no. 1 (2004): 23–56.

Johnson, Aaron. *Ethnicity and Argument in Eusebius' "Praeparatio Evangelica."* Oxford: Oxford University Press, 2006.

Junod, Eric. "L'Apologie pour Origène de Pamphile et la naissance de l'origénisme." StPatr 26, no. 2 (1993): 267–86.

Kannengiesser, Charles, ed. *Politique et Théologie chez Athanase d'Alexandrie: Actes du colloque du Chantilly 23–25 Septembre 1973.* Théologie Historique 27. Beauchesne: Paris, 1974.

Kannengiesser, Charles. *Arius and Athanasius: Two Alexandrian Theologians.* Hampshire: Variorum, 1991.

Kannengiesser, Charles. "Eusebius of Caesarea, Origenist." In Attridge and Hata, *Eusebius*, 435–66.

Karageorghis, Vassos. *Salamis in Cyprus: Homeric, Hellenistic, and Roman.* London: Thames and Hudson, 1969.

Karageorghis, Vassos. *Cyprus: From the Stone Age to the Romans.* London: Thames and Hudson, 1982.

Karmann, Thomas. *Meletius von Antiochien: Studien zur Geschichte des trinitätstheologischen Streits in den Jahren 360–364 n.Chr.* Regensburger Studien zur Theologie 68. Frankfurt am Main: Peter Lang, 2009.

Katos, Demetrios. *Palladius of Helenopolis: The Origenist Advocate.* Oxford: Oxford University Press, 2011.

Kelly, John. *Early Christian Creeds.* London: Longmans, 1950.

Kelly, John. *Jerome: His Life, Writings, and Controversies.* London: Duckworth, 1975.

Kelly, John. *Golden Mouth: The Story of John Chrysostom: Ascetic, Preacher, Bishop.* London: Duckworth, 1995.

Kim, Young Richard. "The Imagined Worlds of Epiphanius of Cyprus." PhD diss., University of Michigan, Ann Arbor, 2006.

Kim, Young Richard. "Epiphanius of Cyprus and the Geography of Heresy." In Drake, *Violence*, 235–51.

Kim, Young Richard. "Reading the *Panarion* as Collective Biography: The Heresiarch as Unholy Man." *VC* 64, no. 4 (2010): 382–413.

Kim, Young Richard. "Bad Bishops Corrupt Good Emperors: Ecclesiastical Authority and the Rhetoric of Heresy in the *Panarion* of Epiphanius of Salamis." StPatr 47 (2010): 161–6.

Kim, Young Richard. "Epiphanius of Cyprus vs. John of Jerusalem: An Improper Ordination and the Escalation of the Origenist Controversy." In *Episcopal Elections in Late Antiquity.* Arbeiten zur Kirchengeschichte 119, edited by J. Leemans, P. Van Nuffelen, S. Keough, and C. Nicolaye, 411–22. Berlin: Walter de Gruyter, 2011.

Kim, Young Richard. "The Pastoral Care of Epiphanius of Cyprus." StPatr 67 (2013): 247–55.

Kim, Young Richard. "Jerome and Paulinian, Brothers." VC 67, no. 5 (2013): 517–30.

King, Karen. What is Gnosticism? Cambridge, MA: Harvard University Press, 2003.

Kinzig, Wolfram. "The Idea of Progress in the Early Church until the Age of Constantine." StPatr 24 (1993): 119–34.

Kinzig, Wolfram. Novitas Christiana: Die Idee des Fortschritts in der Alten Kirche bis Eusebius. Forschungen zur Kirchen- und Dogmengeschichte 58. Göttingen: Vandenhoeck und Ruprecht, 1994.

Knorr, Ortwin. "Die Parallelüberlieferung zum ‚Panarion‘ des Epiphanius von Salamis. Textkritische Anmerkungen zur Neuausgabe." Wiener Studien 112 (1955): 113–27.

Koch, Glen. "A Critical Investigation of Epiphanius' Knowledge of the Ebionites: A Translation and Critical Discussion of Panarion 30." PhD diss., University of Pennsylvania, Philadelphia, 1976.

Kofsky, Aryeh. Eusebius of Caesarea against Paganism. Jewish and Christian Perspectives Series 3. Leiden: Brill, 2000.

König, Jason and Tim Whitmarsh, eds. Ordering Knowledge in the Roman Empire. Cambridge: Cambridge University Press, 2007.

Kopecek, Thomas. A History of Neo-Arianism, 2 vols. Cambridge, MA: Philadelphia Patristic Foundation, 1979.

Kösters, Oliver. Die Trinitätslehre des Epiphanius von Salamis: Ein Kommentar zum "Ancoratus." Forschungen zur Kirchen- und Dogmengeschichte 86. Göttingen: Vandenhoeck und Ruprecht, 2003.

Kruit, Nico and Klaas Worp. "The Spathion Jar in the Papyri." BASP 38 (2001): 79–87.

Kyrris, Costas. History of Cyprus. Nicosia: Nicocles Publishing House, 1985.

Laminski, Adolf. Der Heilige Geist als Geist Christi und Geist der Gläubigen: Der Beitrag des Athanasios von Alexandrien zur Formulierung des trinitarischen Dogmas im vierten Jahrhundert. Erfurter theologische Studien 23. Leipzig: St. Benno-Verlag GMBH, 1969.

Layton, Bentley. The Gnostic Scriptures. New York: Doubleday, 1987.

Layton, Richard. Didymus the Blind and His Circle in Late-Antique Alexandria: Virtue and Narrative in Biblical Scholarship. Urbana: University of Illinois Press, 2004.

Lebon, Joseph. "Sur quelques fragment de letters attribuées à S. Épiphane de Salamine." In Miscellanea Giovanni Mercati, Vol. 1. Bibbia-Letteratura Cristiana antica, 145–74. Studi e Testi 121. Vatican City: Biblioteca Apostolica Vaticana, 1946.

Le Boulluec, Alain. La notion d'hérésie dans la littérature grecque (IIe–IIIe siècles), 2 vols. Paris: Études Augustiniennes, 1985.

Lenski, Noel. Failure of Empire: Valens and the Roman State in the Fourth Century A.D. Transformation of the Classical Heritage 34. Berkeley: University of California Press, 2002.

Levine, Lee. Caesarea under Roman Rule. Studies in Judaism in Late Antiquity 7. Leiden: Brill, 1975.

Liebeschuetz, J. H. W. G. "Friends and Enemies of John Chrysostom." In *Maistor: Classical, Byzantine and Renaissance Studies for Robert Browning*. Byzantina Australiensa 5, edited by A. Moffatt, 85–111. Canberra: Australian Association for Byzantine Studies, 1984.

Liebeschuetz, J. H. W. G. *Barbarians and Bishops: Army, Church and State in the Age of Arcadius and Chrysostom*. Oxford: Oxford University Press, 1990.

Lienhard, Joseph. "*Ousia* and *Hypostasis*: The Cappadocian Settlement and the Theology of 'One *Hypostasis*.'" In *The Trinity: An Interdisciplinary Symposium on the Trinity*, edited by S. Davis, D. Kendall, and G. O'Collins, 99–121. Oxford: Oxford University Press, 1999.

Lienhard, Joseph. *Contra Marcellum: Marcellus of Ancyra and Fourth-Century Theology*. Washington, DC: Catholic University of America Press, 1999).

Lietzmann, Hans. *Apollinaris von Laodicea und seine Schule: Texte und Untersuchungen*. Tübingen: Verlag von J.C.B. Mohr (Paul Siebeck), 1904. Reprint, Hildesheim: Georg Olms Verlag, 1970.

Lim, Richard. *Public Disputation, Power, and Social Order in Late Antiquity*. Transformation of the Classical Heritage 23. Berkeley: University of California Press, 1995.

Limor, Ora and Guy Stroumsa, eds. *Christians and Christianity in the Holy Land: From the Origins to the Latin Kingdoms*. Cultural Encounters in Late Antiquity and the Middle Ages 5. Turnhout: Brepols, 2006.

Lieu, Judith. "The Forging of Christian Identity." *Mediterranean Archaeology* 11 (1998): 71–82.

Lieu, Judith. "Epiphanius on the Scribes and the Pharisees (*Pan*. 15.1–16.4)." *JTS* 39, no. 2 (1988): 509–24.

Lieu, Judith. *Christian Identity in the Jewish and Graeco-Roman World*. Oxford: Oxford University Press, 2004.

Lieu, Samuel. *Manichaeism in Mesopotamia and the Roman East*. Religions in the Graeco-Roman World 118. Leiden: Brill, 1994.

Lipsius, Richard. *Zur Quellenkritik des Epiphanios*. Vienna: Wilhelm Braumüller, 1865.

Long, Anthony. *Hellenistic Philosophy: Stoics, Epicureans, Stoics*. 2nd ed. Berkeley: University of California Press, 1986.

Louth, Andrew. "St Athanasius and the Greek *Life of Antony*." *JTS* 39.2 (1988): 504–9.

Lyman, Rebecca. "A Topography of Heresy: Mapping the Rhetorical Creation of Arianism." In Barnes and Williams, *Arianism after Arius*, 45–62.

Lyman, Rebecca. "The Making of a Heretic: The Life of Origen in Epiphanius' *Panarion* 64." StPatr 31 (1997): 445–51.

Lyman, Rebecca. "Origen as Ascetic Theologian: Orthodoxy and Authority in the Fourth-Century Church." In Bienert and Kühneweg, *Origeniana Septima*, 187–94.

Lyman, Rebecca. "Ascetics and Bishops: Epiphanius on Orthodoxy." In *Orthodoxy, Christianity, History*. Collection de L'École Française de Rome 270, edited by S. Elm, E. Rebillard, and A. Romano, 149–61. Rome: École française de Rome, 2000.

Lyman, Rebecca. "Hellenism and Heresy." *JECS* 11, no. 2 (2003): 209–22.

Lyman, Rebecca. "The Politics of Passing: Justin Martyr's Conversion as a Problem of

'Hellenization.'" In *Conversion in Late Antiquity and the Early Middle Ages: Seeing and Believing*, edited by K. Mills and A. Grafton, 36–60. Rochester, NY: University of Rochester Press, 2003.

Manns, Frédéric. "Joseph de Tibériade, un judéo-chrétien du quatrième siècle." In *Christian Archaeology in the Holy Land: New Discoveries*. Studium Biblicum Franciscanum Collecto Maior 36, edited by G. Bottini, L. di Segni, and E. Alliata, 553–60. Jerusalem: Franciscan Printing Press, 1990.

Manor, T. Scott. "Epiphanius' *Alogi* and the Question of Early Ecclesiastical Opposition to the Johannine Corpus." PhD diss., University of Edinburgh, 2011.

Manor, T. Scott. "Epiphanius' Account of the *Alogi*: Historical Fact or Heretical Fiction?" StPatr 52 (2012): 161–70.

Maraval, Pierre. *Lieux saints et pèlerinages d'Orient: Histoire et géographie des origines à la conquête arabe*. Paris: Éditions du Cerf, 1985.

Maraval, Pierre. "The Earliest Phase of Christian Pilgrimage in the Near East (before the 7th Century)." *Dumbarton Oaks Papers* 56 (2003): 63–74.

Markschies, Christoph. "Epiphanios von Salamis." In *Der Neue Pauly, Band 3*, c. 1152–53. Stuttgart: Verlag J.B. Metzler, 1997.

Markschies, Christoph. *Gnosis: An Introduction*. Translated by J. Bowden. London: T&T Clark, 2003.

Markus, Robert. "How on Earth Could Places Become Holy? Origins of the Christian Idea of Holy Places." *JECS* 2, no. 3 (1994): 257–71.

Marrou, Henri. *Histoire de l'éducation dans l'antiquité, deuxième edition*. Paris: Éditions du Seuil, 1950.

Martin, Annick. "Athanase et les Mélitiens (325–335)." In Kannengiesser, *Politique*, 31–61.

Martin, Annick. *Athanase d'Alexandrie et l'église d'Égypte au IVe siècle (328–373)*. Collection de L'École française de Rome 216. Paris: École française de Rome, 1996.

Martin, Annick. "Les témoinages d'Épiphane de Salamine et de Théodoret à propos de Mélèce d'Antioch." In *Epiphania: Études orientales, grecques et latines offertes à Aline Pourkier*, edited by E. Oudot and F. Poli, 147–71. Paris: De Boccard, 2008.

Martin, Dale. *The Corinthian Body*. New Haven: Yale University Press, 1995.

Martin, Dale and Patricia Cox Miller, eds. *The Cultural Turn in Late Ancient Studies: Gender, Asceticism, and Historiography*. Durham, NC: Duke University Press, 2005.

Mayer, Wendy. "John Chrysostom as Bishop: The View from Antioch." *JEH* 55, no. 3 (2004): 455–66.

Mayer, Wendy. "The Making of a Saint: John Chrysostom in Early Historiography." In *Chrysostomosbilder in 1600 Jahren: Facetten der Wirkungsgeschichte eines Kirchenvaters*. Arbeiten zur Kirchengeschichte 105, ed. M. Wallraff and R. Brändle, 39–59. Berlin: Walter de Gruyter, 2008.

Mayer, Wendy. "Religious Conflict: Definitions, Problems and Theoretical Approaches." In *Religious Conflict from Early Christianity to Early Islam*. Arbeiten zur Kirchengeschichte 121, edited by W. Mayer and B. Neil, 1–19. Berlin: Walter de Gruyter, 2013.

Mayer, Wendy and Pauline Allen. *John Chrysostom*. The Early Church Fathers. New York: Routledge, 2000.

Mayerson, Philip. "Epiphanius' *Sabitha* in Egypt: Σάμβαθον/cάμφαθον/cάμαθον." *BASP* 35 (1998): 215–18.

Mayerson, Philip. "A Note on Syriac *Sabitha* and *Kollathon* in the Papyri." *BASP* 36 (1999): 83–86.

Mayerson, Philip. "Κα(μ)ψάκηc in the Papyri, LXX and *TLG*." *BASP* 36 (1999): 93–97.

Mayerson, Philip. "Measures (μετρηταί) and Donkeyloads of Oil in *P. Wisc.* II.80." *Zeitschrift für Papyrologie und Epigraphik* 127 (1999): 189–92.

McGowan, Andrew. "Tertullian and the 'Heretical' Origins of the 'Orthodox' Trinity." *JECS* 14, no. 4 (2006): 437–57.

McLynn, Neil. *Ambrose of Milan: Church and Court in a Christian Capital*. Transformation of the Classical Heritage 22. Berkeley: University of California Press, 1994.

Megaw, Arthur. "Byzantine Architecture and Decoration in Cyprus: Metropolitan or Provincial?" *Dumbarton Oaks Papers* 28 (1974): 57–88.

Meinhold, Peter. "Pneumatomachoi." In *Paulys Real-Encyclopädie der classischen Altertumswissenschaft, neue Bearbeitung* 21, no. 1, 1066–101. Stuttgart: J.B. Metzler, 1951.

Mena, Peter Anthony. "Insatiable Appetites: Epiphanius of Salamis and the Making of the Heretical Villain." *StPatr* 67 (2013): 257–63.

Metcalf, D. Michael. *Byzantine Cyprus 491–1191*. Cyprus Research Centre Texts and Studies in the History of Cyprus 62. Nicosia: Cyprus Research Centre, 2009.

Mitford, Terence. "Roman Cyprus." *Aufstieg und Niedergang der römischen Welt* 7, no. 2 (1980): 1285–384.

Momigliano, Arnaldo. "Pagan and Christian Historiography in the Fourth Century A.D." In *The Conflict between Paganism and Christianity in the Fourth Century*, edited by A. Momigliano, 79–99. Oxford: Oxford University Press, 1963.

Morales, Xavier. *La théologie trinitaire d'Athanase d'Alexandrie*. Collection des Études Augustiniennes, Série Antiquité 180. Paris: Institut d'Études Augustiniennes, 2006.

Mosshammer, Alden. *The "Chronicle" of Eusebius and Greek Chronographic Tradition*. Lewisburg, PA: Bucknell University Press, 1979.

Mosshammer, Alden. *The Easter Computus and the Origins of the Christian Era*. Oxford: Oxford University Press, 2008.

Mouriki, Doula. "The Cult of Cypriot Saints in Medieval Cyprus as Attested by Church Decorations and Icon Painting." In Bryer and Georghallides, *"The Sweet Land of Cyprus,"* 237–77.

Moutsoulas, Elias. "Der Begriff 'Häresie' bei Epiphanius von Salamis." *StPatr* 7 (1966): 362–71.

Moutsoulas, Elias. "La lettre d'Athanase d'Alexandrie a Épictète." In Kannengiesser, *Politique*, 313–33.

Moutsoulas, Elias. "L'oeuvre d'Epiphane de Salamine "De mensuris et ponderibus" et son unité littéraire." *StPatr* 12 (1975): 119–22.

Moutsoulas, Elias. "La tradition manuscrite de l'oeuvre d'Epiphane de Salamine *De mensuris et ponderibus*." In *Texte und Textkritik: Eine Aufsatzsammlung*, 429–40. Texte und Untersuchungen zur Geschichte der altchristlichen Literatur 133. Berlin: Akademie Verlag 1987.

Mühlenberg, Ekkehard. *Apollinaris von Laodicea*. Forschungen zu Kirchen- und Dogmengeschichte 2. Göttingen: Vandenhoeck & Ruprecht, 1969.

Murphy, Francis. *Rufinus of Aquileia (345–411): His Life and Works*. The Catholic University of America Studies in Mediaeval History, New Series 6. Washington, DC: Catholic University of America Press, 1945.

Nautin, Pierre. *Hippolyte et Josipe: Contribution à l'histoire de la littérature chretienne du IIIe siècle*. Paris: Éditions du Cerf, 1947.

Nautin, Pierre. "La Date du *De viris inlustribus* de Jérôme, de la mort de Cyrille de Jérusalem et de celle de Grégoire de Nazianze." *Revue d'histoire ecclésiastique* 56 (1961): 33–35.

Nautin, Pierre. "Épiphane (Saint) de Salamine." In *DHGE* 15, c. 617–31. Paris: Letouzey et Ané, 1963.

Nautin, Pierre. "Eutychius, évêque d'Éleuthéropolis en Palestine." In *DHGE* 16, c. 95–97. Paris: Letouzey et Ané, 1967.

Nautin, Pierre. "Études de chronologie hiéronymienne (393–397)." *Revue des études augustiniennes* 18, nos. 3–4 (1972): 209–18.

Nautin, Pierre. "L'excommunication de saint Jérôme." *Annuaire de l'école pratique des hautes études Ve section—sciences religieuses* 80–81 (1972–73): 7–37.

Nautin, Pierre. "Études de chronologie hiéronymienne (393–397)." *Revue des études augustiniennes* 19, nos. 1–2 (1973): 69–86.

Nautin, Pierre. "Divorce et Remariage chez Saint Épiphane." *VC* 37, no. 2 (1983): 157–73.

Nautin, Pierre. "L'activité littéraire de Jérôme de 387 à 392." *Revue de théologie et de philosophie* 115 (1983): 247–59.

Norris, Richard. "Heresy and Orthodoxy in the Later Second Century." *Union Seminary Quarterly Review* 52 (1998): 43–59.

Nutton, Vivian. "From Galen to Alexander: Aspects of Medicine and Medical Practice in Late Antiquity." *Dumbarton Oaks Papers* 38, Symposium on Byzantine Medicine, edited by J. Scarborough (1984): 1–14.

Nutton, Vivian. "The Drug Trade in Antiquity." *Journal of the Royal Society of Medicine* 78 (1985): 138–45.

Nutton, Vivian. *Ancient Medicine*. New York: Routledge, 2004.

Osburn, Carroll. *The Text of the Apostolos in Epiphanius of Salamis*. The New Testament in the Greek Fathers 6. Atlanta: Society of Biblical Literature, 2004.

Pagels, Elaine. *The Gnostic Gospels*. New York: Random House, 1979.

Painchaud, Louis. "L'écrit sans titre du codex II de Nag Hammadi (II.5) et la *Symphonia* d'Épiphane (*Pan*. 40)." StPatr 18, no. 1 (1985): 263–71.

Papageorghiou, Athanasios. "Foreign Influences on the Early Christian Architecture of

Cyprus." In *Acts of the International Archaeological Symposium "Cyprus Between the Orient and the Occident," Nicosia, 8–14 September 1985*, edited by V. Karageorghis, 490–503. Nicosia: Department of Antiquities, Cyprus, 1986.

Papageorghiou, Athanasios. "Cities and Countryside at the End of Antiquity and the Beginning of the Middle Ages in Cyprus." In Bryer and Georghallides, *"The Sweet Land of Cyprus,"* 27–51.

Parvis, Sarah. *Marcellus of Ancyra and the Lost Years of the Arian Controversy, 325–345*. Oxford: Oxford University Press, 2006.

Patterson, Lloyd. *Methodius of Olympus: Divine Sovereignty, Human Freedom, and Life in Christ*. Washington, DC: Catholic University of America Press, 1997.

Pearson, Birger. *Gnosticism and Christianity in Roman and Coptic Egypt*. Studies in Antiquity and Christianity. London: T&T Clark, 2004.

Perrone, Lorenzo. "'Rejoice Sion, Mother of All Churches': Christianity in the Holy Land during the Byzantine Era." In Limor and Stroumsa, *Christians and Christianity*, 141–73.

Potter, David. "Η ΚΥΠΡΟΣ ΕΠΑΡΧΙΑ ΤΗΣ ΡΩΜΑΪΚΗΣ ΑΥΤΟΚΡΑΤΟΡΙΑΣ." In *ΙΣΤΟΡΙΑ ΤΗΣ ΚΥΠΡΟΥ, ΤΟΜΟΣ Β': ΑΡΧΑΙΑ ΚΥΠΡΟΣ, ΜΕΡΟΣ Β'*, 763–864. ΛΕΥΚΩΣΙΑ: ΙΔΡΥΜΑ ΑΡΧΙΕΠΙΣΚΟΠΟΥ ΜΑΚΑΡΙΟΥ Γ', 2000.

Pourkier, Aline. "Une méthode pour aborder scientifiquement l'hérésiologie d'Épiphane et un aperçu des résultats obtenus." In *Mélanges Étienne Bernand*, 351–61. Paris: Diffusion Les Belles Lettres, 1991.

Pourkier, Aline. *L'hérésiologie chez Épiphane de Salamine*. Christianisme Antique 4. Paris: Beauchesne, 1992.

Pourkier, Aline. "Un grand hérésiologue: Épiphane de Salamine." *Connaissance des Pères de l'Église* 60 (1995): 19–23.

Prawer, Joshua. "Christian Attitudes toward Jerusalem in the Early Middle Ages." In *The History of Jerusalem: The Early Muslim Period, 638–1099*, edited by J. Prawer and H. Ben-Shammai, 311–48. Jerusalem: Yad Izhak Ben-Zvi, 1996.

Prinzivalli, Emanuela. "The Controversy about Origen before Epiphanius." In Bienert and Kühneweg, *Origeniana Septima*, 195–213.

Puech, Henri-Charles. "Archontiker." In *Reallexikon für Antike und Christentum* 1, c. 633–43. Stuttgart: Hiersemann Verlags, 1950.

Quasten, Johannes. *Patrology, Vol. 3*. Westminster, MD: Newman Press, 1960.

Raban, Avner and Kenneth Holum, eds. *Caesarea Maritima: A Retrospective after Two Millennia*. Documenta et Monumenta Orientis Antiqui 21. Leiden: Brill, 1996.

Rapp, Claudia. "The *Vita* of Epiphanius of Salamis: An Historical and Literary Study." 2 vols. DPhil diss., Worcester College, Oxford University, 1991.

Rapp, Claudia. "Epiphanius of Salamis: The Church Father as Saint." In Bryer and Georghallides, *"The Sweet Land of Cyprus,"* 169–87.

Rapp, Claudia. *Holy Bishops in Late Antiquity: The Nature of Christian Leadership in an Age of Transition*. Transformation of the Classical Heritage 37. Berkeley: University of California Press, 2005.

Raven, Charles. *Apollinarianism: An Essay on the Christology of the Early Church*. Cambridge: University Press, Cambridge, 1923.

Rebenich, Stefan. *Hieronymus und sein Kreis: Prosopographische und sozialgeschichtliche Untersuchungen*. Stuttgart: Franz Steiner Verlag, 1992.

Rebenich, Stefan. "Jerome: The 'Vir Trilinguis' and the 'Hebraica Veritas.'" *VC* 47, no. 1 (1993): 50–77.

Rebenich, Stefan. *Jerome*. The Early Church Fathers. New York: Routledge, 2002.

Riggi, Calogero. "La figura di Epifanio nel IV secolo." StPatr 8, no. 2 (1966): 86–107. Texte und Untersuchungen zur Geschichte der altchristlichen Literatur 93.

Riggi, Calogero. "Il termine 'hairesis' nell'accezione di Epifanio di Salamina (*Panarion*, t. I; *De fide*)." *Salesianum* 29 (1967): 3–27.

Riggi, Calogero. "Nouvelle lecture du Panarion 59,4 (Épiphane et le divorce)." StPatr 12 (1975): 129–34.

Riggi, Calogero. "Catechesi escatologica dell'Ancoratus di Epifanio." *Augustinianum* 18 (1978): 163–71.

Riggi, Calogero. "Formule di fede in Sant'Epifanio di Salamina." *Salesianum* 41 (1979): 309–21.

Riggi, Calogero. "La catéchèse adaptée aux temps chez Epiphane." StPatr 17, no. 1 (1982): 160–68.

Riggi, Calogero. "La διαλογή des Marcelliens dans le Panarion, 72." StPatr 15, no. 1 (1984): 368–73.

Riggi, Calogero. "Différence sémantique et théologique entre ΜΕΤΑΜΕΛΕΙΑ et METANOIA en Épiphane, Haer. LIX." StPatr 18, no. 1 (1985): 201–6.

Riggi, Calogero. "La scuola teologica di Epifanio e la filologia origeniana." In *Crescita dell'uomo nella catechesi dei padri (Età Postnicea): Convegno di studio e aggiornamento Facoltà di Lettere cristiane e classiche (Pontificium Institutum Altioris Latinitatis), Roma 20–21 marzo 1987*, edited by S. Felici, 87–104. Rome: LAS, 1988.

Riggi, Calogero. "La 'lettera agli Arabi' di Epifanio pioniere della teologia mariana (Haer. 78–79)." In *La mariologia nella catechesi dei Padri (Età postnicena). Convegno di studio e aggiornamento Facoltà di Lettere cristiani e classiche (Pontificium Institutum Altioris Latinitatis) Roma 10–11 marzo 1989, XXV dell Facoltà*. Biblioteca di Scienze Religiose 95, edited by S. Felici, 89–107. Rome: Editrice LAS, 1991.

Ritter, Adolf. *Das Konzil von Konstantinopel und sein Symbols: Studien zur Geschichte und Theologie des II Ökumenischen Konzils*. Forschungen zur Kirchen- und Dogmengeschichte 15. Göttingen: Vandenhoeck und Ruprecht, 1965.

Robinson, Thomas. *The Bauer Thesis Examined: The Geography of Heresy in the Early Christian Church*. Lewiston: Edwin Mellen Press, 1988.

Rousseau, Philip. *Ascetics, Authority, and the Church in the Age of Jerome and Cassian*. Oxford: Oxford University Press, 1978. 2nd ed., Notre Dame, IN: University of Notre Dame Press, 2010.

Rousseau, Philip. *Pachomius: The Making of a Community in Fourth-Century Egypt*. Transformation of the Classical Heritage 6. Berkeley: University of California Press, 1985.

Rousseau, Philip. *Basil of Caesarea*. Transformation of the Classical Heritage 20. Berkeley: University of California Press, 1994.

Roux, Georges. *Salamine de Chypre XV: La basilique de la campanopétra*. Paris: De Boccard, 1998.

Rubenson, Samuel. *The Letters of St. Antony: Origenist Theology, Monastic Tradition and the Making of a Saint*. Bibliotheca Historico-Ecclesiastica Lundensis 24. Lund: Lund University Press, 1990.

Rubenson, Samuel. "Origen in the Egyptian Monastic Tradition of the Fourth Century." In Bienert and Kühneweg, *Origeniana Septima*, 319–37.

Rubin, Ze'ev. "The Church of the Holy Sepulchre and the Conflict between the Sees of Caesarea and Jerusalem." *The Jerusalem Cathedra: Studies in the History, Archaeology, Geography and Ethnography of the Land of Israel* 2 (1982): 79–105.

Rubin, Ze'ev. "The See of Caesarea in Conflict with Jerusalem from Nicaea (325) to Chalcedon (451)." In Raban and Holum, *Caesarea Maritima*, 559–74.

Russell, Norman. *Theophilus of Alexandria*. The Early Church Fathers. New York: Routledge, 2007.

Scarborough, John. "Nicander's Toxicology I: Snakes." *Pharmacy in History* 19, no. 1 (1977): 3–23.

Scarborough, John. "Nicander's Toxicology II: Spiders, Scorpions, Insects and Myriapods." *Pharmacy in History* 21, no. 1 (1979): 3–34, 73–92.

Scarborough, John. *Pharmacy and Drug Lore in Antiquity: Greece, Rome, Byzantium*. Burlington, VT: Ashgate, 2010.

Schneemelcher, Wilhelm. "Epiphanius von Salamis." In *Reallexikon für Antike und Christentum, Band 5*, c. 909–27. Stuttgart: Hiersemann, 1962.

Schott, Jeremy. "Heresiology as Universal History in Epiphanius' *Panarion*." *ZAC* 10 (2007): 546–63.

Seibt, Klaus. *Die Theologie des Markell von Ankyra*. Arbeiten zur Kirchengeschichte 59. Berlin: Walter de Gruyter, 1994.

Shaw, Teresa. "Wolves in Sheep's Clothing: The Appearance of True and False Piety." StPatr 29 (1997): 127–32.

Shaw, Teresa. "Askesis and the Appearance of Holiness." *JECS* 6, no. 3 (1998): 485–500.

Simon, Marcel. "From Greek Hairesis to Christian Heresy." In *Early Christian Literature and the Classical Intellectual Tradition: In Honorem Robert Grant*, edited by W. Schoedel and R. Wilken, 101–16. Paris: Beauchesne, 1979.

Simonetti, Manlio. *La crisi ariana nel IV secolo*. Studia Ephemeridis "Augustinianum" 11. Rome: Institutum Patristicum "Augustinianum," 1975.

Simonetti, Manlio. "Il concilio di Alessandria del 362 e l'origine della formula trinitaria." *Augustinianum* 30 (1990): 353–60.

Simonetti, Manlio. "Eusebio nella controversia ariana." In Covolo, Uglione, and Vian, *Eusebio*, 155–79.

Sivan, Hagith. "Who Was Egeria? Pilgrimage and Piety in the Age of Gratian." *HTR* 81, no. 1 (1988): 59–72.

Sivan, Hagith. "Holy Land Pilgrimage and Western Audiences: Some Reflections on Egeria and Her Circle." *Classical Quarterly* 38, no. 2 (1988): 528–35.

Sivan, Hagith. *Palestine in Late Antiquity*. Oxford: Oxford University Press, 2008.

Sizgorich, Thomas. *Violence and Belief in Late Antiquity: Militant Devotion to Christianity and Islam*. Philadelphia: University of Pennsylvania Press, 2009.

Spät, Eszter. "The 'Teachers' of Mani in the *Acta Archelai* and Simon Magus." *VC*, no. 1 (2004): 1–23.

Sperber, Daniel. *The City in Roman Palestine*. Oxford: Oxford University Press, 1998.

Speyer, Wolfgang. "Zu den Vorwürfen den Heiden gegen di Christen." *Jahrbuch für Antike und Christentum* 6 (1963): 129–35.

Spoerl, Kelley. "A Study of the 'Κατὰ Μέρος Πίστις' by Apollinarius of Laodicea." PhD diss., University of Toronto, Toronto, 1991.

Spoerl, Kelley. "The Schism at Antioch since Cavallera." In Barnes and Williams, *Arianism after Arius*, 101–26.

Spoerl, Kelley. "Apollinarius and the Response to Early Arian Christology." StPatr 26 (1993): 421–27.

Spoerl, Kelley. "Apollinarian Christology and the Anti-Marcellan Tradition." *JTS* 45, no. 2 (1994): 545–68.

Sparks, Hedley, ed. *The Apocryphal Old Testament*. Oxford: Oxford University Press, 1984.

Stead, G. Christopher. *Divine Substance*. Oxford: Oxford University Press, 1977.

Stefaniw, Blossom. "Straight Reading: Shame and the Normal in Epiphanius's Polemic Against Origen." *JECS* 21, no. 3 (2013): 413–35.

Sterk, Andrea. *Renouncing the World Yet Leading the Church: The Monk-Bishop in Late Antiquity*. Cambridge, MA: Harvard University Press, 2004.

Stone, Michael. "Concerning the Seventy-Two Translators: Armenian Fragments of Epiphanius, *On Weights and Measures*." HTR 73, no. 1 (1980): 331–6.

Stone, Michael. "An Armenian Epitome of Epiphanius's *De gemmis*." HTR 82, no. 4 (1989): 467–76.

Stylianou, Andreas and Judith Stylianou. *The Painted Churches of Cyprus: Treasures of Byzantine Art*. London: Trigraph for the A.G. Leventis Foundation, 1985.

Tardieu, Michel. "Épiphane contre les gnostiques." *Tel Quel* 88 (1981): 64–91.

Taylor, Joan. *Christians and the Holy Places: The Myth of Jewish-Christian Origins*. Oxford: Oxford University Press, 1993.

Tetz, Martin. "Über nikäische Orthodoxie. Der sog. *Tomus ad Antiochenos* des Athanasios von Alexandrien." ZNW 66, nos. 3–4 (1975): 194–222.

Tetz, Martin. "Athanasius und die Vita Antonii: Literarische und theologische Relationen." ZNW 73 (1982): 1–30.

Tetz, Martin. "Ante omnia de sancta fide et de integritate veritatis: Glaubensfragen auf der Synode von Serdika (342)." ZNW 76 (1985): 243–69.

Tetz, Martin. "Ein enzyklisches Schreiben der Synode von Alexandrien (362)." ZNW 79 (1988): 262–81.

Thornton, Timothy. "The Stories of Joseph of Tiberias." *VC* 44 (1990): 54–63.

Tiersch, Claudia. *Johannes Chrysostomus in Konstantinopel (398–404): Weltsicht und Wirken eines Bischofs in der Hauptstadt des Oströmischen Reiches.* Studien und Texte zu Antike und Christentum 6. Tübingen: Mohr Siebeck, 2000.

Trevett, Christine. "Fingers up Noses and Pricking with Needles: Possible Reminiscences of Revelation in Later Montanism." *VC* 49, no. 3 (1995): 258–69.

Trevett, Christine. *Montanism: Gender, Authority and the New Prophecy.* Cambridge: Cambridge University Press, 1996.

Vaggione, Richard. *Eunomius of Cyzicus and the Nicene Revolution.* Oxford: Oxford University Press, 2000.

Vallée, Gerard. *A Study in Anti-Gnostic Polemics: Irenaeus, Hippolytus, and Epiphanius.* Studies in Christianity and Judaism 1. Waterloo, ON: Wilfrid Laurier University Press, 1981.

Van Dam, Raymond. "From Paganism to Christianity at Late Antique Gaza," *Viator* 16 (1985): 1–20.

Van Dam, Raymond. *Kingdom of Snow: Roman Rule and Greek Culture in Cappadocia.* Philadelphia: University of Pennsylvania Press, 2002.

Van Dam, Raymond. *The Roman Revolution of Constantine.* Cambridge: Cambridge University Press, 2007.

Van Den Broek, Roelof. "Archontics." In *Dictionary of Gnosis and Western Esotericism,* edited by W. Hanegraaff, 89–91. Leiden: Brill, 2006.

van der Eijk, Philip. "Principles and Practices of Compilation and Abbreviation in the Medical 'Encyclopedias' of Late Antiquity." In *Condensing Texts: Condensed Texts.* Palingenesia 98, edited by M. Horster and C. Reitz, 520–54. Stuttgart: Franz Steiner Verlag, 2010.

VanderKam, James. *The Book of Jubilees.* Sheffield: Sheffield Academic Press, 2001.

VanderKam, James and William Adler, eds. *The Jewish Apocalyptic Heritage in Early Christianity.* Compendia Rerum Iudaicarum ad Novum Testamentum 4. Minneapolis: Fortress Press, 1996.

Van Nuffelen, Peter. "The Career of Cyril of Jerusalem (c. 348–87): A Reassessment." *JTS* 58, no. 1 (2007): 134–46.

Van Nuffelen, Peter. "Theophilus against John Chrysostom: The Fragments of a Lost Liber and the Reasons for John's Deposition." *Adamantius* 19 (2013): 139–55.

van Ruiten, Jacques. *Primaeval History Interpreted: The Rewriting of Genesis 1–11 in the Book of Jubilees.* Supplements to the Journal for the Study of Judaism 66. Leiden: Brill, 2000.

Verheyden, Joseph. "Epiphanius on the Ebionites." In *The Image of the Judaeo-Christians in Ancient Jewish and Christian Literature.* Wissenschaftliche Untersuchungen zum Neuen Testament 158, edited by P. Tomson and D. Lambers-Petry, 182–208. Tübingen: J.C.B. Mohr (Paul Siebeck), 2003.

Verheyden, Joseph. "Epiphanius of Salamis on Beasts and Heretics: Some Introductory Comments." *Journal of Eastern Christian Studies* 60, nos. 1–4 (2008): 143–73.

Vessey, Mark. "Jerome's Origen: The Making of a Christian Literary *Persona*." StPatr 28 (1993): 135–45.

Vinzent, Markus. *Asterius von Kappadokien, Die theologischen Fragmente: Einleitung, kristischer Text, Übersetzung und Kommentar.* Supplements to Vigiliae Christianae 20. Leiden: Brill, 1993.

Vivian, Tim. *St. Peter of Alexandria: Bishop and Martyr.* Studies in Antiquity and Christianity. Philadelphia: Fortress Press, 1988.

von Staden, Heinrich. "Hairesis and Heresy: The Case of the *hairesis iatrikai*." In *Jewish and Christian Self-Definition, Vol. 3: Self-Definition in the Greco-Roman World*, edited by E. Sanders, 76–100. Philadelphia: Fortress Press, 1982.

von Stockhausen, Annette. "Athanasius in Antiochien." ZAC 10 (2006): 86–102.

Wacholder, Ben Zion. "Biblical Chronology in the Hellenistic World Chronicles." HTR 61 (1968): 451–81.

Wälchi, Philipp. "Epiphanius von Salamis: *Panarion haereticorum* 25." *Theologische Zeitschrift* 53, no. 3 (1997): 226–39.

Walker, Peter. *Holy City, Holy Places? Christian Attitudes to Jerusalem and the Holy Land in the Fourth Century.* Oxford: Oxford University Press, 1999.

Washburn, Daniel. "Tormenting the Tormenters: A Reinterpretation of Eusebius of Vercelli's Letter from Scythopolis." *Church History* 78, no. 4 (2009): 731–55.

Watts, Edward. *City and School in Late Antique Athens and Alexandria.* Transformation of the Classical Heritage 41. Berkeley: University of California Press, 2006.

Weingarten, Susan. "Was the Pilgrim from Bordeaux a Woman? A Reply to Laurie Douglass." *JECS* 7, no. 2 (1999): 291–97.

Weischer, Bernd. "Die Glaubenssymbole des Epiphanios von Salamis und des Gregorios von Thaumaturgos im Qërellos." *Oriens Christianus* 61 (1977): 20–40.

Weischer, Bernd. "Die ursprüngliche nikänische Form des ersten Glaubenssymbols im Ankyrōtos des Epiphanius von Salamis: Ein Beitrag zur Diskussion um die Entstehung des konstantinopolitanischen Glaubenssymbols im Lichte neuester äthiopistischer Forschungen." *Theologie und Philosophie* 53, no. 3 (1978): 407–14.

Weischer, Bernd. *Qērellos IV.2: Traktate des Epiphanios von Zypern und des Proklos von Kyzikos.* Äthiopistische Forschungen 6. Wiesbaden: Franz Steiner Verlag, 1979.

Weischer, Bernd. "Ein arabisches und äthiopisches Fragment der Schrift 'De XII gemmis' des Epiphanios von Salamis." *Oriens Christianus* 63 (1979): 103–7.

Wilken, Robert. *The Christians as the Romans Saw Them.* New Haven: Yale University Press, 1984.

Wilken, Robert. "Early Christian Chiliasm, Jewish Messianism, and the Idea of the Holy Land." *HTR* 79, nos. 1–3 (1986): 298–307.

Wilken, Robert. *The Land Called Holy: Palestine in Christian History and Thought.* New Haven: Yale University Press, 1992.

Wilkinson, John. *Egeria's Travels.* London: S.P.C.K., 1971.

Wilkinson, John. "Christian Pilgrims in Jerusalem during the Byzantine Period." *Palestine Exploration Quarterly* 108, no. 2 (1976): 75–101.

Williams, Daniel. *Ambrose of Milan and the End of the Nicene-Arian Conflicts.* Oxford: Oxford University Press, 1995.

Williams, Megan. *The Monk and the Book: Jerome and the Making of Christian Scholarship.* Chicago: University of Chicago Press, 2006.

Williams, Michael. "The *Life of Antony* and the Domestication of Charismatic Wisdom." *JAAR Thematic Studies* 48, nos. 3–4 (1982): 23–45.

Williams, Michael. *Rethinking "Gnosticism": An Argument for Dismantling a Dubious Category.* Princeton: Princeton University Press, 1996.

Williams, Rowan. "Arius and the Melitian Schism." *JTS* 37, no. 1 (1986): 35–52.

Williams, Rowan. *Arius: Heresy and Tradition.* London: Darton, Longman, and Todd, 1987.

Williams, Stephen and Gerard Friell. *Theodosius: The Empire at Bay.* New Haven: Yale University Press, 1995.

Wipszycka, Ewa. *Moines et communautés monastiques en Égypte (IVᵉ–VIIIᵉ siècles).* The Journal of Juristic Papyrology, Supplement 11. Warsaw: Faculty of Law and Administration of Warsaw University, Institute of Archaeology of Warsaw University, Raphael Taubenschlag Foundation, 2009.

Wisse, Frederik. "The Nag Hammadi Library and the Heresiologists." *VC* 25, no. 3 (1971): 205–23.

Wisse, Frederik. "Gnosticism and Early Monasticism in Egypt." In *Gnosis: Festschrift für Hans Jonas*, edited by B. Aland, 431–40. Göttingen: Vandenhoeck & Ruprecht, 1978.

Young, Frances. "Did Epiphanius Know What He Meant by Heresy?" StPatr 17, no. 1 (1982): 199–205.

Young, Frances. *Biblical Exegesis and the Formation of Christian Culture.* Cambridge: Cambridge University Press, 1997.

Zachhuber, Johannes. "The Antiochene Synod of AD 363 and the Beginnings of Neo-Nicenism." *ZAC* 4, no. 1 (2000): 83–101.

Zachhuber, Johannes. "Basil and the Three-Hypostases Tradition: Reconsidering the origins of Cappadocian theology." *ZAC* 5, no. 1 (2001): 65–85.

Zionts, Richard. "A Critical Examination of Epiphanius' 'Panarion' in Terms of Jewish-Christian Groups and Nicander of Colophon." PhD diss., Pennsylvania State University, University Park, 2002.

Dictionaries and Reference Works

Blaise, Albert and Henri Chirat. *Dictionnaire latin-français des auteurs chrétiens.* Turnhout: Brepols, 1954.

Glare, P. *Oxford Latin Dictionary.* Oxford: Oxford University Press, 1968.

Lampe, Geoffrey. *A Patristic Greek Lexicon*. Oxford: Oxford at the Clarendon Press, 1961.

Liddell, Henry and Robert Scott. *A Greek-English Lexicon*, rev. Oxford: Oxford University Press, 1996.

Talbert, Richard, ed. *Barrington Atlas of the Greek and Roman World*. Princeton: Princeton University Press, 2000.

Subject Index